The Drama
of the Baltic Peoples

August Rei

The Drama of the Baltic Peoples

KIRJASTUS VABA EESTI

Published in 1970 by

Publishing House Kirjastus Vaba Eesti

Box 16 211, S-103 24 Stockholm 16, Sweden

First printing 1970
Second printing 1972

Printed in Finland

AB SYDVÄSTKUSTEN - ÅBO 1972

CONTENTS

PREFACE

BY EUGENE LYONS

The ordeal of the Baltic states, especially in this our tormented century, has been deeply tragic. Denied any possibility of affecting the course of events, they were preordained by sheer geography to be always the victims of European power struggles.

Make an inventory of the principal afflictions visited upon mankind in our times: fascism, communism, war, imperialism. The Baltic humanity has been subjected to all of them, and always in the most brutal fashion. Even their period of national independence between the two World Wars — lamentably brief, as history is reckoned — was shadowed by Soviet harassments from the east, the pressures of German and Polish ambitions from the other sides. Despite this, the three republics showed remarkable results in building good and viable societies.

Reading this history, one is struck by the miracle that the Baltic peoples have survived — as peoples if not as states — under the burdens of cumulative disasters. They have not merely survived but retained their sense of national identity and cohesion, as well as a capacity for sustained anger and resistance.

One expects that peoples so consistently attacked and oppressed, exploited and humiliated, would lose their self-esteem and be reduced to meek abjection. This has not occurred. On the contrary, the Baltic zeal for national and personal freedom has remained robust under the most luckless circumstances — often driven underground by monstrous duress, as at present, but breaking to the surface at the first opportunity.

At every critical turn in European history, the Lithuanians, Estonians and Latvians have struck out, against impossible odds, for national independence and human rights. They were recalcitrant, troublesome subjects to the Tsarist despots; to the Bolshevik tyrants in the first year of communist occupation in 1940—41, to the Nazi sadists in the war years; and since then to the Kremlin gauleiters in the second and prolonged Soviet occupation.

The short interval of independent statehood was not a free gift from the victors in the First World War. It was won by courageous fighting and heavy casualties in desperate struggle. August Rei, in dealing with that period, writes: »Lithuania, like Estonia and Latvia, went out empty-handed to meet the invasion of the Red Army in the last days of December, 1918.«

Resistance was no less desperate and daring after the Second World War. Baltic guerrilla formations, drawing their strength from the people, fought the Red Army and the MVD for at least five years after their countries had been driven behind the prisonwalls of the Soviet empire. The Lithuanian Freedom Army was operating from forest hideouts as late as 1952. In Estonia, guerrilla resistance persisted until 1956. Considering the power and the ferocity of the conquerors, this speaks volumes for the valor and tenacity of the Balts.

The depredations of Moscow's terror machine in the three Baltic countries were larger and more hideous than in any other of the captive East and Central European nations. Executions and mass deportations were on a scale horrifying even by communist standards of inhumanity. More than 500,000 — over 10 percent of the aggregate Baltic population — were uprooted and dispersed. That was the measure of the Kremlin's fear of Baltic resistance. The magnitude of Soviet cruelty, indeed, can be seen as an unintended Kremlin tribute to the spirit and stamina of these captives. No one familiar with Baltic history, as set forth in this valuable book, can doubt that the Lithuanians, Estonians and Latvians, though conquered and enslaved, have not surrendered in their hearts.

August Rei ends his posthumous history with the incorporation of the Baltic republics into the USSR in 1940. But a concluding seventy-page chapter by the eminent historian Evald Uustalu takes up the narrative and carries it to the present time. At one point he makes an observation of special interest to citizens of the West. It was the suppression of the heroic Hungarian uprising in 1956, he attests, that marked the end of the anti-Soviet guerrilla activity in Estonia — because »it destroyed the last hopes of any help from the Western democracies.»

The sad truth is that the West did not raise a finger in support of the insurgents. It had stood aside similarly during the East German insurrection in 1953, and would remain passive in 1968, when Soviet and satellite armies invaded Czechoslovakia. Moreover, it accepted meekly, almost indifferently, the announcement of the Brezhnev Doctrine, under which Moscow arrogated the right to intervene with military force in any »socialist» country. The eclipse of hope of Western help for the captive peoples is by now total.

We should recall that in World War II the Allies had an alternative to the betrayal of East-Central Europe. Winston Churchill was not alone in proposing that Germany be attacked through the Balkans, the »soft underbelly of Europe», in order to block Soviet domination of East Europe. But President Roosevelt, having fatefully misjudged the nature of communism, rejected this strategy and his decision prevailed.

The West, and the United States in particular, thus cannot shrug off their share of responsibility for the Soviet enslavement of nearly a hundred million Europeans, the Baltic peoples among them. The painful reality is that during and after the war the victorious democracies deliberately consigned an array of East-Central European nations to the tender mercies of Stalin and his butchers. That was the shabby price they paid, in the national freedoms of others, under the delusion that they were buying safety and freedom for themselves.

Even as *Realpolitik*, the surrender of East-Central Europe to communism was a short-sighted blunder. Having won the war against one brand of totalitarianism, the Allies lost the peace by permitting the expansion of another brand. In effect they gave an unobstructed right of way to communist imperialism and ever since have been continually engaged, in consequence, in fending off its aggressions throughout the world, from Berlin to Cuba to Vietnam.

However this may be explained and justified in terms of expediency, the conduct was then, and remains today, utterly immoral in human terms. The complicity of the West in the cruel fate of nearly a hundred million East and Central Europeans, confirmed and extended by twenty-five years of eager groping for *detente* with the prison-world of communism, makes it a partner in guilt for the servitude and suffering imposed on the victims. The Baltic peoples, like all the other captive peoples, have in effect become expendable chips in the game of flattering and appeasing their Red masters.

This fact weighs heavily on the conscience of millions of us in the free world, and will not be lifted until the victimized states regain both independence and freedom.

I am among those who are convinced that history has not said its last word. Hungary and Czechoslovakia, though beaten down, hold portents for the future. So do the clear evidences of intellectual and political ferments in Soviet Russia itself. Those who read this Rei-Uustalu history will not be astonished to learn, as news of growing dissidence in the USSR reaches us across the Iron Curtain, that it is especially strong among the Baltic peoples.

I

THE BALTIC PEOPLES THROUGH THE MILLENNIA

A glance at the map of languages and nationalities of Europe shows that between Western Europe, inhabited predominantly by Romanic and German peoples, and Eastern Europe, populated by Slavic peoples, there stretches, from north to south, an intermittent belt of peoples of heterogeneous language and character. This long and alternating belt is no temporary and passing phenomenon on the ethnographic map of Europe; it has subsisted since the beginning of the historical period and probably even for quite a long time before.

One section of this belt, inhabited by the Estonians, Latvians and Lithuanians, forms a fairly uniform geographical unit which can properly be called the East-Baltic region. It is a part of the eastern coast of the Baltic Sea, running from the Gulf of Finland in the north to the south-eastern corner of that sea. The region is divided into two halves by the Gulf of Riga. The main part of the northern half is inhabited by the Estonians, the southernmost part of the southern half by the Lithuanians. The Latvians people the middle of the region round the Gulf of Riga and its hinterland along the river Daugava (Dvina, Düna).

Notwithstanding all the changes that have occurred during their long history, these three countries have always remained distinct from one another and their surroundings with respect to the nationality of their inhabitants, and have always formed political and administrative units apart. Until the end of the twelfth century they were populated by tribes of different languages frequently at war with one another. For the last centuries of the Middle Ages, and since then until the end of the first World War, they have been living in greater or lesser dependence upon foreign conquerors. But irrespective of whether the Order of the German Knights or Denmark, Sweden, Poland, or Russia has exercised sovereign power over it, the East-Baltic region has always constituted a clear-cut territorial unit, subdivided into three component parts, corresponding to the three peoples, Estonians, Latvians and Lithuanians. The first World War brought about conditions which enabled these peoples to establish their self-governing, free and independent states.

By the beginning of 1939 the areas and population of the three Baltic republics were:

	Area in square miles:	Population in millions:
Estonia	18,400	1.1
Latvia	25,500	2.0
Lithuania	20,500	2.5

While Latvia is the largest of the three republics with respect to area, Lithuania has the largest population. Estonia occupies the third place in both respects. The density of population diminishes from south to north as everywhere else in Europe. As to population, Latvia and Lithuania are not much behind Norway and Ireland, and in area each of the three Baltic states is larger than Denmark, Belgium, Luxemburg, Switzerland, Liechtenstein or Albania. Estonia, the smallest of the three Baltic republics, has a population larger than Albania, Luxemburg or Iceland. The areas of the three republics added together exceed that of Czechoslovakia, Hungary, Bulgaria, Greece or Portugal, and their populations added together exceed that of Finland, Denmark, Ireland or Switzerland.

The fact that the three Baltic peoples have been able to preserve their languages and national individualities as well as the main part of their areas over thousands of years, can be attributed partly to the geographical and physical conditions of their countries and partly to their national character and their relations to the surrounding world.

The East-Baltic region forms part of an extensive plain surrounding the southern half of the Baltic Sea and stretching far into central and northern Russia. The surface is lowest on the Estonian islands and the western coast of the mainland, especially round the south-eastern coast of the Gulf of Riga. Here the line denoting 65 feet above sea level lies at a distance of 18.5—21.5 miles from the shore. The northern coast of Estonia, as well as that of the Kurland peninsula, rises more steeply. Inland there are several unconnected elevations, the highest of them attaining 490—1.040 feet above sea level. Between these elevations there are lower lands opening onto the shores of the Gulf of Finland, the Gulf of Riga, or the Baltic Sea. Of special importance is one of these lowlands which stretches along the eastern frontier of Estonia, that of Peipus with the broad, shallow lake Peipus, from which the river Narova falls into the Gulf of Finland. In the south, the lowland of Peipus stretches along the river Velikaya into Soviet Russia.

In the northern part of Estonia and on the islands west of the mainland, the subsoil consists of limestone strata, covered with a thin layer of stony or sandy earth. In southern Estonia and in Latvia the subsoil is partly red sandstone, partly limestone, covered with considerably thicker clayey moraine coating. Geologically Lithuania is the youngest part of the Baltic region. Here the subsoil consists mainly of layers from the chalk period, thickly covered with fertile moraine. In all the three Baltic states the best arable land is to be found on moraine elevations, but their fertility, and correspondingly the proportion of the cultivable land in the total area, increases from north to south.

Even with respect to climate the southern part of the Baltic region is considerably more favoured than the north. In accordance with temperature cycles the summer vegetative period of such great importance for agriculture is longest in the south-western part of the region, in western Lithuania and Kurland. To the north and northeast it diminishes, being shortest in northern and north-eastern Estonia.

As to the total rainfall and its seasonal distribution, there are no great differences between the three Baltic states. On the whole this region suffers rather from superabundance of humidity than from dryness. Diverting excess water is a problem of considerable importance for agriculture in Estonia.

The Atlantic zone of mild climate characteristic of Western and Central Europe reaches to the Baltic and its eastern shore. The greater part of the area of the Baltic states falls within this milder climatic zone. The lowland areas with large lakes, forests and marshes which separate the Baltic countries from Russia, are of some importance in this respect.

The Estonians, Latvians, and Lithuanians have resided in their pre-

sent areas for the whole duration of the historical period, since remote antiquity. In earlier times these areas stretched farther to the
east and south, but the most densely populated, central part of their
habitat on the shores of the Baltic Sea has been preserved by these
peoples throughout. In the first centuries of the Christian Era it was[1]
known that there were peoples of other languages to the east and
north-east of the areas peopled by the Germans on the coast of the
Baltic Sea and in its hinterland. The forested zone of Eastern Europe
was sparsely populated by these peoples, whose settlements reached
in the south to about the 52nd parallel of northern latitude. Finno-
Ugric tribes constituted the main element in the population of this
vast area. The south-western region of the lower Vistula and the
upper Dnieper had been settled c. 2000 B.C. by the so-called Baltic peoples, Lithuanians and Latvians who had opened the fertile
moraine elevations for agriculture in what are now East Prussia, Lithuania and Kurland. The coast of the Kurland peninsula and Livonia,
north of Daugava, remained in the possession of a Finno-Ugric tribe,
the Livs, north of whom the Estonians lived in the land they still
inhabit.

Less is known of the southern neighbours of the Baltic peoples and
Finno-Ugric tribes in pre-historic times. The Passarge river in East
Prussia is assumed to have been the border between the Germans and
the most south-westerly Baltic tribe, the Lithuanians. To the south
from here begins the area between the Vistula and the Dnieper which
was in the first centuries of the Christian Era inhabited by Slavic
tribes, rather distantly akin to the Baltic peoples with respect to language. In older documents of classical antiquity and the early Middle
Ages they are designated "Veds" or "Ants". Scholars disagree as
to how far the area they peopled stretched to the south and south-
east in the direction of the Black Sea. During the great migration of
peoples in the early Middle Ages, the area of the Slavs swelled considerably to the west as well as to the south and south-east, reaching
to the Balkan peninsula and the Black Sea. In the period between the
5th and the 9th centuries the Slavic tribes settled in the region of the
Berezina and the Dnieper began to widen their areas towards the
north. At first they penetrated into the areas of the higher Daugava,

---

[1] The ancient Greeks knew them too — see "The Golden Fleece" by R. Graves.

where the eastern Lithuanian and Latvian tribes are presumed to have lived. From there they soon penetrated into the territory of the Finnish Vatya tribe on the river Lovat and Lake Ilmen. Novgorod on the river Olhava (Volkhov), which flows out of Ilmen and into Lake Ladoga, became a commercial and administrative centre of these northern Slavic tribes. From here communication by river was established with the Black and Caspian Seas. Thus a Slavic wedge was driven between the Baltic and Finno-Ugric tribes settled on the Baltic and those living between the river Volga and the Ural mountains, the former being now separated from the latter and embedded between the Germans and the Slavs.

The question arises: why did not the Slavs manage to expand over the whole vast plain between the Baltic Sea and the Ural mountains, but instead, contenting themselves with the above-mentioned, gradually widening wedge, left the area on the Baltic alone? The reasons for this must obviously be sought in those same circumstances which have enabled Estonia, Latvia, and Lithuania to preserve themselves since time immemorial as a region apart.

Let us consider: does the eastern boundary of this region coincide with any clear-cut topographical border-zone which might have obstructed communications from east to west, from the areas conquered by the Russians to those on the Baltic coast? Such a border-zone is clearly discernible, though it is not uninterrupted. In the first place Lakes Peipus and Pskov with the marshy and wooded lowlands fall within this zone. Communications between Estonia and Russia over these lakes and their nearest surroundings have always been very poor if they existed at all. Russian settlements spread rather early from the area of the river Lovat and Lake Ilmen up to the eastern shore of the lakes Peipus and Pskov, but here their expansion stopped. Between Lake Peipus and the Gulf of Finland there is, however, a strip of more elevated limestone ground at the height of the town Narva, where the river Narova streams down the limestone terrace in a waterfall. This limestone terrace is like a bridge and a comfortable communication between northern Estonia and the elevation of Ingermanland, east of the Estonian frontier. Similarly there is an elevation of the ground south of Lake Pskov where, analogously to Narva, the town Pskov is situated on a limestone terrace astride the river Velikaya which streams in rapids down the terrace. This forms a second convenient link between the region of Novgorod and Pskov and Livonia, and in fact this way has always been used by the Russians for incursions into Livonia.

South of Pskov there is in the eastern part of Livonia a long belt of marsh and forest with the large, shallow Lake Luban in its midst. This belt has always, especially in olden times, presented an obstacle to east-west communications from Russia to southern Livonia. Nowadays, however, two railway-lines and several highways pass along this belt. East of the Luban lowland rises the high Latgale moraine elevation, which continues to the north-east in the elevation between the lakes Peipus and Ilmen, and crosses the river Daugava at Daugavpils (Dvinsk). Across this elevation a number of convenient highways run from the region of Opoczka, Velikye Luki and Polotsk into Latgale, to the river Daugava and further into Kurland. Consequently the south-eastern part of Latvia has no protective borderland sheltering it against invasion from the east. The same moraine elevation runs on along the greater part of the eastern frontier of Lithuania, alternating with river valleys and marshy lowlands of smaller dimensions. Only in the farthest south-eastern section of the frontier, on the middle Nemunas (Niemen), is there a broader marshy lowland.

From these briefly stated facts it is clear that the topographical character of the eastern border of the Baltic region can hardly in itself have constituted an obstacle to the efforts of the Russians to submerge and swallow up these countries. There must have been other factors which have deflected Russian colonization from the Baltic area, directing it to the Lovat, Ilmen and Olhava region. In order to discover them we must first try to throw light upon the forces which set the Slavs in motion, driving them northwards from their warmer and more fertile areas into the less propitious conditions of the forest belt settled by the Latvian, Lithuanian, and Finnish tribes.

According to the prevailing opinion of historians, this northward movement of the Slavs was part of the great migration of peoples which opened the Middle Ages. In the first centuries of the Christian Era Slavic tribes settled between the Vistula and the Dnieper were in the sphere of interest and power of the Goths. The invasion of the Huns into the steppes on the Black Sea and the downfall of the power of the Goths gave impetus to the peoples of Eastern and Central Europe. This in turn inevitably brought about a pressure of the Slavs on their northern neighbours, though their main masses moved west and south, into the areas of the decaying empire of the Huns. On the other hand it must be remembered that since time immemorial very important commercial routes had connected the Baltic Sea with the Black and the Caspian Seas along the rivers passing through northeastern Russia. In order to pass from the basin of one river to that of another at the rather narrow and low watersheds, boats and unloaded goods were dragged or carried overland. Armed guard had to be set on the unloaded goods while the boats were being trailed over, and to reduce trouble and labour part of the goods were willingly bartered for local products. Thus permanent commercial settlements arose on the watersheds where passage from one river basin to another was easiest. Similar commercial establishments also arose at other convenient places along the rivers. These facts were well known to the Slavs settled between the Vistula and the Dnieper. They knew that the boats of merchants coming up the Dnieper from the Black Sea would go by a tributary of the Dnieper, Berezina, into the Vilya or the Nemunas, or from the upper Dnieper by the Kasplya, a tributary of the Daugava, into that river or into the Lovat, and that there were permanent commercial establishments on watersheds where local products could be bartered for goods of southern or eastern origin. It was more than natural for the younger enterprising elements in the Slavic tribes, when once exposed to strong pressure, to set out along the rivers for the watersheds in the north and from there on into the basins of other rivers in search of better conditions of life and activity. The areas round the Vilya and the Nemunas were, however, densely populated by the Lithuanians, and those round the lower and middle Daugava by the Latvians. Both these peoples had long been sedentary agriculturists and there was no room in their areas for newcomers. Better opportunities of penetration and settlement were offered by the region of the upper Daugava and the upper Volga as well as on the Olhava-Lovat system. The region of these rivers was at that time still much more sparsely populated, partly by the eastern Latvian tribes, but mainly by the Finnish tribes Vatya, Vepsa and partly, perhaps, the Mari (Merya) tribes who supported themselves to a great extent by nomadic hunting and fishing. Into these areas the Slavs could penetrate much more easily and in much greater numbers.

2

Slavic expansion therefore took place in the direction of the region of the upper Daugava and the Lovat, Lake Ilmen and the Olhava. Step by step the Slavs broadened their territories from the Lovat—Olhava line to the west, into the basin of the river Velikaya, possibly driving the Estonians somewhat farther west. North of Pskov the lakes Pskov and Peipus and the river Narova above Narva, became the definitive border between the Estonians and the Russians. The lower Narova and the lower Luga, Ingermanland limestone plain, and the river Neva with the southern coast of Ladoga remained for centuries in the possession of the Finnish tribe Vatya. There was no commercial intercourse worth mentioning over the lakes Peipus and Pskov and along the rivers Narova, Plyussa and Luga, since these lakes and the upper reaches of these rivers were not in sufficiently close and easy contact with the systems of the rivers Daugava, Lovat and Olhava. Moreover navigation on the rivers Narova and Luga was impeded by waterfalls and rapids and, what was perhaps of still greater consequence, they flowed into the broad, open expanse of the Gulf of Finland, unprotected against storms and therefore avoided by open boats. As it is well known, the commercial route from Sweden to lake Ladoga went along the northern shore of the Gulf of Finland, sheltered by numerous islands, into the Gulf of Viborg or the mouth of the Neva.

Thus Estonia lay out of the way of the main lines of Russian expansion. For this reason the Estonians managed to preserve their home on the coast of the Baltic Sea. It is scarcely necessary to stress that if the Estonians had been submerged by Russian colonization, the Latvians and the Lithuanians would very soon have shared their fate, exposed to pressure from east and north over frontiers lacking natural defences. As it was, preserving their Baltic homes, their languages and national individualities, these peoples continued to maintain their contacts with the western world. And the cultural impulses which they have received without interruption from the west, have essentially contributed to the formation of their national character. Marked individualism and self-reliance, a rather cool and critical attitude to any mass movement and collectivist initiative, and an inclination to seafaring activities are conspicuous among the traits of their character. These features, common to all the three peoples in question, clearly distinguish them from the inhabitants of the vast plains of the East-European inland.

Between the 9th and the 12th centuries the Russians made frequent predatory incursions into Estonia and Latvia, seeking to subjugate these countries. Incursions into Estonia came in earlier times almost invariably from the south-east, i.e. via Pskov and Irboska.[2]

This aggression was interrupted in the second quarter of the 13th century when the Russian principalities themselves were invaded and dreadfully devastated, and subsequently overrun by Mongols. Attempts were made by the Mongols to invade even Lithuania. They were defeated, however, and let the Baltic countries alone. Thanks to the Mongols the Baltic peoples gained respite from the attacks from the east for nearly 250 years, i.e. for the whole duration of the Mongol rule over Russia.

To protect themselves against incursions, the Estonians, Latvians and Lithuanians had erected in easily defensible locations hundreds of strongholds which were used as shelters for the population and bases for retaliatory action against the invaders. The construction and maintenance of these strongholds as well as measures for repelling attackers or invading enemy territory were undertaken by tribal leaders, called *rex, princeps, dux* or *senior* in Latin chronicles of the 13th century, with the assistance of the heads of the leading families in the tribe, called in the chronicles *meliores* or *seniores.* In times of more serious danger coalitions or temporary unions of tribes were formed for common defence, and political development showed a marked gravitation towards uniting into common national states. However, before this goal was attained in Estonia and Latvia, the development was interrupted by the emergence of a danger much more disastrous than the encroachment of the Russians or the earlier incursions of the Scandinavians.

Already in the last decades of the twelfth century merchant groups from German towns on the North and Baltic Seas, accompanied by mercenaries and Catholic monks, had occasionally appeared in the country around the estuary of the Daugava. The merchants and mercenaries were after spoils, whereas the monks came to preach the

---

[2] The region of Narva first became an arena for encounters in the 15th century, after Moscow had conquered Novgorod with its dependency, Ingermanland ("Votskaya Pyatina" — the area of the Vatya tribe).

Gospel to the Livs and other pagan tribes and to conduct them into the fold of the Holy Catholic Church.

At the same time, however, even the Russian principalities which had adopted Christianity from Constantinople, were making strenuous efforts to impose the Byzantine version of Christianity upon the peoples on the Baltic coast. In this rivalry between the two Churches Rome got the better of Constantinople by taking the decisive step: subduing these peoples and establishing its permanent domination over them.

Crusades being the order of the day, a crusade to convert the Livs and other peoples on the Baltic coast to Christianity was proclaimed by the Pope. Thus the fate of these peoples was sealed, because the mighty Catholic Church was in a position to supply the crusaders with practically unlimited reinforcements by exhorting people from thousands of pulpits to join their ranks. There were more than enough people ready to follow these exhortations — hardly so much out of religious fervour as out of greed for the booty to be grabbed in the pagan countries. The peasant armies of the heathen peoples were by far inferior in armament to the iron-clad knights of the crusading armies. Considering all these circumstances one cannot but wonder how these peoples nevertheless managed to resist for nearly thirty years, the resistance of the Estonians not being definitively broken till 1227. There cannot be any doubt that the resistance was fierce, superhumanly heroic and death-despising.

The territories of the vanquished Estonians, Livs[3] and Latvians constituted henceforward the State Confederation of Livonia, forming a part of the Holy Roman Empire, through its separate members, bishoprics, and the so-called Livonian Order, formed of the crusaders at the very beginning of the conquest and later merged with the Teutonic Order and transformed into its local, Livonian branch. Since the Livonian Order soon usurped a leading position in the Confederation, the latter was often called "the Order State". Repeated revolts

---

[3] From the Livs who were the first tribe met and subdued by the crusaders, the whole of the conquered territory, which comprised the present day Estonia and Latvia, got the name of Livonia. Having thus bequeathed its name to posterity, this tribe was absorbed by the surrounding Latvians and nearly completely melted away. There were but a few Livonian speaking villages in north-western Latvia a quarter of a century ago.

against the invaders were crushed and the subjugated peoples step by step deprived of their rights, became the bondsmen of their foreign rulers.

As to the Lithuanians, the German knights did not succeed in subduing them. For nearly six centuries from the time when the Livs, Estonians and Latvians were subjugated, the history of the Lithuanian people diverged from theirs. We shall later return to this subject.

The first thing the Russians did after they had managed to throw off the shackles of the Mongol rule (1480), was to invade Livonia again. This occurred in the spring of 1481. The country was horribly devastated and uprecedented atrocities were committed. This incursion, however, was but a foreboding of the resumption of Muscovy's expansionist drive for the subjugation of Livonia. Unfortunately the Order State was far from equal to this perilous situation. The native population having been reduced to serfdom and, in consequence, being of little, if any value as warriors, the noble knights were far too few in number to defend the country against the Muscovite hordes. Increasingly on the decline in military strength, the Order State was in mortal danger of being submerged in the flood of the Russian expansions. However, under the guidance of a highly able leader, the Master of the Livonian Order, Wolter von Plettenberg (1494—1535), who exerted its financial resources to the utmost to hire a large number of mercenaries and also employed diplomatic manoeuvres with great success, it managed to hold off the onslaught and secure an unstable peace for fifty years.

At last the catastrophe so long impending occurred: in 1558 the armies of Ivan the Terrible invaded Livonia. After hopeless, though often valiant resistance almost the whole country fell into Russian hands and the Order State crumbled (1561). At this juncture, however, the Polish-Lithuanian union and Sweden intervened and the war went on for twenty years, frightfully ravaging the unfortunate countries, until the Tsar found himself finally obliged to conclude peace (1582—1583), and give up all the territory he had seized during the hostilities.

The inheritance of the Order State was divided between Sweden and the Polish-Lithuanian union, the former getting the main, northern part of Estonia, the latter its southern part and the whole of Latvia. Later, after a clash and prolonged struggle between Sweden and Poland the latter relinquished even the southern part of Estonia and that part of Latvia north of the Daugava (1629).

Swedish rule over northern Estonia lasted about one hundred and fifty years, and over its southern part as well as north Latvia about seventy five years. For the inhabitants of these areas this was relatively the happiest time in the seven hundred years of foreign rule, from the beginning of the thirteenth century to the recovery of their national freedom in 1917–1920. A series of measures were taken by the Swedish government to ameliorate the lot of the peasant population and promote education in Livonia.

The Great Northern War (1700–1721) put an end to this respite, which for two hundred years was remembered by the Estonian people as "the good old Swedish time". This war had been desired and welcomed by the Livonian land-owning aristocracy, who were roused to anger by the reforms the Swedish government carried out especially for the reversion to the crown of all estates to which the occupants were unable to show legal title. This reform, prompted by the desire and the necessity to restore the country's shattered finances, dispossessed the majority of the noble landowners. This section now hoped that as a consequence of the war Livonia would be annexed by the Polish state, the Swedish reforms abrogated and the confiscated estates restored to their former owners. The outcome of the war, however, was that Livonia, i.e. the whole of Estonia and north Latvia came under Russian rule (the peace treaty of Nystad, 1721). Even the southern part of Latvia, which at the extinction of the Order State had become a semi-independent Polish vassal state under the name of the Duchy of Kurland, became soon after the conclusion of the treaty of Nystad in fact, if not in name, a Russian vassal. When at the third partition of Poland (1795) this Duchy was formally incorporated into Russia this was but confirmation of a reality which had come about seven decades earlier.

The peace treaty of Nystad guaranteed to Livonia provincial autonomy and the restoration of the reverted estates to their former owners.

The history of Lithuania from the 13th century to the end of the 18th century can very succinctly be summarized as follows:

As already mentioned, the German knights proved unable to subdue the Lithuanians, who managed to maintain their liberty and several times to defeat them. This they owed to the fact that the Order had given them a short breathing space which was exploited by one of their chieftains, Mindaugas (1217—1263), with admirable results. He succeeded in bringing all the Lithuanian tribes under his control, organized an efficient army and a fairly well ordered state, of which he was crowned the first king. Skilfully manoeuvering also on the diplomatic chessboard, he raised Lithuania to the status of a Power able not only, under his successors, to inflict crushing defeats on the German Knights, as e.g. in the famous battle of Tannenberg (1410), which stopped the German *Drang nach Osten*, for five centuries, but to become for a time one of the mightiest factors in Europe.

The evolution of this state subsequently deviated, however, on a track which took it into a blind alley and finally to ruin. One of its kings, Yogaila (Yagiello) was elected King of Poland by the Polish lords in 1385 and thus a union of these two states was established. From an independent state Lithuania turned into a minor partner of the Polish-Lithuanian union, in which the Polish element became more and more predominant, ultimately overshadowing the Lithuanian national element. The noble landowning magnates who emerged soon after the establishment of the union fell under the spell of Polish civilization, adopted the Polish language and became spiritually denationalized, cutting adrift from the bulk of their own people. For this same reason, however, this aristocracy proved unable notably to bias the ingrained democratic turn of mind of the Lithuanian people, especially as the Lithuanian Grand Dukes created a counterweight to this magnate class in conferring the status of nobility on a great number of ordinary farmers who thus came to constitute a numerous petty aristocracy. This nobility became accustomed to taking an active part in the election of rulers, municipal officials, judges etc, and to discussing public affairs.

It is true that even the Polish-influenced nobleman regarded themselves as Lithuanians, citizens of the Lithuanian state, which they by no means wanted to see submerged and devoured by Poland. It was nevertheless an unhealthy situation and the great mass of the people were reduced to illiterate bondsmen. Furthermore, through the spiritual kinship of the Lithuanian ruling noblemen with the Polish lords Lithuania was drawn into the anarchical state brought about by the claims of these lords for excessive privileges, a situation which was to bring an end to real freedom and lead the Polish state to destruction. Thus the ruin of Poland engulfed Lithuania too.

When the Polish-Lithuanian State was finally partitioned, Lithuania was incorporated in Russia. Even Latgale, the eastern part of Latvia, which had been a Lithuanian province since 1629, became now a Russian province.

Thus by 1795 all the three peoples in question had come under Russian rule.

Whereas "the good old Swedish time" in Estonia and northern Latvia had been the happiest, or rather the least unhappy of the seven hundred years of foreign domination, the Russian turned out to be the unhappiest. All liberal reforms carried out by the Swedish government were abrogated and the Baltic-German noble landowners gained practically unlimited control over the peasant population, who lost the last remnants of human rights and were reduced to utter destitution. A reliable witness, the Evangelic-Lutheran clergyman and diligent writer A. W. Hupel, describes the condition of the peasants in Livonia in 1777 in the following terms: "The Estonians and Latvians are not persons, but slaves, merchandise and objects which are sold or bartered against horses, dogs, pipe-bowls etc. Men are cheaper in Livonia than negroes in the colonies." There was no exaggeration in this testimony, for it could be corroborated by much conclusive proof[4].

The change for the worse was still more painfully felt in Lithuania, where there had never been serfs bound to the soil. There had been only serfs who owed labour duties to the estates, regulated as to the number of working days and the type of work to be done. These had been free to move to other estates or to the cities if there were substitutes willing to perform their duties to the estates. After the incorporation into Russia not only this class but even free tenants who had been paying a fixed rent, were firmly bound to the soil and became

---

[4] Suffice it to point to the following advertisement in the *Rigascher Anzeiger* on Jan. 15, 1788: "Four families of serfs to be sold cheap. Buyers asked to apply to the Government officer, 51 Schloss Strasse."

actually slaves who could be gambled away by their owners in card games or in some similar manner.

Driven to despair, the peasantry several times rose in rebellion, only to be mercilessly put down by force of arms. In Lithuania the peasant-serfs took an active part in the insurrection which broke out in Poland in November 1830 and soon spread into Lithuania, being however quickly crushed by Russian forces.

At last the economic interests of the noble landowners themselves began to suffer from this unhealthy state of affairs. The axiom that slave labour is highly unproductive proved true also in this case. A few enlightened persons among the Baltic Germans began already in the second half of the eighteenth century to realize this and argue that serfdom was uneconomical and unprofitable even to the landowners themselves. They remained, however, lone voices crying in the wilderness. Nor did the passionate condemnation of serfdom hurled out by a noble-minded representative of the German "enlightenment", Garlieb Merkel, in his famous book *The Letts, especially in Livonia, at the End of the Philosophic Century*, published in Leipzig in 1796, prevail upon the landowning nobility and induce them to alleviate the lot of the serfs[5]. At last, however, a kind of agrarian crisis which began to spread in the Baltic area at the turn of the century caused the landowners to rack their brains for measures which might help them out of the straits they had got into. When, at about the same time, the Tsar Alexander I, who then sympathized with liberal ideas, began to exhort them to emancipate their serfs, they discovered a way of yielding to the whim of the autocrat which also involved the prospect of advantage to themselves.

According to the laws passed by the representative bodies of the landowning aristocracy, the Estonian and the Livonian Diets, and sanctioned by the Tsar in 1816 and 1819 respectively, the peasants were, of course, emancipated from serfdom, or rather slavery, but at the same time also deprived of any right to the land they and their forefathers had tilled from time immemorial. Instead of improving the condition of the peasants these laws, by which the entire peasant

---

[5] Just as ineffectual proved a counterpart to Merkel's famous book, published six years later by C. J. Petri under the title *Estonia and the Estonians*. It is true that this book was written with less talent and verve than Merkel's.

population became landless proletarians, rendered it still more unendurable. Never has the Estonian and the Latvian peasantry been so poverty-stricken as during the forty years after the "emancipation".

The abolition of serfdom in Estonia and Latvia was echoed also in Lithuania, where the gentry were willing to follow the example given by their neighbours. However, the Tsarist government forbade them even to discuss such "revolutionary measures" at their local diets. Serfdom was abolished in Lithuania only in February 1861, when it was abolished in the whole of Russia.

At last in the eighteen sixties, when a number of rather important reforms were carried out in the Russian Empire, the government found it necessary to intervene also in Estonia and Latvia. A number of laws were enacted for the protection of the peasantry, and soon a slow improvement set in. The peasants began to acquire land, managing to pay, thanks to superhuman exertion, the excessive purchase prices exacted by the monopolist landowners. In this way landowning peasantry arose.

At the same time industrial development got under way in the Baltic area. Owing to circumstances dependent mainly on their geographical situation it advanced more rapidly in Latvia and Estonia than in Lithuania. Latvia was especially favoured in this respect. Her situation on that section of the Baltic coast which lies nearest to Central Russia around Moscow induced the Russian government as early as the eighteen fifties to build the two railway-lines Riga—Dvinsk and Riga—Vitebsk which, by connecting Latvia with the vast Russian hinterland, gave a considerable impulse to the industrial and commercial development of this province of the Empire. A number of large industrial enterprises arose already between 1870 and 1890, mainly in Riga, among them some branch-establishments of German industry.

High import duties on manufactured goods, repeatedly raised in the eighteen eighties and nineties, in combination with low costs of transport by sea of raw materials and fuel into the sea-ports of Latvia and Estonia, and the abundance of cheap and yet fairly efficient labour, created favourable conditions for the development of industry in these provinces. Notwithstanding the unsound agrarian order, which was an ever-flowing source of proletarianized rural masses in

Latvia and Estonia, the country was considerably ahead of the Russians with respect to education.[6] As a result, and surely still more owing to the diligent habits acquired by the Baltic peoples in countless generations under the pressure of their far from generous natural environment, their labour was of considerably higher efficiency and productivity than that of the Russians. For these reasons western industrialists too, whose exports to Russia were increasingly burdened by rising import duties and who therefore found it profitable to invest their capital inside Russian territory, readily established branch-enterprises in Latvia and Estonia.

It is not surprising, then, that by the eve of the first World War Latvia had become one of the most industrialized regions of the Russian Empire. The capital of Latvia, Riga, was at that time the greatest timber port in the world, fed by the Daugava (Dvina) and its waterways, topping not only the rich forests of Latvia herself but also supplies from Russia proper. According to the census taken in 1910 there were 782 industrial enterprises in Latvia, with 93,343 workers, metal, timber, chemicals, textile, stone, and earthenware being the main fields involved.

Though Estonia was somewhat less favoured by her geographical situation and other natural conditions, with respect to the development of industry she nevertheless made considerable progress. A number of large industrial enterprises arose, mainly in Tallin, in the 'eighties and 'nineties, and then, immediately before the outbreak of the World War, three shipyards of considerable size were built in that port, intended to serve the needs arising from the projected expansion of the Russian Navy, in 1910. The number of her industrial workers was 45,370 in 1913.

Lithuania, on the other hand, having no sea-port towns, lacked those geographical conditions which promoted the development of industry in Latvia and Estonia. Nor was she rich in mineral deposits

---

[6] Whereas, according to the census taken in 1897, the percentage of persons above the age of nine years able to read and write was 27 in the whole of Russia, it was 95 in the province of Estonia, the highest in the Empire, 93 in the province of Livonia, the northern part of which was inhabited by the Estonians and the southern by the Latvians, and 85 per cent in the province of Kurland (the southern half of Latvia).

which might have given rise to manufacturing and industry. The number of her industrial workers before the first World War was estimated at thirteen to fourteen thousand, so that she remained almost entirely an agricultural country. What there was of industry, like the leather factories at Siauliai and Tillmann's iron foundries at Kaunas, were dependent on the markets of the Russian Empire and had little connection with the local Lithuanian market and the needs of the Lithuanian people. It must also be borne in mind that the oppression of Russian rule lay considerably more heavily on the Lithuanian people than on the Estonians and Latvians, particularly after the unsuccessful insurrections of 1831 and 1863. Hundreds of thousands of Lithuanians emigrated to the New World in order to escape this unbearable despotism and the wretched social conditions.[7] This continuous drain inevitably weakened national strength and slowed down economic progress, especially the industrialization of the country.

Nonetheless, in consequence of the development briefly referred to, all the three peoples had already by the eve of the World War developed on the one hand their own national bourgeois class, still far from being financially strong, yet accumulating wealth year by year, and on the other a native industrial proletariat growing more and more numerous, as well as a fairly numerous and swiftly expanding educated class. All these sections of the population were growing increasingly self-conscious and nationally minded. The peasants toiled upwards with fanatical energy in order to pay off the heavy debts they had incurred in purchasing their farms and to become really independent and prosperous. And their exertions were bearing fruit. Adapting their production to the requirements and tendencies which had emerged on the world market in the last two decades of the 19th century, the peasants began at the turn of the century to shift the centre of gravity of their production from the cultivation of grain to livestock breeding. In this they succeeded fairly well, owing mainly to a net of co-operative associations they hastened to establish. A considerable number of co-operative societies of different kinds came

---

[7] It is estimated that one third of the Lithuanians moved abroad in the fifty years preceding the World War I (v. Brit. Enc., vol. 14, p. 213).

into existence in a very short time, nearly all of them in the last ten years of Russian domination. The fields they represented were:[8]

	in Latvia (1914)	in Estonia (1918)	in Lithuania (1914)
Co-operative dairy societies	88	50	x
Associations for common use of agricultural machinery	178	173	x
Co-operative credit associations	249	134	155
Co-operative consumer societies	151	149	52
Milk control associations	294	14	x

(x: figures not available)

These associations, which owed their origin to the enterprising spirit and practical turn of mind of the peasants, reflected the economic progress this class had made.

At the same time the sons of the peasantry were no less industriously acquiring higher education. A large number of these young Baltic intellectuals were employed in the liberal professions, civil service, industry, banking, commerce, etc., throughout the vast Russian Empire, and were appreciated as dependable and efficient employees. And so by the time the autocratic order broke down in Russia, these peoples were amply provided with countrymen who had acquired both theoretical knowledge and practical experience in various branches of administrative, professional and social activity, and were fully able to establish and administer democratic, autonomous self-government in their homelands.

As a clear manifestation of the growing self-consciousness of these peoples this period saw the rise of literature and fine arts, as well as research into national antiquities, folklore in the first instance, national history, mother tongue, etc. Since in this, as in many other respects, the development proceeded on almost identical lines in Es-

[8] E. Zolmanis *Latvia Among the Baltic States*, Riga 1931 (p. 79); *Estonia* (Reprint from the *Estonian Encyclopedia* — in Estonian), Geislingen, 1949, vol. 3, p. 144; A. Simutis *The Economic Reconstruction of Lithuania After 1918*, New York 1942, pp. 32, 33.

tonia and Latvia, diverging somewhat in Lithuania, we shall first consider the former two and thereafter turn to the latter.

Invaluable preparatory work which greatly contributed to the rise
of national literature, fine arts, and scholarly research, had been done
in Estonia and Latvia in the first decades of the 19th century by a
group of intellectuals immigrated from Germany, in whose universities
they had been imbued with enthusiasm for the ideas of German Enlightenment of the so-called »storm and stress» *(Sturm und Drang)*
period. A direct spur to action had been given to these "esto-, resp.
letto-philes", by one of the leading spirits and champions of the
"storm and stress", J. G. Herder (1744—1803) who among other inspiring ideas had propagated a loving interest in and a careful study
of popular songs, folk tales, and folklore in general of all peoples as
the most adequate expression of their spiritual essence and substance.
Having in the prime of his life passed five years (1764—1769) in Riga,
Herder had had an opportunity to acquaint himself with the popular
poetry of the three Baltic peoples and to learn to appreciate their
poetic value. In a collection of folk songs of a number of peoples,
published in 1778 under the title of *Volkslieder I* he introduced
some specimens of the popular poetry of these peoples to the public.

Under the influence of Herder, the letto- and estophiles began to
take down folk songs, popular fairy tales and folklore of any kind
among the Baltic peoples, to inquire into their past, to cultivate their
languages with the ambitious aim of turning them from the coarse
vernaculars of illiterate serfs into cultivated languages, vehicles adequate to convey every shade of human thought, and every emotion
of the human soul. One of the most enthusiastic and active estophiles, Dr. J. W. Luce, went to the length of declaring (in 1815) that it
would be normal and commendable for educated Germans in Estonia
to use, even in their intercourse among themselves, the Estonian
language, which, in his opinion, was not only rich in its vocabulary
and amenable to development in every respect, but also the most
euphonious of all languages.

That Dr. Luce's ideas concerning the possibility of development
inherent in the despised vernaculars of the serfs was not an idle daydream, was adequately demonstrated a few decades later in the works
of literature composed by the first prominent Latvian and Estonian
poets: a young Latvian, Juris Alunanis, who in 1856 published a col-

lection of lyric poems containing also a number of fine translations of masterpieces from the western world, and "the father of Estonian poetry", Dr. Fr. R. Kreutzwald, who in the following year brought before the public the first part of a romantic poem, *Kalevipoeg*, a work based on national legends and folksongs freely recast. This work, the last part of which came out in 1861, became, as the Estonian national epic, a mighty stimulant to the national self-consciousness of Estonians.

In the wake of these two real founders of a truly national literature, a number of authors soon made their appearance. Their ranks were steadily increased, the quality of their works improving at the same time at an equal pace. By the turn of the century the literature of the three peoples was already linked in the common stream of world literature. It was the same with other fine arts. National music, painting, sculpture, scenic art etc., which had grown hand in hand with the literature, developed rapidly, especially after the turn of the century, and by the outbreak of the World War, the Baltic peoples had produced works by no means inferior to those of the leading civilized nations of the world. It is true that the number of authors and artists as well as of their works was still rather modest compared with those of peoples whose development had taken place under more favourable auspices. But how could it have been otherwise, since it was but a beginning? It was, however, a sowing, promising rich harvest in a not too distant future, especially if — as there seemed to be every reason to hope — the fetters of the superannuated, reactionary old order of Tsarist Russia, long felt to be an intolerable hindrance in every sphere of life, were to be burst by the irresistible pressure of oppositional and revolutionary forces.

Lithuania has suffered many more fickle and tragic vicissitudes than Estonia and Latvia as regards the development of literature, fine arts, and ethnic research.

The dawn of nationalism among the Lithuanian people cast its first rays in the eighteenth century. Here, too, it was the interest in folklore, popular customs, and the historical past of the nation which gave the first impulses to a national consciousness. As the first initiators and promoters of this awakening a few scholars at the university of Königsberg were outstanding. They began to publish Lithuanian folk songs and to study the Lithuanian language and ethnography.

Translated into German, Lithuanian folk songs aroused the interest of Lessing, Herder, Goethe, and other prominent poets and thinkers in Germany. It is worthy of mention that Immanuel Kant himself lent a helping hand in the publication of the first Lithuanian dictionary, contributing to it even with a foreword in which he praises enthusiastically the national character of the Lithuanian people. As a sympathetic echo to the activity of these scholars at Königsberg the first really notable Lithuanian poet, Kristionas Duonelaitis (1714–1780), wrote and published his wonderful poems.

The national catastrophe involved in the extinction of the Polish-Lithuanian state by its third and final partition in 1795 interrupted this development for a time, but a new movement of national renaissance set in soon after the turn of the century. A group of scholars centering round the university of Vilnius resumed research work into folklore, national traditions and the historical past of the Lithuanian nation. The first works of Lithuanian scholarship were published in the Lithuanian language, among them the *History of Lithuania* in two volumes and *Lithuanian popular customs* by Simonas Daukantas, two books which exerted a lasting influence on the growth of the nation's self-consciousness.

These promising beginnings, however, were brutally trampled down by the Tsarist authorities after the unsuccessful rebellion of 1831. Even the university of Vilnius was closed in 1832. A new revival became possible only in the 'fifties, when the reverses suffered by Russia in the Crimean war and the death of the Tsar Nicholas I, one of the most reactionary rulers the Russian Empire ever had, brought a certain abatement in the oppression imposed on the Lithuanians as on all the non-Russian peoples in the Empire.

However, even this new wave of national revival was to be of very short duration. It was the second unsuccessful rebellion of 1863 which gave rise to a real bacchanal of persecution aiming at the annihilation of the Lithuanian nation by its russification and forcible conversion to the Greek-Orthodox creed. Since the catholic clergy formed the backbone of national opposition to this policy, the catholic church became the main target of persecution. A number of churches, chapels, and monasteries were closed and even demolished. Riots and bloodshed were provoked by this policy.

One of the oppressive measures taken deserves to be mentioned, not only because it brought fines, imprisonment, banishment to Siberia, and other penalties and repressions to thousands of Lithuanians but also because it was no less preposterous than revolting. In the delusive, silly belief that this would hasten the russification of the Lithuanian people, from 1865 on it was prohibited to produce any kind of printed matter in the Lithuanian language with Latin characters. Only printing in Russian characters was permitted. However, people obstinately refused to read the few books printed under the auspices of the Russian government in Russian characters. Lithuanian patriots then began to publish books and periodicals in Latin characters in that minor part of ethnographic Lithuania which in the thirteenth century had fallen under the domination of the German Knights of the Cross. Though a policy of intensive germanization was being carried on in this so-called Lithuania Minor, it was still possible to publish there Lithuanian books and periodicals. From there they were smuggled into Russian Lithuania. Even catechisms, prayer books, and other works of religious literature had to be secretly introduced into Lithuania in face of the dangers of such a traffic. Repressions and penalties hung like the sword of Damocles over the smugglers as well as over those who had the illegal literature in their possession. It hardly need be stressed that even though this barbarous policy proved a notable hindrance to the development of Lithuanian national culture, it fanned the patriotic fervour of the Lithuanian people and filled them with intense hatred and contempt for the existing order and for Russia.

In Lithuania in spite of the particularly heavy oppression, a not inconsiderable degree of economic progress had been realized even in that country, thanks to the singular industriousness of its population, to say nothing of Latvia and Estonia with their more favourable natural conditions and the less heavy oppression hanging over them. An indication of this is to be found in the statistics of co-operative associations adduced above. However, the reverse side of the coin ought not to be lost sight of. Though in comparison with the conditions prevailing in the middle of the 19th century the advance was, of course, material, nevertheless social conditions had become shockingly antiquated and unjust by the eve of the first World War. Instead of being mitigated by the advancement of economy and culture, discontent and bitterness were actually increasing. The main reasons for the growing dissatisfaction were on the one hand the utterly abnormal distribution of landed property between the owners of great estates and the peasants, and the completely outmoded system of local government on the other.

As to the former, the following facts may suffice to give an idea how unendurable the conditions had become.

In Estonia barely 4,531,468 acres or 42 per cent of the total of land were owned in 1910 by 51,640 Estonian farmers, whereas 1149 large estates, owned by noble families mainly descended from German knights, covered 58 per cent (5,999,468 acres). The 42 per cent owned by the Estonian peasants were, besides, overburdened with mortgage debts representing the unpaid remainders of the purchase-prices. According to estimates these debts amounted in 1904 to about fifty per cent of the purchase-prices in the more fertile southern half of the country and to more than eighty per cent in its northern half. Moreover, it had to be taken into consideration that as monopolist sellers of land the noble owners of large estates had forced the purchase-prices considerably above the real value of the land. The excess valuation of the land was estimated to amount to 33 per cent of its real value in the southern and 75 per cent in the northern half of Estonia. Furthermore, by common agreement of the sellers a series of rights normally appertaining to the ownership of land, e.g. milling, hunting, marketing and distilling rights, had been withheld from the purchasers. Thousands of farms, burdened with heavy debts, were sold by auction in the eighteen nineties. 23,028 lessees farmed leasehold land on conditions which the noble lords had chosen to dictate. Roughly two thirds of the rural population were reduced to proletarianized and exploited classes lacking all social security. The plight of this landless rural proletariat was so woeful that masses of them had to seek salvation in emigration. No less than 572,000 Estonians emigrated to Siberia, the Caucasus, and Southern Russia between the years 1881–1897.

Not much better were conditions in Latvia. According to the records of the Latvian Board of Statistics there were in 1913 1410 large estates in that country, covering 7,808,360 acres, i.e. 48.1 per cent of the land, whereas 83,000 farmers owned 6,384,528 acres, i.e. 39.3 per cent. (The remaining 12.5 per cent consisted mainly of State property

and church estates). There were latifundia which spontaneously recalled medieval princely domains, e.g. the estate of Dundaga with
172,500 acres and those of Pope and Vilaka with 126,000 and 120,000
acres respectively. Moreover, there were numerous families who owned a number of estates, the extreme case being that of a Baron Wolff
with no less than 36 estates, covering 716,328 acres.[9] South of Daugava nine noble Baltic German families owned twenty per cent of the
land.

In Lithuania, as has already been mentioned, serfdom was abolished
nearly half a century later than in Estonia and Latvia. In return,
emancipated serfs were not deprived of any rights to land. They were
allotted plots at a definite rental and received the right to redeem them
in 49½ years. Moreover, in the process of implementation of the reform the Tsarist government in a manner favoured the peasants at the
expense of the gentry, who had been the main supporters of the rebellion in 1863 and were regarded as the chief obstacle to russification.
The peasants, distrustful of the gentry, had maintained a rather passive attitude towards the rebellion. In consequence the distribution
of landed property was not so disgracefully unjust as in Estonia and
Latvia. Still, conditions were bad enough and a radical agrarian reform was urgently needed. Suffice it to say that about forty per cent
of the land was held in large estates and that about 450 families
possessed 3.5 milion acres or twenty two per cent of the total landed
property, each of them possessing more than two thousand acres,
whereas most peasants were insufficiently provided for, their small
allotments not permitting rational and economic husbandry.

Moreover, the fact that many estates had been confiscated after the
rebellions of 1831 and 1863, and either converted into entailed estates
and turned over to Russian noble families or parcelled and dealt out
to Russian colonists, was still felt by the Lithuanian nation like an
open sore.

As to local administration, all three peoples were debarred from any
participation in it. Only small rural districts had elected local boards

[9] Cf.: *Estonia,* op. cit., pp. 14 and 41; Ojamaa—Varmas *Estonian History,*
Stockholm, 1946 (in Estonian), p. 268, 224 etc; Prof. P. Starcs *Les résultats écono-
miques de la réforme agraire en Lettonie,* Riga, 1939, pp. 87—88; Prof. A. Schwabe
Histoire du peuple letton, Stockholm, 1955, p. 192 etc.

which, however, though attending also to certain inconsiderable local needs, were rather the petty executive organs of the state administration than organs of self-government in the accepted sense of the word. When a kind of local self-government was introduced in Russia proper in 1864, this reform was not extended to either Estonia and Latvia or to Lithuania. Often in Lithuania Russians were appointed even to the posts of secretaries of local rural boards.[10]

No space need be devoted here to exposing the monstrous, truly disgraceful antiquation and injustice of the state of affairs prevailing in all the three countries regarding local administration, particularly in Latvia and Estonia, where local government was exercised by a caste, vanishingly small in numbers and alien to the local population, while the bulk of that population had no share in it. The question of a certain modernization of this system of government in the two provinces had been raised and discussed more than once in St. Petersburg, but the selfish, narrow-minded leaders of the Baltic landed nobility had always succeeded in frustrating the rather half-hearted initiatives taken by the Tsarist government to this end. The main argument against any reform was the pledge given by Tsar Peter the Great in article IX of the Treaty of Peace Russia and Sweden concluded at Nystad in 1721, which runs as follows: "His Imperial Majesty, moreover, promises to maintain all the inhabitants of the provinces of Livonia, Estonia, and Oesel, nobles and roturiers, cities, magistrates, and the guilds of artisans in all their privileges, customs, and prerogatives which they enjoyed under the domination of the King of Sweden."

No wonder the revolutionary conflagration ingnited in 1905 by the inconsiderately provoked war with Japan raged with particular violence in the Baltic area, most violently in Latvia.

There is an Italian proverb: out of a great evil springs a great good. Since their needs were in a more than unsatisfactory way served by the existing organs of local government from which they were completely debarred, the three peoples in question had to rely mainly on their own initiative, individual as well as collective, for the management of matters normally attended to by public authorities —

[19] Cf. Thomas G. Chase *The Story of Lithuania*, New York 1946, pp. 222—228; A. Zimutis, op. cit. p. 25.

by the organs of local government in particular. What an eminent Lithuanian leader, deputy to the Russian State Duma, Andrius Bulotas, wrote in an article on Lithuania published in 1915 in the Russian *New Encyplopedia* under the editorship of a group of liberal professors (vol. 24, p. 688), fully corresponded to the conditions in Latvia and Estonia, too. The statement of Mr Bulotas runs as follows: "Peasants willingly combine into agricultural unions, associations for spreading knowledge, credit associations, and co-operative societies, with a sphere of action often stretching over a number of districts. These societies have stores of agricultural implements and there are agronomists in their service. Addresses are delivered, courses of lectures on agriculture started, experimental fields organized".

The above-mentioned co-operative associations, established in the years 1901—1918, bear witness to this statement.[11]

This habit of relying on their own initiative and combining efforts in the attainment of common ends had doubtless developed, like the habit of hard work, under the pressure of the natural environment which had required it as an indispensable condition for survival. However, the deplorably bad system of local government under which they had had to live during centuries of foreign rule, especially under the 120—210 years of Russian domination, surely contributed greatly to this habit's striking still deeper roots. It goes without saying that it has stood the Baltic peoples in good stead, proving an asset of inestimable value in their fight for national freedom in 1918—1920, as well as in their efforts to establish well-ordered states with sound economy and finances, creditable social conditions, and flourishing national culture.

[11] A characteristic fact deserves to be mentioned: that the quoted article contained a number of blanks. By this the oppositionally minded publishers, displaying their indignation, wanted to bring it to the notice of the public at large that cuts had been made by the military censor. Any reasons of military character which would have justified the cuts were quite out of the question. Obviously they had been made solely because the article was running counter to the reactionary and chauvinistic policy of the government.

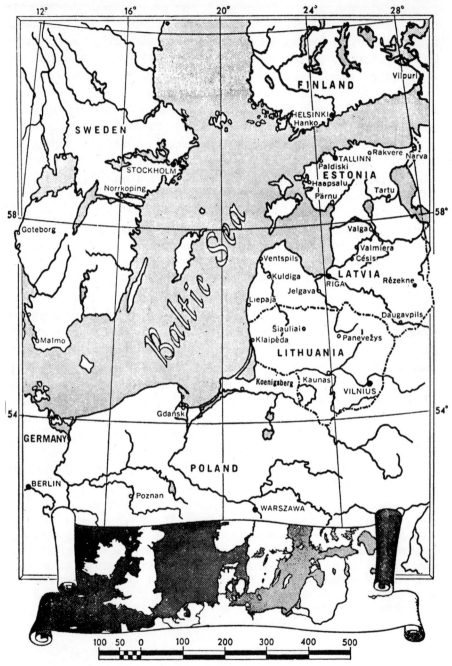

The Baltic States.

II

IN THE WHIRLWIND OF THE WORLD WAR

The downfall of the Tsarist autocracy came as no surprise to the Baltic peoples. Already by the autumn of 1915 it was obvious that Russia was not able to cope with the tremendous difficulties the great war had plunged her into. Suffering heavy losses, the Russian armies were driven back deep into Russia and the whole of Russian Poland and Lithuania were abandoned to the enemy. The railway service grew more and more ineffective and the supply of the towns with food and fuel began to break down. By the late autumn of 1916 the chaos in the administration of the vast empire and the dissatisfaction in all classes of the population had attained such proportions that the upheaval was clearly imminent.

By chance Estonia was at that juncture in a more favourable position than Latvia and Lithuania with regard to opportunities for exploiting the new conditions created by the overthrow of the Tsarist régime and the rather extensive liberty that suddenly succeeded the most rigid and oppressive regimentation. No such possibilities were offered to the Lithuanians, since the whole of their country had been occupied by the German armies from the summer of 1915 until the end of the war. As to the Latvians, their country had been cut into two nearly equal halves by the battle-front in the same summer, its northern half, north of the river Daugava (Dvina), being still held by the Russians, while the southern half was under German occupation. Only the Estonians, whose country in its entirety was still under Russian rule, had the possibility of taking action to obtain concessions from the new rulers of Russia. By quickly turning the new situation to account they managed to force through a highly important reform which was to have far-reaching beneficial consequences not only for Estonia, but also indirectly for her two Baltic neighbours.

The Estonian political leaders had given timely consideration to what they would have to do on the day after the overthrow of the Tsarist autocracy. They had decided that the first thing should be to take appropriate steps to wrest the local administration from the semi-feudal Baltic-German land-owners and making the Estonian people masters in their country by establishing free, autonomous and democratic local government. A fortnight after the Russian Provisional Government had entered into office, a bill on the autonomous self-government of Estonia was drawn up in its final shape at a conference of the leaders of the Estonian political parties and presented to the Provisional Government with an urgent request to enact it without delay.

After the overthrow of the old reactionary régime it would have been a downright scandal to tolerate, even for a very short time, a continuation of the monopoly of the barons in local administration in Estonia and keep ninety eight per cent of the population debarred from it. And this the more so as, since the very outbreak of the war, these barons had been denounced in the Russian press — not wholly without reason — for German sympathies and disloyalty to Russia, and a considerable number of them, convicted of disloyal behaviour, had been deported to Siberia, whereas no doubts had arisen as to the loyalty of the Estonians themselves. With regard to these circumstances it was well nigh impossible to decline the request presented. After some bargaining the bill was enacted with a few slight alterations. By the Law on Estonian Autonomy, issued on April 12th, 1917, the Estonian people acquired an autonomous self-government with fairly extensive authority. The two central organs of this self-government were to be a democratically elected assembly, the National Council (the Diet), and executive organ, the National Administration, appointed by the former.

Owing to this reform, which hardly would have been granted in the same liberal shape a few months later,[1] Estonia by the time of the overthrow of the Provisional Government by the communists (in November 1917), was in possession of democratically elected lawful organs of autonomous self-government enjoying the full confidence

---

[1] It is positively known that regrets of the "precipitate" granting of autonomy to the Estonians were expressed in Provisional Government circles later on, particularly when even the Ukrainians most resolutely began to demand autonomy. It is also

and support of the people, entitled to speak and empowered to act on their behalf. This circumstance endowed the Estonian people with a national cohesion which enabled them to withstand very great dangers and trials during the stormy years which were to follow the shortlived era of freedom in Russia.

From the very first days after the downfall of the Tsarist régime Estonian officers and soldiers began to take steps towards a withdrawal from the Russian army and the formation of Estonian national units. A number of Latvian regiments had already been formed in the summer of 1915 when the indomitable steamroller of the German offensive was driving back the Russian armies and a most critical situation had arisen on the whole Russian front. The fact having been observed that on Latvian soil Latvian soldiers were fighting with incomparably greater tenacity and gallantry than the Russians, the experiment was made of setting up a few companies of Latvian soldiers under the command of Latvian officers. This experiment having brought excellent results, two Latvian infantry brigades were formed, which turned out to be perhaps the staunchest units on the whole Russian front. The Latvian soldiers and officers, defending their native country, fought the enemy to the last drop of their blood. The question as to whether it might not be advisable to seek permission for the setting up of similar national units of Estonians had been discussed by the Estonian leaders already in the summer of 1916, when the danger was envisaged of a German thrust aiming at the occupation of Estonia. For a number of tactical reasons, however, the suggestion was declined by the majority of these leaders. With the downfall of the Tsarist government these considerations had vanished. At the same time an order permitting the setting up of Estonian

worth adding that an impressive manifestation organized on April 8th, 1917, by the Estonian colony in Petrograd played a considerable part in getting the bill of Estonian autonomy enacted by the Provisional Government. The exemplary order kept by the demonstrators, especially the splendid view of the 15,000 Estonian soldiers and officers of the Petrograd garrison, very favourably contrasting with the Russian soldiers who were already showing noticeable marks of dissolution of discipline, made a strong impression on the public in the Russian capital and without any doubt even on the Provisional Government, to whom the explicit demand to enact the bill in question was submitted by a delegation sent by the demonstrators.

national units could more easily be obtained from the liberal and rather weak Provisional Government than from the Tsarist government. At the urgent demand of Estonian officers and soldiers an Estonian infantry regiment was set up in May 1917, although consent to this measure was rather reluctantly given by the Provisional Government, since a tendency towards a dismemberment of the Russian Empire was scented behind such endeavours.

The immediate reason for the desire of the Estonian soldiers and officers to form Estonian military units was the fact that, widely differing in their temper and outlook from the Russians, they did not mix well with them in the Russian units, especially when after the downfall of autocracy the Russian army, fretted by the defeatist propaganda of the communists, began to disintegrate, and the atmosphere prevailing in the Russian units grew more and more displeasing to the Estonians, who instinctively disliked disorder and anarchy, while defeatism was quite unpalatable to them. Defeatist propaganda could only help the Germans to win the war, and this was the very last thing the Estonians wanted, since there could be no doubt but that a victorious Germany would annex Estonia as well as Latvia and the rule of the Baltic barons with their superannuated social privileges would be perpetuated. Even more than that: they knew that the incorporation of the Baltic provinces with Imperial Germany would sound the death-knell of the Baltic peoples.[2]

Very soon after the revolution, however, another powerful motive emerged for doing what could be done towards detaching Estonian soldiers and officers from the Russian units and bringing them together in national units: the comprehension that only by having their own military force at their disposal would the Estonian people have a chance of keeping aloof from the chaos spreading in Russia, which was certain to entail grave dangers and afflictions for the population and might even put the very existence of the Estonian people in jeopardy. Before long the overwhelming majority of Estonian soldiers

[2] The Pan-German nationalists were openly discussing in their propaganda-literature, published in the first years of the World War, how by settling a couple of million German colonists in the Baltic area and by forcing the use of the German language upon the native population, Estonia and Latvia could be completely denationalized in a couple of decades. A certain Herr P. Rorbach was especially outspoken in propagating such ideas.

and officers shared this realization — either consciously or instinctively. The Russian Provisional Government, however, continued in its
negative attitude towards the dissolution of the army into national
units.

In order to render more efficacious the measures designed to overcome this attitude of the Provisional Government, a Supreme Committee of Estonian Military Men was elected by the delegates of the
Estonian soldiers and officers from all army corps on the front and
units in the rear, and assembled in a congress in Tallinn on July
1st—4th, 1919.

The Supreme Committee developed a very active programme to attain
the ends for which it had been elected. This proved far from easy. If
the resistance of the Provisional Government and of the High
Command of the Army began to give way, this was due more to the
development of military and political events than to the very
numerous steps taken by the Committee to this end. What induced
the Russian authorities gradually to give way on this matter was
mainly the fact that the Estonian officers and soldiers with very few
exceptions were practically immune to the defeatist propaganda being
spread in the army in harmonious collaboration by both communists
and the Germans. Right up to the day of the seizure of power by
Lenin, the Provisional Government and the High Command still
cherished the hope that it would ultimately prove possible to maintain
the Russian army in existence until the end of the war, even though
its fighting value was nearly nil. Units with exceptionally strong
power of resistance to defeatist propaganda, such as the first Estonian
regiment had proved to be, were therefore of particular value, a value,
moreover, which rose in proportion to the progressive decomposition
of the army. Hence the resistance of the authorities to the formation
of the Estonian units gradually waned, and by the end of the year
there was already an Estonian infantry division, consisting of four
regiments, an artillery brigade, and a cavalry regiment.

If it had been a hard task to obtain from the Russian authorities the
orders for setting up the Estonian units, hardly less toil was required
for the actual formation of these units: to select the most able and
deserving among the Estonian officers in the different Russian armies,
to build the backbone of the first units, to get them released from the
Russian units, to organize the home-coming of the Estonian rank and

file from the Russian units and so on. Without this extensive staff work it would hardly have been possible to realise the plan, but with its successful implementation the foundation of the Estonian army was laid.

When the staff of the Estonian division was formed in early November 1917, most of this work was taken over by that staff.[3]

Happily enough the Estonian units formed as a result of the endeavours of the Supreme Committee and of the Staff of the Estonian Division were not disbanded by the first Estonian Soviet government, established in November 1917. That government hoped to convert them to dependable communist troops. This miscalculation gave them the requisite time for developing into a force in which both men and officers were well knitted together before they were disbanded by the German occupational authorities in early April 1918. Thus no time was needed to weld them into efficient fighting units when they were called up at the outbreak of the war eight months later. This circumstance was to prove of inestimable value, since in November—December 1918 the only chance of survival of the young Estonian state lay in the speed with which efficient troops could be drawn up and marched out against the invading Red Army.

Tsarist Russia has been called "the prison of nations" by her minorities. The name shows clearly enough what their feelings towards her have been. To them she personified reaction, corruption, and nationalist oppression. Yet at the moment of the downfall of the Tsarist régime the optimistic hope was widely fostered that a new and entirely different Russia would arise, a free and democratic commonwealth, in which the rights and liberties of the national minorities would find recognition and protection. For a few months even a considerable part of the Estonian people, the Estonian soldiers and officers among them, shared these optimistic illusions. It was not long, however, before stern reality shattered them. With every week it became clearer that the indispensable pre-requisites of a free and

---

[3] It is worth mentioning that the Commander of the division and his Chief of Staff were the two Estonian officers of the Russian General Staff who later, in the War of Liberation, commanded the Estonian army as its Commander-in-Chief and Chief of Staff, Colonels Johan Laidoner and Johan Soots.

democratic order did not yet exist in Russia. In the summer of 1917 it was clear that Russia was sinking into a chaos of civil war and anarchy and that no forces existed able to check this fatal course. No reasonable person could doubt the ultimate outcome. A new and presumably more detestable despotism was not only possible and probable: it was the inevitable result unmistakably foreseen. Nobody in his senses could continue to cherish the illusion of a co-existence of nations in a free and democratic Russian commonwealth.

By the autumn of 1917 there was no longer a Russian army able to defend the Empire against the enemy. From an instrument protecting the country against powers without and maintaining order within it had turned into an anarchical, unbridled, armed mass that grew daily more dangerous to peaceful citizens. When at the beginning of October 1917 the Germans occupied the Estonian islands Saaremaa (Ösel) and Hiiumaa (Dagö), the Russian forces, utterly demoralized by communist defeatist propaganda, offered no resistance. Instead of defending the country against the Germans the savage Russian soldiery devastated and pillaged it. In this tragic situation the Estonian National Council took a decisive step: falling back on the inalienable right to self-determination which in a solemn Declaration by the Soviet government on November 15th, 1917, had been explicit extended to all nationalities living in Russia, even to the point of separation from the Russian empire and the establishment of independent states, the National Council proclaimed itself the provisional supreme power in Estonian territory until the convocation of a Constituent Assembly which would finally determine the political structure of the country. At the same meeting the National Council addressed an urgent appeal to Estonian soldiers on all battlefields, calling them to return and form Estonian military units to defend their own country against the ravages of the dissolute Russian soldiery.

At the same time the National Council decided immediately to proclaim elections for the Constituent Assembly.

The National Council had hardly been able to make these decisions when it was dispelled by a mob of Soviet Russian soldiers and sailors at the instigation of the Estonian communists. The National Council and the National Administration were proclaimed dissolved and replaced by the workers' and soldiers' soviets, and an Estonian Soviet government. However, the National Council and the National

Administration continued their activities underground, directing the resistance of the Estonian people to the rule of the Soviet-collaborators supported by Russian bayonets.

The Estonian Soviet government did not cancel the decision of the National Council about the elections to the Constituent Assembly. The communists hoped that their demagogic propaganda, supported by a ruthless use of public means and power, would carry the day. However, their plan miscarried. They had not succeeded in either duping or frightening the people. The communists obtained no more than 35 per cent of the votes, the noncommunist parties whose participation in the elections had still been admitted, gathering 65 per cent. Seeing this unwelcome result of the elections, the Soviet government did not take the trouble to convoke the elected Constituent Assembly.

This first, short-lived Estonian Soviet government, raised to power by the demoralized Russian soldiery that was its only support, only deepened the prevailing anarchy and chaos. One of its actions deserves to be mentioned, since it considerably influenced the attitude of the Estonian people towards the communists: the outlawing of all Baltic noblemen and noblewomen. This act of manifest lunacy, published on January 28th, 1918, might easily have been understood as an incitement to kill the "outlaws", though the proclamation only declared that everyone was entitled and even obliged to arrest the "outlaws". Happily enough no case of murder occurred, although about two hundred "outlaws", detained in Tallinn, were within a hair's breadth of being massacred by the Russian soldiery, enraged by reckless communist demagogy. Hundreds of noblemen and noblewomen were taken into custody and deported to Russia. A number of well-known Estonians who had nothing to do with the Baltic barons, were deported together with them. A few months later all the deported "outlaws", the barons as well as the Estonians, were sent back to Estonia by the Soviet Russian authorities at the demand of Berlin.

The reason behind this act of folly was that representatives of the Baltic—German land-owning aristocracy had implored the German government to occupy Estonia, this being, in their opinion, the only way to save the lives and property of the members of their class. The efforts of the agents of the nobility to get their petitions for the occupation of Estonia signed even by Estonians brought little result, since the Estonians considered such an occupation a great national calamity

The danger of German occupation growing daily more imminent, the Estonian leaders had for some time been discussing the idea of proclaiming the independence of Estonia, hoping that this move might avert the impending misfortune, or at least turn the future of Estonia into a problem of international politics, and in this way improve the prospects of getting rid of the Germans at the end of the war.

When on February 18th, 1918, after the negotiations for a peace treaty with Soviet Russia had entered a blind alley, Germany cut short the armistice and resumed her attack, the moment had arrived to carry out the carefully considered plan. On Feb. 24th 1918, the National Council proclaimed Estonia a sovereign democratic republic, determined to observe strict neutrality in its relations to other states and hoping that these latter would equally respect its neutrality. The first Provisional Government, headed by Mr. Konstantin Päts, was formed on the same day. The Estonian Soviet government had fled to Russia the day before. The national military units organized in 1917 as the armed force of the Provisional Government, disarmed the demoralized Russian troops.

Imperial Germany, however, animated by annexationist greed, had no intention of respecting the independence of Estonia. It is scarcely necessary to stress that the military strength of the young republic was puny in face of the Germans who landed on the mainland of Estonia and occupied the whole country in a few days. The Provisional Government had to suspend its activities, since Berlin had other plans for Estonia than independence. The Provisional Government, however, continued its activity underground, directing passive resistance to the occupation forces. When it was disclosed by an unfortunate accident that Prime Minister Päts was personally leading this activity, he was arrested and sent to a concentration camp in Poland, where he was detained until the capitulation of Germany. A delegation secretly sent abroad by the Provisional Government, succeeded in May 1918 in obtaining the *de facto* recognition of the Republic of Estonia by Great Britain, France, and Italy.

Eight days before the proclamation of the independence of Estonia, on February 16th, 1918, the Council of Lithuania (Lietuvos Taryba), elected by a National Assembly convened at Vilnius in September, 1917, referring to the generally recognized right of nations to self-determination, proclaimed the restoration of Lithuania as a sovereign state. It is true that this Assembly had not issued from democratic elections, for such were out of the question while the country was occupied by Germans. It is likewise true that having been convened with the permission of the German authorities, the Assembly, as well as the Taryba elected by it, had of necessity to pay deference to Imperial Germany. Thus the Taryba, hard pressed by the Germans, had to declare, in a document issued on December 11th, 1917, that it was "in favour of a lasting and sound alliance with Germany". All the same, the Assembly was a faithful organ of the Lithuanian nation, since all prominent and well-known men, representatives of the various parties, classes, and professions, 214 in all, attended it. No less qualified was the permanent organ elected by the Assembly, the Taryba, whose twenty members belonged to the very flower of the Lithuanian nation.

No less than the Estonians and Lithuanians the Latvians desired to constitute their own sovereign state. However, the fact that the territory of Latvia since the summer of 1915 had been cut into. two halves, unable to communicate with one another, impeded them from convening an assembly endowed with the requisite authority for proclaiming, on behalf of the Latvian people, the independence of Latvia. Only when with the capitulation of Germany the separating front disappeared, did it become possible for the Latvians to convoke such an assembly in their capital, Riga. This assembly, called The People's Council, attended by representatives from all Latvian political parties except the communists, proclaimed on November 18th, 1918, the independence of Latvia. Until such time as the constitution was drawn up and came into force the People's Council, in which national minorities, too, were represented, was to be the bearer of the supreme power. The Council was presided over by Mr. Janis Chakste, who later on was elected the first President of the Republic. The Provisional Government, appointed by the People's Council, was headed by Prime Minister K. Ulmanis.

It is, however, worth mentioning that a declaration demanding the election of a Latvian Constituent Assembly for the establishment of an autonomous Latvian state, had been adopted exactly twelve months earlier, on November 18th, 1917, by a conference held in Valk, a small town on the Estonian—Latvian border, and attended by representatives of those sections of the Latvian political parties which had been acting in the northern half of the country, still held by the Russian armies. This conference had also appointed a provisional Latvian National Council which should take all requisite steps for the establishment of a free, autonomous state. As a delegate of this body, Mr. Z. Meyerovics, who was later to direct the foreign policy of the Latvian state, had been sent to London on the mission of securing the recognition of the independence of Latvia by Great Britain and other Western Powers. A week before the official declaration of the independence of Latvia, on November 11th, 1918, Latvia was recognized as a *de facto* independent state by His Britannic Majesty's Government.

In the first half of the year 1918, having defeated Russia and Rumania and occupied vast territories in the east, the government and the military leaders of Germany were confident of final victory. Plans were drawn up as to how, among other things, the Baltic countries could be incorporated into a Greater Germany as a satellite state. According to these plans local administration was to remain the monopoly of the Baltic-German land-owning nobility. A couple of million German soldiers were to be settled in the Baltic area, which was to be denationalized in less than twenty years.

The Baltic peoples, on the other hand, were no less firmly convinced that all these grand plans would very soon come to naught. Looking foward with passionate longing to the defeat of Germany, they welcomed every piece of news boding the imminent collapse of Imperial Germany, and when this at last occurred, it came like a vivifying, splendid sunrise after a gloomy night.

The Estonian Provisional Government, which had continued its activity underground, resumed it openly on November 11th, the very day of Germany's capitulation. The two most urgent tasks it had to grapple with were the re-establishment of the administrative apparatus, smashed and thrown into chaos by the Estonian Soviet government, and the restoration of the economy, heavily damaged by the years of war, revolutionary disorders, the pillaging Russian soldiery, and the ruthless extortions of the German occupational authorities. However, the Provisional Government had not been able to devote its energy to these tasks for more than eleven days when suddenly, on November 22nd, the German companies which were still holding the front on the border of Soviet Russia, east of Narva, were without warning attacked by Soviet Red Army units manifestly bent on the capture of Narva.

This assault was repulsed by the Germans, but it appeared immediately thereafter that a concentration of Red Army forces was gathering in front of Narva, and on November 28th a new and considerably stronger attack took place. This time very few Germans were still in the trenches, the great majority of them having set out for their homes in Germany. Although the Provisional Government, among its other urgent tasks, had paid due attention to the re-establishment of the military units formed from April 1917 to March 1918, and two days after the first assault of the Red Army partial mobilization had been proclaimed in the Narva district, there had been no possibility to form military units worthy of the name in a few days. About a thousand hastily gathered men, an embryo of, and raw material for, an infantry regiment, had been sent to Narva to replace the Germans who had left. This feeble force was far too insufficient to hold its ground and repulse the attack, which was supported by artillery whereas the defenders had not a single gun. The inevitable result was the fall of Narva to the Red Army (on November 28th). The Estonian War of Liberation had begun.

One cannot emphasize strongly enough that the same Soviet Government that almost exactly a year before had explicitly recognized the inalienable right of all nations of the Russian Empire to national self-determination, even unto separation from Russia, and the establishment of independent states, now entirely disregarded the fact that the freely and democratically elected assembly of representatives of the Estonian people, referring to that very inalienable right, had proclaimed Estonia an independent, democratic state. It was impossible to deny that the Estonian National Council, freely elected according to democratic franchise, was the authoritative spokesman of the Estonian people, fully entitled to act on its behalf. But instead of entering into negotiations with the lawfully constituted organs of the Republic of Estonia, the Soviet Russian Government embarked upon unprovoked aggression against Estonia without even declaring war upon her, let alone presenting her an ultimatum, even a trumped-up one. Judged by the standards of international morality and decency which at the Nurnberg trials, with the participation of the Soviet Union, were constituted rules of International Law, this wilful aggression was a punishable international crime.

No more justifiable was the aggression started by Soviet Russia simultaneously against Latvia and Lithuania. Although the bodies by which the independence of these two states had been proclaimed, had not originated from democratic general elections, this was in no way the fault of the peoples concerned, since circumstances beyond their control had prevented such elections from being held. Thus the authoritative representatives of the political parties of these peoples, giving expression to the will of the respective nations, incontestably had the power to proclaim their determination to separate from Russia and constitute independent states. Besides, the Soviet Government itself has later, in peace treaties concluded with all the Baltic States in 1920, recognized that these states had come into existence on the strength of the right of all nations to decide their own destinies, a right proclaimed by the Federal Socialist Soviet Republic of Russia (art. 2 of the said peace treaties). This was a retroactive recognition on the part of Soviet Russia that the bodies which had proclaimed the independence of Latvia and Lithuania, let alone the lawfully elected Estonian National Council, had been expressing the will of the three peoples and acting on their behalf.

To justify this unprovoked aggression a trumped-up explanation was put into circulation at the same time as the attack was going on. It has been repeated ever since and is to be found, e.g., in the third volume of the *History of Diplomacy*, published in Moscow (in Russian) in 1945, viz. that the Estonian workers, together with Red Army detachments, liberated Estonia and established there a Soviet government which soon thereafter, on Dec. 8th, 1918, was recognized by the Russian Soviet government, and that Lavia and Lithuania, too, having been "liberated" in the same way, had their independence recognized by the Russian Soviet government *(Hist. of Dipl.,* v.3, p.56). How wide a gulf separates these allegations from reality and truth, may be seen from the following facts.

As to the Estonian workers, they never dreamed of liberating Estonia together with the Soviet Red Army detachments, for this could mean nothing other than helping the Red Army to conquer Estonia and incorporate it into Soviet Russia. What in actual fact occurred was an attempt to subdue the three Baltic peoples, who for themselves desired nothing but to be left alone. It was an aggression embarked upon by those in power in Soviet Russia in the name of the "world revolution", the fantastic idea of which had originated, during the first World War, in the brains of their leader, already then undoubtedly seriously affected by the incurable ill-omened disease which a few years later turned him into a living corpse and soon did away with him. That this aggression had absolutely nothing to do with either the Estonian or the Latvian and the Lithuanian workers, is incontrovertibly proved by a frank pronouncement in *Izvestia*, the official organ of the Central Executive Committee of the Soviet of the Deputies of the Workers, Peasants and Soldiers, then the highest authority of the Soviet State, on December 25th, 1918, i.e. at the very time the Red Army was attempting to subjugate the three Baltic peoples with fire and sword. This pronouncement reads as follows: "Estonia, Latvia, and Lithuania are directly on the road from Russia to Western Europe and are therefore a hindrance to our revolution, because they separate Soviet Russia from Revolutionary Germany ... This separating wall has to be destroyed. The Russian Red proletariat should find an opportunity to influence the revolution in Germany. The conquest of the Baltic Sea would make it possible for Soviet Russia to agitate in favour of the Social revolution in the Scandinavian countries so that the Baltic Sea would be transformed into the sea of the Social Revolution."

As to the Red Army, on the other hand, it never succeeded in "liberating" Estonia. Neither was any Soviet government established in Estonia. It is true that a so-called Estonian Soviet government was carried to the Estonian frontier in the train of the Red Army, among its other paraphernalia, but it never got into Estonia. In Narva, on the Estonian frontier, it was awaiting the fall of the Estonian capital Tallinn in order to be conveyed there. When, instead of capturing Tallinn, the Red Army was forced to beat a hasty retreat from Narva as the Estonian army made a rapid advance upon on it, this puppet and tool of the Soviets, too, fled to Russia, where it was disbanded a few months later when Moscow discovered it to be a useless and even annoying toy.[4]

III

FIGHT TO THE DEATH

To be or not to be was the question raised for the Baltic peoples by the Red Army aggression. Whether to take up arms against it or to submit without resistance, considering it hopeless to contend against the mighty Russian Empire even though it was plunged in the chaos of civil war and anarchy.

It is small wonder that there were also those in Estonia who were inclined to choose the second path out of the dilemma, seeing no possibility of resistance to the aggression. As already mentioned, the Estonian military units had been disbanded by the Germans and their weapons taken away. There was no money in the Treasury — or rather, there was no Treasury at all. The administrative apparatus of the Republic had been shattered by the Estonian Soviet government in November, 1917, and had not been re-established by the Germans. How to wage war without army, weapons, money, administrative apparatus, when, moreover, the economic life of the country had been thrown out of gear by four and a half years of war, revolutionary disorders and the ruthless plundering of a foreign occupation?

But knowing what they did of communist Soviet rule through their own experience during the four months in the winter of 1917—1918, as well as from reports of the horrible conditions it created in Russia, there could be no hesitation for the Estonians. Submission without resistance to a power that would outlaw and deport whole groups of citizens without giving anyone the chance of defending himself and

---

⁴ A curious parallel to this Estonian Soviet government of the year 1918—1919 was constituted by O. W. Kuusinen's "government" of the "Democratic People's Republic of Finland" twenty one years later. This puppet and tool of the Red Army, too, never got any farther into Finland than the small summer resort Terijoki on Finland's frontier, where it was proclaimed. After a few months it was just as slightingly dropped and disbanded.

refuting the charges brought against him was out of the question. Only a people like the Russian, who had lived from time immemorial under despotic rule and had never had occassion to acquire the habits of respect for law and order, could stand such a power and such an order.[1] The Estonian people, as well as the two other Baltic peoples who have always belonged to western European culture by virtue of their religion and their developed sense of personal responsibility, justice and order, will never endure such a power. Indeed it was a grave mistake on the part of communists if they had imagined that by outlawing the Baltic barons and thus indulging the Estonian people in their deep-rooted bitter feeling towards that privileged caste, they would gain great popularity. Lynch law was unacceptable and repugnant to the Estonian people, even if applied to the members of the ruling class for whom they felt no sympathy.

But one decision could therefore be taken by the Estonian as by the Latvian and the Lithuanian peoples: armed resistance to the unprovoked imperialist aggression to the last drop of their blood, even if a start must be made with bare hands! There was even more reason for taking this stand, for civil war was raging in Russia and the Red Army had to fight on other, very extensive fronts besides the Baltic.

Organizing the army became now the most important task of the Provisional Government. In this as well as in everything else the National Council, summoned to an extraordinary session on November 20, 1918, proved a really invaluable support. Through it the Estonian nation spoke, giving its unanimous, inspiring support to the Government and the army, its fifty members so many emissaries and ardent organizers of the nation's exertions for survival as free men and women.[2]

---

[1] A few lines from a book by a Russian historian may deserve to be quoted in this context: "What this legal anarchy meant can hardly be exaggerated ... We may recall in this connection the prophetic words of Count Witte in an address delivered in 1905: 'Woe to the country whose people have not learnt to respect the principles of legality and the right of property, and where a system of collective ownership prevails that is regulated by obscure custom and arbitrary judgment; such a country may become sooner or later the scene of unparalleled calamities' ". (M. Florinsky, *The End of the Russian Empire*, Yale Univ. Press, 1913, p. 127).

[2] Communist members had fled to Soviet Russia.

Considering the fact that a totally new situation had arisen with the Soviet agression, the Provisional Government resigned and the National Council appointed a new cabinet with Mr. K. Päts as Prime Minister and myself as Deputy Prime Minister and Minister of Labour We had already been in close and harmonious collaboration in the preceding year, Mr. Päts having been elected Chairman of the Supreme Committee of the Estonian Military Men and I Vice-Chairman. Having soon thereafter been elected Chairman of the National Administration, Mr. Päts, attaching great importance to the work being done by that Committee, continued to devote to it as much of his time as the duties of Chairman of the Administration left him.

There were tens of thousands of Estonians who had received their military training in the Russian army and on the battlefields of the great war. As to weapons and munition, they had to be procured from without and the Provisional Government took appropriate steps to obtain them. The first, though moderate, quantity of them came from Finland. The first delivery of rifles and of a few guns with adequate munitions arrived in Tallinn before the end of November, 1918. An incomparably larger quantity of arms, most valuable among them one thousand light machine-guns, were handed over to the Estonian army by the British admiral Sinclair, who put into Tallinn's roadstead with a squadron on December.[3]

These deliveries of arms made it possible to start forming regiments armed with modern weapons. Their formation and drilling took place with great energy and feverish haste. Fortunately there was an ample supply not only of younger officers exercised in battle in the ranks of the Russian army, but also of senior officers, among them a number who had graduated with distinction from the Russian military academies and acquired vast experience both in commanding units on the battlefield and in staff work. And it was natural that the most able among these staff officers, a man whose brilliant talents had

[3] One cannot pass over in silence the fact that the Estonian authorities could not secure the return from the Germans of the rifles and guns taken away when the Estonian military units had been disbanded in April, 1918. Not being able to take these weapons along when they were leaving Estonia, the Germans made them unusable by throwing the gunlocks into the sea, from where a certain quantity of them was later rescued by Estonian divers.

attracted attention already in the Academy of the General Staff in St. Petersburg, Colonel Johan Laidoner, should now be appointed Commander-in-Chief of the Estonian army.

However feverish the haste with which the formation and training of the military units proceeded, it could not be carried out in a couple of weeks, the less so as there were no accumulated supplies to equip the units with all the necessary kit. Even the Army Commissariat had to be created out of nothing at the same time as the fighting units were being formed and drilled. In the meantime nothing could be done other than try to make the best use of the scant and still very insufficiently trained, rather guerilla than regular forces, available for fighting on the battle-front, to delay the advance of the enemy as long as possible. With this end in view, every natural barrier and every conceivable device was made use of to gain time while regular troops were equipped, drilled and welded into plucky units, thus preparing for the day when it would be possible to stop the retreat and launch the counter-offensive.

For all that it would have been utterly careless to reckon that the enemy would not forestall this plan by hastily concentrating an overwhelming superiority of forces on the Estonian front and smashing the feeble defence with one massive stroke. Assistance in military units from abroad seemed therefore indispensable in the initial phase of the war and at the very beginning of the Soviet aggression the Provisional Government turned to the Finnish government, since only from that country was it conceivably possible to get such help. The Finnish government, however, declared that in the prevailing states of affairs it was able to give only a limited supply of arms and financial help. Instead, a Committee for Aiding Estonia was set up by a number of prominent persons in order to raise volunteers and form companies to be sent to Estonia. Although thousands of young men enlisted in these companies, the activity of the Committee was in the beginning handicapped by the hostile attitude taken towards it by the Finnish Socialist Party and trade-unionists, very inadequately informed about the rather complicated situation in Estonia and grossly mis-informed by Soviet propaganda. This propaganda, zealously spread not only in Finland and Sweden, but also everywhere else, depicted the Estonian Provisional Government as a clique of reactionaries who in collusion with the heinous Baltic barons sought to drown in blood the working people risen in rebellion to set up a free, democratic order in Estonia.

To counter these brazen lies I drafted on Christmas Eve, on behalf of the Estonian Socialist Party, an appeal to the Socialist Parties of Finland and Sweden and another, which was adopted two days later by the National Council, to the democracies of the world. In these appeals I unmasked the shameless mendacity of the Soviet propaganda. Immediately after that, with the warmest blessing of the Prime Minister, I went to Finland, where, attending as a guest the congress of the Finnish Socialist Party, I succeeded in persuading the Finnish Labour leaders that Estonia was defending her national freedom against an unjust, unprovoked aggression. From this time on the Finnish Labour Party took a benevolent attitude to the Estonian War of Liberation and desisted from obstructing the efforts of the Finnish Committee for Aiding Estonia.

Warm moral support to the cause of Estonia was also given, on behalf of the Socialist Party of Sweden, by its great leader Hjalmar Branting in a telegram sent in reply to my telegram from Helsinki and the appeal of the Estonian Socialist Party, and the leading paper of the Party condemned the Soviet aggression against Estonia and the two other young Baltic States in very strong terms.

The counter-offensive of the Estonian forces was launched, at last, on January 7th, 1919. Even then units had to be sent into battle still sorely in need of continuation training. There was, however, no choice. They had to complete their training on the battlefields, since the front was already nearing the ganglion of the defences of the country, the capital Tallinn. Its nearest point was but seventeen miles from Tallinn; at night the flashes of batteries in action could be seen on the horizon from the town. The first units of volunteers, some six hundred men, had just arrived from Finland. These volunteers proved to be very tough soldiers and were of great help in the counter-offensive started the very day they reached the battlefront. Most inportant, however, was the heartening and inspiring effect of their arrival on the morale of the Estonian troops, inevitably affected to some extent by the six weeks of disheartening retreat under the pressure of an enemy far superior in numbers and equipment.

The offensive was supported by batteries of field-artillery, although still in far from sufficient strength, and three armoured trains built by the Estonian workers in the workshops of Tallinn. Moreover, a nucleus of the Estonian navy had in the meantime come into being as a result of an attempt to penetrate into Tallinn's roadstead made on December 27th, 1918 by two Soviet destroyers which had fallen an easy prey to Admiral Sinclair's naval squadron. Magnanimously handed over to the Estonians, and manned by Estonian sailors, under the command of Estonian officers, these destroyers very effectively supported the offensive by repeatedly performed landings behind the hastily retreating enemy front. The result was a complete discomfiture of the invaders. The Red Army troops, who after six weeks of toilsome offensive had come almost in sight of the steeples of Tallinn, were routed and in twelve days driven back over the border of Estonia, leaving behind them rich booty. It took a few more weeks to drive off also those enemy forces which had penetrated into Estonia from the south-east, via Pskov. On the first anniversary of the proclamation of independence, on February 24th, 1919, the Commander-in-Chief was in a position to announce that there was no longer a single enemy soldier on the soil of Estonia, apart of course from the considerable number of prisoners.

Soviet aggression had more success in Latvia, where conditions for resistance were far worse or rather quite non-existent. Neither had it been possible to call into being a democratically elected autonomous local government nor to build up its apparatus, nor had the Provisional Government, appointed on November 18th, 1918, any organized cadres of officers and soldiers at its disposal, from which it would have been possible speedily to set up military units able at first to slow down the advance of the Red Army and then to repulse it. Moreover, arms and munitions were completely lacking. Whereas practically all Estonian soldiers and officers, obeying the call of the Estonian National Council, had come home from the Russian army before the country was occupied by the Germans in February 1918, the great majority of Latvian soldiers and officers had stayed on in Soviet Russia, their country having been occupied by the Germans and the frontier between Russia and Latvia closed.

In such a situation there was practically no chance of survival for the young state unless it got military assistance from without. There was, however, hardly any prospect of this from the western Allied Powers, whose peoples, exhausted by the long-drawn-out war, impatiently demanded prompt demobilization as soon as Germany had capitulated. Neither was it conceivable to obtain help from any other state — except Germany, to whom the conquest of Latvia by the Red Army and her transformation into a province of the communist Soviet empire would have been highly unwelcome for several reasons. On the one hand the wildfire of communist subversive propaganda could easily spread from a Soviet Latvia to the adjacent East Prussia. Of still greater weight was the fact that the Baltic area in general, and quite especially Latvia with her sturdy German minority, had for seven centuries been a highly important bastion of Germany in the east. Germany, whose ambitious aspirations to world domination had come to nothing with the defeat on the western front, could hardly countenance the obliteration of this old, venerable outpost of German civilization on the other side. Germany still had, even after the capitulation, a powerful military force and ample stores of arms and munitions at her disposal, being fully capable of putting a stop to the conquest of Latvia by the Red Army. Nor had the victorious Western Powers any serious objections to such a manœuvre by Germany, as they were equally interested in stemming the expanding wave of the communist World Revolution, and especially as they themselves were unable to intervene with their own forces in Latvia.

While drawing up the terms of armistice they had therefore appreciated the need to allow German troops to stay in the Baltic area for some time to bar the Red Army from further advance and to afford the Baltic nations the time they needed to arm themselves and assume their own defence. An article (12) had been inserted in the Conditions of Armistice with Germany, signed on November 11th, 1918, according to which "all German troops at present in the territories which before the war formed part of Russia", were "to return to within the frontiers of Germany as soon as the Allies shall think the moment suitable, having regard to the internal situation of these territories", — consequently to stay there until instructions were given them to return to Germany. For the same reason the Treaty of Peace signed at Versailles on June 28th, 1919 contained the same clause in its art. 433.

No complications would have arisen if Germany had had the honest intention of observing the terms of armistice and of the peace treaty. Unfortunately this was not the case. Instead of devoting their endeavours to the tasks assigned to them by the terms of armistice, the German troops left in the Baltic area began, with the knowledge and consent of their new republican government, to pursue their own quite different and dubious aims.

The spokesman of Germany in the Baltic area was a certain Herr A. Winnig, one of those right-wing German socialists who had adopted the annexionist aims of the Pan-German ruling circles.[4]

Already in the summer of 1918, when Hindenburg and Ludendorff were still actually controlling the policy of Germany, this queer socialist had been considered a man fit to represent Imperial Germany as her plenipotentiary in the Baltic area, with his seat in Riga. With this gentleman the Latvian Provisional Government had now to negotiate agreements on the assistance to be rendered by German troops for the defence of Latvia against Soviet aggression. The fact that it was only by this assistance that the submersion of the country by the Red Army could be warded off, was exploited to the full by Herr Winnig, who imposed upon the Latvian government conditions which, far from promoting the effective defence of the country, were highly detrimental to that defence and could result only in its breakdown. Of course, what Herr Winnig had in mind and was aiming at was the preservation of the dominant position of the Baltic-German land-owning nobility with its latifundia and semi-feudal privileges. That such a policy must inevitably arouse caustic bitterness among the owerwhelming majority of the Latvian people and ruin all prospects of united, impassioned efforts to repel the Soviet aggression, ought to have been manifest to anyone in his senses. Herr Winnig and his advisers were, however, unable to understand this. They of course envisaged quite a different way out of the mortal dangers which threatened Latvia and the whole Baltic area.

According to the aggreement concluded by Herr Winnig with the Latvian Provisional Government on December 7th, 1918, Germany undertook to assist Latvia by forming a volunteer armed force

---

[4] No wonder that he was praised as "a great patriot" by one of the most enthusiastic admirers of Hitler, and warmest adherents of his nazi-gospel, General R. von der Goltz, of whom there will be occasion to speak more further on (v.v.d. Goltz's book *Als politischer General im Osten*, Leipzig, 1936, p. 81).

consisting of a home guard, called *Die Baltische Landeswehr*, and a military unit, called The Iron Brigade (soon after renamed The Iron Division). Both were to be commanded by German officers.

As do the *Landeswehr*, an embryo of it had already come into being in the middle of November, 1918, a few days after the capitulation of Germany. The initiative towards this had been taken by a body called the *Baltischer Vertrauensrat*, actually a quasi-regency, appointed by the German Government in the summer of 1918 when preparations were being made for the creation of a German satellite state out of the three Baltic "provinces", with a Hohenzollern prince at its head. According to the agreement of December 7th the *Landeswehr* was to consist of Latvian, German and Russian companies. No mobilization of the *Landeswehr* was admitted by Herr Winnig. Rendering lip-service to the fact that the overwhelming majority of the population consisted of Latvians, he agreed to a clause according to which the number of men in Latvian companies could attain to double that in the Baltic-German companies. This clause, however, remained inoperative. Since the command was in the hands of the Germans, who controlled also the enlistment of the volunteers, and moreover, all supplies were to come from the sixth German reserve-corps, so that the Latvian companies were wholly dependent upon Germans, the latter had full liberty to enlist as many or as few men in the Latvian companies as they liked. Actually the number of men in the Latvian companies was but a fraction of that in the German ones.

As to the Iron Division, it was to be formed of volunteers enlisted among the soldiers and officers of the German sixth reserve-corps stationed in Latvia. However, intensive propaganda for enlistment into this division was started also in Germany and enlistment offices were opened in a number of German towns. Already in early March the division numbered four thousand men. Consisting of soldiers and officers who were German citizens, this troop was a purely German unit.

In short, the whole armed force was to be an instrument firmly in German hands, whereas the rightful masters of the country, the Latvians, had to content themselves with the part of fifth wheel of the coach.

But even this was not the whole story. According to a complementary agreement concluded on December 29th, 1918, the volunteers of the Iron Division were to acquire not only Latvian citizenship, but also the right to allotments of agricultural land for settlement as farmers if they had fought on Latvian soil against Soviet aggression for four weeks. In order to render the allotment of land to these German settlers possible, the official representation of the land-owning nobility of Latvia passed a resolution according to which all owners of large estates were to sacrifice one third of their land to this end. In this way convenient opportunities were to be opened for settling thousands of German colonists in the country and thus strengthening the German minority in Latvia.

All these conditions had doubtless been set up by Herr Winnig on the advice and at the instigation of the leaders of the German minority of Latvia, among whom the owners of the latifundia were playing first violin. Moreover, this minority, though constituting only 3$^1/_2$ per cent of the population, was to have from twelve to fifteen per cent of the mandates in the provisional organ of the sovereign power, the People's Council, and assurances were to be given that institutions of nobility were not to be suppressed and no agrarian reform was to be carried out.

The Latvian Government had to swallow all these conditions. It had no choice. It was in the position of a drowning man who has to accept any conditions the only possible rescuer might put forward. Neither Herr Winnig, nor those on whose advice the agreement was drawn up, ever asked themselves whether the Latvian Government would feel any moral obligation to carry out such extortionate conditions. Of course this question did not arise for them, since they believed that they would before long be able to do away with this government and with the free and sovereign Latvian state as well as with the other two Baltic states.

As it was, the Red Army made haste to overrun the country before adequate armed resistance could be organized. By the end of December it had already flooded the northern half of the country and on January 3rd, 1919, the same fate befell the capital Riga.

The Latvian Provisional Government removed to the seaport town Liepaja (Libau), where the German 6th reserve-corps had its headquarters. Before long the the whole country was overrun and occupied by the Red Army, barring Liepaja with a rather limited area round it.

On February 18th the Latvian government made an agreement with the Estonian government according to which Latvian citizens residing in Estonia could be mobilized into Latvian units to be formed in Estonia. Until they passed over onto Latvian territory and under the command of their own government these units were to owe their allegiance to the Estonian Commander-in-Chief, but were to be used only in operations in the southern front of Estonia, i.e. against the Latvian Red Army. Estonia was to provide them, against Latvia's account, with weapons and other necessities, as far as her own needs and resources would permit. Two Latvian infantry regiments, two batteries of artillery, and a squadron of cavalry were formed by virtue of this agreement. These units were able to take part in the operations against the *Landeswehr* and the Iron Division in June, to the story of which we shall come further on.

In early February the 6th reserve-corps had a new commander appointed, the above-mentioned General R. v. d. Goltz, who twelve months before had commanded a German expeditionary corps in Finland. Being a staunch monarchist and arch-reactionary, this "political general" cherished far-reaching, rather fantastic plans: to organise first, jointly with Russian counter-revolutionary white forces, a crusade to overthrow the Soviet government and restore the monarchy in Russia; then having in that monarchy won a faithful friend and ally to Germany, he was to march on Berlin and restore the monarchy there too; after the accomplishment of these exploits the two allied monarchies were to resume the fight against the western Allies and liberate Germany "from the shackles of the Versailles treaty". . . These visionary schemes of his were frankly revealed later by v.d. Goltz himself in several passages in his book, especially on p. 165.[5]

It was not to be wondered that v. d. Goltz was anything but kindly disposed to the Latvian government. Its very existence was a hindrance to the realisation of his preposterous plan, which must be tackled without delay. Every possible occasion was used for obstructing

[5] By the way, v.d. Goltz obviously in good earnest believed it to be possible to carry out these odd plans behind the back or rather before the eyes of the gullible and unsuspecting victorious Allies as can be inferred from the violence of the abuses which he in his book heaps upon the latter for having seen through and thwarted his clumsy plots.

the Government and hampering its activity. All the same the authority of the Government was slowly but steadily rising among the people. V. d. Goltz therefore decided to get rid of it. On April 16th, 1919, a Baltic German troop withdrawn from the battlefront of Liepaja all of a sudden surrounded the seat of the Government, attempting to arrest its members, and declared it deposed. With great difficulty v. d. Goltz managed to keep down the civil war which was almost precipitated, and it proved still more difficult to find any Latvians of reputation willing to compromise themselves by agreeing to appointment as members of a puppet government by the grace of v. d. Goltz. At last a "government" was appointed, headed by an arch-reactionary Latvian clergyman, A. Niedra, who could rightly claim the honour of being the archetype of the species well known since the second world war under the designation of "Quisling". The plot miscarried, however, as far as the planned arrest of the members of the government was concerned: the Prime Minister K. Ulmanis and several members of his Cabinet succeeded in escaping to the British Legation, from where they passed over to and settled down on a Latvian steamer *(Saratov)* in the roadsteads of Liepaja, under the protection of British men- of- war.

It is worth mentioning that the Allied Powers reacted at the *coup d'état* in Liepaja, demanding of the German government the immediate re-establishment of the lawful Latvian government with the liberty of carrying out its duties and the power of enrolling Latvian troops. Unfortunately they refrained from taking any vigorous steps to enforce these demands when the German government, advancing evasive and deceptive explanations, omitted to carry them out. As a result of this failure the Quisling-government of Herr Niedra was to have a couple of months of grace before it was flung on the rubbish-heap of history.

It goes without saying that the Estonian government continued to consider the cabinet of Mr. Ulmanis as the lawful government of Latvia.

Here we must interrupt our account of the events in Latvia and pass over to Lithuania.

Lithuania, like Estonia and Latvia, went out empty-handed to meet the invasion of the Red Army in the last days of December, 1918. The

Provisional Government had neither any organized and trained military units, nor weapons and munitions at its disposal. When the Germans evacuated the Lithuanian capital Vilnius, the Provisional Government had to retire to Kaunas, the largest town but one of the country, situated about sixty miles to the west of Vilnius. Any possibility of repelling the invaders and preventing the capture of the city was, of course, out of the question. On January 5th it was occupied by the Red Army.

With regard to the fact that only very scant volunteer units, utterly inadequately provided with weapons and munitions in some way or other acquired from German soldiers, were offering resistance to the invaders during the first two months, one cannot but be astonished that not the whole country, but only its northern and eastern areas were overrun and occupied by the Red Army. Either the Soviet government was of the opinion that no significant military force was needed for the subjection of the weaponless country, and placed its reliance mainly upon the dissolving effect of subversive communist propaganda, or the Red Army troops were more badly needed on other fronts in the Russian civil war. The fact, at any rate, remains.

Already in February the Lithuanian volunteer units managed to inflict the first, rather serious defeats upon the enemy: on February 7th at Kedainai, and on February 14th at Alytus. These successes were rendered possible by the fact that more normal, if still far from adequate supplies of weapons and munitions to the fighting units had been secured by a treaty which the government had succeeded in concluding with Germany. After the enactment of compulsory enrolment (on March 5th), the Lithuanian army began to reconquer the territory which had fallen into the hands of the enemy. By early June about half of the invaded territory was recaptured and the Lithuanian army was preparing to envelop Vilnius from the north and south.

However, already in this early phase of the struggle of the Lithuanians for their national freedom friction with Poland developed which boded ill for the Lithuanian cause.

Before the extinction of the Lithuanian state and its swallowing up — mainly by Russia — in 1795, as already mentioned, it had been a minor partner in the Polish-Lithuanian Union, concluded in Lublin in 1569. After the breakdown of the Tsarist "prison of nations" the Lithuanians aspired to restore their own sovereign statehood. How-

ever, there can scarcely have been a single Lithuanian who also desired to see the old Polish—Lithuanian union re-established. At any
rate no Lithuanian of any standing is known to have given expression
to such a desire. Quite the contrary: already in that very first declaration of December 11th, 1917, in which, as already mentioned,
the restoration of the Lithuanian state was demanded, the authoritative organ of the Lithuanian nation, the Taryba, stressed in unequivocal terms that "all political bonds which at any time had linked
Lithuania with other states would be abandoned". The same announcement was repeated word for word in the declaration of independence, issued by the Taryba on February 16th, 1918, and presented
to the governments of Russia, Germany and other states.

This was, of course, the only conceivable attitude the Lithuanians
could take. The memories left behind by the Lublin union were not
such as to arouse a longing for its restoration. Besides, the Lithuanians
were no longer what they had been at the moment of the extinction
of the Lublin union at the end of the eighteenth century — a mass
of illiterate rustics with a sprinkling of gentry, who, though of Lithuanian descent, were fused with the Polish gentry, having adopted
its language, turn of mind, and manner of living. As already pointed
out, Lithuania too had seen the emergence of the classes of modern
industrial society, as well as of a national literature, national arts, national research and national self-consciousness — this in the teeth of
all hindrances placed in their way by the chauvinistic and reactionary
Tsarist government. Like all culturally more advanced national minorities of the Russian Empire the Lithuanians were irresistibly roused
by the call for national self-determination which in the course of the
great war had become one of the most loudly resounding and most
effective rallying-cries of the democratic Powers. The Lithuanians
wanted to be masters in their own house and not minor partners in
a union.

That is not to say that the Lithuanians had become unfriendly to
the Poles. Far from that. Centuries of close ties had left behind a
comprehensive legacy of common feelings, and among the stimulating
impulses which the growing Lithuanian civilization was receiving
from without, those radiating from Poland played, if not a predominant, at any rate an eminent part. It is worthy of note that it was a
widespread custom among educated Lithuanians to speak Polish in

family circles. For all these reasons, and – last but not least — with regard to the common dangers threatening both nations from east and west, there was every prospect of not only good-neighbourly, but really hearty relations developing between the two resuscitated states. An indispensable condition, however, was that the Poles, making allowance for the national feelings and aspirations of the Lithuanians, would abstain from attempts to impose upon them, in particular from putting pressure to bear upon them to restore the Lublin union extinguished in 1795.

Unfortunately indications were soon to appear that the leaders of the restored Poland had different views and were entertaining designs which must inevitably bring about a highly regrettable conflict, difficult of solution. Like an incurable festering sore this conflict embroiled and envenomed the relations of the two states for the whole interwar period. In view of its disastrous consequences, it is appropriate to report on the origin of this conflict at some length. This is indispensable, in particular if we are to judge fairly upon the attitude of Lithuania in subsequent years.

Already a couple of months after the commencement of the Soviet expansionist drive to "pull down the wall separating Soviet Russia from revolutionary Germany", the Polish forces began to penetrate into and occupy areas which for centuries had been Lithuanian territory, omitting to take any steps to agree on these moves beforehand with the Lithuanian government. Thus in early March they occupied Gardinas (Grodno) and six weeks later took possession of the old capital of Lithuania, Vilnius, having expelled the Soviet forces which had been holding both this city and the surrounding district since early January. Two days after the capture of Vilnius the head of the Polish state, J. Pilsudski, issued a declaration in which, disregarding the declarations to the contrary by the Lithuanian Taryba already referred to, it was made clear although not expressly stated that the Lublin union was to be restored.

Since the Polish forces continued to intrude upon the territory of Lithuania, giving rise to recurrent clashes with the Lithuanian forces, the Supreme Council of the Allied and Associated Powers felt called upon to intervene. Three times it tried to put an end to the encounters and to prevent their recurrence by drawing lines of demarcation not to be crossed by either side. The Poles, however, failed to respect these lines.

As the interdependence of events renders it appropriate to go back to what was in the meantime happening in Estonia, it seems necessary to break off this account of the development of Lithuanian—Polish relations. We shall revert to them at an appropriate moment further on.

During the first three months after it had been turned out of Estonia, the Red Army made desperate attempts to regain lost ground, and the Estonian army had to exert all its strength to repel its fierce attacks. With the exception of a few irruptions into the Estonian lines, each time quickly liquidated with heasy losses, the enemy never succeeded in penetrating into Estonia again. Similar to armour forged of resilient steel, the Estonian army protected the country; the Red Army proved unable to pierce it.

The secret of this strength of the Estonian army lay in its patriotic ardour and democratic spirit. The "founding fathers" of the Estonian Republic had been endowed with sufficient political instinct and acumen to appreciate the extent to which victory in the War of Liberation depended upon the ideology and the spirit pervading the nation. By the time the Soviet aggression started, the communists in power in Russia had not yet managed to build up a well-disciplined Red Army out of the remnants of the Tsarist army, the disintergration and demoralization of which they themselves had very thoroughly effected. Moreover, the Red Army forces at the disposal of Lenin's government were engaged on numerous fronts in the Russian civil war. Thus in undertaking aggression against the Baltic states the Soviet leaders placed their hopes of an easy victory less in the power of their arms than in the embittered and fermenting landhungry proletarianized masses in the states, easily to be won over to their side, as they presumed. Especially they sought, by unbridled, demagogic propaganda among the Latvian and Estonian masses, to cast suspicion on their governments, whom they defamed as striving, in collusion with the "barons", treacherously to frustrate yet again the hopes of a long-coveted, thorough agrarian reform. That those who wished to become free and independent farmers, tilling their own plot, could hope to see this dream fufilled only in turning their arms against their own governments and helping the Red Army to conquer the Baltic States, was preached in countless proclamations sent across the battle-front and spread among the soldiers of the Baltic states. Taking into consideration the impatience spread among the proletarianized rural masses as well as the habitually distrustful mentality of these masses it would have been unpardonable and indeed criminal neglect to underestimate the danger of this propaganda.

There was but one means to ward off the peril: a consistent democratic ideology and a realistic program of social reform, able to inspire and fill with inflexible determination the overwhelming majority of the nations in question. Such an ideology and such a program were to be set against the utopian Soviet ideology and the demagogical, braggart promises generously made by the aggressors to the "toiling masses" of the Baltic states. And more than that: it was urgently necessary to set about the program of reforms — in the first place its cardinal point, the agrarian reform — without waiting for the end of the war. Though every nerve must be strained in winning the War of Liberation, and nobody could be unaware how complicated a task the implementation of the reform would present, its planning and realisation could not be deferred to the end of the war. Not only was its planning to be set on foot at the same time as arms were taken up to stave off Soviet aggression, it was even necessary to commence its enforcement while the death-struggle was raging on the fronts. It was not inconsiderate impatience that dictated this course of action: only in this way could the mendacious propaganda of the enemy be disproved — by manifest actions.

It was regarded as an axiom in all three states that a Constituent Assembly was to be elected on the basis of democratic franchise as soon as possible, its task being to establish the constitution and enact fundamental laws, the agrarian reform among them. In Latvia and Lithuania, however, in consequence of the wayward political events and military entanglements already partly touched upon, the elections could not be held before April 1920. Only in Estonia did it prove possible to elect the Constituent Assembly as early as the beginning of April, 1919. Even before the election of this Assembly, the first measures manifestly aiming at the liquidation of large estates had been taken by the National Council and the Provisional Government. These measures had been occasioned by the fact that a considerable number of estates had been abandoned by owners not courageous enough to remain and brave the impending danger of falling under the terroristic rule of the Soviets. There were no less than 229 such abandoned estates, covering 24 per cent of the total area of the estate lands. On these destitute estates production was breaking down and coming to standstill. The state was obliged to take measures to prevent their further dilapidation, since the falling off of so large a proportion of agricultural production threatened the country with famine. Regulations to this effect were enacted by the National Council on November 27th, 1918, i.e. the day before the capture of Narva by the Soviet Red Army and the beginning of the real Soviet aggression. In February and March, 1919, the said estates were parcelled out to those willing to engage themselves to till the plots allotted.

Similar measures were taken in Latvia, where a decree analogous to the Estonian regulations of November 27th, 1918 was enacted by the Provisional Government on February 27th, 1919, though there was obviously little possibility of executing it before July, 1919, when v.d. Goltz's domination over Latvia collapsed. It is worth mentioning that the number of abandoned estates, as well as their combined area, was still greater in Latvia than in Estonia: no less than 629 estates, comprising altogether 1,977,892 acres, or 25.3 per cent of the total area of the large estates were taken under the guardianship of the state by the end of 1920, to be divided and distributed to landless peasants. About 77 per cent of this combined area was actually leased; the remainder, about 23 per cent, consisting mainly of forests, was kept by the state under its own management.

In Lithuania likewise the agrarian problem was tackled already in 1918, when a decree was issued by the Provisional Government, proclaiming all the land confiscated by the Russian government after the uprising of 1831 and turned over, as entailed estates, to families of the Russian nobility, the property of the Lituanian state, to be parcelled out to landless and insufficiently landed peasants, the latter category including all who owned less than twelve acres.

Though all the measures referred to were formally of provisional character, to be sanctioned and completed later on by democratically elected Constituent assemblies, they furnished unequivocal evidence that the governments were not going to shrink from resolute and drastic measures with respect to the large estates in questions of vital importance to the nation. And indeed these measures did evoke confidence in their young states and governments among the land-hungry masses and they proved a very effective antidote to the enemy propaganda. The sympathetic echo evoked among the broad masses of people in general and the soldiers in the trenches in particular doubtless contributed notably to the victory at the elections of the parties determined to carry out a land reform which would thoroughly sweep away the intolerable, superannuated, semi-feudal agrarian order, above all the socialists, who secured 39 per cent of seats in Estonia and 36 per cent in Latvia. In Estonia, moreover, 25 per cent of the seats fell to the share of the radical-democratic Labour Party, a no less resolute advocate of radical agrarian reform.

The Estonian Constituent Assembly, well aware of the impatience with which the soldiers in the trenches and the whole nation awaited the reform, set about elaborating the reform law without delay. The debates on the bill and the rapid progress of its elaboration, followed with breathless attention by the fighters at the battlefront, mightily enhanced the confidence of the people in their government, and when, on October 19th, 1919, the Agrarian Law was passed, not only were the demagogic fables about the collusion of the Government with the "barons" with a view to frustrating the hopes for an agrarian reform now finally confuted, but also a mortal blow was dealt to the credibility of any kind of propaganda spread by the enemy. More than this, any chances of the communists' ever being able to gather broad masses of the Estonian people under their banner were now lost for good.[6]

There was yet another stimulant to the unbending determination of the Estonian soldiers and officers to die rather than to yield to the enemy: the abhorrence aroused by the inhumanity of the Soviet authorities re-established for a few weeks in districts occupied by the

---

[6] As a matter of fact the votes cast for communists appearing under different signboards, only once, when the country had to wrestle with extraordinary difficulties, viz. in May 1923, reached 9.5 per cent. Usually the percentage oscillated between five and six per cent. Moreover, it is clear that not all these five to six per cent were convinced adherents of the communist ideology. Many of those who voted for the communists did so only in order to give vent to discontent occasioned by various causes having nothing to do with the aims of the Communist Party.

Red Army during its advance. The Estonian communists, well aware that there was no hope of gaining the support of the majority of the Estonian people, by whom they were loathed as detestable traitors and tools of a foreign power, seeking to enslave Estonia, had decided to break the resistance by ruthless terror. With this end in view "commissions for combating counter-revolution" had been appointed. Composed of mentally deranged fanatics, these commissions began executing wholesale, without any trial and judgment, any persons suspected of entertaining sympathies to the "white-guardists", as those loyal to the lawful authorities were abusively called. The terror grew particularly bloodthirsty at the last moment before the precipitate flight of the Soviets and the Red Army to Russia. Hundreds of innocent victims taken into custody were indiscriminately slaughtered. Thus, to mention but a few examples, when the university town Tartu (Dorpat) was liberated by the Estonian army on January 14th, 1919, about fifty persons, among them the Greek-Orthodox Archbishop Platon, and there other priests, one of them a professor of divinity, were found butchered in the cellar of a bank where they had been detained along with about 350 other persons. These horrors had been committed at the very moment when the Estonian army, having broken the resistance in the outskirts, was pouring into the town. There can be little doubt that the surviving 350 owed their lives only to the precipitate flight of the murderers, who had had to break off their beastly work in order to escape falling into the hands of the approaching avengers. In another place, near the town of Valk on the Estonian—Latvian border, all prisoners had been mowed down by machine-gun fire in the cellar of a manorhouse where they had been detained. In a third place, the small town of Rakvere in northern Estonia, one hundred and eighty corpses were dug out of three mass-graves. According to the testimony of a few persons who by a miracle had escaped death, the mass-executions had been carried out with a cruelty and lack of human feeling that defy description.

To what extent communists already then, after but one year of tyrannical Soviet totalitarianism, had shaken off any respect for the sanctity of the human person, is shown by the fact that the leader of the Estonian communists, J. Anvelt, later, at a conference of the Estonian Communist Party held in Soviet Russia behind the frontline of the Red Army in March 1919, instead of deploring these massacres as regrettable excesses, declared it to have been a blunder that executions had not been numerous enough.[7]

It is well to stress, by the way, that the appalling inhumanity to which the horrible butcheries referred to bear witness, cannot be regarded as an outburst of momentary and transient moral insanity called forth by passions kindled in the extreme vehemence of the struggle for power. Still less could it be imputed to the national character of those who committed these abominations. A sufficient number of crackbrained sadists, able and willing to carry out the most horrible brutalities under the protection of Soviet Red Army bayonets and tanks, will be found even among the most highly civilized nations. This bestiality is obviously inherent in and inseparable from the ruthless mentality of those whose brains have been intoxicated and bedevilled by fanatical totalitarian ideas, be they of red or brown colouring. If it were not so, the humanity that is proper to any normal individual as well as to any civilized community, would have been restored to its place of honour in the Soviet state after the final victory of the communists over their opponents and the definitive extinction of any resistance. There are, however, ample proofs that totalitarian rule has continued in the Soviet Union without the least mitigation of its barbarous inhumanity. Suffice it to point to the horrors of the mass-graves detected at Vinnitsa when the Ukraine was occupied by the Germans in the Second World War. All the tens of thousands of Ukrainan peasants, workers, and intellectuals whose mutilated corpses were dug out of these graves had been murdered several years before the outbreak of the war. If such blood-curdling mass-murders had been perpetrated in peacetime, it is not to be wondered at the bestialities committed by the Soviet police and Red Army forces in the summer and autumn of 1941, in their hasty retreat before the advancing Germans from the Baltic states and other occupied territories. We shall later refer to these atrocities, which put into the shade all that had been done by the communists in 1918–1919.

[7] One cannot help seeing the well-deserved revenge of impartial justice in the fact that Anvelt himself ended his life in the cellar of the GPU in March 1938, as one of the innumerable victims of Stalin's Great Purge.

When Soviet aggression commenced at the end of November 1918, some Russian "white" units, formed under German patronage in the German-occupied town of Pskov, near the south-eastern corner of Estonia, had retreated into Estonia under the pressure of the advancing Red Army. Since Estonia at that time actually had no army, every fighter against the invader was welcome and the Commander-in-Chief of the Estonian army, Colonel Laidoner, took these Russians under his command. They constituted a special unit, numbering about 3000 bayonets, under the name of the Northern Corps. Being reactionary minded, hardly concealing their hostility to the independence of Estonia and displaying mediocre fighting spirit, they proved to be of rather questionable value in Estonia's fight for national freedom.

While in March and April, the two months with the highest casualties in all the thirteen months of the War of Liberation, the Estonian army was repelling persistent heavy attacks by the Red Army, Laidoner, mindful of the time-honoured precept of the art of war concerning the best defence, was planning and preparing a vigorous offensive. In the projected operations a rather important part was assigned to the Northern Corps, whose fighting value had considerably increased owing to measures taken in the meantime to improve its discipline and efficiency. The Corps had to mount an offensive over the river Narova, in the direction of Leningrad (at that time Petrograd), with the aim of liberating from communist rule as broad a zone as possible of Russia to the north-east of Estonia. It was presumed that it would be possible to develop this zone into an autonomous, self-governing unit where the Northern Corps might move, using it as its base for further operations against the Red Army. If the corps managed to attain this end, Estonia would be rid of this rather embarrassing lodger. The Estonian army was to mount a synchronised offensive on the southern front of Estonia against the Soviet Latvian army, and in the direction of Pskov against the Soviet Russian Red Army.

The offensive started on May 13th 1919. Direct assistance was rendered to it by two Estonian regiments stationed on the coast of the Gulf of Finland, who had the task of shielding the left flank of the Northern Corps, while the forces concentrated on its right flank were to strike the main blow upon the Red Army. Moreover, one unit of the Estonian army, the Baltic battalion, formed of Baltic—German citizens of Estonia, pro tem. transferred to the N. Corps, participated in its offensive, which Estonian naval units most effectively supported with landings in the rear, along the coast of the Gulf of Finland and Lake Peipus, being themselves protected against the attacks of the Soviet navy by British squadrons patrolling in the Gulf of Finland.

The well-prepared offensive proved a great success. Whole regiments of the Red Army either disintegrated or went over to the N. Corps. The enemy suffered heavy losses and a considerable area was conquered.

Three days after the start of the offensive of the N. Corps the two Estonian divisions holding the southern front against Soviet–Latvia were ordered to assume the offensive too. Here the enemy was considerably superior to the Estonian forces both numerically and in fire power, as well as with regard to technical equipment. Moreover, the Latvian communist regiments were less demoralized than the Russian Red Army units. For these reasons no spectacular victories could be won in the very first days of the offensive, notwithstanding the far higher morale of the Estonian troops. The rather stubborn resistance of the enemy began, however, to give way after a few days of pertinacious assault from the Estonian forces, and before long it broke down completely. Almost simultaneously two important junctions were captured: the old Russian town Pskov, at the eastern end of the front, on May 25th, and Valmiera in the centre, in northern Latvia, on the following day.

In the meantime, while the Latvian communist forces had to exert all their strength to ward off the onslaught of the Estonian army, General v.d. Goltz, exploiting the favourable situation, made a sudden assault on Riga and captured it on May 22nd. In consequence the spectre of encirclement and annihilation rose suddenly before the communist forces in northern Latvia, north of the Daugava. Seized with panic they took to flight to the east, planning to escape to Soviet Russia. In order to cut off their escape and complete the rout the left wing of the Estonian army immediately after the capture of Pskov began to drive a wedge deep into the eastern confines of Latvia, running a race with the enemy troops now fleeing in disorder.

The advanced point of this wedge, consisting of one cavalry regiment, a battery of field artillery, and a company of Danish volunteers, reached the Daugava at Krustpils (Kreutzburg) on June 5th. When two days later this vanguard was overtaken by infantry troops, among them the first Latvian regiment formed in Estonia, the town of Krust-pils was handed over to this regiment.

Only a fraction of the communist troops succeeded in getting out of the trap before the railways and highroads to Soviet Russia were cut off. Most of them surrendered, throwing away arms and muni-tions. The Latvian Soviet government and other communist heads had been farsighted enough to put themselves out of harm's way in time. The communist rule with its gruesome terror had come to an end in Latvia.[8]

However, for a while it was not a free and democratic Latvia that was to succeed the bloody rule of the communists. It was to be a Lat-via ruled by v.d. Goltz with his menial, Herr Niedra. "A veritable reign of terror was begun in Riga by Major Fletcher, who was ap-pointed Governor. He took the opportunity to execute large numbers of Letts under the pretext that they were Bolshevists"; so we read in a Memorandum Respecting the Situation in the South Baltic States, compiled by the British Foreign Office on July 11th, 1919, and pub-lished in Documents on British Foreign Policy 1919—1939, I. Series, vol. 3 p. 5 (Major Fletcher was the Commander of the *Landeswehr*).

As soon as he had established himself in Riga, v.d. Goltz began to move his forces north towards the line' of the Estonian forces in northern Latvia as well as towards the open flank of the Estonian and Latvian troops advancing to the south in eastern Latvia, pursuing the hastily retreating enemy. On June 1st reconnaissance detach-ments of the *Landeswehr* made their appearance in the region of Cesis (a town on the Tallin—Riga railway, about half-way from the Estonian border to Riga), occupied a day before by the Estonian troops and held by the second Latvian regiment formed in Estonia. They were politely but firmly told by the commanding officer on the spot that the zone of Latvia north of this town had been cleared of com-munist forces by the troops under the command of the Estonian

---

[8] How inhuman this rule had been appeared from the fact that no less than 3632 persons had been shot in the four and a half months of this first Latvian Soviet republic, as its leaders themselves later on boasted (v. A. Schwabe *Historie du peuple letton*, Stockholm, 1953, p. 181).

Commander-in-Chief and as it was in the immediate rear of the Estonian army, the *Landeswehr* was to keep aloof from it.

Disregarding this admonition, the *Landeswehr* went on concentrating its forces towards Cesis, which was the centre of the Estonian frontline in northern Latvia.

At that time the vanguard of the Estonian forces operating in eastern Latvia had crossed the railway connecting Yeriki (Ramockoye), a station a couple of miles south of Cesis on the Tallinn—Riga railway, with Pytalovo, on the Leningrad—Warsaw railway, about 55 miles south of Pskov. As long as these forces were operating in that region, it was imperative for the Estonian High Command to have this railway at its undisturbed disposal, since it was the main and indispensable line of communication of these forces with their rear. General Laidoner therefore advised General von der Goltz that for the reasons just mentioned the *Landeswehr* was to remain clear of the zone of operations of the troops under the Estonian High Command, to wit the river Koiva (Aa) from its mouth up to the station Segewold and from there in a direct line to Schwaneburg, a junction on the Yeriki—Pytalovo railway, in the region where the Estonian—Latvian troops were operating in eastern Latvia. He admonished v.d. Goltz, instead of moving his troops to the north, towards Estonia, to send them to the front against the Soviet Red Army in eastern Latvia, and in this way to relieve the Estonian troops on that front, who for tactical reasons, i.e. to complete the rout of the beaten and fleeing enemy, had had to advance into that region.

These exhortations fell, however, on deaf ears. The venturesome plot von der Goltz was forming admitted of no dawdling. After Latvia, Estonia too was to be laid under his heel, and this was to be done as soon as possible, circumstances being at that very moment, and maybe only for a very short time, particularly opportune for a stab in the back of the Estonian army. The Estonian forces were involved in battles with the Red Army over long stretches of front and were therefore apparently an easy prey for an annihilating, treacherous blow from behind.

On June 5th the *Landeswehr* opened hostilities. After four days of initial skirmishes, at the prompting of an Allied Military Mission sent by the Allied Supreme Council in Paris an armistice was concluded with a view to seeking an amicable settlement of the conflict.

The dispatch of this mission was a sign that the Supreme Council had begun to pay somewhat closer attention to what was going on in the Baltic area. As a matter of fact the situation in the Baltic states stood very often on the order of the day at the meeting of the Council of Four, i.e. of the heads of the governments of the four principal Allied and Associated Powers, France, Gt. Britain, USA, and Italy, as well as at those of the foreign ministers of these Powers. At the overthrow of the Latvian government at Liepaja on April 16th, the attention of the Supreme Council had been attracted to this region, and it was inevitable that the victorious Allied Powers should begin to look more attentively into the doings of von der Goltz and his myrmidons.

On May 23rd the Supreme Council had agreed that the execution of the Allied military policy in the Baltic area should be controlled by a British Military Mission to Finland and the Baltic states, to which officers of the other three Powers were to be attached. General Sir Hubert Gough, who was appointed chief of this mission, having arrived in the Baltic area at the very moment when the Landeswehr opened hostilities against Estonia, was thus in a position to report forthwith to the Supreme Council on this event. After a preliminary discussion of the matter at its meeting on June 7th, and an examination by military experts, the Supreme Council decided on June 13th (only the points relevant in this connection are quoted):

1. Marshal Foch should order the Germans to cease all further advance northwards towards Estonia;
2. The local national forces of the Baltic Provinces should be supported with equipment, arms, ammunition, clothing and supplies generally;
3. Military Representatives in Versailles should advise as to what supplies should be sent and by whom.

In the meantime General Gough, having acquainted himself with the situation and forthwith seen through v.d. Goltz's foul play, had sent him on June 10th an aerogram ordering him to withdraw his troops behind the line indicated by the Estonian Commander-in-Chief as delimiting the zone of operations of the forces under his command, to wit the river Koiva (Aa) – Segewold — Schwaneburg. On June 13th General Gough's plenipotentiary, Colonel Tallents, attending a meeting of the authorized representatives of the Estonian High Command and of the *Landeswehr*, expressly re-iterated that order to the Commander of the *Landeswehr*, and communicated another order from his chief, requiring the contesting parties to refrain from any offensive operations save those against the Soviet Red Army and prolonging the truce until further notice.

V.d. Goltz, raving at the "insolence" of a British general arrogant enough to give orders to a German general, was in no wise inclined to comply with them. No wonder: compliance with these orders was tantamount to the collapse of his magnificent plans — from the crusade to Soviet Russia and the restoration of monarchy in both Russia and Germany, to the crowning achievement of his golden dreams, the resumption of hostilities and the defeat of the western Allied Powers. For him retreat was therefore out of the question. The planned operation was to be brought to its conclusion: the death-blow aimed at Estonia was to be dealt without any further delay.

There was, however, a vexatious check which must be avoided in some way or other. An undisguised assault upon Estonia carried out by German troops under German command, in defiance of the explicit prohibition twice issued on behalf of the Allied Supreme Council, would ineviably provoke an intervention by the victorious Allied Powers. It was obviously too dangerous to brave these Powers openly at this early stage of the plot. Apprehension of the possible intervention of these Powers had indeed probably been the main reason why the first attacks on Estonia on June 6th—9th had been made by the *Landeswehr* alone, without the participation of the undeniably German Iron Division, especially as it was more than questionable whether even the former really could be designated a Latvian unit.[9] Another reason, of course, might have been that v.d. Goltz, who in his memoirs bitterly complains about the unsatisfactory quality of the intelligence work of his forces concerning Estonia, had in pure

[9] The memorandum of the British Foreign Office quoted above, gives the following information about the *Landeswehr*: "The main support of the German policy was the Balt *Landwehr*, a force recruited locally from the Balt (=Teutonic) element of the country and containing a large number of German soldiers who had been pressed into its ranks as a stiffening. A great number of the officers were ex-German officers, and the whole force was commanded by Major Fletcher, a Prussian". (V. Documents on British Foreign Policy 1919—1939, First Series, v. 3, p. 5).

arrogance presumed it would be easy for the *Landeswehr* alone to crush the Estonian army.

However, the skirmishes between June 6th and June 9th had shown that the troops commanded by General Laidoner were tougher than had been imagined and that it was far from certain that the *Landeswehr* alone would be able to cope with them. The Iron Division had consequently to be sent in. To avoid or at least reduce the danger of Allied intervention an ingenious expedient was hit upon: on June 18th the Iron Division was nominally detached from v.d. Goltz's command and "hired out" for two weeks as a mercenary unit to the "Latvian" Niedra-government. By this hocus-pocus the division was as if by a motion of a magic wand turned into a Latvian unit which consequently could be used against the Estonians, and its assault upon Estonia had been transformed into an armed clash of a mock Latvian republic of Herr Niedra with Estonia, of which the German government could wash its hands. Actually, however, v.d. Goltz was acting in collusion with this new, "democratic" government of the Latvian republic, as he later revealed in his above-quoted memoirs.

To perfect the "masquerade", as this knavish trick was styled by v.d. Goltz himself, the Iron Division an the *Landeswehr* also received a Latvian sham "Commander-in-Chief" for the campaign against Estonia. This was a man who had consented to play the part of minister of war in Niedra's puppet-government, a civilian without a semblance of knowledge or experience in military matters. He now received the honour of acting the part of Commander-in-Chief of the Latvian armed forces in that campaign, in which, by the way, not a single Latvian company of the *Landeswehr* was assigned to take part — of course for the good reason that their desertion to the adversary at the first opportunity could be anticipated with certainty. It hardly need be mentioned that v.d. Goltz himself was the real commander-in-chief behind this ludicrous dummy.

The day after the hiring out of the Iron Division, on June 19th, the *Landeswehr* broke the armistice. Hostilities were opened by the Iron Division, who attacked the right flank of the Estonian and Latvian forces, whereas the onslaught of the *Landeswehr* upon the centre and left flank was to follow at the appropriate moment. The Iron Division succeeded in pressing the Estonian and Latvian units somewhat back in some places. These insignificant initial successes, however, not only did not contribute to the victorious issue of the expedition, but, on the contrary, in conjunction with an erroneous report by aerial reconnaissance, proved fatal to the whole campaign. On account of this report the *Landeswehr* was sent in prematurely, contrary to the plan worked out beforehand. V.d. Goltz himself has given the following judgement on this fatal mistake: "In consequence of the false report the Landeswehr alone, reinforced only by a new German free company, was sent in, fell with the second and third of its three columns into an ambush and had to give up the fight. Although the whole reserve of the corps was drawn up the retreat to Riga had to be embarked upon in the following days." (Polit. General etc, p. 129.)

In violent attacks and counter-attacks around Cesis, which raged almost without intermission for about thirty-six hours, the offensive push of the *Landeswehr* was broken, and when, on June 22nd in the afternoon, the Estonian and Latvian forces mounted an impetuous general counter-offensive, the *Landeswehr* was routed. Along with the Iron Division it had to take to flight. Like avenging sprits of Greek mythology the victors relentlessly pursued the remnants of the beaten enemy, depriving them of the possibility of reforming, resting and reorganizing for a resumption of the campaign. How pertinacious and harassing the pursuit was and how thoroughly undermined the fighting spirit of the forces of v.d. Goltz, might be seen from the following quotations from the first edition of his memoirs, in which the clash with Estonia is more fully treated than in the second, revised edition: "The higher command issued an order to the Iron Division to build a bridgehead north of Hintzenberg and concentrated a strong shock force (five battalions) on its left wing with a view to retrieving the situation with an attack on the right flank of the pursuers. However, owing to an unpropitious fate the enemy managed to break into the middle of the dead tired troops in the night of June 23nd; the commander of the Iron Division considered the situation so serious as to beg permission to withdraw the whole division beyond the river Aa (Koiva). This ruined all plans of the High Command for the offensive . . . The Landeswehr made an attempt to hold its ground in the old trenches at Hintzenberg. This, however, proved impossible, the troops being overstrained and several seconds-in-command proving to have completely lost their selfcommand." (Quoted after the Swedish translation, KRIGSMINNEN FRÅN FINLAND OCH BALTICUM, Helsingfors, 1920, vol. 2, p. 235).

The casualties of the troops under the Estonian High Command in the decisive battles round Cesis and in the pursuit of the beaten enemy, from June 19th to June 23rd, amounted to 445 men, those of the Estonian troops being 16 officers and 373 soldiers of the rank and file, the corresponding numbers for the Latvian units being 5 and 51. The losses of the Iron Division and especially of the *Landeswehr*, two thirds of which, as mentioned, had fallen into an ambush, were doubtless much higher. In all probability the heavy losses sustained were the main reason for the almost complete collapse of the fighting efficiency and morale of both the *Landeswehr* and the Iron Division as mirrored in the facts mentioned by v.d. Goltz himself, a few samples of which have been quoted above.

The discomfiture was so thorough that v.d. Goltz had to swallow his arrogance and apply to the Estonian High Command for an armistice. The first application was, of course, made — doubtless by his orders — by the dummy commander-in-chief who now declared himself ready to accept the terms demanded by the Estonian Commander-in-Chief in early June, to wit the withdrawal of the *Landeswehr* and the Iron Division behind the line Koiva—Segewold—Schwaneburg. This overture was declined by the Estonian Commander-in-Chief, who refused to conclude an armistice with an adversary who but a few days ago had broken an armistice already made. Then a German-Balt delegation beseeched General Gough at Liepaja to take steps to bring about an armistice, and v.d. Goltz himself, having in the meantime "officially resumed the command of his troops", in his capacity of an allegedly "neutral commander" personally requested the American military mission "to stop the civil war" (*Politischer General . . .*, p. 129).

General Gough, with good reason considering the suspension of hostilities to be in the true interest of Estonia too, complied with the request and the Estonian government, reluctantly but thinking it proper to give way, concluded the armistice. The Estonian troops, however, who were standing at the gates of Riga and making their last preparations to take that city by assault, were rather bitter at being deprived of the occassion to deal a final blow to the odious enemy. They had a kind of instinctive presentiment that unless this mortal foe of the free, democratic Baltic states were wiped out, he would go on devising mischief and conjuring up new dangers which might imperil the very existence of these states. That this presentiment was not a delusion was very soon manifest.

According to the terms of the armistice concluded after obstinate and hot debates in the small hours of the morning of July 3rd, the *Landeswehr* as well as all German officers and troops were to leave Riga at once. This evacuation was to be completed by six p.m. on July 5th. The *Landeswehr* was to withdraw to the south of the river Daugava. All German forces were to be clear of Latvia as soon as possible and no advance on their part was to be made in any part of Latvia, except against the troops of the Soviet Red Army. The Estonian army was not to advance beyond the positions they occupied at the moment the armistice was signed.

The *Landeswehr* was not to be disbanded. The Allied Military Mission still entertained the hope that its strength could serviceably be used in the struggle against the Soviet Red Army. To effect its reorganization, indispensable after the heavy defeat sustained, as well as to make sure that it would not be used to other ends than the fight against the Red Army, it was to be put under the command of an Allied officer. A highly qualified British officer, who a quarter of a century later was to be one of the most brilliant Allied generals in the Second World War, at that time Lt. Col. H. R. Alexander, was appointed to this post. The headquarters of the *Landeswehr* was moved to the former residence of the Dukes of Kurland, Yelgava (Mitau), a town about thirty miles south of Riga.

Seeking to vindicate his honour as a general, v.d. Goltz asserts in his memoirs that his defeat was occasioned by the great superiority of the Estonian—Latvian forces both in numbers and in technical equipment, the Estonians having been copiously supplied with the most modern machine-guns, manned by experts. *(Politischer General*, p. 20). Unless these allegations are deliberate untruths, they only confirm v.d. Goltz's complaints about the very poor state of his intelligence concerning Estonia. How matters really stood concerning technical equipment appears from the exact data compiled by the Committee on the History of the Estonian War of Liberation and published in the second volume of the book *The Estonian War of*

Liberation 1918—1920 (In Estonian, Tallinn, 1939). These data are given in the following table:

The Arms of the Parties on June 19th, 1919:

(over and above rifles and sabres):

	Guns	Machine-guns	Mortars	Armoured trains	Airplanes
The Iron Div. and the *Landeswehr:*	48	310	16	1	Unknown
The Est.—Latvian forces:	30	189	0	2	0

As this table shows it was the forces of v.d. Goltz himself that were in great superiority as to technical equipment and fire power. As to numerical strength, it is true that the number of bayonets and sabres in the whole Estonian third division, to whom the task had been assigned of heading off his attack, was 6357 as against 5250 enemy. However, this division was spread over about sixty five miles of front to cover all conceivable lines of attack. A number of battalions out of the way of the actual attack of the Iron Division and far from Cesis had therefore to remain inactive and did not take part in the decisive engagements of June 21st—22nd in which the forces of v.d. Goltz were routed. For these reasons those subordinate sections of the third division which actually took part in these engagements were not only in equipment and fire-power, but also numerically inferior to v.d. Goltz's forces.

What decided the issue was not numbers and equipment, but the fighting morale of the troops and the spirit animating them. Every Estonian and Latvian officer and soldier was fighting for the heart-stirring ideals of national freedom, democracy, and social justice. Every man thirsted to rush upon the perfidious enemy, and it was a common rule that the wounded went on fighting as long as they had strength left and went to the dressing stations only at the end of the encounter.

The *Landeswehr,* with its considerable admixture of German mercenaries, and the Iron Division, consisting wholly of such mercenaries, stood no comparison with the undaunted fighters they had to cope with. How incomparably superior in morale and fighting value the Estonian—Latvian troops were appears also, quite contrary to his intention, from the memoirs of v.d. Goltz himself. He cannot help admitting that "the Estonians fought passionately against the Germans and the Balts". In several of his own troops, on the other hand, he complains, the feeling that it made no sense for Germans to die for Baltic Barons had gained a foothold. Many of his soldiers, he says, had volunteered to the Baltic troops merely to enrich themselves, and there were units which on the first skirmish lost confidence in their commanders and dispersed. He mentions four cases personally known to him, of outbursts of catastrophical panic which compelled the higher command to sound the retreat. (*Krigsminnen*, pp. 125, 143 and 144).

No wonder that an army impaired by such heavy defects was beaten by an adversary inferior in numbers and especially in equipment, but far superior in morale and moreover, with a command displaying at all levels, from the highly talented Commander-in-Chief to officers commanding the companies, far superior skill in conducting operations. It is worth mentioning that not a single case of panic, let alone catastrophical panic, ever occurred with the Estonian or Latvian troops, not even when, on June 21st, the two above-mentioned columns of the *Landeswehr* succeeded in making a rather broad and deep inroad into the Estonian lines, — a momentary success for which they paid a very heavy penalty, and which, as already mentioned, entailed the wreck of the whole campaign.

The defeat of v.d. Goltz's forces also decided the fate of Herr Niedra's "government". Availing themselves of the circumstance that only a few Russian companies of the *Landeswehr*, loath to interfere in Latvian internal affairs, had been left in v.d. Goltz's domain, Liepaja, the lawful government of K. Ulmanis already on June 27th alighted from the steamer *Saratov*, on board which it had resided since the *coup d'état* of April 16th, and resumed its activity. On June 8th the Government returned to Riga, and Niedra with his accomplices had to flee abroad.

In the meantime events had been taking place in Estonia which were eventually to have far-reaching consequences affecting not only the future of the Baltic states, but even the policy of the Allied Great Powers.

However strong was their determination to die rather than to yield to the enemy, neither the Estonians nor the other Baltic peoples would have been able to withstand Soviet aggression if they had been thrown exclusively upon themselves, receiving no help and assistance from without. As they had hoped, they met with sympathy from the western world, which provided them with weapons and munitions.[10] As to Estonia, barring the rifles and guns which she received from Finland in the first days of the war, all weapons and munitions were supplied to her by Great Britain. Of quite inestimable value was the assistance rendered to her by the British naval units operating in the Baltic Sea, corking up the Soviet Red Navy in its base at Kronstadt. This eliminated the danger of raids by the Red Navy on the coast of Estonia and Latvia. Neither was the Red Army able to get its operations supported by the actions of the Red Navy in the rear of the Estonian front.

However, if it did not prove especially difficult to obtain the indispensable weapons and munitions from the western world, this help was given, at any rate in the beginning, and for a considerable time, not with a view to enabling the Estonians and the other Baltic peoples to secure their national freedom and independence, but in order to keep them fighting against the Soviet government, thereby contributing to the efforts of the Russian anti-communist forces to overthrow the Soviet order in Russia.

By the spring of 1919 there were three Russian "white" armies waging war against the Soviet government: General Denikin's so-called "Volunteer army" in the south, Admiral Kolchak's army in the east, and the so-called "Northern army" in the north, — the last-mentioned, of course, half-British, since half of its units were British.[11] All these armies had also their own governments attending to the civil administration in the rear. Through the successful offensive of the Northern Corps, a fourth "white" Russian front had actually come into being.

---

[10] Conditions were, however, so contradictory that Lithuania had to apply for and actually was obtaining arms and munitions from Germany.

[11] As a matter of fact, the British Government in July, 1919, decided to evacuate these troops. When this decision, announced in the House of Commons on July 29th, was carried out about three months later, the offensive of the Red Army wiped out both this army and the Government attached to it.

The Northern Corps having in its entirety removed from Estonia to the Russian area it had liberated from communist rule, and there being no longer any necessity of its being under his command, General Laidoner, on June 19th, resigned the High Command of the Corps, which a few days later assumed a new, more high-sounding name: from July 1st on it was to be called the North-Western Army. Its new Commander-in-Chief was to be General Yudenitch, who in the World War had commanded Russian armies on the Caucasian front and soon after the Bolshevik October revolution had succeeded in escaping to Finland, where he had since been living a retired life in Helsingfors. On June 5th, while the Northern Corps was still under the High Command of General Laidoner, General Yudenitch had been appointed "Commander of all Russian forces operating in the Baltic area" by Admiral Kolchak, whose government, which he personally headed, had only a few days before been recognized as the "All-Russian Government" by General Denikin's administration and the Government of the Northern Front.

All the leaders of the Russians white forces were, however, tooth and nail against separation from Russia and the establishment of the sovereign states on the Baltic, nor did they wish other peoples subdued in the course of centuries and incorporated into the Tsarist Empire to achieve their separation. Their pass-word was "the one and indivisible Russia". It was well within the interests of these white forces that the non-Russian peoples of the former Tsarist Empire should fight against Soviet aggression, thus binding considerable Red Army forces to their fronts and thereby increasing the chances of victory for the Russian counter-revolution. However, they made no secret of their absolutely negative attitude to the aspirations of these peoples towards national freedom and their own independent statehood. There could not be any doubt that these peoples were destined for their old cells in the "prison of nations"; they were to be forced to this, if need be, by arms.

It was no secret that the same attitude had prevailed also in the Northern Corps from its very beginning. The first thing to do after the overthrow of the "Jewish-Bolshevik" rule would be to turn their bayonets against Estonia and drive her back into the fold of the "one and indivisible Russia"; so the officers and the rank and file of the

Corps openly boasted, especially when inebriated. No wonder that the Estonian soldiers and officers heartily disliked these allies of theirs.

Their dislike turned into a deep mistrust bordering on hatred when, on June 8th and 9th, i.e. at the very time when the first encounters of the Estonian–Latvian forces with the *Landeswehr* were going on round Cesis, three German airplanes were forced down near Narva by the fire of the Estonian detachments and proved to have started from v.d. Goltz's and Herr Niedra's Latvia and to be conveying certain Russian leaders, known as reactionary Germanophiles, sent as emissaries on some mysterious mission to the command of the Northern Corps. There was thus reason for the gravest suspicions about the intentions of these emissaries, although the mission with which they had been entrusted could not be made out at their examination. That the aims of the *Landeswehr* in its treacherous assault on Estonia, the annihilation of Estonia as a free, democratic state and the perpetuation of the former semi-feudal order, were meeting warmest sympathy from the leaders of the Northern Corps, was a foregone conclusion, especially as the ranks of the higher officers of the Corps swarmed with the scions of the Baltic land-owning nobility. The Russian reactionaries would hardly have scruples about requiting with the blackest ingratitude the assistance generously tendered to the Northern Corps by the Estonian army in the offensive, as well as the hospitality the Corps had enjoyed in Estonia.

In the meantime the offensive of the Northern Corps had come to a stop. On July 3rd General Gough reported to London: "Military situation has completely changed. Bolshevik forces are now pressing back Russian Northern Corps whose collapse is imminent." (Op. cit. p. 412). By the end of July most of the area captured by the Northern Corps in May and June was reconquered by the Red Army.

This, of course, had been inevitable. The initial success of the offensive had a chance of becoming lasting and leading to victory over Soviet tyranny only so long as the sympathies of the population in the liberated area were won by the establishment of social and political conditions undeniably better than those under Soviet rule, and provided not only that good order and discipline were maintained in the army, but that it really proved to be a liberating army, animated by the ideals of freedom, democracy, and social justice. It hardly need be said that the Command of the North-West Army, as well as the political leaders around it, absolutely failed to appreciate, let alone carry out, these imperative demands of the moment. The provisional local administration appointed by the Army Command swarmed with the offspring of land-owning nobility, who as a rule were reactionary-minded people, moreover for the most part lacking in administrative experience as in other qualifications requisite for the satisfactory performance of their duties. The generally clumsy arrangements made by these unskilful administrators, and the death-sentences passed profusely and, according to general opinion without sufficient reason, by the organs of the Army, very soon turned the enthusiastic sympathy with which the liberators had originally been met, into apathy and eventually pure hatred.

Lacking popular support, floating in a political and social vacuum and being no longer bridled by the wise and masterly command of General Laidoner, the Army was rapidly deteriorating. In consequence of nepotism, rank in the Command of the Army was becoming worthless, while the mutual intrigues and quarrels among the higher officers, growing ever more acute, rendered the fighting efficiency of the Army daily less reliable.[12]

However, hardly had the first unsuccessful offensive come to an end when the need for a new offensive in the direction of Petrograd arose and grew more pressing day by day. General Denikin, who had dangerously extended his front, urgently needed a diversion elsewhere to relieve the pressure of the Red Army on his own forces. Neither Kolchak nor the Northern Army was able to produce such a diversion, the former owing to continuous reverses suffered since May, the latter in view of the publicly announced imminent evacuation of the British troops. An offensive aiming at the old capital of the Tsarist

[12] In a letter sent to General Yudenitch on August 4th, General Gough demanded in very strong words that an end be put to quarrels in the Army and all its forces be concentrated on fighting the Bolsheviks. General Gough threatened even to suspend all supplies to the Army if what he demanded was not done. This letter is quoted in *The Estonian War of Liberation* — in Estonian — Tallinn, 1939, vol. 2, p. 230). In a report sent from Tallinn by Colonel Pirie-Gordon to the Foreign Secretary, Earl Curzon, on August 18th, we read that the leaders of the North—West Army "have devoted much time and energy to political intrigue, to the detriment of their military duty". (Br. Doc., vol. 3, p. 505).

Empire, which was also an important industrial centre and had been the cradle of the Bolshevik revolution, seemed to be the only conceivable diversion eventually able to bring the much-needed relief. However, the North-Western Army, weakened and dispirited after the retreat, was manifestly unable to mount a second offensive.

In the second half of May, when the initial success of the offensive of the Northern Corps had become known, the political coterie around Yudenitch had entered upon negotiations with the Finnish government with a view to inducing it to render the Corps assistance by joining the offensive. Quite exceptional importance was attached by Yudenitch and his friends and advisers to Finnish assistance, especially because they were perfectly convinced that with the Finns joining the offensive the Bolsheviks would certainly be turned out of Petrograd and this disaster would deal the death blow to the communist Soviet power.[13] The eagerly sought Finnish assistance was therefore to consist in an advance by Finnish troops on Petrograd and the capture of the city.

Considering the passionate hate of Russia and all things Russian which the Tsarist government had aroused in Finland by its brutal trespasses upon her autonomy and its cynical violations of her laws in the last twenty years of Russian supremacy over that country, it would have been reasonable to expect that Yudenitch would not have the slightest chance of getting the assistance of the Finns. Actually, however, matters stood quite differently. There were influential people in Finland willing to render that assistance. General Mannerheim himself, who was then Finland's Regent, i.e. Head of the State, had a strong inclination to embark upon the adventure of an intervention

---

[13] This was a wide-spread or rather generally shared illusionary belief of the Russian "white" leaders. "The capture of Petrograd would mean the collapse of the Bolshevik power", wrote e.g. Admiral Kolchak in a note sent to the Allied and Associated Powers on June 27th. General Yudenitch was doubtless of the same opinion, as was apparent from the reasonings about "Petrograd as the vital centre of Bolshevism" and "the immense strategical importance of the Baltic front", adduced in his letter to the British Prime Minister Balfour of Sept. 12th (Br. Doc., vol. 3, pp. 403 and 546). If in that letter it was said that "with the taking of Petrograd *and Moscow* (italics furnished) Bolshevism would be crushed", Moscow probably had been added to obviate eventual objections by critically-minded people.

in Russia. Still more enthusiastic about a daring advance on Petrograd was his entourage, which consisted of conservative Germanophile activists.

One cannot help wondering how any Finns in their senses could be ready to help these "white" Russian leaders, who aimed to restore the same "one and indivisible" Russia which with barbarous ruthlessness had trampled under foot Finland's rights and privileges. Could there be any doubt that the restored "one and indivisible", far from tolerating the independence of Finland, would use every means to force her back into the restored "prison of nations"?

The riddle was, however, easy to read. The restoration of the "one and indivisible" Russia was to be the first essential step towards the realization of the ambitious plans under way in the incorrigible imperialist and militarist circles in Germany: the restoration of Tsarist monarchy in Russia, to be followed by the march on Berlin, the restoration of the monarchy there too, and the rending of the "Versailles shackles". The most prominent exponent of these German circles was General v. d. Goltz, who therefore at least as ardently as Yudenitch wished the Finns to embark upon an intervention in Russia and most certainly did his best to prevail upon them to do this. He was held in highest esteem in Finnish conservative circles, since, as the commander of a German corps sent to Finland in the spring of 1918, he had helped overthrow the communist government established there by forcible seizure of power at the instigation of Lenin, and had assisted in driving out the main armed support of this government, the bolshevized Russian soldiery. The esteem for this general, who was considered to have saved Finland from drowning in the bog of anarchy spreading from Bolshevik Russia, was in many cases so uncritical, not to say ecstatic, as to suspend normal reasoning. Persons in such a state of mind could easily be persuaded that the help rendered at that decisive moment to the fighters for the restored German and Russian monarchies would be rewarded by the recognition of Finland's independence by these Powers. This was at any rate the very gospel v. d. Goltz preached to Finnish leaders. He thought it proper to address it even directly to the Finnish government, who, as was well known, was far from being enthusiastic about the policy of intervention in the Russian civil war.[14] There is every reason to presume that numbers of letters were sent to his friends and admirers in Finland, urging them to bring pressure to bear upon the government to induce it to give up its negative attitude towards the advance on Petrograd.[15]

However, public opinion in Finland was unmistakably averse to an adventure which, far from being of benefit to her, could only put her very existence as a free country in jeopardy. With the exception of the numerically insignificant Germanophile activists, the whole people was in the sway of an "obstinate desire for a policy of strict defence", as Yudenitch himself had to admit in his telegram sent to Kolchak on July 8th (v.p. 435 of the quoted Br. Doc., vol. 3). This was also the main reason why General Mannerheim received only fifty votes in the first presidential elections in the Finnish Diet in July, 1919, whereas the rival candidate, Professor Ståhlberg, was elected with the overwhelming majority of 143 votes. The new President and the Government appointed by him, being fully alive to all the dangers

---

[14] Cf. the following cipher telegram of the Finnish Minister in Berlin to his government, shown by the Foreign Minister R. Holsti to the British Chargé d'Affaires, Sir C. Kennard, on Oct. 21st, 1919, and published in the Br. Doc., vol. 3, p. 191: "V.d. Goltz urges that it will be of advantage to Finland to intervene at once in Russia in co-operation with White Russian Government. Apart from other reasons v.d. Goltz represents that Finnish intervention now will assure the recognition of Finnish independence by future Russian Governments." — It might be appropriate to add that what the Russian "white" leaders really thought of Finland's claim for independence was very expressively disclosed by the following exclamation of Kolchak's Foreign Minister Sazonoff in his conversation with the British Foreign Secretary Earl Curzon in early June, 1919: "The Finns are asking for a great deal, but they shall have nothing, absolutely nothing!" (Op. cit. p. 361).

[15] In a private conversation with Sir C. Kennard in early September Dr. R. Holsti mentioned that two prominent Finnish leaders, the ex-Premier Ingman and General Ignatius, were bitterly opposed to Estonian independence (Brit. Doc., p. 108). This attitude of these two gentlemen must surely have been imposed from without since it was hard to explain how any Finnish statesman could consider the suppression of the independence of Estonia to be in the interest of Finland. The idea suggests itself readily that v.d. Goltz was in all probability the source of this inspiration. After the crushing defeat of his forces by the troops commanded by the Estonian Commander-in-Chief, who had dashed to pieces his first important action in the realization of his ambitious plot, v.d. Goltz hardly ever missed any opportunity of giving vent to the rage that gnawed in him against Estonia.

that a military expedition into Russia must entail, were decidedly against such an unwarrantable hazard, as the Foreign Minister R. Holsti told Sir C. Kennard in the above-mentioned conversation. Actually this fact had already become clear by the middle of July, as appeared from the telegrams sent to London by General Gough. Although the activists who advocated the intervention continued to agitate for some time, by the end of July it was already quite obvious that their efforts were doomed to failure.[16]

But there was the Estonian army. It was quite possible and rather probable that with its assistance Petrograd could be captured.[17] And this army drew for its supply of war materials upon the Allied Supreme Council in Paris, who did everything in their power for the support of the Russian counter-revolutionary forces, bestowing upon them lavish grants of war material and other goods of every kind. It was therefore easy to exert pressure upon the Estonian government to induce it to give the military help Yudenitch bitterly needed.

Such pressure was also brought to bear upon Estonia at the insistence of the Russian "white" leaders as it grew increasingly apparent that chances of getting assistance from the Finns were vanishing.

This pressure posed a deeply perplexing problem for the Estonian government. What was to be done? Flatly refuse to render any help to Yudenitch? One could not brush aside the possibility of a stoppage of the deliveries of arms and munitions to Estonia by an angry Supreme Council. On the other hand, unqualified military assistance to Yudenitch was out of the question. The Estonia army simply could not be ordered to render such help. The Estonian soldiers and officers were not robots, blindly executing any order given. They were critically-minded citizens of a free country. They had given evidence

---

[16] "With the fall of General Mannerheim the project (of the advance upon Petrograd) has received its *coup de grâce*" (death blow), it was stated in Earl Curzon's dispatch to the Prime Minister Balfour of August 21st, 1919 (Brit. Doc., p. 525).

[17] General Laidoner was of the opinion that this was possible. However, having had the opportunity of getting well acquainted with the Russian "white" leaders, he entertained grave doubts as to their ability to remain masters of the vast city, to wit adequately to organize its administration and successfully to repel the counter-attacks of the Red Army.

of the highest heroism in many heavy battles, but only because inspired by the firm conviction that they fought for the most valuable good on this earth, national freedom. How could they be ordered to help to victory an army unmistakably hostile to the independence of Estonia, an army from whose ranks threats had frequently been heard of turning its bayonets against Estonia to annihilate her the moment this same victory was won?

The only solution to the dilemma which could make it possible for Estonia to render the assistance desired by the North-Western Army was quite correctly pointed out in an article headed "Yudenitch's Army at a Crisis", sent from Tallinn to *The Times* by the paper's own correspondent on August 22nd, 1919. In this article it was said: "The Estonian, who can fight like a lion, was willing to turn the Bolshevist out of his country. It he is to go further, he must see clearly what he is to get out of it. And what he wants out of it quite clear — the recognition of the independence of Estonia by the Russians and the Allied Powers."

That this claim of the Estonians was an entirely legitimate one had been realized by such a quick-witted man of sound judgment as the venerable head of the British Military Mission, General Gough, already by late July. On July 25th, he had sent a telegram to London "advocating recognition of Estonian independence", as noted in the British Documents (vol. 3, p. 509–). The text of this telegram has not been printed there, but some excerpts from it have been published in the official history of the Estonian War of Liberation. They are well worth quoting here. They run as follow: "The (leaders of the) Baltic states have displayed far more skill and farsightedness in organizing their states than any Russian group whatsoever, be it monarchist, bolshevik, liberal, or social-democratic. I have been pleasantly impressed by the great energy and sober discernment with which these young states are tackling the problems before them and by their eagerness to learn the views of the Allies and to follow their advice." On the "white" Russians, on the other hand, General Gough, having had occasion to observe the North-West Army at close quarters, passed in that telegram the following severe judgment: "They are lacking in organizing ability, energy, faith in themselves, sober reasoning, and even requisite honesty." Having come to the conviction that "the best way to the restoration of order and peace in the split-off and blood-stained parts of former Russia would be to organize every part separately in as large areas as according to circumstances would prove possible, with their own local governments in each such part, and to leave the problem of their melting together to the future to solve", he empasized the advisability of recognizing the independence of the Baltic states and of promoting their collaboration in every possible way.[18]

General Gough repeated this recommendation in a telegram sent to Prime Minister Balfour on August 10th, in which he said *inter alia:* "Estonians, who are the only good troops in the Baltic, do not understand what they are fighting for. They have forced out Bolsheviks and Germans and they are now asked to march on Petrograd and save Russians who have quarrelled with and threatened them ever since the Estonians gave them help which was refused by every other small state, including Finland. My views of the above are as follows: ... that to keep the essential aid of the Estonians it is desirable to recognize independence." (Br. Doc. p. 56).

At the very time this telegram was sent, negotiations were being carried on in Tallinn under the auspices of the Allied Military Mission, between on the one hand General Yudenitch with the Russian circle around him, and the Estonian government on the other, on the question of the military aid to be given to the North-West Army by Estonia with a view to liberating Petrograd. For the reasons indicated above, the Estonian government declared itself unable to render any assistance unless an adequate guarantee of Estonian independence was first obtained from the Russians. Looking for a way out of the impasse, Yudenitch and the coterie around him, yielding to the necessity of circumstances, as well as to the persuasions of the Allied Military Mission, on August 12th formed a professedly democratic North-West Russian government who issued a declaration recognizing the independence of Estonia and applying to the Estonian government for military aid for the deliverance of Petrograd from Bolshevik tyranny.

[18] *The Estonian War of Liberation* (in Estonian), vol. 2, pp. 248—249. Since the above-quoted utterances of General Gough have been translated first from English to Estonian and then back to English, it is possible and even probable that they differ slightly from the original as to their verbal expression but not, we hope, in substance.

This body, headed by a former Russian industrialist, Lianozov as Prime Minister, Yudenitch being Minister of War and Commander-in-Chief of the N.-W. Army, pretended to undertake the functions of governmental authority in the "North-Western Province of a United Russia" which was to comprise the provinces (counties) of Petrograd, Novgorod, and Pskov. Actually there was under its control but a tiny fraction of this extended area, hardly more than two thousand square miles, on the western edge of this region, with only one small country-town, Gdov.[19]

It goes without saying that the recognition of Estonian independence by a local Russian government, of whom the British Prime Minister Balfour in view of the circumstances just mentioned most pertinently remarked that it "looked rather like the prospectus of a bubble company",[20] could by no means be considered as *adequate* recognition by the Russians. A different thing would have been, of course, if the so-called All-Russian government of Admiral Kolchak had recognized Estonian independence. Yet the Estonians could not content themselves even with this. They were too well acquainted with the Russians to put their confidence in their declarations. As quite rightly mentioned in the article in *The Times* quoted above, the Estonians wanted the independence of their state to be recognized not only by the Russians, but also by the Allies. This latter recognition was, to tell the truth, but a matter of course if Kolchak's All-Russian government gave its recognition, since in that case there would no longer have been any reason for withholding recognition.

However, neither was Admiral Kolchak willing to recognize the secession from Russia of Estonia or of any other state, nor were the Allies ready to grant their recognition, since they still entertained the hope that the Russian "white" generals would succeed in overthrowing the Soviet government. Therefore they sided with Kolchak's government.

[19]   There was, of course, in that region a somewhat larger town, about seventy miles south of Gdov, to wit Pskov. As already mentioned, it was captured in late May and still held — until August 25th — by the Estonian army, the N.-W. Army being unable to assume its defence.

[20]   Mr. Balfour's telegram to Earl Curzon, sent from Paris on August 19th, 1919, — Brit. Doc., vol. 3, p. 514.

On August 16th the Estonian government gave its only conceivable reply to the N.-W. Army as well as to General F. G. Marsh, representative of General Gough: that it was unable to co-operate with that army as long as the full independence of Estonia was not recognized by the Allied Powers.

Thereupon General Gough sent a new telegram to the Supreme Council in which he again emphasized the urgent need to recognize the full independence of Estonia, adding that "unless this was done at once, the collapse of the Russian (N.-W.) Army might be expected and the situation would be impossible to control." At a meeting of the Supreme Council held on August 20th, where this telegram was read and in connection with it the situation in the Baltic states discussed, it was decided to keep to the benevolent attitude towards Admiral Kolchak taken in late May — "unless and until other arrangements are made."[21]

In these last words a ray of hope, though a rather dim one, could be discerned, since at least the possibility of an eventual change in the attitude of the Supreme Council was admitted as conceivable. There was the greater reason to hope for such a change as at the same time the first promising signs of a veering of public opinion came to light in the Allied countries. No less a paper than *The Times* not only readily published articles rather favourably disposed to the Estonian demand for recognition, articles like the one quoted above, but also, three days later, on August 22nd, referring to the declaration of the North—West Russian Government of August 12th, wrote in its editorial: "This Russian—Estonian agreement removes one obstacle to the granting of such recognition to the Estonians as the circumstances and our duty to Russia may warrant."

However, the Allied Military Mission continued to press the Estonian government to do what it had declared itself unable to do. The threat to stop all deliveries of arms, munitions, and other necessities hung the whole time over the Estonian government.

On August 26th, a military conference was held in Riga, with General F. G. Marsh in the chair, and attended by representatives of the

[21] "Papers Relating to the Foreign Relations of the US: The Paris Peace Conference 1919", vol. 7, pp. 730—734.

Estonian, Latvian, and Lithuanian forces, an envoy from General Yudenitch, and a quasi-"Colonel" Bermondt-Avaloff, who at that time was in command of certain Russian forces quartered at Yelkava (Mitau), along with the German troops of v.d. Goltz. The plan of a joint offensive against the Soviet Red Army was discussed and agreed upon. To each of the forces represented at the conference, a section of the common front was assigned, and the joint offensive was to start on September 15th.

However, this offensive was not carried out.

By the end of September the N.—W. Army was far from being ready to set about a general offensive. It needed time to reorganize, re-equip and train its troops. Estonia was not particularly interested in this offensive — she agreed to take part in it only under the pressure of the Allied Powers. The Latvian and Lithuanian armies had other things to concern them, and Bermondt, in collusion with v.d. Goltz, was forming his plot against Latvia.

Well informed of these developments, the Soviet government, no less interested in preventing the participation of the Estonian army in the envisaged offensive against Petrograd than was Yudenitch in its taking part, hurried to make an ingenious diplomatic move. On August 31st it officially proposed to the Estonian government, by wireless, the commencement of negotiations on the conclusion of a peace treaty by which Soviet Russia would recognize the full independence of Estonia.

No wonder that the Allied Powers, vitally interested in the success of Denikin's offensive, at the time still in progress, felt worried about the Soviet peace proposal. It was as clear as day that the conclusion of such a peace by Estonia, with the other Baltic states in all probability soon following suit, threatened a severe blow to the Russian counter-revolutionary generals, since in that case not only would any help from the Estonians to the North—West Army be out of the question, but this army itself must either disband or remove from Estonia to some other base.

Therefore the Allied Powers, keeping to their policy confirmed anew on August 20th, sought to induce Estonia not to enter into peace negotiations but instead to give its assistance and support to the offensive of the North—Western Army. Particularly insistent were the French, which was rather easy to understand considering their anxiety about their ample loans to Russia and the belief that only the victory of the counter-revolutionary generals would leave some hope of saving these billions of francs.

But however weighty reasons there might have been for distrusting the honesty of the Soviet Government and its diplomatic and other moves, it was downright inconceivable for Estonia and the other Baltic states to decline the Soviet proposal. Estonia was not fighting to overthrow the Soviet government, only to repulse an aggression and secure her independence. By proposing peace negotiations the aggressor had expressed his willingness to put end to the aggression on terms which could be agreed upon. Neither the Estonian army, nor the Estonian people, would have been able to understand and approve of the refusal of the Estonian government to enter into these negotiations. Answering therefore in the affirmative, the Estonian government at the same time, however, suggested that the same proposal should also be made to Finland, Latvia and Lithuania. The Soviet government agreed to this and acted accordingly.

When the first peace talk took place in Pskov on Sept. 17th, 1919, Denikin's offensive was in full swing. The Allied Powers doubled their pressure on Estonia, admonishing her to break off or at least to delay the peace negotiations. Both the French and the British governments advised Estonia not to take any steps towards the conclusion of peace.

However, in reply to a note of September 21st, 1919, in which the Estonian Foreign Minister explained why the Estonian government could not refuse to enter into peace negotiations, the British government readily admitted that they felt they were not entitled to exercise any pressure upon the free initiative of the Baltic states, whose governments must be at liberty to decide upon such action as might be most conducive to the preservation of their own national existence (Note of Sept. 25th, 1919, Br. Doc., pp. 569—570).

The British government not only kept to the policy expressed in this note, but also showed a benevolent understanding of the actions the Estonian government considered its duty to undertake, and on many occasions gave its support to these actions.

All Estonian political leaders, with the exception of the communists, of course, had from the very outset been convinced that the new states which had seceded from Russia would have a chance of maintaining their national freedom and independence only if they joined into a union. In their opinion it was of particular importance that the three Baltic states, against whom Soviet Russia had started aggression simultaneously, should jointly enter into peace negotiations and carry them on with one accord. Since the Finnish, Latvian, and Lithuanian governments had not yet had time to send off their replies to the proposal of the Soviet government, the peace conference was, on the demand of the Estonian delegation, suspended pending receipt of the replies of those governments.

The respite, however, grew rather long. The attitude of the three governments concerning the peace negotiations was, for different reasons, irresolute, although they did not deem it suitable to decline the offer of the Soviet government. In a common radio message the Estonian, Latvian, and Lithuanian governments proposed joint negotiations to commence at the latest on October 25th. In the meantime, however, events took place which removed the peace negotiations from the order of the day for a somewhat longer time.

The remnants of the Iron Division whom the intervention of the Allied Military Mission had saved from complete annihilation by the joined Estonian and Latvian forces, and other German troops under v.d. Goltz's command had in the meantime been reorganized and considerably reinforced by an influx of German soldiers and war material from Germany, in defiance of the repeatedly issued orders of the Supreme Council, commanding all German forces to evacuate from the Baltic area in as short a time as possible, and forbidding the entry of fresh German troops. Parallel to this, Russian prisoners of war in Germany were being recruited into Russian "white" or "kolchakist" units which were being formed in that part of the Baltic area which still was under v.d. Goltz's occupation, under the command of the above-mentioned "Colonel, Prince" Bermondt in Yelgava (Mitau), and of a Russian colonel Vyrgolich in north-western Lithuania.[22] It was

[22] Concerning this "colonel" and "prince" the following information is worth mentioning. According to a report sent to Earl Curzon by Colonel Tallents on Sept. 1st, 1919, Bermondt had been before the war a subaltern in the 1st Lancers and was believed to have no right to either the rank of colonel or the White Cross he conspicuously wore on his uniform. (Br. Doc. p. 86). According to a reliable Estonian

an open secret that money for the maintenance and equipment of
these forces was supplied by big German industrialists who dreamt
the same day-dreams as v.d. Goltz: the overthrow of Lenin's regime
in Russia by an alliance of German volunteer troops with Russian
"white" forces, and the radiant perspective of a thoroughly Germanized Russia, open to the exploitation of her resources for Germany's
benefit.[23] Being wholly dependent upon this German money, these
Russian troops were actually but tools in the hands of v.d. Goltz, who,
as mentioned, was regarded as the exponent and leader in these industrial circles.

In the meantime, however, the Supreme Council, kept constantly
informed by General Gough and his subordinates of the German—
Russian intrigue in Latvia, began harder and harder to press the German government to carry out the evacuation of all German troops
from Latvia. Realizing that it was high time to put an end to this
dangerous plot, the Supreme Council on Sept. 27th sent a formal ultimatum to the German government threatening to stop all supplies
of foodstuffs and raw materials to Germany, to refuse her all financial
facilities she was enjoying or seeking from the Allied and Associated
Powers, and, if necessary, to take other measures if the evacuation of
all German troops, as well as of all German soldiers and officers enlisted in Russian units organized in the Baltic states, was not immediately commenced and without interruption continued.[24]

This language of the strong arm told.[25] On October 3rd the German
government dismissed General v.d. Goltz, whose recall from the Bal-

source, the well-documented book *"The Birth of the Independence of Estonia"* (in
Estonian) by E. Laaman, Tallinn, 1932, he had been a bandmaster in a Russian regiment in Tsarist time, lacking any right to the title of Prince.

[23] Cf. the report sent by the Chief of the Brit. Mil. Mission in Berlin, General
Malcolm, to London on Aug. 8th, and the Foreign Office Memorandum of Oct. 9th,
Brit. Doc. pp. 53 and 142.

[24] v. the text in *Papers Relating...*, vol. 8, p. 420.

[25] As the German government expressed itself in a proclamation addressed to
those German soldiers in the Baltic area who were reluctant to obey the order calling them home, the measures referred to in the ultimatum threatened Germany with
the renewal of the blockade "which ravaged our ranks more murderously than all
other weapons in the war". Millions would fall victims of unemployment and famine would break out on the very threshold of winter. (Br. Doc., pp. 134—135). Al-

tic area had three times been demanded by the Allied and Associated Powers but still not effected. At the same time the German government found themselves compelled to propose that the Supreme Council create a mixed commission to supervise and carry out the expeditious completion of the evacuation. This latter step by the German government proved the lever which at last moved the matter from the dead point, the mixed commission, constituted soon thereafter, putting an end to the interminable tergiversations by which the German authorities had been purposely delaying the evacuation.

By the measures imposed by the Supreme Council, v.d. Goltz had been put in the same critical situation in which he had found himself by the middle of June, when a veto had been interposed by General Gough on behalf of the Supreme Council at the very moment when, after the completion of all preparations, he was ready to strike the mortal blow to the Estonian republic. "The troop was in a state of passionate irritation", we read in his memoirs. "All were waiting for, the attack scheduled to take place in a few days . . . To beat a retreat was no longer possible." (*Politischer General*, p. 152). He took the same desperate resolution he had taken in June, a resolution which like the former was to lead to a well-deserved catastrophe: to stake his all. He resolved to defy the order of the Supreme Council and strike the planned blow, come what might. To make the analogy complete, he resorted to a "masquerade", analogous to his clumsy trick of "hiring out" the Iron Division to Herr Niedra's "Latvian" government: all those German soldiers and officers who were foolish enough to join their leader in his mad enterprise, exchanged their German shoulder-traps for Russian ones and joined Bermondt's forces as "Russian volunteers". Let us listen to v.d. Goltz's own words: "I ordered on Oct. 3rd that from this time forth Prince Avaloff-Bermondt was to take the command of all the troops who stayed on. By this it was given out that from Oct. 3rd forth the Baltic venture was a Russian one. In this way I hoped to keep Germany and the German government aloof from the whole story and thus to elude the demands of the Entente." (p. 151).

though perhaps the paint had been laid too thick in this proclamation, to render it more impressive, there could not be any doubt that any further tergiversation with regard to the evacuation from Latvia and Lithuania would threaten Germany with very grave consequences.

With regard to the eventual danger of Allied intervention as well as to the approaching winter it was necessary to act with full speed. On Oct. 8th Bermondt, as commander of a "Russian West Army", opened an attack on Riga. Two of the three columns of this "Russian" army were, according to v.d. Goltz's testimony, "the German Legion of the United German Free Companies" and our old acquaintance, the Iron Division. The third column, a Russian one on the left flank, was obviously but an appendage, useful for enabling the whole army to pass as Russian. Calling a spade a spade this was v.d. Goltz's army, the sham-colonel Bermondt being but a figure-head, as counterfeit as his colonel's rank and prince's title.

If not the fate of free, democratic Latvia, then at all events that of Riga seemed to be sealed. Against Bermondt's force of 8600 bayonets and sabres, provided with 56 guns, 201 machine-guns etc, the Latvian command was able to concentrate no more than 6400 bayonets and sabres, with 16 guns and 64 machine-guns. Bermondt's forces were consequently considerably superior in numbers and by far the superior in fire power. Moreover, Bermondt had a vast reserve of trained soldiers to draw upon, since the total of his forces, according to reliable information, amounted to no less than 50,000, all richly supplied with German arms and munitions. Moreover, the great majority of the soldiers and officers of this army had fought in the ranks of the German army in the world war. The Latvian army, on the other hand, was suffering from rather acute lack not only of equipment and war materials but even clothing and footwear. Further, most of the Latvian units, having been formed only after the return to power of the lawful Ulmanis government in the middle of July, had not yet got either full military training or their baptism of fire on the battle-fields.

In defiance of all these adverse conditions the Latvian troops fought with the courage of despair, as can be inferred from what v.d. Goltz utters in his memoirs on the initial battles from October 8th to 10th. "The fighting was hard and fought by the enemy with an unexampled cruelty, obviously animated with not only fanatical hatred of the Germans, but partly also Bolshevik brutality.[26] However, against the

---

[26] As to the alleged "unexampled cruelty" and "Bolshevik brutality" of the Latvians, v.d. Goltz can hardly be regarded as a trustworthy witness. It was, of course, possible that cruelties were committed by the Latvian soldiers, thrown into a

overwhelming superiority of the enemy forces they could not hold their ground. Next day after the start of the offensive, on October 9th, the suburbs of Riga on the southern bank of Daugava were in Bermondt's hands.

But the Estonian government, well aware that the very existence of not only a free Estonia, but Latvia too was at stake, sent without delay, at the urgent request of the Latvian government, two armoured trains, whose crews were classed among the best troops of the Estonian army, to the assistance of their neighbour and ally in mortal danger. When these trains, after midnight on October 9th/10th, arrived at the last station before Riga, about 18 miles from it, they learned that the Latvian army was in full retreat, having been ordered to take up positions on the line of the river Jägel and a few small lakes, four to five miles north of the city. As it was said that the Commander-in-Chief of the army was still in Riga, the trains, taking all appropriate precautions against sudden attacks, continued their advance towards the city, where they observed but few Latvian patrols on the quiet streets. No enemy forces had yet come over the river. After placing outposts at all the bridges and along the river bank, the commander of the trains, Captain **Hinnom**, was taken to the Commander-in-Chief's quarters, where the **Prime Minister** and the **Foreign Minister** were also present. It turned out that the units, not yet tempered on the battle-fields, had been so demoralised by the retreat under heavy fighting against overwhelming enemy forces that all hope had been given up of their being able to hold their ground and preventing the fall of the capital. It took Captain Hinnom considerable trouble to persuade the high dignitaries that it was worth while to try to fight the enemy rather on the broad Daugava than on the much less easily defensible line mentioned above, and to prevail upon them to cancel the order to retreat. They agreed to this only when he had declared that his trains would at any rate stay on fighting at the Daugava and retreat only if the enemy's fire rendered this unavoidable.

passion by the treacherous attack of the Bermondt forces. However, v.d. Goltz, who according to the testimony of the British Foreign Office had established "a veritable reign of terror" in Riga after its capture on May 22nd, was the last person to rant about the cruelty and brutality of others.

When in the early hours of the morning the news of the arrival of
the Estonians spread in the city and the Latvian troops returned
public feeling began hastily to veer round. The transient crisis of des-
pondency was overcome. Machine-gun nests commanding all bridges
and other places where the river could be crossed were hurriedly
constructed and trenches dug all along the quay.

The enemy, being in the dark as to the strength of the forces that
had come to the assistance of the Latvians, dared not make any serious
attempt to cross the Daugava. There was, moreover, the danger of
being caught in a trap, since the British men-of-war riding in the
mouth of the Daugava could blow up the bridges behind any forces
which crossed the river. There was the more reason to apprehend this
danger as already on the same Oct. 10th, when the Estonian armoured
trains took action in Riga, it became apparent that the Allied Powers
were not going to remain passive onlookers in these events. A blockade of German ships, to wit the suspension of all passage of German
vessels in the Baltic, was declared on that day by the Allied Naval
Armistice Commission — "in consequence of the attack on Riga" as
was expressly stated in the telegram. All German vessels were to be
recalled at once and those thereafter found at sea were declared liable
to seizure by the Allies. (Brit. Doc., p. 157).

Not knowing what to do in the blind alley he had got into, Bermondt offered a truce to the Latvian government as early as the morning of Oct. 11th. The latter did not deign to answer this offer, made
by the way in most insolent terms. Before long the British Navy intervened. In an ultimatum sent over the air and by messengers on Oct.
13th, the Commanding Officer of the squadron, Admiral Cowan, required the German forces on the river Daugava to withdraw by noon
on Oct. 15th, failing which he intended to shell them. As only an
evasive answer was received, the fortress Dünamünde on the southern
bank of the mouth of Daugava was bombarded by Cowan's ships at
the time indicated. Soon arms and ammunition as well as equipment
needed by the army began to stream in more abundantly than before.
This enabled the Latvian High Command more intensively to form,
equip, and train new units.

In the meantime the enemy, doomed to immobility on the southern
bank of the Daugava, since an advance across the river was out of the
question for the reasons indicated above, was giving vent to his im-

potent rage by insensately bombarding the open town of Riga, causing considerable damage to buildings as well as many casualties, mainly among the civilian population.

The idleness to which Bermondt's forces were doomed could not but demoralize and weaken them, whereas at the same time the strength of the Latvian army was growing day by day. By early November, the Latvians were already able to mount a vigorous offensive. In violent battles which lasted three days, from Nov. 6th to 8th, supported by the fire of the Allied navy, the Iron Division was thrown back in disorder to Olai, midway between Riga and Yelgava, leaving behind considerable numbers of guns, trench mortars, machine guns etc. Riga was at last freed from a bombardment which had continued without rhyme and reason for four weeks. (Br. Doc., p. 223).

Then the mixed commission of the Allied Powers and Germany, headed by the French General Niessel, established an effective check on the Latvian—German frontier and cut off Bermondt's stream of supplies of arms, ammunition etc. which had all the time been flowing in from Germany. This was the final mortal blow to v.d. Goltz's intrigues in the Baltic area, as the latter himself avowed in his memoirs. What decided the fate of Bermondt's adventure, he wrote in that book, was not the intervention of the Allied navy (though called "fatal" in the same breath). "What proved decisive was the closure of the frontier. The armed forces "rapidly" dwindled away,[27] clothing and footwear wore out and were not replaced. Many men had no overcoats, no woollens, no change of linen. Therefore not only the fire of the enemy, but also, and still more, pneumonia, gastric complaints, bad provisioning and icy weather decimated the troop. Very soon ammunition too ran short." (*Politischer General*, p. 155).

The bandmaster had to break off his mad performance and retire to Germany with the remnants of his beaten army.

In a report sent to London on December 9th, when the evacuation of German—Russian forces from Latvia and Lithuania was nearing

---

[27] This somewhat ambiguous sentence, with the word "rapidly" in inverted commas, was in all probability merely a euphemism, purposely chosen to express in a milder way what in reality was but desertion spreading like wildfire. Of course, the chain-reaction of a general desertion was unavoidable as soon as the mass of this army became alive to the hopeless, insensate adventure they had been lured into by their irresponsible leader.

completion, the following judgment upon the v.d. Goltz—Bermondt intrigue was given by the British representative on Gen. Niessel's commission, General A. J. Turner: "The Baltic Adventure has been entirely controlled and planned by the Military Party. The German War Office, the Reichswehr Commander at Koenigsberg and the VIth Corps Commander at Tilsit are all thoroughly implicated. Bermondt has been a mere puppet. The ostensible reason — that of fighting Bolshevism — was merely a red herring across the trail, to deceive their own people in Prussia, to gain the support of the gullible Russian Party at Berlin and to help their intrigues in Russian affairs generally." (Br. Doc. p. 249)

In its proclamation to the German soldiers in the Baltic area quoted above, the German government had declared that it was its order, dictated by the interests of Germany, that all German citizens who had joined volunteer units in that area, should leave this foreign country. It was added that all means at the command of the Government would be used to enforce the evacuation of the Baltic Provinces. All those German soldiers and officers who did not obey this order were consequently to be regarded as mutineers. As a matter of fact, summonses to return to Germany had already earlier been addressed, on behalf of the government, to v.d. Goltz's troops, among whom, however, a "movement of refusal to return to Germany" had sprung up, and the idea spread that "entering into Russian service" would be a method of evading the necessity of complying with the Government's order. From a speech made by v.d. Goltz at Yelgava on Sept. 1st, on the occasion of the parade of the Iron Division, it was clear that he was fully at one with this "movement", although he could not help calling it "disobedience", for which reason he "could not set himself at its head". A convincing proof of his sympathy for this movement was a secret Corps order issued a day before, forbidding any agitation against accepting Russian service. (Br. Doc., pp. 102 and 95). As a Prussian general he was, of course, well aware of the truism that disobedience tolerated in an army destroys its very foundations. In the speech in question he said himself that "the danger lurks in it (disobedience) that all other bonds of discipline and cohesion may disappear". It was not long before these words of his were to come true in a really hideous way — when, after the collapse of his and Bermondt's dream, their mercenary army fell to pieces.

In General Turner's reports we read: "Colonel Dosse has supplied further information as to the conduct of the German troops. This is based not only on his personal observation, but also on the facts reported by a small Allied Commission detailed to investigate the reports received. The Germans throughout the whole area they have occupied have committed wholesale robbery, pillage, and destruction. Horses, cows, poultry, carts, and even furniture have been removed. Nothing is left to the peasant but the few things he has been able to hide. The various Frei Corps are the most unruly, outdoing the Iron Division and the Bermondt troops in violence. They are now bands of cut-throats of the worst type — armed to the teeth and brooking no interference with their actions. The control of the railways by Allied Officers is in many areas a mere farce, as any officer endeavouring to examine a wagon is at once threatened with rifles or bombs. Bombs and stones are thrown at the Allied officers from wagons. General Eberhardt's[28] officers even if they wished could do little to put a stop to it and at times receive similar attentions themselves, two of the staff officers having been wounded by bombs." "The whole country, according to reports of the Allied Control officers has been entirely devastated, all livestock removed and the inhabitants systematically robbed and ill-treated. The peasants have been left without the means of tilling their fields, and measures of relief will be necessary without delay." (Br. Doc. pp. 246, 252).

V.d. Goltz has in his memoirs tried to make the reader believe that Bermondt's intention was not to cross the Daugava and capture Riga, but solely to get his flank secured by the river Daugava against possible attacks of the "unfriendly Latvians", before turning with his forces against the Red Army. To refute this assertion suffice it to quote what the president of Bermondt's "Central Council", Count Pahlen, has told the representative of the Allied Military Mission at Yelgava, Lt.-Col. J. J. Grove. According to the latter's report of October 16th, "it is perfectly apparent from the admissions that Count Pahlen has made at various times that the object was to upset the Ulmanis government and to settle at once and definitely any question of independence for Latvia and annex that country as a Russian Pro-

---

[28] A general who by order of the German government had taken over the command of the 6th Reserve Corps from v.d. Goltz.

vince. In one conversation Count Pahlen observed that the re-annex-ation of these provinces would have necessitated hard fighting if post-poned until after the restoration of Russia." (Br. Doc., p. 165). That v.d. Goltz's allegation is but a clumsy attempt to misrepresent obvious and undeniable facts is in any case clear without Lt.-Col. Grove's evidence.

At the very time when Bermondt opened his sudden attack on Riga, Yudenitch was starting his advance upon Petrograd. Though the necessary preparations had not yet been properly completed, the offensive could be delayed no longer. The possibility that the nego-tiations opened on Soviet initiative might lead to the conclusion of peace between Estonia and Soviet Russia, could not be left out of consideration. For the reasons indicated above, such an eventuality would have meant catastrophe for the North—Western Army. A successful offensive, on the other hand, crowned by the capture of Petrograd, was the most efficacious means of averting this disaster. Moreover, on Denikin's front too the point had been reached which would decide either victory or defeat and ruin. If Denikin could still be helped by a diversion on some other front, this help was to be rendered without any further delay. Yudenitch thus had no choice.

The offensive of the North—Western Army started on Oct. 10th. In order to fufil the obligations assumed at the military conference held in Riga on August 26th, Estonia had assigned considerable forces, among them a number of the very best units of the Estonian army, to take part in the joint offensive. These Estonian forces, advancing along the coast of the Gulf of Finland, and the Estonian naval forces operating in that gulf, covered the left flank of the North—Western Army. In accordance with the decisions of the conference of August 26th, Estonian forces simultaneously took the offensive west and south of Pskov. Substantial support to the offensive was rendered, furthermore, by the British naval squadron operating in the Baltic, which not only forced the Red Navy to remain in Kronstadt under the protection of the batteries of that naval station, but also assisted the offensive by the bombardment of Red Army entrenchments on land.

The offensive proved in its initial stage more successful than there had been reason to anticipate. On October 20th the army stood at the approaches to the last defensible line before Petrograd, a row of hills stretching to right and left of the Russian observatory Pulkovo. An order of the day had been signed by Yudenitch, assigning to the army the task of carrying by assault the last line of defence of the Red Army and breaking into the city on the following day.

In the meantime, however, the Command of the Red Army had managed not only to levy about twenty thousand volunteers in Petrograd, but also to reinforce the defence of the city by conveying to it several shock units from the Moscow district, about 9000 bayonets in all. This was made possible by the fact that the vitally important task of cutting off the Moscow—Petrograd railway-line, entrusted to one of the divisions, had not been carried out. The commander of the division, fascinated by the view of the Petrograd cupolas, and anxious to be among the first to break into the city, had deflected the bulk of his force in this direction, and the remainder had proved unable to accomplish the task assigned. After three days of violent fighting, the North—Western Army had to sound a retreat which very soon turned into a complete rout. Only the Estonian troops taking part in the offensive maintained order and discipline, as well as their fighting spirit and strength during the retreat and in the repulsion of the onslaughts of the Red Army on the line beyond Narova, which with provident care had been chosen and fortified in due time.

There was nothing to do with the demoralized remnants of the routed army but to disarm them and disband the whole army. A request made by Yudenitch and emphatically supported by the Allied Military Mission as well as by the Supreme Council, not to disarm his army, but to grant him leave to reorganize it on Estonian territory, was rejected by the Estonian government. Of course it would have been sheer madness to tolerate a foreign army, deeply hostile to a free and independent Estonia, and yet in possession of its weapons, behind the frontline of the Estonian army which as it had to exert all its strength to repulse the fierce attacks of the Red Army. Moreover, the disarming and disbanding of this army was an imperative necessity, since Estonia had made up her mind to conclude peace with Soviet Russia as soon as an acceptable agreement on terms could be reached. Owing to the tact and firmness with which the operation was carried out, the Estonian Command succeeded in disarming and disbanding the remnants of the North—Western Army without any incidents worth mentioning.

It proved, of course, considerably more difficult to solve the very complicated problem of how to accommodate the human flotsam of the wrecked army, thrown on the shores of Estonia — tens of thousands of unhappy men — with lodgings, food, sanitation, etc. With the help of the Allied and Associated Powers this problem too was somehow mastered.

In view of these events, and especially of the fact that the Latvian government had to use every effort to combat Bermondt, it proved impossible to re-open the peace conference at the set time, on October 25th. The conference was therefore pro tem adjourned.

Soon after that date some hints from Moscow which seemed to prove that the Soviet government was really interested in concluding peace with Estonia and the other Baltic states, reached the Estonian government. Nonetheless it took another six weeks before the peace conference met at Tartu on December 5th, 1919. The Latvian and the Lithuanian governments were irresolute and hesitating. Their attention was still concentrated on the clearance from their territory of the remnants of v.d. Goltz—Bermondt's forces.[29] Estonia, however, could not take the risk of overstraining her army, which had born the brunt of the battle for eleven months, staving off Soviet aggression. The Estonian government was convinced that any hesitation and irresolution over the conclusion of peace, once acceptable terms could be reached, would expose Estonia to unavailing and unjustifiable dangers. It did not flinch from the decision to conclude peace even when M. Philippe Berthelot, on behalf of the French government, on December 17th, 1919, in a talk with the Estonian diplomatic representative, hinted in unmistakable words at the probable penalization of Estonia with an economic blockade should the peace negotiations lead to recognition of the Soviet government, in other words, to the conclusion of peace. The Estonian government had, however, succeeded in the meantime in getting possession of trustworthy information that there was hardly any danger of the British government bringing pressure to bear upon Estonia should she make peace with Soviet

---

[29] Their evacuation was not completed until December 16th (Br. Doc. p. 258).

Russia. There was reason to believe that the blockade with which M. Berthelot had threatened Estonia would never be enforced.

It was nearly four weeks before an agreement on the armistice was reached. This occurred on December 31st, 1919, and the cease fire was sounded on January 3rd, 1920. In the meantime battles had raged at the front, more violent and furious than ever during the preceding months of the war. Unsparingly flinging ever new cannon fodder into battle, the Soviet government hoped to force upon Estonia terms of peace which would render her hardly viable from the economic and quite defenceless from the military point of view, an easy prey to communist propaganda as well as to new aggression. However, the Estonian delegation at the conference did not let itself be impressed either by the fury of the attacks of the Red Army at the front or by the arrogance and grandiloquent boastfulness of the Soviet delegates at the conference table. The sang-froid displayed by the Estonian delegation in face of the threats of the Soviet delegates to crush the Estonian front by conveying to it such and such a number of fresh divisions, gradually told: step by step the Soviet delegation gave up the terms which the Estonian from the very beginning had declared to be unacceptable, and at last an agreement was reached which could be recognized by both parties as just and honourable, as it was stated in the preamble to the treaty.

Significantly enough, however, a new and unexpected demand was presented by the Soviet delegation a few days before the signature of the convention of armistice, when agreement on all its articles had already been reached. It very soon came to light that the only purpose of this delay in signing the agreement was to give the Red Army an opportunity of trying once more to break the resistance of the Estonian army. For three days, December 18th—30th, masses of Red Army troops recently conveyed to the front assaulted the Estonian lines with the ruthlessness and prodigality in squandering lives ever characteristic of the Russian army. Wave after wave of assailants was flung under the murderous fire of the Estonian army. The only outcome were heaps of corpses in front of the Estonian lines and such heavy losses inflicted on the attacking units that they would no longer have been serviceable even for guard duty, as the commander of the 7th Soviet Army reported to his superiors. As soon as the failure of these attacks was manifest and the command of the Red Army had to sound the retreat, the Soviet delegation dropped the new demand and signed the armistice.

The armistice convention contained the most essential part of the peace treaty and the real moot point which it had had to solve: the agreement upon the frontier between Estonia and Soviet Russia. It took a further month to reach agreement upon economic and other rather complicated questions connected with the secession of Estonia from Russia. The peace treaty was signed on February 2nd, 1920.

A fortnight before the termination of the peace conference, on January 16th, 1920, the economic blockade of Soviet Russia was lifted by the Entente Powers.

It is now time to return to the development of the Lithuanian—Polish relations, interrupted to devote attention to the momentous events in Estonia and Latvia in the summer of 1919.

It was mentioned that the Supreme Council of the Allied and Associated Powers made several attempts to put an end to present and prevent subsequent clashes between the Polish and the Lithuanian forces by drawing lines of demarcation between them, not to be crossed by either of them. The first two lines were drawn conforming to the lines actually held by both forces. The Poles, however, failed to respect these lines. Then, on December 8th, 1919, a new line of demarcation was drawn up, based on a closer investigation of the national areas actually existing within the region in question. This line was to be a provisional frontier of Poland which was to separate the indubitably Polish areas from those with predominantly non-Polish population. The establishment of such a provisional frontier was considered necessary to enable the Polish government to set up regular administration in these areas, which would certainly be assigned to the Polish state when, after the termination of the civil war in Russia and of the chaotic conditions resulting from it, it became possible to agree upon the permanent eastern frontier of Poland.

Corresponding to its general aim the main part of this so-called Curzon line,[30] to wit the stretch running due south from the point where it touched the river Niemen, marked off the indisputably Polish areas from those inhabited by the White—Ruthenians and the Ukrainians. Its north-western section, on the other hand, from its be-

---

[30] It became known under this designation owing to the prominent part played at its fixing by the British Foreign Office, whose head at that time was Earl Curzon.

ginning at the frontier of Prussia to the river Niemen, had been drawn up so as to correspond, as exactly as practicable, to the actually existing watershed separating the Polish areas from the Lithuanian ones. Gardinas as well as the city and district of Vilnius lay on the outer, i.e. non-Polish side of this line.

As a matter of fact Poland had no justified claims to either of these two districts, for, as the latest available Russian statistics reveal, the percentage of Poles was only 10.1 in the district of Gardinas and 8.2 in that of Vilnius. In the city of Vilnius itself it was, of course, considerably higher, but still no more than 30.1, i.e. less than one third of the total number of inhabitants. It is true that the Lithuanians too were a minority in the district of Vilnius and indeed almost non-existent in the district of Gardinas, their percentage being 17.6 in the former and only 0.2 in the latter. This, however, in no wise substantiated Poland's claims to these districts. The bulk of the population in both areas consisted of a people quite distinct from the Russians, the White-Ruthenians, whose percentage was 61.1 in the district of Vilnius and 71.2 in that of Gardinas.[31] The White-Ruthenians had for centuries been citizens of the Grand Duchy of Lithuania, and enjoyed civil rights fully equal with those of the Lithuanians. White-Ruthenian grandees had played a prominent part at the court of the Lithuanian Grand Dukes in the late Middle Ages. Their influence at this court was so great that for a long time the official documents of these Grand Dukes were written in White-Ruthenian. One of the great chieftains of the Lithuanians, Gediminas (1316-1342), was accustomed to style himself *Rex Lithuaniorum et multorum Ruthenorum* (The King of the Lithuanians and many Ruthenians). — Whether the White-Ruthenian majorities of the two districts in question were willing to be included in the restored Lithuanian state or rather wanted to belong to their own sovereign national state — provided their nation proved able to establish such a state — with the probable consequence of a partition of the Vilnius region according to the principle of nationality, — these were questions concerning the White-Ruthenians and Lithuanians, and to be decided by them, whereas the pretensions of the Poles to these districts lacked any fair ground.

[31] The above statistical data are taken from the Russian *New Encyclopedia* quoted above, vol. 10, p. 542 and vol. 15, p. 75.

The Poles, though accepting the Curzon line, made no haste to deliver either Gardinas or the city and district of Vilnius to the Lithuanians. Then of a sudden a violent trial of strength broke out between Poland and Soviet Russia, the Poles starting a strong offensive against the latter in late April, 1920. Though successful in the beginning this offensive was stopped about three months later by a Soviet counteroffensive, and then the Polish armies were pushed back in heavy battles along the whole front almost to the very gates of Warsaw. In the general retreat the Poles had to withdraw also from the Vilnius district, which fell into the hands of the Red Army.

While the chance of war was still in abeyance, the Soviet government considered it opportune to make an ingenious move: it took the initiative of concluding peace with Lithuania as well as with Latvia.

As to the former, no military actions had taken place between her and Soviet Russia since April, 1919, when the Polish army had occupied the eastern confines of Lithuania, separating her army from any contact with the Soviet Red Army. In the meantime the Lithuanians had had to guard against the Poles in the east and the unruly Russian—German troops of Vyrgolich and others in the north-western part of the country. As to Latvia, she had managed with the assistance of the Polish army to force the Red Army out of her eastern province, Latgale, in January, 1920, and thereafter, on February 1st, succeeded in concluding an armistice with Soviet Russia. It proved, however, more time-consuming to get the treaty of peace concluded. The Red Army, having in the meantime got the better of all the counter-revolutionary "white" generals, was no longer so acutely interested in concluding peace with Latvia and Lithuania as it had been in the case of Estonia in the last months of 1919. If then, quite suddenly, on July 12th, peace was concluded with Lithuania, and on August 11th with Latvia, Lenin had obviously considered this necessary to secure the neutrality of these two states in his conflict with Poland.

Towards Lithuania Lenin displayed a magnanimity rather uncommon with communist leaders: in the treaty of peace signed in Moscow on July 12th, Soviet Russia recognized the Vilnius and Gardinas areas as integral parts of Lithuania. Moreover, "taking into consideration the fact that during the world war Lithuania had been almost entirely ruined, and that Lithuanian citizens were deprived of the possibility even of re-establishing their homesteads, their partly destroyed and gutted buildings, owing to the destruction of the forests of Lithuania", the Soviet government "granted the Lithuanian government the right to cut timber, for a period of twenty years, over an area of 270,000 acres of the Soviet territory", and undertook "to make over to the Lithuanian government three million gold roubles".

A timber concession over an area of equal extent was granted by the Soviet government to Latvia in the peace treaty of August 11th, 1920, — "with a view to assisting the Latvian peasants in the restoration of buildings destroyed in the course of the war", as well as four million gold roubles to cover the sums due to her as compensation for various property evacuated to Russia during the war.

It cannot be passed over in silence that the Soviet government had been still more generous towards Estonia, to whom a sum five times larger than that received by Lithuania and an area ten times larger for cutting timber had been granted by the peace treaty. This admirable liberality towards Estonia obviously depended upon the incomparably greater interest of the Soviet government in peace with Estonia than it displayed in the subsequent negotiations with Lithuania and Latvia. Of course, peace with Estonia was to cut the first hole in the net of the blockade drawn around Soviet Russia. Since for this reason the position of Estonia was rather strong, the Soviet delegation failed in its attempts to smuggle into the text of the treaty all the high-flown words of Soviet propaganda about the assistance of the peasants in the restoration of their buildings, destroyed in the course of war, etc., which were later inserted in the peace treaties with Lithuania and Latvia.

Another fact, too, deserves to be mentioned. All the concessions granted to three states for cutting timber in Soviet Russia proved nothing but castles in Spain. All attempts to agree upon "the fixing of detailed conditions for the cutting of timber", which by the treaties of peace had been left to be decided by mixed commissions, proved futile. Not a single one of these millions or hundreds of thousands of acres granted by treaties, was ever exploited by any Estonian, Latvian, or Lithuanian concessionaire.

It need hardly be added that the three milloin roubles paid by the Soviet government to Lithuania was so derisively insignificant compared with the value of the evacuated property that it would be an exaggeration to call it even a token compensation. Still less of a sacrifice for Lenin was doubtless the recognition of the Vilnius and Gardinas districts as integral parts of Lithuania, since he was perfectly convinced that the Lithuanian workers would very soon overthrow their "white-guardist" government and proclaim their country a Soviet republic, which without any delay would either join Soviet Russia or conclude with her a new treaty. Moreover, when the peace treaty was being signed in Moscow, Vilnius was still in the hands of the Poles. Two days later, however, the latter withdrew and Vilnius was occupied by the Red Army, who again a few days later passed it over to the Lithuanians. Within a fortnight the Lithuanian forces were in possession of practically all the territory on their side of the Curzon line.

In the nick of time, however, the Poles by a supreme effort succeeded in averting defeat and inflicting so severe a blow upon the Red Army that it had hastily to back off. Yet clashes between the Polish and the Lithuanian forces had been going on, even while fortune still favoured the Soviet forces and catastrophe threatened the Poles. In the middle of September, 1920, on the initiative of the Polish government, an attempt was made "to find an amicable solution" to the discord and put an end to hostilities. Negotiations, however, came to naught. Then a fortnight later a new conference was held at Suvalkai (from September 30th—October 7th). Here the two states agreed upon a line of demarcation "under no pretext to be passed by the troops of the contracting parties", and along the entire length of which hostilities were to cease. For the western part of this line the parties accepted the north-western stretch of the Curzon line from the frontier of Prussia until the point where, at Niemen, it turned to the south. From that point on they drew it, by mutual consent, east-north-east, but no further than Bastouny, a station on the railway from Vilnius south to Lyda. As to why the line was broken off at that point, the agreement referred to the fact that the region to the east of the said railway was still held by the Soviet troops. The agreement contained, however, a clause according to which the establishment of the line of demarcation to the east of Bastouny and the cessation of hostilities along this line was to be regulated by a special agreement, and, moreover, the contracting parties reserved the right to appeal to the League of Nations to determine these questions if they themselves should fail to come to an agreement.

It goes without saying that an agreement on a line of demarcation between the armed forces of two states with a common frontier still in abeyance does not determine this frontier itself. And indeed this was explicitly declared in the Suvalkai agreement: the line of demarcation fixed below "does not decide beforehand what are the territorial rights of the two contracting parties". This could not, however, be taken to mean that this line and the frontier to be fixed were things having no bearing upon each other. There could hardly be any doubt that the line of demarcation was to be an approximation or a rough draft of the frontier line, to be amended where reasons should be found, and in this way fixed as the definitive frontier. That this was so is reflected in the above-mentioned fact that the parties had accepted as the western part of the demarcation line the respective section of the Curzon line drawn up in conformity with the ethnical character of the areas it divided. It would have been obviously inconsistent not to follow the same criterion when the line of demarcation was being continued to the east of Niemen. But be this as it may, by engaging themselves to suspend hostilities along the entire line already agreed upon and deciding, moreover, to commit the establishment of its eastern remainder to the League of Nations, if they themselves failed to agree upon it, the contracting parties had undertaken to determine their common frontier and to settle their reciprocal territorial claims concerning it in an amicable fashion, by way of negotiations, refraining from a military solution to these matters.

Along certain parts of the line of demarcation hostilities had been already suspended before the Agreement was signed at Suvalkai on October 7th, as appears from its text.[32] However, instead of taking measures for a cease-fire along the remainder of the line before noon on October 10th, when the Agreement, according to its concluding chapter, was to come into force and hostilities were to be suspended along the entire length of the line, on the very day after the signature of the Agreement, while the ink was still wet as it were, the Polish

[32] The Agreement has been reproduced, in English translation, in *Lithuania Past and Present* by E. J. Harrison, London 1922, pp. 207—209.

army all of a sudden launched a strong offensive from south to north along the railway-line Lyda—Vilnius, with the obvious aim of capturing Vilnius. It should be mentioned that Vilnius is situated about fifty five miles to the north of Bastouny, i.e. of the eastern end of the line which, according to the Agreement signed the day before, was "under no pretext to be passed by the troops of the two contracting parties".

Appreciating the overwhelming superiority of forces — five Polish divisions against three Lithuanian battalions and one battery — the Lithuanians began hastily to evacuate Vilnius, and on the following day the city was occupied by the Poles in spite of violent rear-guard actions. With the withdrawal of the Lithuanian forces and authorities from the city of Vilnius the region to the east of it automatically fell into the hands of the Poles. The latter advanced also into the Lithuanian territory west of Vilnius, meeting with growing resistance.

The capture of the city and district of Vilnius was thinly camouflaged as a self-willed act of a general of the Polish army, L. Zeligovski, at the head of a freebooting army formed of allegedly insubordinate Polish divisions. An allegedly autonomous territory of "Central Lithuania" was proclaimed with a kind of government. The camouflage was, however, so transparent that no one of normal intelligence can have been taken in by it. No wonder therefore that only two years later the clumsy subterfuge was cast away by none other than Marshal J. Pilsudski, who in 1920 was the Head of the Polish state. In an interview given to the diplomatic representatives of the Allied Powers in Warsaw in December, 1922, he frankly avowed that Zeligovski had acted on his orders. This declaration of his was cited by one of those to whom it was made, the Italian Minister in Warsaw, Signor E. Tommasini, in his memoirs published in 1925.

In January, 1922, elections to a "Constituent Assembly" were held in "Central Lithuania", the Vilnius district, by order of the administration appointed by Zeligovski. Only a tiny minority took part in these elections, whereas the overwhelming majority, to wit practically all Lithuanians, White-Ruthenians, and Jews, boycotted the polls, considering that the conditions requisite to honest elections were lacking in a territory subdued by force of arms and held under military occupation. Although the Assembly could therefore in nowise be recognized as an authorized expression of the will of the inhabitants, nevertheless made bold to apply, in the name and on behalf of the people, to the Polish Sejm for the incorporation of "Central Lithuania" into Poland, and the Polish Sejm likewise made bold to satisfy this demand on March 22nd, 1922. Lithuania refused to recognize this incorporation of the district of Vilnius into Poland. Neither was this act ever approved by the League of Nations, who, however, lacked the power to redress the wrong done.

IV

THE HEALING OF THE WOUNDS AND THE BUILDING UP OF THE YOUNG STATES

The War of Liberation had been a very heavy strain on the Baltic nations. While the struggle raged at the battle-fronts, all organs of state administration had to be built up out of nothing and set functioning under high pressure to answer the demands of the life-and-death conflict. All this had to be done in great haste, there being no time for close and thorough consideration of all the details. If slips were made, they could be amended after the war. Even the enactment of the constitutions had to be carried out in two stages. As already mentioned, only in Estonia did it prove possible to hold elections for the Constituent Assembly as early as April, 1919. However, when the Assembly met on April 23rd, it was to such an extent overburdened with the most pressing current tasks directly connected with the conduct of the war, that it proved advisable first to enact a provisional constitutional law, establishing a transitional system of government pending the working out of the constitution. This provisional law was passed on June 4th, 1919, and the constitution about six months after the end of the war, on June 15th, 1920. In Latvia and Lithuania the elections could not be held until April 1920. Following the example of the Estonian Constituent Assembly, the Constituent Assemblies of Latvia and Lithuania also enacted provisional constitutional laws, on June 1st and 10th, 1920, respectively, whereas the Constitutions were passed in 1922, on February 15th and August 1st respectively.

On these constitutions it might be appropriate to make the following observations.

All three Baltic nations owed the attainment of their independent statehood to the inspiring idea of the inalienable right of nations as well as individuals to freedom, and their constitutions were being elaborated and enacted at a time when the democratic form of government was in triumphal procession making headway in the world. It was therefore a foregone conclusion that the constitutions to be enacted were to be true and unadulterated expressions of liberal and democratic ideas. All three proclaimed their states democratic republics in which the ultimate power was vested in the people. The will of the sovereign people was to be expressed through parliaments elected by universal, equal, direct, and secret vote, as well as by the people's power of plebiscite. No second chamber of parliament was created, since it was considered that through one single chamber the will of the people would find more direct and unhindered expression. The Estonian as well as the Lithuanian constitution contained a rather lengthy enumeration of the fundamental rights of citizens, among which were, over and above the freedom of the press, of speech, of worship, of assembly, etc., also the right of national minorities to education in their mother tongue, and their right to form autonomous institutions for the promotion of their national culture and welfare. In Latvia, too, all these freedoms and rights were no less firmly established by special laws, though for some reason or other their list was not included in the Constitution. It is noteworthy that Latvia was the first state in Europe to enact (on Dec. 8th, 1919) a law which granted cultural autonomy to her national minorities.

As to the executive power, in Latvia and Lithuania it was vested in the President of the Republic, elected by the Parliament and the Cabinet of Ministers. The latter, designated by the President, had to enjoy the confidence of Parliament. A vote of non-confidence entailed the resignation of the Cabinet or of one of its members respectively. The President of the Republic himself was rather dependent upon the Parliament, which not only elected him, but had also the power to dismiss him by a two-thirds vote. The Estonian constitution excluded a President altogether in the governmental structure, vesting the usual functions of President in the Prime Minister.

These brief remarks might suffice to show that on the one hand, the three Assemblies were inspired by the desire to produce constitutions which would be the nearest approach possible to the ideal of the democratic form of rule, and, on the other hand, that in this undertaking they were guided almost exclusively by abstract reasoning and theoretical considerations, which indeed was not to be wondered at, in view of the fact that they were completely lacking in practical experience of the management of state affairs. It was not long before the shortcomings of the constitutions came to light, causing tensions and leading to constitutional crises to which we shall return in due course.

The same procedure as that used with regard to the constitutions was also to be adopted regarding the agrarian reform laws, which, in view of their vital importance to the peoples concerned, could in justice be marked as no less fundamental than the former. In Estonia, it is true, the Agrarian Law had already been passed by the Constituent Assembly before the end of the war, on October 19th, 1919, This law, however, left a number of important details to be regulated by special laws eventually to be enacted by the administration. In Lithuania and Latvia, even the first sections of the agrarian reform law were enacted after the end of the war, in August and September of 1920 respectively, and the concluding sections which confirmed the whole reform were passed in April and May of 1922 respectively.

A much more complicated and difficult task than the elaboration and enactment of these fundamental and important laws was, however, the restoration of economic life, thrown out of gear by nearly six years of war and revolutionary disorders. How strenuous were the efforts needed can properly be realized only if one has an idea of the extent of the devastation inflicted on the country and the losses sustained in the terrible years from 1914—1920. We shall therefore try to furnish a brief account of this devastation and these losses.

It is obviously impossible to state with certainty which of the three countries had suffered most, since there is no possibility of assessing exactly the damage suffered by each of them, statistical data being often very unsatisfactory and on occasion completely lacking. One can only say that Estonia suffered less severely than the two other countries, since she was spared from becoming a theatre of war. Even when she was occupied by the German army in February 1918, the disintegrated remnants of the Russian army retreated without offering any resistance. As to which of the two, Latvia or Lithuania, suffered the deeper wounds, only inconclusive, subjective opinion can be expressed. Keeping this proviso in mind the following statement nevertheless deserves attention as it has been made by a neutral witness with ample opportunity to ascertain facts on the spot and in whose case there seems to be no reason to call in question either the veracity or the faculty of judgement. "Lithuanian territory was destined to bear the brunt of hostile attack, and in proportion to area and population, no country has suffered more severely or made greater sacrifices." It is an Englishman, Mr. E. J. Harrison, who makes this statement in his book *Lithuania Past and Present*, published in London in 1922. Mr. Harrison came to Lithuania in August 1919 as secretary to a commission sent to the Baltic area by the British government, and was soon thereafter appointed acting British vice-consul in Kaunas. He travelled all over the country in 1919 and 1920, when nothing had yet been done towards removing the traces of devastation, and eye-witnesses to the events which had wrought the havoc could be questioned on the spot. It might be noted that Mr. Harrison, who during the war had worked in St. Petersburg as assistant correspondent for *The Times*, according to his own statement possessed a very sound knowledge of Russian, at that time spoken by practically every Lithuanian belonging to the educated classes, and soon learnt also Lithuanian. He was thus able to communicate with the Lithuanians themselves, dispensing with intermediaries. Before coming to Lithuania he had spent a couple of months in Latvia and Estonia.

The following excerpt from Mr. Harrison's book might suffice to give an idea of the tragedy of the Lithuanian people in the years 1914—1920.

"During the Russian offensive in East Prussia (in Sept.—October 1914, A.R.) the Lithuanian provinces suffered terribly. Flourishing towns and villages were completely destroyed by artillery fire. Fifteen thousand persons, the majority Lithuanians, were deported by the Russians into the interior of the country, the brilliant idea underlying this policy being to leave the advancing Germans nothing but desert." Then, in the summer of 1915, the Germans invaded Lithuania, forcing the Russians out. "As ill luck would have it, the German offensive coincided with the harvest season. During their retreat the Russians destroyed everything which they were unable to remove, with the result that the output of an entire year's hard work was lost to the inhabitants. Fighting raged all over Lithuania for several months, and artillery fire above all caused wholesale devastation. The western districts of Kaunas and Suvalkai in many places resembled a desert. The towns of Kalvarija, Kibartai, Sirvintai, Naumiestis, Sudarga, Sakiai, Siauliai, Jurbarkas, Taurage, Kretinga, Gogzdai, and others were burnt or otherwise reduced to ruins. The region of the Nemunas (Niemen), where the fortresses of Kaunas, Alytus, and Gardinas were situated, offered a frightful spectacle of devastation. In the parish of Kalvarija alone fourteen large villages with their estates were entirely obliterated. — The western part of the Vilnius government and the district of Ezerenai (Zarasai) in the Kaunas government fared no better. These regions suffered severely under the tactics of the retreating Russians. Villages and farms were given to the flames, machinery and implements were carried off, and unspeakable miseries began for the inhabitants of these desolated areas."

In the following three years of the war the country was ruthlessly looted by the German occupation armies. "Enormous quantities of timber were removed from the country. The forests bordering the lakes, roads, and rivers were almost completely razed to the ground. In the same manner the land was denuded of horses and cattle through constant requisitioning not only for the needs of the army of occupation but for purposes of export to Germany. The value of this form of loot, reckoned at the present exchange, would run into billions of marks».

It has been mentioned that industry was very little developed in Lithuania by the outbreak of the war. Of the little there was hardly anything worth mentioning was left behind: machinery was for the most part either carried away or destroyed, often along with the factory buildings. "Three-quarters of the town of Siauliai were destroyed by fire, and this flourishing industrial centre of 30,000 inhabitants counts now only a few thousands. — In Kaunas province 144 mills were razed to the ground; in Vilnius 235; in Suvalkai 87."

Summing up what he had seen as well as heard from eye-witnesses Mr. Harrison stated: "What with the inevitable devastation wrought by gunfire, and the deliberate plundering of so-called friends and open foes, Lithuania in the wake of the war was reduced to little better than a desert. The countryside, through lack of working hands, wore a wild and savage aspect. According to the testimony of Dr. Bartuska, who visited the country as an American delegate, Lithuania at that time seemed entirely ruined. In the district of Suvalkai, owing to the destruction of houses, the inhabitants were forced to dwell in the abandoned trenches."

The deep wounds inflicted upon agriculture, which was the main occupation of the population and the mainstay of the national economy, were mirrored in the decrease of livestock in 1919 as compared with 1913. Happily enough, however, these wounds could be healed in a very short span, since this could be achieved solely by the exertions and toil of hundreds of thousands of peasants, without the injunction of capital, though this would have been highly desirable to accelerate the process of recovery. So in fact the recovery was not long in coming, as can be seen from the following table:

There were in Lithuania (in 1000 head):

Year	Horses:	Cattle:	Pigs:	Sheep:
1913	373	766	1138	1152
1919	280	480	750	806
1920	335	604	1118	894
1922	421	955	1414	1191

It appears from this table that as to livestock, more than half of the way back to the pre-war level had already been made by the following year, 1920, and this level had even been surpassed by 1922. The number of horses had, in fact, already slightly outstripped the pre-war level in 1921: there were 376,000 horses in 1921 as against 373,000 in 1913.

It goes without saying that grain culture, too, suffered considerably in the conscription of men in the prime of manhood, the requisition of livestock, the ensuing reduction of manuring, the cutting off of imports of artificial fertilizers, etc. Statistics are lacking, however, to show the extent of this setback as well as the process of recovery in this department in the years immediately following the end of the war.

As to industry, according to an *Album of Diagrams*, published by the Lithuanian Central Statistical Board in 1928 under the title of *Lithuania in Numbers*, about the same number of workers earned their livelihood in industry as before the war. Though certain branches such as the metal and timber industries had been reduced, the former by 2000 and the latter by 500 workers, the gap had been filled by other newly established branches.

Fearful though the afflictions fallen upon the Lithuanian people were, however, and with all respect to the testimony of Mr. Harrison, who in going to print in March 1922 hardly had at his disposal statistics relevant to the matter, there is reason to ask if the sufferings and losses sustained by the Latvians were not still more severe. At any rate the economic damage as mirrored by statistics was doubtless in general more grievous than that suffered by the Lithuanians. It could hardly be otherwise, since, whereas no military operations took place on Lithuanian territory from the summer of 1915, when she was occupied by the Germans, until the end of the war in November, 1918, in Latvia they went on unabated along the front which had cut the country into two parts thoughout the same summer of 1915. Moreover, compared with Lithuania there was also much more to be laid waste in Latvia, which country had reached a considerably higher level of economic development and welfare.

It was the flourishing industry of Latvia that was hit hardest. The numerous cellulose and match factories, papermills, sawmills and distilleries were, in the majority of cases, ruined or dismantled during the war. When in 1915 the southern half of the country was occupied by the Germans and Riga lay close to the battlefront, the Russian government, in July, 1915, ordered a total evacuation of industry from Riga in order to prevent its falling into the hands of the enemy. About 20,000 railway trucks filled with costly machinery and equipment estimated to have valued five hundred million dollars rolled eastwards to Russia. Even raw material and manufactured goods ware carried away, in many cases along with all the employees. In a word, the industry of Latvia, predominantly concentrated around Riga, was virtually wiped out.

Though agriculture had been less severely hit than industry, the damage suffered was still frightful. In the southern half of the country, Kurland, over half of the farms were destroyed or stood empty and the population as well as the cultivated area had diminished to one third at the time of the German occupation. The whole country had lost nearly forty per cent of its population, mainly by emigration after the German invasion. Hardly 300,000 of those who had emigrated returned after the end of the war. Nearly 650,000 perished.

How the cultivated area and the harvests had sunk is clear from the following table:

Land Used for Various Crops (in 1000 acres):

Year	Rye	Wheat	Barley	Oats	Potatoes	Flax
1909—1913 (aver.)	867.3	81.5	472	756.1	197.1	173
1920	484.3	39.5	305.4	533.7	121.1	74.1

Harvests (in 1000 metric tons):

Year	Rye	Wheat	Barley	Oats	Potatoes	Flax fiber	seed
1919—1913 (aver.)	325	38	173	219	639	30	25
1920	119	11	66	113	375	10	10

The decrease in livestock, on the other hand, was rather moderate in comparison with the fall in harvests. The following table shows the extent of this loss as well as the recoverary after the war.

Stock of Domestic Animals in Latvia (1000 head):

Year	Horses	Cattle	Pigs	Sheep
1913	320	912	557	996
1920	261	768	481	978
1923	341.2	910.9	487	1488.2

As we gather from this table, the gap struck in the livestock by the war was already filled up, with the exception of pigs, by 1923, as to sheep even before that date: their number had by 1921 already surpassed the pre-war level by fourteen per cent. As to the produce of the field, the pre-war harvest was surpassed: in potatoes in 1921, when it was 673,800 tons as against 639,000 tons in 1909—1913, wheat in 1925, when it was 44,600 tons as against 38,000 tons in 1909—1913, and oats in 1925, when it was 303,850 tons as against 279,000 tons before the war. In 1925 also the harvest of rye and wheat added up surpassed the pre-war level, being then 393,930 tons as against 374,000 tons before the war.

In Estonia the stock of domestic animals had been considerably thinned by requisitions repeatedly carried out for the needs of the armies, the Russian until the spring of 1918, and the German from then to the end of the war. The extent of the fall in livestock is clear from the table given below. The year 1916 in this table has been chosen because an agricultural census was taken that year and data for all categories of livestock are thus available. For the year 1914, on the other hand, only the number of beef cattle and dairy cows are available.

There were in Estonia (in 1000 head):

Year	Horses	Cattle	Pigs	Sheep
1916	178.3	518.8	304.2	620.8
1919		406		
1920	167.6	465.1	266.7	551.5

The number of cattle surpassed already in 1922 that of the year 1916 as well as the pre-war level, and by 1925 both years had been by far surpassed also with respect to horses, pigs, and sheep. (There were 527,368 cattle in 1922, and 223,747 horses, 338,648 pigs, and 719,785 sheep in 1925).

For the same reasons as in Lithuania grain culture doubtless suffered also in Estonia. Unfortunately statistical data showing the extent of this setback are lacking in Estonia too.

Industry suffered in Estonia still more seriously than agriculture, notwithstanding the fact that no real military operations had taken place on Estonian territory. It also took considerably more time before the pre-war level of development was reached and surpassed in this department. The hardest, as well as the most insensate, blow struck to the industry of the country was the destruction of a cellulose factory *Waldhof* in the town of Pärnu in the south-west corner of Estonia. This enterprise, one of the largest and technically most up-to-date in northern Europe, had been mined by order of the Russian military command to ensure its annihilation at short notice in case there was imminent danger of its falling into the hands of the Germans. In 1916 the commander of the Russian forces on the spot, scared by a couple of shots fired from a German destroyer penetrating into the waters near the town, gave the fateful order and in half an hour the factory was turned into heaps of rubble. Then, in the autumn of 1917, pursuant to an order given by the Provisional Government in anticipation of an early occupation of Estonia by the Germans, most of the machinery and equipment of the three shipyards and of a large railway-carriage factory were evacuated from Tallinn to Russia. This brought unemployment to about ten thousand workers. There was, however, a considerable percentage among the workers in the shipyards of such who had moved in from Russia proper and now preferred to go back whence they had come. This circumstance proportionally reduced the number of those in Estonia unemployed because of the seizure. On the other hand, even if the machinery and equipment had not been evacuated, there was hardly any prospect of these shipyards being able to continue production since they were specially built to serve the needs of the Russian navy. They could be kept running only if thoroughly reorganized and adapted to the requirements of Estonia, mainly for building commercial vessels, and there would hardly have been work for all of them. Their partial liquidation was therefore in any event unavoidable in the changed conditions. It was, of course, different with the railway-carriage factory, which in all probability would have been kept running if its machinery had been spared.

From the tables given above an idea can be formed of the process of recovery which set in in the field of agriculture after the end of the War of Liberation. It was their traditional, inveterate habit of hard work, their enterprising spirit and self-reliance to which the three peoples owed the gratifyingly rapid recovery here as in all other fields. Their efforts were mightily enhanced by a new factor: the long coveted and finally accomplished national freedom. Instead of the organs of the reactionary Tsarist government putting obstacles of every kind in the way of their national endeavours they had now their own national governments and organs of local self-government doing everything in their power to promote the well-being and progress of their peoples. Well aware of the axiom that economic strength is an indispensable condition of progress in all other departments of national life, these organs considered it their primary and urgent task to set the shattered economic life of their countries on its feet; this of course, was to be but the first step on the way towards further progress.

It goes without saying that industry could not be reconstructed as fast as agriculture in any of the three states. This would have been feasible only by the investment of large amounts of new capital in it in order to replace what had been destroyed or carried away. But where was such capital to come from? The war had done away with most of even that rather scanty floating capital accumulated by 1914 in these far from well-off countries. The Estonian people, for instance, had lost, at a low estimate, over one hundred million dollars in bank deposits alone. It can safely be presumed that the losses of the Lithuanian people were hardly less, whereas those of the Latvian people were in all probability considerably greater. On the other hand there was hardly any real prospect of foreign capital beginning to flow in from a world still shaken by the aftermath of the greatest war ever experienced by mankind, and least of all into small countries adjacent to a Great Power in the convulsions of civil war showering sparks from its conflagration over the whole world and of course the more thickly the nearer the countries were lying.

Clearly, then, the reconstruction of industry was to demand incomparably more ingenuity, more adaptability to the quickly changing conditions, more patience and more time. Even those industrial enterprises which had not lost their equipment found themselves in entirely new conditions; in order to adjust to these they had to make considerable alterations in their structure and invest no small amount of new capital. Having till then been working for the vast Russian market, under the protection of high customs tariffs, they had had no close connexions with the economic life of the Baltic area. When the Russian market was closed to them and the protection of the Russian custom duties removed, they had to look for markets outside Russia as also to take an interest in the countries in which they were situated. The home market of these new states was too limited and it was far from easy to work into the new foreign markets.

It goes without saying that the governments, though well aware of their inability to help industry to regain its pre-war health in a short span, did everything they could under the prevailing circumstances for its furtherance. They were well acquainted with the elementary truth that without normally expanding industries their countries were condemned to remain backward and poor. Moreover, there was the problem of how to do away with unemployment, a matter of grave concern economically and socially as well as politically, since the communists did not miss the opportunity of exploiting the distressing predicament of the unemployed to stir them with ruthless, demagogic propaganda against their governments and their own statehood.

Yet for all that the restoration of agriculture was chosen as the task to be tackled first and foremost. Apart from the fact that this could be accomplished in a fairly short time, whereas the restoration of industry must needs be a rather protracted business, agriculture was also the occupation of the great majority of the population. Moreover, the urgently needed thorough agrarian reform must be taken in hand without further postponement, not only for the weighty political and social reasons stressed in the preceding chapter, but also in order to raise the country to a considerably higher level of productivity within a short time. It was of course easy to anticipate the fanatic fervour with which the beneficiaries of the reform would set to work on the land they would now receive as their property. The implementation of the agrarian reform was therefore set in the van of the government's activities in all the three states as soon as the war was over.

We shall therefore concern ourselves first with the agrarian reform and the economic and social changes brought about by it, returning to the development of industry a little later.

It was inevitable that the owners of large estates and the publicists who defended their interests should sharply criticize the reform. They argued that the large estates were pioneers of progress and rational methods in agriculture and maintained that their liquidation and parcellation would therefore entail first stagnation and very soon even a decline in agricultural production, and that the end would be famine. This gloomy prophecy was not however taken seriously, since the argument upon which it rested did not hold water. Only a slight fraction of the large estates were intensively managed and could be classed among the standard-bearers of modern and rational methods of agriculture. It was common knowledge that most great estates were losing concerns which, for the most part, made ends meet only by selling forests bit by bit. There was therefore every reason to expect that the liquidation of large estates, far from lowering the general level of agricultural productivity, on the contrary would notably raise it. There could hardly be any doubt that the land would be tilled more rationally by farmers than it had been by the owners of the large estates. Their forebodings thus had no echo and the land reform was carried through without hesitation.

About the reforms the following details might be appropriately adduced.

By the Estonian Agrarian Law, which entered into force on October 25th, 1919, 5,828,187 acres of land were nationalized and turned over to a State Land Fund for parcelling into viable farms which could be worked by the farmer's family and two horses, or homesteads for craftsmen, labourers etc. Priority in the allotment of land was given to those who had fought in the War of Liberation and to the families of men fallen in the defence of their country.

Eighty three per cent of the nationalized land, i.e. 4,780,589 acres, had been the property of private persons, the estate owners. The remainder consisted of 757,534 acres which had been the property of either the Russian State or the Russian Peasants' Land Bank, together with 260,063 acres which had been the property of churches or of the corporations of the nobility. The question of compensation for the nationalized land was reserved to be decided by a special law. This law was enacted in 1926, the former owners feeling the compensation it provided to be inadequate. It was, of course, rather moderate. However, the state was hardly able to afford more under the prevailing circumstances. No prophet could foretell the development of market conditions for the products of agriculture. To charge the settlers with heavy mortgage debts for the land they received would have been both unreasonable and dangerous.

The former owners lodged a complaint against the Law to the League of Nations, alleging the reform to be a deliberate injustice directed against the Baltic German national minority and consequently non-observance of the assurances given by Estonia when she was admitted in 1921 to the League of Nations, namely to treat her national minorities on the same footing as the majority. This contention was, however, without any foundation in fact, since all

categories of estates enumerated in the Agrarian Law were nationalized regardless of the nationality of the owner. And indeed there
were among the expropriated estates also a few owned by pure Estonians who had purchased them, having managed to amass a certain
fortune. It was a social reform brought about to meet the demands
of a serious social situation, and the complaint was rightly dismissed
as groundless by the League of Nations.

How radical a change was produced by the reform is clear from the
following table, which shows the classification of farms in 1939,
according to the agricultural census taken that year.

The Classification of Farms by Size in 1939:

The size of the farms (in acres)	The number of farms	Percentage of the to-tal number of farms	Combined area of the farms (in acres)	Percentage of the combined area
1— 12.35	22,051	16.0	213,605	2.8
12.36— 24.71	23,869	17.1	542,105	7.0
24.71— 74.13	65,703	46.9	3,350,222	43.2
74.13—123.55	21,704	15.5	2,326,842	30.0
123.55—247.1	6,215	4.4	1,089,078	14.0
over 274.7	442	0.3	234,537	3.0
Total:	139,984	100	7,756,389	100

Instead of the 1149 large estates with a combined area of six million
acres in round numbers, making an average size of 5,222 acres, there
were in 1939 but 442 holdings with an area exceeding 247.1 acres,
with a combined area of 234,537 acres, and consequently 530.6 acres
on an average. These larger farms had been created with a view to
furthering various special branches of agriculture, e.g. the breeding
of thoroughbred horses and cattle, the development of high productivity seed-grain, disease-resisting potatoes, etc. 56,203 new farms had
been created by the agrarian reform, all the 23.722 leasehold farms
converted into freeholds, while 14,363 dwarf allotments had received
additional plots with a view to making them more viable. About
96,000 households all in all had either been created by the agrarian
reform or derived direct advantage from it. Though in fact it is a
rather low figure to estimate four persons per household on an

average, we may say that about 400,000 persons, or one third of the whole population, directly benefited from the reform, not to mention the advantages derived by other social classes from the considerably increased purchasing-power of the rural classes.

In *Latvia* no compensation was paid to the former owners of the expropriated estates. When, on April 14th, 1924, the law on the compensation to be paid to the former owners was being voted in the Constituent Assembly, the Baltic German deputies, inspired by uncompromising and irreconcilable opposition to the reform, abstained from voting for the clause providing for compensation, thus helping the votes against compensation to carry the majority, whereas with the votes of the abstainers added to those cast for the clause this would have passed. Behind these desperate tactics lay the hope that if land was nationalized without compensation, a decision condemning the Latvian agrarian reform could more easily be obtained from the League of Nations, to which the estate-owners intended to appeal. Yet this scheme came to nothing: the League of Nations dismissed the complaint and the outcome was that no indemnification was paid to the owners of the nationalized land.

In this respect the agrarian reform was more radical in Latvia than in Estonia. On the other hand, however, the estate-owners in Latvia were left with 123.5 to 247 acres of land, with all necessary farm buildings and all the implements as well as with industrial enterprises attached to their former estates. In Estonia, former owners had no claim to any part of their former estates. For the apportionment of land they had to apply, like all other citizens seeking allotments, to the local organs charged with the implementation of the reform. Neither were any implements left to them. Their estates were expropriated along with all the implements, for which they received compensation according to legal enactments.

By the Latvian Agrarian Reform Law, 9,168,431 acres were turned over to the State Land Fund. 7,452,161 acres, or 81 per cent of the total, had belonged to the large estates, 17 per cent was the property of the state. A limit of 54.4 acres was fixed for the new farms to be created out of the land turned over to the State Land Fund. Farms already existing which were smaller than 54.4 acres could be enlarged to this limit if they adjoined the land of the State Land Fund. Moreover, 7.4 acres of forest land could be allotted to the farms over and above the limit of 54.4 acres. Four fifths of the forests, which covered about 27 per cent of the total area of Latvia, were retained by the State. In Latvia as in Estonia, priority was given in the allotment of land to those who had fought in the War of Liberation and to the families of those fallen in the defence of their country.

As to the changes in the social stratification of agriculture brought about by the reform, the census taken in 1935, when the implementation of the reform had been practically brought to a close, showed the following picture:

The Classification of Farms by Size in 1935:

The size of the farms (in acres)	Number of the farms	Percentage of the to-tal number of farms	Combined area of farms (in acres)	Percentage of the combined area
Up to 12.355	78,567	28.5	273,755	2.5
12.355– 24.71	40,089	16.0	830,758	7.5
24.71 – 49.42	77,856	28.2	2,872,616	25.9
49.42 – 74.13	59,750	21.7	4,430,197	39.9
74.13 –247.1	14,365	5.2	2,314,825	20.9
upw.of 247.1	1,071	0.4	365,137	3.3
Total:	275,698	100	11,087,298	100

As seen at a glance from this table, social conditions brought about by the agrarian reform in Latvia were almost identical with those which had developed in Estonia. Through the reform 54,128 new farms and 41,751 homesteads for handicraftsmen, horticulturists, fishermen, etc. as well as holdings for various public and cultural uses were created in the countryside, and moreover, 16,508 holdings on the administrative territory of the towns, all in all 112,387 holdings. Adding to this the 31,024 insufficiently landed holdings which had received additional plots and the 9,754 leasehold farms converted into freeholds, we get a total of 143,441 holdings either newly created or supplemented by the reform. This constituted 52 per cent of the total number of holdings according to the census taken in 1935. All in all 4,004,000 acres had been allotted to 144,681 persons.[1]

[1] These data as well as the above table are taken from the essay *Les résultats économiques de la réforme agraire en Lettonie* by Prof. P. Starcs, Riga, 1939.

It is no exaggeration to say that in the agrarian reform the social stratification of the rural population of Estonia and Latvia was changed past recognition. Communities of free and independent farmers, contented and enjoying a creditable measure of social security, emerged in place of a superannuated, semi-feudal order, undermined by deep bitterness and revolutionary discontent, threatening to explode at the first propitious occasion. Hardly ever has an agrarian revolution of such thoroughgoing character and so successful and beneficial in its economic, social, and cultural effects been accomplished in any other country. (To these effects we shall recur later in the proper connection.) However, this revolution was carried out in a fully lawful and peaceable manner, without a sign of violence or commotion.

In Lithuania the agrarian problem was tackled at the end of 1918 by the Provisional Government, who issued a decree which ordained that all land converted by the Russian decrees of 1835 and 1842 into entailed estates should be turned over to the Lithuanian State for distribution among the landless and insufficiently landed peasants, the latter class comprising those who owned less than twelve acres.

This decree, issued as a measure of provisional character, was sanctioned by the Land Reform Law enacted by the Constituent Assembly in March 1922. Besides, the lands which belonged to the former Peasants' Land Bank and Nobles' Bank were proclaimed the property of the Lithuanian State and taken over without indemnity. Moreover, from the estates owned by private persons all land in excess of 321 acres was expropriated for the purpose of the reform.

The declared aim of the reform was the creation of conditions favourable to the development of agriculture, more particularly to further the medium-sized farm (from about 20 to 50 acres). Such persons or the legal successors of such persons from whom land had been seized by the Russian government after the rebellions of 1831 and 1863, were to receive priority. Each head of a family could receive not more than 49.4 acres. The recipients had to pay equal annual instalments for the land allotted, payable over 36 years. There was, however, an exception from this rule — all volunteer soldiers in the Lithuanian War of Independence: they and their families were exempted from all payments.

For the land expropriated for the purpose of reform the estate owners were entitled to fair compensation based on valuations existing in the period between 1910 and 1914. The compensation was to be paid in government bonds, bearing three per cent interest and redeemable at any time not later than thirty six years from the date of issue. The so-called Oberost Mark, put into circulation during the war by the German occupation authorities, being the legal means of payment at the time of the passing of the Land Reform Law, the compensation was to be paid in this currency. However, owing to the rapid deterioration in the value of the Oberost Mark, the compensation dwindled down to quite modest amounts. It is estimated that a sum amounting to four million US dollars in all was paid for the total of the expropriated land.

Out of the total of 1,744,100 acres expropriated for the purpose of the reform, about sixty nine per cent was distributed to settlers for the establishment of new farms, to employees and labourers for building homesteads, to owners of small farms, to render them solvent, and so on. The remainder was assigned to various public uses. It is estimated that over 45,000 new farms were established through the land reform and over 200,000 persons, including the new settlers and their families, were provided with regular occupations and permanent homes.

In short, there is every reason to agree with the following appreciation given to this auspicious reform by the Lithuanian author A. Simutis in his book *The Economic Reconstruction of Lithuania After 1918* (Columbia University Press, N.Y., 1942), from which most of the above information has been derived: "This has undoubtedly brought beneficial results to the social and economic life of the country. Moreover, the land reform has undoubtedly been a means of substantially raising the country's productivity, to the benefit of both the state and the individual farmer." This appreciation is fully borne out by the wonderful progress achieved by Lithuanian agriculture and national economy in general in the years after the reform, most convincingly evidenced by statistical data to be adduced further on in the proper connection.

V

THE THREAT FROM THE EAST

Among the reasons why the ravages of the war and its aftermath could not be made up for as quickly in the field of industry as in that of agriculture, there was yet another passed over in silence in the preceding chapter. In comparison with agriculture, industry was vastly more dependent upon what was going on in the world at large. A considerable portion of the produce of agriculture was consumed by the producers themselves, and most of the rest was sold on the home market. Moreover, as long as the losses sustained during the years of war and revolutionary change had not been made good, there was hardly any surplus worth mentioning after the needs of the drained home market were met. As to industry, on the other hand, only certain small, craftsman-type enterprises had survived and could live by the sale of their products on the local, home market. All enterprises of more importance had been working for the market of the Russian Empire.

It would have been not only most natural, but also in the mutual interest of both parties if after the conclusion of peace with the Baltic States, Soviet Russia had resumed the old ties and collaboration with them making her market easily accessible to their industries. Having for decades been working for the Russian market and being therefore both best acquainted with its requirements and fairly well equipped to meet the demands, they could best serve it. By resuming and developing the exchange of services with the industry of Soviet Russia the industrialists of the Baltic states could best have solved the rather knotty problem of their markets. This would have offered them welcome prospects for the rapid redress of the losses and damages sustained. Such continued collaboration would thus have been to the advantage of both parties. At the same time it would have been the most effective way to establish really good neighbourly relations between Soviet Russia and these new states.

However, it soon became evident that the rulers of the Kremlin had intentions of quite a different kind regarding the relations of Soviet Russia with the Baltic states. On the very day of the signing of the peace treaty with Estonia, in which the Soviet government declared in black and white that "Russia voluntarily for ever renounces all rights formerly held by Russia over the Estonian people and territory", Lenin in his report to the Central Executive Committee of the Soviets unblushingly stated that this treaty was not to be a long-lived one. The Estonian workers, he said, would soon overthrow their government and form a Soviet Estonia which would conclude a new treaty with Soviet Russia. There could scarcely be any doubt that the first task this new Soviet Estonia anticipated by Lenin was to assume, was that indicated by the Central Executive Committee in the decree by which on December 23rd, 1918 it had recognized the "independence" of the Estonian, Latvian, and Lithuanian "Soviet republics", proclaimed in December 1918: "to form a free, voluntary, and inviolable union of workers of all peoples inhabiting the territory of the former Russian Empire". In other words and in plain language: to give up their national independence and to resign themselves to being swallowed by the Russian Empire, restored under the label of the Russian Socialist Federative Republic.

At the time it could still be presumed that Lenin's ill-boding utterance was perhaps but a flourish used to calm certain hot-headed elements among his listeners. However, clear evidence that he spoke in full earnest was soon forthcoming.

In the course of the year 1920 Soviet Russia had managed to conclude peace with Estonia, Latvia, Lithuania, Finland, and the Transcaucasian republic of Georgia. Even the Polish—Soviet war which had flamed up again in April 1920, had come to a factual end on October 12th, 1920, when a preliminary treaty of peace had been signed in Riga.

Ascribing all these achievements to the love of peace of the Soviet government, *Pravda* wrote in its New Year's leader on Jan. 1st, 1921: "The principle of national self-determination, unswervingly maintained by the Soviet Power, is the cornerstone of all our foreign policy. The sincere realization of this principle secures us peace with all border countries which do not dance to the piping of bellicose circles in the Entente".

At the very time when *Pravda* was thus offering incense to the Soviet government for its alleged unswerving respect for the principle of national self-determination, carefully planned preparations were nearing completion for treacherously trampling underfoot the national freedom of one of those nations whose right of self-determination had been solemnly recognized by the Soviet Union but a few months earlier.

Among the achievements of the peaceful policy of the Soviet government *Pravda* boasted, as mentioned, of the peace concluded with the Republic of Georgia. It was a just peace, profitable to both parties; so the same official organ of the Soviet government had declared in the editorial of the issue in which the text of the treaty was published (on May 9th, 1920). The treaty contained a declaration by the Soviet government that Soviet Russia, mindful of the right of all nations to self-determination, unreservedly recognized the independence of the Georgian State and engaged herself to abstain from interference in her internal affairs. Notwithstanding this, Soviet Russia had already by December 1920 concentrated on the frontier of Georgia such considerable Red Army forces, and made such extensive military preparations, that the Georgian government felt called upon to proclaim partial mobilisation of its armed forces, as could be gathered from an official declaration published in *Pravda* on December 21st, 1920. Both the concentration of the Red Army forces and military preparations near the frontier of Georgia were denied by the Soviet government in the said declaration. However, it is hardly conceivable that the small Georgian republic would find it well-advised to provoke her mighty neighbour by proceeding to mobilize her armed forces in the frontier regions if there had not been very weighty reasons for doing so. That the anxiety felt by the Georgian government had not been unwarranted, grew ever more evident a few days after *Pravda's* eulogy of the Soviet government for its respect for the right of all nations to self-determination.

A downright barrage of hateful aspersions was opened in the Soviet press against Georgia, loaded with malicious accusations and abuse of every kind. The Georgian government was charged with infringing the peace treaty, persecuting communists and worrying the personnel of the Soviet legation. Conditions in the country were depicted as dreadful and quite insufferable. The dissatisfaction of the workers and peasants was said to be growing more and more acute and the country rapidly approaching revolution. Such humbug was published in *Pravda* and, of course, in the whole Soviet press every other day.

After such preparatory bombardment for six weeks, the Soviet press suddenly, at the end of February, published a sensational piece of news which there had been reason to apprehend for a long time: that Georgian "workers and peasants" had risen in rebellion. From the following day on news of the successes of the "insurgents" in their fight against the governmental forces began to pour in. After three weeks of battles the resistance of the Georgian army was broken. Georgia was proclaimed a Soviet republic by the insurgents, who did not waste time in applying to Moscow for incorporation of this new Soviet republic into Soviet Russia. No hint was ever made in the news of the "insurrection" that the Soviet Red Army had had anything to do with it.

Twelve months later, however, no less a person than the Commander-in-Chief of the Red Army, L. Trotsky, then Lenin's closest collaborator and heir presumptive, made the following cynically open avowal: "There is no doubt that the Soviet upheaval in Georgia has been carried out with the active participation of the Red Army. It would have been treason not to give assistance to the workers and the poorest peasants of Georgia with armed force if we had it. We did not and could not see any obstacle on principle to introducing, at the request of the revolutionary vanguard of Georgia, the Red Army into that country and helping to throw down their wretched democracy with as little delay as possible."[1]

Trotsky's assertion that the Red Army had been "introduced into Georgia at the request of the revolutionary vanguard of that country" etc., was obviously pure invention and brazen hypocrisy. The invasion of Georgia was an absolutely unwarrantable aggression in flagrant violation of the peace treaty, prepared for and carried out in

---

[1] L. Trotsky, *Mezhdu imperializmom i revoluciej* (Between Imperialism and Revolution), Berlin, 1922, p. 117. The foreword to this book is dated Feb. 20th, 1922.

cold blood by the Soviet rulers with a view to subduing Georgia and incorporating it into Soviet Russia. Hardly any communist-controlled disorders worth mentioning had ever been possible in Georgia, where communists had always constituted a minority of quite insignificant adherence and influence. And even if disorders had occurred in Georgia or even an insurrection, the duty of Soviet Russia would have been to abstain from interfering in them since she had assumed this explicit obligation by the peace treaty.

The danger manifestly overhanging the Republic of Georgia could not but arouse anxiety in the Baltic States. In the same month of January, 1921 when the aggression against Georgia was openly being prepared by the campaign of aspersion in the Soviet press, the first Soviet envoy in Latvia, A. Yoffe, considered it necessary to publish a statement in the Latvian press in which he declared that "the rumours spread by provocateurs that Soviet Russia is concentrating armed forces against Estonia, Latvia, and Lithuania, are groundless." Russia, the envoy said, wanted more than ever to dedicate all her forces to the work of internal economic reconstruction. (*Pravda*, 1.12. 1921.)

No thoughtful person in the Baltic states could accept this reassuring declaration at its face value. Moreover, its falsehood was soon most convincingly displayed by the aggression started against the Republic of Georgia.

It was not difficult to understand why Soviet imperialism had picked out a Transcaucasian republic and not any of the Baltic states for its first victim. The out-of-the-way Republic of Georgia had hardly any prospect of getting effective assistance from outside in her struggle against the Muscovite invaders, whereas there was every reason to surmise that the Baltic states would, in the case of a new Soviet agression, again receive substantial support from the western Powers from whom they had got substantial aid in their War of Liberation in 1918–1920. They were considered essential links in the chain of the *cordon sanitaire* separating the Soviet state from the western world. Moreover, they had proved to be tough adversaries with well organized armies, steeled in victorious battles. On the other hand, was it not likely that success in this first attempt would inspire the rulers of Soviet Russia to proceed on the way of aggression and "imperialist robbery", to use Lenin's favourite expression? Were not the Baltic states to be the next victims?

However, internal conditions in Soviet Russia had in the meantime grown utterly adverse to such adventures. Although more than two years had passed since the end of the World War, no sign of the world revolution prophesied by Lenin as its inevitable outcome, was visible anywhere. Instead of this Lenin's forcible seizure of power had produced results of a quite different kind: a civil war in Russia with all its baleful consequences. Growing economic chaos and decay had resulted in a famine which could no longer be passed over in silence. Even in January 1921 one came across articles in *Pravda's* columns under headlines like "Fight against Hunger" and even "Succour Must be Given to the Starving Countryside". If a countryside which had always not only fed itself and the urban population of Russia, but also produced an exportable surplus, was now itself starving and in need of help against famine, conditions had obviously grown alarming. The same sailors of Kronstadt who had been Lenin's most arduous supporters in 1917 and mightily contributed to the success of his *coup d'état*, rose in rebellion against the Soviet government in early March, 1921. This revolt and the general catastrophic conditions in Soviet Russia induced Lenin to carry out an abrupt change in the economic policy of the Soviet government. In order to overcome chaos and decay, private interest and incentives to gain, which had been stifled and gradually eliminated, were given somewhat larger scope again.

However, before this *New Economic Policy (NEP)* had had time to produce its healing effect, a very serious trial broke out. It was signalled in an alarming leader published in *Pravda* on June 30th, 1921, under the headline: "Against Hunger and Filth!" which opened with the following words: "A new misfortune, an evil legacy of past times, now looms over Soviet Russia: drought". One cannot refrain from the comment that if the old régime had incontestably deserved blame for not having taken any effective steps for developing methods of agriculture in Russia which might have rendered it less vulnerable to drought, now and again recurring in rather wide regions of the Empire, Lenin and his proselytes were far more to be blamed for the hunger catastrophe in the drought year 1921. That the famine had such an extent and cost the lives of so many people, — the num-

ber of those who died from starvation was estimated at half a million,
— was the direct result of the ravages caused on the one hand by the
civil war ignited in wanton levity by Lenin, and on the other by the
preposterous communist experiments which had throttled the interest
of the peasant in maintaining his production even on the low level
it had attained, let alone developing it to higher level.

Drought and famine turned out to be so severe that according to
estimates no less than ten million people would have died of hunger
if the USA and other Western countries had not organized relief
action on a vast scale[2]. That the Soviet government was well aware
of the extreme gravity of the predicament, was shown by a series of
short statements to all and sundry, published by Lenin himself and
placed, to attract the special attention of readers, in capital letters in
the middle of the columns of *Pravda*. To give an idea of the tenor
and tone of these statements, suffice it to quote but one of them.
"We are in a state of such destitution, over-fatigue, and enfeeblement
of the main productive forces of our peasants and workers that for
a time everything must be subordinated to the one fundamental consideration: at all costs to increase production. Lenin." (*Pravda*, 16.7.
1921). The exhortation "Into the Fight against Hunger!" was thereafter an oft recurring headline in Pravda.

It was easy to guess that because of this unforeseen, desperate predicament the Soviet leaders found themselves constrained to refrain
for the time being from the staging of a spurious "rebellion of the
workers and peasants" in the Baltic states and "introducing the Red
Army into these states in order to throw down their wretched democracies with least possible delay" — after the pattern applied in Georgia. Such a counterfeit "Soviet upheaval" had willy-nilly to be put off
to a more propitious time.

All the same, the Soviet government showed no inclination to renounce the belief in the world revolution and to desist from pursuing this daydream. Quite on the contrary: longing for its early
realisation grew all the more intense since this seemed to be the only
means of escaping from the catastrophic impasse into which the vast

---

[2] "The crop failure was reckoned to have affected an area inhabited by 20 to 30
million people. Unless help was forthcoming, not less than 10 million seemed
doomed to perish from starvation before spring." (British Encyclopedia, vol. XIX,
p. 738).

country was plunged by the heedless seizure of power and the subsequent rash experiments. Therefore it was daily asserted that the communist world revolution, though, of course behind time, was at last on the point of breaking out. "We are brought up against a new wave of revolutionary movements in Germany"; wrote K. Radek in an article under the significant heading "Signs of Storm In Germany" (*Pravda*, 25.3.1921). There was much talk about the rising wave of revolution in almost every copy of Pravda, and when, on April 6th, the paper had to avow that "even this time the new explosion of revolutionary movement in Germany did not end with the victory of the proletarian revolution", it had forthwith a comfort within reach: "Even before the thunder of revolution had ceased in Germany, a new storm-cloud had arisen over the world — the general strike of miners in Great Britain." The leader of the paper ended with the following words: "The whole capitalist world is nowadays a grandiose volcano that makes the ground tremble without interruption."

The attempt to subdue the Baltic states undertaken in 1918—1920 had failed. If the rulers of Soviet Russia in 1921 believed and hoped that a new wave of world revolution would rise in the near future and overwhelm the capitalist world, then the old task for which the aggression had been started against the Baltic states in 1918 remained before them: to tear down the wall separating Russia from Western Europe, trembling now in the fever of revolution. If it was felt that this new wave was already rising, the task must come to the fore again in the immediate future. The Soviet leaders were therefore by no means interested in developing and strengthening friendly relations with the Baltic states. On the contrary, it was appropriate to fan hostile feelings against them among the Soviet citizens and in every conceivable way to undermine and weaken the power of resistance of these states in order to render their subjugation easier and avoid a repetition of the failure met by the aggressors in 1918—1920. All this was actually being done in the Baltic states through Moscow's docile tools, the local communists. Subversive activity was carried out in the Baltic states with even greater intensity than anywhere else. Their geographical contiguity to Soviet Russia, better knowledge of their conditions, and a series of other circumstances seemed to promise particularly good results in these states.

In these schemes Moscow could rely on rather numerous cadres of fanatics, in their primitive simple-mindedness firmly convinced that a communist world-revolution would break out, if not to-morrow, then the day after, and willing to contribute to its early outbreak body and soul, believing moreover that their merits would not be forgotten but deservedly rewarded after the expected victory. Being well aware that the Soviet order could be forced upon their peoples only with the aid of Soviet Russia, by means of ruthless terror, they placed themselves at the disposal of Moscow as its obedient instruments, ready to carry out any order given to them by the prophets of world revolution.

Things being so it is easy to understand that the establishment of normal, friendly economic collaboration with the Baltic states and the opening of the Soviet market to the products of their industry were far from suited to the designs of the Soviet leaders. Not only had they no interest in the rapid recovery of their industries and the alleviation of unemployment, or in the ensuing rise in the general welfare of these states; from their point of view it was desirable that industrial output in these states decrease, the living standard of the broad masses sink, and unemployment swell. The larger the number of unemployed and the greater their distress, the more promising seemed to them the prospects of communist subversive propaganda.

As a matter of fact, unemployment was one of the most serious problems the governments of the Baltic states had to tackle as soon as the War of Liberation had come to an end.

The setback sustained by industry and the extent of unemployment caused by it is revealed in the following statistics.

In Estonia the two paramount branches of industry, textiles and metal, were most severely hit. In the textile industry the number of workers had shrunk to 7800 by 1922, when the first census was taken by the Estonian authorities, where in 1913 they had numbered 19,000. In the metal industry the number had diminished from 16,700 to 7000. Thus in these two branches alone, in which in 1913 eighty per cent of the industrial workers of Estonia had been employed, numbers had decreased by 20,900. This of course had been unavoidable, since the enterprises in question had been established and actually working for the market of the Russian Empire, where also the lion's share of their production had been sold, and this market had now dropped off. Since in the meantime, however, other branches of industry which in Russian times had to a greater extent or even predominantly been working for the local market, had now somewhat expanded, the fall in the number of workers in the total of the large-scale and medium-sized industries was 4030 less than that which had taken place in the two above-mentioned industries: from 45,370 in 1913 this number had diminished to 28,500, a total decrease of 16,870.

This did not, however, mean a burden of over sixteen thousand unemployed left as a legacy of the war. As already mentioned, several thousand Russian workers who had swelled the ranks of industrial workers of Estonia when a few years before the outbreak of the World War three shipyards had been constructed in Tallinn, had gone back to Russia in the winter 1917/1918. Then at the end of the War of Liberation, a new outlet was opened to those left without a livelihood through the grievous shrinkage of industry in Estonia. The implementation of the agrarian reform, i.e. the parcelling of the large estates and the distribution of land to those willing to settle was put into speedy operation immediately after the conclusion of peace with Soviet Russia. Since nearly all Estonian industrial workers had grown up in the countryside either as labourers or as sons of the farmers, it was most natural for those out of work to avail themselves of the opportunity to become masters of their own farms or homesteads. So much the more so as the state, by granting loans at low interest and lending assistance in various other ways, also helped the settlers to erect farm buildings, to provide themselves with livestock and to overcome other initial difficulties. (It goes without saying that similar provisions were made at the same time in Latvia and Lithuania.) Though no statistics are available as to the number of industrial workers who owing to the agrarian reform returned to agriculture as settlers, one can safely estimate it at several thousand.

Nevertheless unemployment reached a figure which could not but be disquieting, considering the troubled circumstances of the time.

The actual extent of unemployment is seen from the following table.

The Number of Unemployed Registered and Vacancies Offered at Labour Exchanges

(Monthly average computed by dividing the total by twelve):

Year:	The number of persons registered as seeking employment:	The number of vacancies registered at the labour exchanges:
1022	850	593
1923	765	645
1924	1674	871
1925	2598	1823
1926	1771	1356
1927	1968	1338
1928	1808	1192
1929	2064	1499
1930	1911	1401
1931	2479	1944
1932	3964	2994
1933	4005	2718
1934	2780	3304
1935	1547	2504

As appears from these data, the number of the unemployed rose considerably in 1924 and 1925, when Estonia was beset with great economic difficulties, and still more sharply during the world depression, 1931–1933, whereas in the years between these two climaxes unemployment was rather stable, oscillating round an average of 1918[3]. From 1934 on unemployment began to recede and the number of vacancies registered at the labour exchanges for the first time outstripped that of the registered unemployed. From about 1936 on unemployment as a chronic social disease could be regarded as overcome.

That it took until 1936 to master the chronic unemployment problem was, for the rest, the consequence of the world economic depression, which as can be deduced from statistical data delayed its removal for at least five years. Of course the number of persons

[3] (1771+2064):2=1918.

occupied in large-scale and medium-sized industries, increasing step by step to reach 36,123 by 1929 and then, carried away by the great slump, falling to 29,945 by 1932, had thereafter begun to increase again and by 1934 had not only overtaken but even slightly outstripped the level of 1929, reaching 36,900. In the following year, 1935, only 6.8 per cent were still lacking from the pre-war number, and in 1936 this goal was already surpassed by nearly ten per cent, being then 48,905 as against 45,370 in 1913. In 1936 unemployment-relief works at public expense were also discontinued as being no longer necessary. Instead of unemployment the scarcity of labour began gradually to make itself felt.

A few observations deserve to be made about the adduced statistics of unemployment.

As a matter of fact unemployment was subject to considerable seasonal fluctuations, the number of unemployed being largest in the winter months and decreasing towards the summer. Since not monthly data, but only monthly averages are given in the Estonian statistical publications, we are left in the dark about seasonal variation. As we shall see from the Latvian labour statistics, which are much more elaborate in general, and in particular on this point, giving monthly data on unemployment, the number of unemployed registered in that country in the months of acutest unemployment was often twice, and one year even thrice the average over the year. Since conditions in Estonia did not notably differ from those in Latvia, we can safely presume that here too the number of unemployed must have been in the months of worst unemployment two or three times the average. Consequently the number of unemployed reached nearly eight thousand in the months of worst unemployment, in winter of 1924–1925 and about twelve thousand in 1933–1934. For a country the size of Estonia this was obviously a figure to cause serious concern.

In order to alleviate the distress of the unemployed, unemployment relief works were organized on grants from public funds and support in cash was given to families in distress. For the unemployment-relief work the following statistical data are available:

Statistics on Unemployment-Relief Work
(yearly average)

Years	The number of partici- pants in the work	Sums expended on the work (in 1000 E.kr.)
1922—1925	3185	814
1926—1929	1958	519
1930—1933	4468	1352
1934—1937	3332	980

Latvian industry was far more severely hit than the Estonian by the war and its aftermath, and this was not of course to be wondered at considering the long and fierce battles fought on Latvian territory. The number of workers employed in Latvian industry in 1922 was but one third of that of the year 1910: 31,800 as against 93,340. Happily enough, however, Latvian industry began to recover at a rather brisk pace, as one gathers from the following table:

The Number of Workers in Latvian Large-Scale and Medium-sized Industry:

Year:	Number of workers:
1922	31,800
1923	40,000
1924	48,100
1925	50,000
1926	57,200
1927	61,156
1928	67,098
1929	71,736
1930	72,100

From 72,100 in 1930 the number went down to 51,604 in 1932, but in 1934 it had risen again to 84,669, and in the following year, 1935, already outstripped the pre-war number: it was then 93,793 as against 93,340 in 1910.

Although industry recovered thus fairly rapidly and the number of workers employed in it increased year by year, in Latvia as in Estonia, unemployment remained a grave problem until the second half of the 'thirties, and unemployment relief works had to be maintained.

Latvian labour statistics give quite an extensive and sound picture of the situation in that country with regard to unemployment and its development, as well as of government measures to fight it and alleviate the distress of the unemployed. The following tables given in these statistics may well be adduced here.

The Number of Unemployed Registered at Labour Exchanges, the Number of Participants in Relief-Works and Sums Expended on these Works.

Year	Monthly average of the un- employed	Maximum (usually Jan. or Febr.)	Minimum (usually June)	The Number of participants in unempl. re- lief works	Sums expended on relief- works (in 1000 Latv. Lats)
1920	1,278	2,354	448		
1921	3,329	5,560	1,488		
1922	4,790	8,764	2,106	1,340	1,612.5
1923	3,023	7,176	701	1,356	912
1924	1,987	3,521	868	657	795.5
1925	2,721	5,097	814	1,193	1,114.6
1926	2,787	5,234	722	1,076	1,108.2
1927	3,131	6,399	944	1,505	1,741.9
1928	4,700	14,030	928	1,685	2,447.2
1929	5,617	12,856	1,205	2,190	2,039.9
1930	4,851	10,022	607	1,947	2,328.8
1931	8,709	21,935	1,584	3,412	5,887.6
1932	14,587	26,335	7,056	7,853	8,731.1
1933	8,156	14,777	3,140	9,533	8,435.5
1934	4,972	10,435	904	5,323	7,104.4
1935	4,825			2,918	6,159.8

A still more instructive table was published in the Latvian Labour Statistics for 1936. It gives a survey of the number of unemployed in the towns during the nine months with the highest level of un- employment, from the winter of 1930/1931 to that of 1935/1936.

Unemployment in Latvian Towns in the Low Employment Seasons (from October to June) 1930/1931—1935/1936

	1930/1931	1931/1932	1932/1933	1933/1934	1934/1935	1935/1936
Maximum	15,170	39,086	34,139	23,295	13,657	12,446
Minimum	1,641	9,217	7,875	4,392	3,659	2,793
Average	10,036	25,272	24,971	15,273	9,090	8,074

The table reveals that the maximum number of unemployed had dropped from 39,086 in January 1932 to 12,446 in February 1936, and the minimum from 9,217 in June to 2,793 in June 1936.

That scarcity of labour was setting in in Latvia instead of unemployment, which thus ceased to be a chronic social evil, is evident from the following table given in the same statistical publication:

Farm-hands Entering the Country from Abroad:

	1933	1934	1935
Men	4,398	8,807	14,142
Women	8,006	14,047	20,067
Total	12,404	22,854	34,209

As to Lithuania, the available statistical publications do not contain any further data complementary to what has already been said. The number of workers who had lost their jobs was, of course, several times less in Lithuania than in Estonia, let alone Latvia. However, in proportion to the pre-war figure for industrial workers, which also was several times less, it was serious enough, offering the communists good opportunity to exploit unemployment in their subversive propaganda and give trouble enough to public authorities.

The governments expended considerable amounts of money in organizing relief works. However, since the public authorities, whose revenues were far from abundant after the years of war and revolution, had to provide for whole series of other highly pressing needs, above all things the realisation of the agrarian reform, but also the erection of schoolhouses (a task unpardonably neglected in Tsarist times), the care of numerous disabled soldiers and the families of the fallen, etc., the grants for unemployment-relief were of necessity so moderate as to secure no more than the most indispensable relief. It goes without saying that the communists sought with particular fervour to exploit the distressing predicament of the unemployed with a view to fanning the discontent of these unhappy men and women and stirring them to revolutionary disorders.

VI

THE FIFTH COLUMNS AND THEIR MASTERS

If the communist fifth columns had contented themselves with agitation against the government and the prevailing democratic order, they would not have been dangerous in the least. No measures against them would have been needed other than matter-of-fact information explaining what the public authorities were doing and what it was possible to do for the benefit of the unemployed. Moreover, communist agitation was finding but feeble echo among the unemployed even without any organized counterpropaganda, since the majority were well aware that the exhausted condition of the national economy rendered it hardly possible to do more for their benefit than was being done. It may be mentioned in passing that even if the grants-in-aid were really moderate, nobody died of starvation in the Baltic states, whereas in Soviet Russia half a million citizens perished during the horrible famine of 1921.

Much worse and more dangerous, however, than the agitation to stir up revolutionary discontent was the fact that every fanatical communist considered it his duty and honour to assist Soviet-Russian espionage, to help organize communist cells in the army to undermine its morale, and to make preparations for the most effective means of paralyzing the defence efforts of their country by well planned and well timed acts of sabotage. Such activities could not be tolerated. The authorities would have made themselves guilty of high treason if in indolent passivity they had looked on while cliques of fanatical fools, enticed by an unscrupulous, tyrannical foreign power, sought to wrest from them the invaluable treasure of national freedom and political independence. It was their sacred duty most resolutely to suppress such activities, not shrinking from the severest measures to this end, if need be.

However, the prospect of prosecution and punishment had little effect on communists who were convinced that a victorious world revolution was imminent. They were, moreover, greatly encouraged by the prospect of escaping in case of need to the adjoining mighty Soviet state and finding asylum there.

More than this: the Soviet government began intentionally to encourage them in their treasonable activities by assuming the role of a high protector of communists convicted of high treason in the Baltic states, and giving wide publicity in the press to the steps it was taking in this capacity. Thus, e.g., the Soviet envoy in Estonia, M. Litvinov, proposed to the Estonian government, on February 21st, 1921, a repeal of the death sentence passed upon three Estonian citizens found guilty of espionage for the benefit of Soviet Russia. This démarche was advertised in *Pravda* on February 26th under the heading "Interference of the Representative of the RSFSR for the Benefit of Sentenced Communists". The paper even published the full text of the diplomatic note in which M. Litvinov had sought to refute the considerations advanced by the Estonian government that this démarche was an interference in Estonian internal affairs.[1]

This interference was an unmistakable intimation to the Estonian communists as well as to those of the other Baltic states that their treasonable activities were highly appreciated by the Soviet government, which, moreover, was taking steps to rescue them from the penalties they might incur.

That time M. Litvinov's proposal came to naught. Not long afterwards, however, conditions arose which rendered it difficult to decline such proposals.

This came about by a concurrence of circumstances in the following way.

The proclamation of the New Economic Policy had roused optimistic hopes in Estonian business circles that the rulers of communist Russia were going to give up their rash experiments in economic policy and gradually restore an economic order based on private initiative and free competition. This, they hoped, would open up the possibility of trade between Estonia and Soviet Russia. In order to

[1] Attention deserves to be drawn to the curious fact that M. Litvinov's démarche was — in all probability by an unintentional irony — called "interference" by the paper itself in the heading under which it published the note.

elucidate such propects and eventually to make use of them, a trade delegation was sent from Estonia to Moscow, where, after rather protracted discussions, Estonian businessmen were granted permission to export articles of food as well as some industrial products to Soviet Russia. (This occurred in 1921, at about the time when *Pravda* had begun to publish its alarming articles about "hunger and filth, destitution, over-fatigue, and the enfeeblement of the main productive forces".) Payment was to be made in Soviet roubles, the Soviet Commissariat of Foreign Trade declaring that payment in any other currency was out of the question for want of it. The Estonian exporters were, however, to be entitled to spend this money on purchases of various raw materials in Soviet Russia and their export to Estonia.

Owing to this agreement the value of exports from Estonia to Soviet Russia rose in 1922 to 13.6 million Estonian crowns, or 22.1 per cent of the total export of Estonia in that year. When, however, the exporters sought to exercise their right to purchase Soviet raw materials and to export them to Estonia, the Soviet authorities in contravention of the assurances given, refused to grant the required licenses for exportation.

It fared no better with those more cautious businessmen who had made arrangements with the Soviet commercial representation (Torgpredstvo) in Tallinn for exports to Soviet Russia on the express condition that they might demand payment in either Soviet roubles or English pounds sterling. The payment in pounds sterling was refused under the pretext that the Torgpredstvo having been entitled to make deals only in Soviet currency, had overstepped its authority in granting the exporters the right to demand payment in pounds sterling. The Estonian exporters had to content themselves with Soviet roubles.

Thus a number of Estonian businessmen found themselves in possession of considerable amounts of Soviet roubles which neither had any value on the world financial market, nor could be used to purchase any export goods from Soviet Russia. Looking for ways to back out of the difficulty and save their money, they came upon the only conceivable though far from certain expedient. Mindful of the announcement made by Lenin when he proclaimed his new economic policy, that the Soviet government was disposed to grant foreign capitalists concessions for the establishment of industrial enterprises in Soviet Russia, they applied for such concessions. They got on lease a brewery in Leningrad and started its exploitation, being among the first foreigners to try their luck as concessionaires in Lenin's communist state. The attempt proved, however, a complete failure. Hardly had the concessionaires started production, having invested the lion's share of their Soviet roubles in the restoration of the dilapidated brewery and in supplementary equipment, when the Soviet authorities began to harass them with various demands, often quite impracticable, especially in matters of taxation. Several lawsuits followed in Soviet courts, and in the end the concessionaires had every reason to consider themselves lucky to get out of Soviet Russia unscathed, though shorn of all the capital invested in the ill-starred attempt to do business with the "base and lever of world revolution".

In connection with these business activities a number of Estonian citizens visited Soviet Russia and stayed there for a longer or shorter time. Latvian businessmen too, no less desirous to avail themselves of the opportunities of trade with Soviet Russia which seemed to be opening there, either personally travelled or sent their representatives there with the same aims in view. Lithuanian businessmen, on the other hand, seem to have displayed less interest in such trade relations. As we shall see further on, the trade of Lithuania with Soviet Russia was rather insignificant during the whole inter-war period.

Several of the persons who went to Soviet Russia to transact business were arrested on some charge or other, and when the Soviet government wished to secure the release and dispatch to Soviet Russia of some Baltic citizen sentenced in his own country for treasonable communist activities, it would propose to barter them for Baltic citizens confined in Soviet Russia. Although such dealings were in principle repugnant, the governments could not for long decline the urgent requests of the families of their citizens languishing in Soviet Russian prisons. It seemed indeed a bargain to get back a citizen who had trespassed neither upon the laws of his own country, nor, in all probability, upon those of Soviet Russia, and at the same time be rid of the burden of keeping in prison, feeding and watching a citizen who refused to obey the law, by banishing him to Soviet Russia and depriving him of citizenship.

Thus a peculiar kind of barter trade in prisoners was struck up between the Baltic states and Soviet Russia. This trade did much to increase the insolence and daring of the communist fifth columns in trespassing laws. The most fanatic among them did not hesitate to commit the gravest crimes, even acts prohibited on penalty of death, as for example armed resistance to the police. In this respect it was worst in Latvia, where conditions for communist subversive activity were more favourable than in Estonia and Lithuania. Since industrial development had begun earlier and made greater progress in Latvia, the labour movement, too, had started there ten years earlier and had from the very beginning a most radically revolutionary character. Consequently this movement had fallen under Lenin's influence. Moreover, as already shown, Latvia had been more harshly hit by the war and especially her industry had suffered very severely. No wonder that Moscow paid special attention to that country, obviously hoping to find there a more fertile soil for revolutionary sowing.

In the light of these circumstances one can hardly condemn the Latvian government, grappling with enormous difficulties, if in order to suppress the seditious activity of the ever more brazen communists it had recourse, in June, 1921, to a quite abnormal and inadmissible measure: ninety seven communist disturbers were conveyed to the eastern frontier and sent over to Soviet Russia — without any foregoing notice given, let alone agreement reached with the Soviet government. Moscow made an energetic protest against such a mode of dealing which could of course in no wise be justified.[2]

Since at the same time a court-martial had sentenced to death seventeen communists, nine of whom had been executed, while the penalty of the remaining eight had been commuted to life imprison-

---

[2] According to *Pravda* the Latvian convoy had even opened fire upon the communists in question in order to force them to walk over to Soviet Russia, and only after this had the Soviet frontier guards realized what the matter was and allowed them to pass the frontier. If this version were true, the Latvian convoy had been firing quite close to the frontier in the direction of and consequently upon the territory of Soviet Russia. It was inconceivable that the Soviet government would have omitted to protest against such a gross trespass upon Soviet territory. Since, however, nothing has been heard of such a Soviet protest, it is obvious that the *Pravda* report was a fraud, devoid of any foundation and set afloat solely with a view to fanning hate against Latvia.

ment, the Soviet government proposed to exchange these eight for Latvian citizens sentenced to death by Soviet courts. A sharp protest had also been made in the same note of the Soviet government against the execution of the nine communists in question since, if one could put any trust in what that paper published, both the Minister of Foreign Affairs and the Home Secretary had, before their execution, agreed to the Soviet Envoy's oral proposal to exchange these, too. The exchange of notes in this matter led before long to agreement on the exchange thenceforth of persons sentenced to death in the two countries.

The text and tenor of this agreement, which in all probability was confidential, is not available. The following characteristic story, related in *Pravda* on August 11th, 1922, shows, however, how the Soviet government interpreted it.

On August 7th, 1922, a certain Arnold Purin, who had been sentenced to death by court-martial, had been executed. Against this execution the Soviet Envoy Yurenev lodged a protest on the grounds that the person named had been included in the list of Latvian citizens sentenced to death in Soviet Russia. The refusal of the Latvian government to exchange a person convicted of the murder of two policemen performing the duties of their office was considered an illicit act by the Soviet government, who "laid the responsibility for it on the Latvian government" as stated in M. Yurenev's note in rather ambiguously threatening terms: As a result of the quarrel aroused by this Purin case the Latvian government was prevailed upon or rather forced to give a promise that the life of all whom the Soviet government might claim in exchange, would be preserved. (*Pravda*, 17.8. 1922.)

There is hardly need to emphasize how great an encouragement such an agreement must have been to the communist fifth columns, not only in Latvia, but indirectly also in the neighbouring states. Bidding defiance to police and judicial power, the communists developed their criminal activities almost openly, making use of the trade unions and other associations they were assiduously founding with this end in view. Actually no trade union movement in the proper, Western European sense had existed in the Baltic countries before they had become independent states, since its indispensable condition, the freedom of association, was almost completely lacking under the

Russian *ancien régime*, although it was in a manner recognized — at least on paper — during the last years of that rule. What there was at this time can well be described as representing the pre-historic period of the trade union movement. No wonder that the trade unions which came into existence at the beginning of the independence of the Baltic states, were utterly weak, lacking as they did both traditions and experienced leaders. Moreover, the prevailing economic conditions, characterized by the shattered state of industry, great scarcity of capital, and — the inevitable upshot of this — acute unemployment, were extremely unfavourable to the trade union movement. Since the unions lacked the power to attract the broad masses of workers, it was easy for the communists to get most of the unions under their control by dint of their customary conspiratorial infiltration tactics. Having succeeded in this they turned them into branch-establishments of the communist party having nothing in common with trade unions in the proper sense. The endeavours to achieve, through the concerted actions of workers organized into unions, conditions like shorter working hours, better wages, collective bargains etc., were for communists a despicable, manifestly pernicious reformism, since they diminished the chances of revolution, which were considered the more favourable the worse the conditions of the workers were.

Trade unions, transformed into organs of the communist party, were used for all the subversive activity which the fifth columns were required by Moscow to carry out. This could not but bring the active and leading members of these organizations to trial. It came to light that plots were under way in the communist fifth columns to create propitious conditions for a new Soviet aggression against their own states. The number of accomplices in these plots runs in some cases to more than one hundred persons. The outcome was a series of criminal proceedings in the Baltic states in the years 1921—1925 with an unusually high number of persons in the prisoner's box. The actual and true accused in all these trials should have been the Comintern and the master and sustainer, the Soviet government, since without their instigation, leadership and material support not a single one of these trials would have taken place. This, however, did not restrain the Soviet press and the Comintern from raising a deafening clamour every time the wretched simpletons cynically beguiled by them were brought to justice in the Baltic states. These States were on such occasions cried down as the lairs of blackest reaction, where the toiling masses were said to be persecuted in the most cruel manner. A couple of examples chosen at random may give an idea of the style of the hate-propaganda that was being poured out in the Soviet papers and from the platforms of Soviet meetings.

Under the heading "Demoratic Paradise" *Pravda's* own correspondent wrote from Kaunas on April 1st, 1921: "The bestial hatred of the petty bourgeois government for communists emerges in its most repulsive shape. Inhuman tortures, pain, flogging." About Estonia on May 25th, 1922: "Arrests continue. Up to twenty persons have been taken into custody. The political police are unleashed, the white terror of 1919 has returned."[3] Concerning the Latvian court-martial which had sentenced a number of communists to death *Pravda* said (on Nov. 5th, 1922) that even Latvian bourgeois barristers would find the Latvian law-courts a thousand times more inhuman and bloodthirsty than those of Tsarist Russia. On all the Baltic states the following sentence is passed in a long correspondence from Riga in *Pravda* on May 28th, 1922: "There is no freedom for the workers in these 'demoratic' states. The communist party is outlawed. Active members of the trade unions are being arrested, banished to Russia, and shot 'attempting to escape'. The growing reaction is achieving unprecedented, monstrous scope, and is threatening completely to annihilate the working classes."

After what has already been said about the constitutions and the agrarian reform being carried into effect at that very time with decision and expedition in all three countries, as well as about the measures taken to relieve the distress of the unemployed, there is hardly any need to dwell upon these outpourings of Soviet propaganda. Their absurdity ought to be obvious to anyone with a minimum of judgement. Suffice it to point to the following facts. By the agrarian reform the privileged, semi-feudal estate-owning class had

---

[3] No such thing as "white terror" ever occurred in Estonia in 1919, in spite of numerous acts of barbarous, inhuman cruelty committed by communists in those parts of the country they had managed to occupy for a few weeks in December 1918 and January 1919. The Estonian authorities never stained their hands by retaliating to this abhorrent red terror.

been completely wiped out. The class of capitalist industrialists, bankers, merchants, etc., on the other hand, was still so sparse and feeble that it would have been downright preposterous even to imagine it capable of gaining power over the broad masses as a reactionary social force. The social stratification was thus as democratic as it ever might be. The policy of the young states was being determined by the free, unhampered will of the broad, democratic masses of peasants, workers, and artisans, as well as of the educated class, the so-called intelligentsia, themselves descended from these social groups. The power of the state was exercised through democratically elected parliaments and governments dependent upon the confidence of the parliaments. How could states with such a social structure and such a form of government be branded as reactionary?

It is true, however, and it seems appropriate to discuss it in this connection, anticipating posterior events, that several years later a constitutional crisis developed in all the three states, which entailed considerable encroachments upon their democratic system of government and turned them for a time into either semi- or fully-authoritarian states.

It is, of course, hardly necessary to stress that these subsequent developments are by no means justification for the abuses heaped upon the Baltic states by Soviet propaganda a number of years before. All the same it is well to give here a brief account of how these authoritarian interludes in the political evolution of these states came about. Even though these deviations from the democratic form of rule ought in justice to be regretted, it is easy to show that they give no occasion for upbraiding the Baltic peoples, let alone vilifying their young states as lairs of the blackest reaction.

We have already hinted at the shortcomings of the constitutions of these states, enacted in the early twenties. They are, of course, obvious. Since parliament was all-powerful, the executive branch was inevitably weak and lacked the requisite stability; this weakness was aggravated, moreover, by the proportional system of representation which gave rise to an overgrowth of political parties. These shortcomings were by no means the result of reactionary tendencies in the Assemblies which drew up these constitutions. Just the reverse: they originated in the desire of these Assemblies to give their states constitutions which would offer their peoples the possibility of expressing their sovereign will in a most direct and unhampered way and be the last word of democratic radicalism. However, lacking practical experience in the management of state-affairs, they omitted to provide for the checks and balances requisite to guarantee the smooth working of a democratic state apparatus. Cabinet crises occurring rather frequently and mostly far from easily solved were thus unavoidable. These crises shook the political life of the country and a growing dissatisfaction made itself felt.

This dissatisfaction certainly played a not inconsiderable part also in Lithuania, where as early as 1926 a *coup d'état* took place which soon turned this state into an authoritarian dictatorship, if in fact a rather moderate one. Since, however, some purely incidental factors were also involved it would be more to the purpose not to dwell upon it here, but to revert to it further on in the proper context.

As to Estonia and Latvia, it would have been a fairly easy matter to make the requisite amendments in the constitutions in the peace and quiet of normal conditions. But how could there be any question of peace and quiet in a world thrown out of gear by the unprecedented economic depression and the danger of a second world war looming on the horizon with Hitler coming to power and growing more and more portentous month by month?

Because of the misery, bewilderment and despair spreading in the wake of the great depression, extreme rightist parties arose in the early 'thirties in the Baltic states as elsewhere. Imitating the German nazis who, for purposes of their own, encouraged and even financially supported them, these extremists started a recklessly demagogic propaganda designed to undermine and overthrow the democratic system of government. Cleverly exploiting the deficiencies of the constitutions they began to carry to extremes the demand — in itself warrantable — for a stronger executive.

In Estonia the draft of a new constitution, submitted to a plebiscite by these rightist elements, carried the day (in October, 1933). Of course the voters, lacking composure at a time when economic depression was at its worst proved unable to grasp the real aim of the motion: to turn Estonia into an authoritarian dictatorship ruled according to the so-called "Führer-principle". Nevertheless, although after this success at the plebiscite the seizure of power seemed to lie within the grasp of the aspiring dictators, they were thwarted and came off losers in the end when the then Prime Minister and Head of the State, Mr. K. Päts, supported by the army and all sound democratic forces, succeeded in outmanoeuvring them.

This, of course, could not be accomplished overnight. It was in fact about four years before the crisis was solved by the enactment of a new constitution elaborated by a National Assembly, elected for this purpose by free, democratic elections held in December 1936.

This new constitution, which restored parliamentary democracy in a new and well-balanced form, came into force on January 1st, 1938. Its most essential features were: a bicameral parliament; a majority system of representation; a president of the republic not depending on the moods of the parliament and entrusted with considerable, though not excessive powers; a skilfully adjusted balance of power of the parliament and the executive.

If it proved possible to solve the constitutional crisis in Estonia without too great difficulties and in a rather short span, this was due to the fact that the semi-authoritarian régime had been introduced not by a violent *coup d'état*, but in a legal form, viz. by the decision of the people in the above-mentioned plebiscite, which had also invested the Prime Minister and Head of the State with extraordinary powers enabling him to take all the requisite steps. Not having broken any laws and consequently not having to apprehend the institution of penal proceedings, Mr. Päts was not prevented from steering the country back to parliamentary democracy.

In Latvia, on the other hand, the authoritarian régime was established by an undisguised *coup d'état*, carried out under cover of darkness in the night of May 15th, 1934, by the Prime Minister K. Ulmanis, with the support of a paramilitary Home Guard as well as of army and police units, in a rather close imitation of Louis Napoleon's well-known "Eighteenth Brumaire" of December 2nd, 1851. Steering the country back to free, democratic rule was of course quite out of the question under such conditions.

Whereas the semi-authoritarian rule of Mr. K. Päts in Estonia was directed against the rightist aspirants to dictatorship, his aim being to make them lose the popular support they gained by the victory at the plebiscite and thereby reduce them to impotence and dissolution, in Latvia, on the other hand, dictatorship was directed against democratically minded groups, socialists in the first instance, who opposed and condemned the irresponsible, reckless gamble of the originators of the *coup*. The first act of the usurpers was to incarcerate a considerable number of their opponents in concentration camps. No wonder that opposition was rather strong and the régime quite soon developed into fullyfledged totalitarianism.

Yet it was far less harsh than the Fascist régime in Italy, let alone German nazism. However severe a judgment may be passed upon the Latvian *coup d'état*, there is no justification whatever for deriding the Latvian people as politically immature and unable to appreciate the inestimable value of a free, democratic form of rule. Opposition growing ever stronger in the broad masses of the people, it was but a question of time before Latvia would resume the safe course of democratic, ordered freedom.

But no matter if these were the developments, in the middle of the 'twenties there was not an iota of justification for heaping the vilifications instanced above upon the Baltic States. The press of the Soviet state, moreover, a system based on naked violence and brutal terror from the very first day of its existence, was the last in the world to raise its voice in protest about the "lack of freedom" and the "terror" in states founded on Justice, Law and Freedom.

However, the democracy which prevailed in the Baltic states, as well as anything their governments did, were anathema to the Soviet Russian communist rulers and to their myrmidons in these states. Among other things it is worth mentioning that they were even strongly against the agrarian reform, an attitude easy in fact to understand. Of course there could be no doubt that the provision of hundreds of thousands of labourers and smallholders, tenant-farmers and cottagers with land enabling them to attain the long-desired status of independent citizens, would deprive communist propaganda of one of its most fertile fields. Well aware of the very great popularity of this reform among the broad masses, communists dared not openly express their dislike. Instead they tried to detect in it as many flaws as possible.

In the eyes of the political leaders of the Baltic States, with their realistic turn of mind inherited from the peasant population from whom almost to a man they were descended, all the visionary plans of world revolution of the Kremlin potentates were nothing but the fever-phantasies of deranged brains. Having seen the horrors of hunger and misery brought about in Russia by the pursuit of this chimera, these leaders were determined to resist to the last drop of blood all attempts to draw their peoples into the same miseries. The governments set up by free, democratic election considered it a sacred duty to keep careful watch over their national freedom and to suppress, in lawful order but with a firm hand, all criminal attempts to destroy it. It was, of course, most regrettable that trials with un-common numbers of persons in the prisoners' box had to be held in those years and severe punishments inflicted on those found guilty. The Soviet government and its uni-directed press, however, were the last ones with any moral right to reproach the Baltic states for this.

The real motive behind the vituperations about "white terror", "tortures", "inhuman persecution of the toiling masses" etc., was vexation at the fact that the authorities of the Baltic states were not slack and foolish enough to allow the fifth columns in Moscow's service to carry on their treasonable activities without impediment. It was for this reason alone that the Soviet press lamented over the "outlawry" of the communist party and "cruel persecutions" of law-fully registered workingmen's associations — actually associations founded as branch-establishments of the communist party with the sole purpose of promoting its seditious ends.

VII

DIPLOMATIC MOVES AND COUNTERMOVES

Neither the communists in the Baltic countries nor their masters in the Kremlin tried to conceal the fact that the subjugation of the whole world under communist totalitarian tyranny was and would remain their aim. The Baltic nations were well aware that they were destined to become the first victims of aggression if Soviet imperialism undertook to spread the world revolution with fire and sword. That the outpourings of Soviet propaganda about the universal upheaval were meant in full earnest and must not be ignored as but a brag uttered for the attainment of some other ends, was convincingly enough reflected in the unremitting activity of the communist fifth columns. This urged the Baltic states as well as other states adjacent to Soviet Russia to look for means of protection against the threatening danger.

The only conceivable effective means was a defensive alliance of all the states who felt themselves threatened. Most natural, however, was an attempt to bring about a Baltic Union, i.e. a union comprising the peoples who had lived in more or less close contact for centuries through the connecting link of the Baltic Sea, from Finland in the north to Poland in the south. The idea of such a union had originated among the leaders of these states during their wars of liberation.

The first conference to discuss the creation of this union was that attended by the official representatives of the five states, Finland, Estonia, Latvia, Lithuania, and Poland, in Helsinki on Jan. 15th, 1920. However, their efforts came to naught. A Baltic Union with the participation of Poland was inacceptable to Lithuania, which had unsettled questions with Poland concerning the common frontier of the two states. A union of Estonia, Latvia, and Lithuania proposed by the latter was not acceptable to the two former since, in their opinion, such a union would be too feeble to guarantee the security of its members. A few resolutions adopted by the conference remained on paper. — No better results were achieved at a second conference held at Bulduri, a seaside place near Riga, in August, 1920.

Despite these failures further attempts were made in which, however, Lithuania no longer took part, as she refused to sit at a conference table together with Poland as long as the seizure of the capital of Lithuania, Vilnius, carried out by the Polish general Zeligovski on October 9th, 1920, had not been redeemed. Since that regrettable event Lithuania considered herself to be in a state of war with Poland, which meant the absence of diplomatic, consular, and other relations and a frontier closed to intercourse between the two states.

Two conferences held for establishing a union of four states, Finland, Estonia, Latvia, and Poland, one in Helsinki in July 1921, the other in Warsaw in March 1922, proved no more successful than the two in 1920. In Warsaw a protocol was adopted on March 17th, 1922, which in rather vague terms purported to establish a kind of defensive alliance, providing in its article 7 for the observance of benevolent neutrality towards any signatory state which might be attacked without provocation on its part and immediate consultation on steps to be taken in such circumstances. The Finnish Foreign Minister R. Holsti considered the creation of such a union indispensable to guarantee the security of the participating states, especially since at that very moment new rumours were abroad of the aggressive plans of Soviet Russia. However, even before the opening of the conference objections were raised in Finland to entering into a union with Poland, and the opposition against this grew still stronger after the conference, when the protocol adopted there became known. The opponents of the Protocol argued that since relations between Poland and Soviet Russia were considerably more strained than those between Finland and Soviet Russia, Finland would incur the risk of becoming involved in conflicts with her neighbour, participation in which might not be justified from the point of view of Finnish national interests. Since the Finnish Parliament refused to approve the Warzaw Protocol, even this attempt to create a union of the four states mentioned came to naught.

No less natural than the endeavours of the states adjacent to Soviet Russia to unite into some kind of defensive alliance or union was the negative attitude of Soviet Russia to such attempts. These attempts were designed to erect a bulwark against what was the highest aim and the very *raison d'étre* of the Soviet state: the spreading of world revolution. The Soviet press did not try to conceal its hostile attitude, depicting the moves as utterly harmful and dangerous. All critical, sceptical or negative comments, wherever made, were invariably reproduced in the Soviet press under approving headings.

Since in view of the catastrophic state of affairs which had set in in Soviet Russia by the summer of 1921, it would have been madness for the Soviet government to dream of warlike adventures and since on the other hand no signs of an impending outbreak of the longed-for world revolution could be detected in the capitalist world, the Soviet government considered it expedient to employ diplomatic manoeuvres which might hamper or even frustrate the adjacent states in their endeavours to unite. With this end in view it took the initiative of summoning conferences of these states.

The first of such conferences, attended by Soviet Russia, Estonia, Latvia, and Lithuania, met in Riga on November 1st, 1921. It discussed questions of economic relations between the participating states, above all aspects of commerce, rail and sea transport, etc. A few resolutions were adopted, and among other things it was decided to create a permanent economic bureau of the participating states. No real, practical results worth mentioning can be pointed to either from the resolutions adopted or from the activity of the permanent bureau, which very soon faded unnoticed into oblivion.

As a countermove to the Warsaw conference, which obviously disquieted Moscow, the latter initiated another conference which met a fortnight later in Riga. The proposal to meet was made by Moscow during the Warsaw conference and sent to all the states participating in it[1]. This conference was attended by no lesser persons than the Commissar for Foreign Affairs, M. B. Tchitcherin himself, his deputy M. Litvinov and M. A. Yoffe, who were passing through Riga on their way to the Genoa conference. Other participants were Estonia, Latvia, and Poland, the latter, however, having sent only a representative with restricted powers, whereas Finland had sent an observer. The protocol of the conference reaffirmed the principle of the sanctity of

---

[1] *History of Diplomacy*, vol. 3, p. 163.

treaties, declared desirable the *de jure* recognition of Soviet Russia and the development of commercial relations with her.

The same judgment is to be given upon this conference as upon the preceding ones: neither did it contribute to the establishment and reinforcement of good relations between Soviet Russia and the Baltic states, nor did it produce any other positive and useful results. But such had not been Tchitcherin's aim. For the Soviet government this conference had importance only in that it declared itself in favour of the *de jure* recognition of Soviet Russia and the development of commercial relations with her, points in which Moscow, in dire need of financial help from the western Powers, was then highly interested. The following lines from the *History of Diplomacy* concerning this conference are worth citing: "The conference succeeded in shaking somewhat the common front of the Baltic countries and wearing down the anti-Soviet edge of the Warsaw conference". Thus even this manoeuvre was appreciated by Soviet diplomacy first and foremost as a means of impeding and frustrating the attempt of the neighbouring states to establish alliances for the preservation of their independence.

A new initiative was taken by Moscow soon afterwards. On June 22nd, 1922 the Soviet government proposed to the same four states, Finland, Estonia, Latvia and Poland, and, moreover, to Rumania, to assemble for a conference in Moscow to conclude a treaty of disarmament. For some reason or other the invitation to attend the conference was sent to Lithuania five months later, in November. At this conference, which met on December 22nd, 1922, the draft of a non-aggression pact was drawn up. Since this treaty, however, was to come into force simultaneously with a disarmament treaty on which agreement was not reached, even the non-aggression treaty came to nothing, and this conference, too, failed to lead to any result.

After the failure of the Warsaw conference no further attempts to build a broader union were made by the Baltic states for the following three years. The abortive conferences held in 1920—1922 had shown the impossibility of establishing either a union of five states or one of four. Thereafter it soon became clear that even a defensive alliance of three states could not be brought about. After the Finnish Foreign Minister R. Holsti had been disavowed by the parliament which rejected the Warsaw Protocol, Finland drifted further and further from collaboration with the states south of the Gulf of Finland. A union comprising Finland, Estonia and Latvia had therefore to be ruled out. Neither was a union comprising Poland, Latvia and Estonia to be thought of, since this combination, if at all conceivable, would have been too artificial to be seriously considered. Moreover, a series of considerations rendered it doubtful whether such a union would not in fact have done more harm than good. The only remaining combination, a union comprising Estonia, Latvia and Lithuania, was in the abstract the most natural one. Actually, however, even this had to be ruled out since Lithuania displayed too little interest in it, her whole attention being centered round her conflict with Poland over the question of Vilnius.

Such being the situation, Estonia and Latvia decided to make a beginning by concluding a defensive alliance contracted in Tallinn on Nov. 1st, 1923. It engaged the contracting parties immediately to lend assistance to the other party in the event of unprovoked aggression. A preliminary economic and customs agreement was concluded at the same time, providing among other things for the coordination of the custom tariffs of the two allied states. This latter pact, however, was never put into effect.

The Soviet government, for its part, obviously considered it superfluous to go on arranging such diplomatic manoeuvres as the two conferences it had initiated in 1922. It neither raised any protest against the treaty of defensive alliance concluded by Estonia and Latvia on Nov. 1st, 1923, nor resorted to any other diplomatic stratagem on this occasion.

VIII

DISAPPOINTED HOPES OF WORLD REVOLUTION
AND THE ADVENTURE IN ESTONIA

The absence of any reaction to the conclusion of the Estonian–
Latvian Treaty of Defensive Alliance may be attributable to the fact
that this event coincided with a sudden surge of optimistic hope in
the Kremlin that the long awaited world revolution was at last on
the point of breaking out. These good tidings were announced by no
less a person than the highest authority on this matter, the president
of the Third International, G. Zinoviev. In his article "The Second
Wave of the International Revolution", published in *Pravda* on Dec.
1st, 1923, he wrote: "Events in Poland, Germany, and Bulgaria signify
the beginning of the second wave of the international proletarian
revolution. The first wave of the years 1917–1920 proved unable to
shatter capitalism to its foundations. After that came the years of ebb
in the revolutionary flood. The years 1921, 1922 and the first half of
1923 constitute the period of the greatest excesses of international
reaction and of the weakening of the working classes. Now we are
manifestly approaching the rising second wave of the international
proletarian revolution. One need be no prophet to anticipate the new
explosion of revolutionary movement among the broad masses in the
winter close at hand and in the spring. The second wave of the
international proletarian revolution will to the last fragment wash
away the foundations of the edifice of capitalism in Europe. This
edifice must inevitably collapse".[1]

What Zinoviev wrote in this article was then an opinion generally
prevailing among Russian communists. This was fully confirmed e.g.
by the correspondent of *The Times* in Riga, one of the persons best

---

[1] The mountebankish quality of Zinoviev's style is to the utmost possible extent
preserved in the translation of this quotation.

informed of what was going on in Soviet Russia. In a correspondence published in his paper on Nov. 8th, 1923 he wrote: "Soviet leaders are firmly convinced of the inevitability of an early and complete communist victory in Germany. Members of the Russian Council of Labour and Defence are continually passing through Riga to Germany. It is stated that Radek is now in Hamburg, where Soviet Russia has accumulated great supplies of propaganda material. General Tukhachevsky is travelling to Germany via Danzig and Yoffe is acting from Danzig, General Noskoff is now in Berlin awaiting the formation of a German revolutionary military Council on Russian lines, when he will serve as a link between the Berlin and Moscow Councils. Several other experienced revolutionary generals are in Moscow, ready to proceed to Germany when it is considered expedient to go; but it is not intended to send armies. Judging by the recent speeches of Soviet leaders, the Soviet is determined to bring about the German revolution now or never."

The belief that a revolution which would bring about an early and complete communist victory was going to break out in Germany at any moment seemed to find confirmation in a series of disorders in a number of German towns, caused by the insufferable misery of all wage-earners and the complete poverty of the middle classes in consequence of inflation, which had reached truly fantastic proportions. Communists did not fail to exploit the situation for fomenting disorders. Fully confirming the information given by the correspondent of *The Times*, a revolt broke out in Hamburg in the second half of November. Far from a spontaneous outburst of the discontent of the masses, it was a well-prepared uprising meant to become the signal for, and the first decisive battle of, the communist revolution in Germany.

The correspondence from Riga published in *The Times*, truthful in all other respects, seems to be erroneous in its the assertion that there had not been any intention to send Soviet armies to Germany. If one takes into consideration how eagerly the Kremlin potentates longed for the advent of the world revolution, it is hard to believe that they had not envisaged intervention by the Red Army at the very moment when Germany, in their opinion, was on the eve of a communist revolution — to kindle its firebrand and give requisite guarantees against its being quenched before it was sufficiently spread.

There are convincing proofs that designs to send Red Army troops to Germany were formed and discussed in the Kremlin and that steps were taken to prepare for this intervention. One indication is to be found in a letter sent by Trotsky a short time before his expulsion from Soviet Russia, on Dec. 16th, 1928, to the Central Committee of the Communist Party of the Soviet Union and published immediately after his arrival in Constantinople (Istanbul). In this letter he upbraided the Committee for "having smoothed over the wretched policy of the international leadership which resulted in the abandonment of excellent revolutionary positions in Germany without battle in 1923."[2] What omitted battles in Germany in 1923 might have been meant in this sentence if not those which the Red Army could have fought in Hamburg to help the revolt to gain ground? — Another proof is given by the well-known Russian historian and émigré-politician B. Nikolayevsky, one of the best experts on Soviet Russia. In his report to the conference of the Institute for the Study of the History and Culture of the USSR, held in New York on March 20th—22nd, 1953, he related among other things that "in 1923, when the uprising was being prepared in Germany, negotiations were being conducted with Latvia about the passage of the Red Army into Prussia."[3] That such negotiations were conducted at that time was mentioned also in the already quoted correspondence from Riga in *The Times,* in which it was said that the Soviet agent Vigdor Kopp was again coming to Riga "in order to continue his efforts to obtain assurances that traffic between Russia and Germany shall not be hindered in case of a communist revolution in Germany." There can hardly be any doubt that Kopp most carefully abstained from mentioning that the "goods" whose unhampered passage he was soliciting, would have been weapons, munitions and the Red Army's soldiers. Nor can there be any doubt that that very kind of "goods" would have begun to roll from Russia through Latvia to Germany if the disorders there had not been put down so quickly. Only because the first flames of revolt in Hamburg were so quickly extinguished by the armed forces of the German republic, did the whole design of sending Red Army troops to Germany to assist the workers and the

---

[2] L. Trotsky *Chto i kak proizoshlo?* (What Happened and How), Paris 1929, p. 54.
[3] *Materialy po izucheniu istorii i kultury SSSR*, Munich, 1953, p. 127.

poorest peasants to throw down German democracy with the least delay have to be abandoned.

Contrary to Zinoviev's forecast, neither the winter of 1923–1924, nor the following spring brought a new explosion of the communist revolution and the collapse of capitalism in Europe. What collapsed were the air-castles of the fantastic hopes of the majority of communists. At this very time the Soviet communist party and the Soviet state sustained a severe blow: the loss of their leader Lenin. It is true that with the exception of a temporary recovery in the short interval at the end of 1922 and the beginning of 1923 he had been incapable of any work. The hope and belief that he would soon recover and begin to lead the party with a firm hand again had helped, however, to keep down disagreements in the party. The unavoidable consequence of this departure was an intensified outburst of these disagreements, bringing the tug of war of the pretenders to the vacant throne. Already during his illness a conspiracy headed by Zinoviev and Stalin had been formed in the party with the aim of precluding Trotsky from becoming Lenin's successor, though he seemed to be both most entitled to and qualified for this. As secretary general of the party, invested with dictatorial powers over all its functionaries, Stalin was in a position to pack all its organs as he liked. With his habitual ruthless brutality he removed the followers of Trotsky from all important posts in the Party. After that it was an easy task to bar him from the leadership of the Party and the Soviet state. He enjoyed, however, immense popularity with the masses. The bulk of the members of the party and especially the officers of the Red Army remembered too well his great merits in the Civil War, in organising the army with unremitting energy and inspiring it with his fiery eloquence to endurance and heroism. This popularity had to be destroyed. A venomous reviling campaign was opened, and a hue and cry raised against him. Although he was soon deprived of any possibility of replying to and refuting the gross lies which were spread about him, it was not less than five years before Stalin dared to strike the decisive blow and expel him from the Soviet Union.

There had been disagreements and passionate debates in the Soviet communist party when questions of high importance had to be decided in highly complicated situations. So it had been in the autumn of 1917, on the eve of the ursurpation of power, when a number of Lenin's closest followers had considered this step to be a fatal mistake and refused to go along. So also when the party and the Soviet government had had to decide whether to accept or decline the Brest-Litovsk peace. However, in all such cases Lenin had managed, thanks to his overwhelming authority, to force his will and with it also a firm and coherent policy upon the party and the Soviet state. Now the party was again faced with an extremely complicated situation and highly intricate problem. What conclusions were to be drawn from the failure of the revolt in Hamburg, to which such high-flung hopes had been attached? Had these hopes been but groundless daydreams, nothing more than wishful thinking? If so, the whole policy of the international communist movement and of the Soviet state would have to be radically changed. A whole complex of deep-rooted ideas and lines of thought must then be thrown overboard. Only a leader with the authority of Lenin could have effectuated such a radical change in the policy of the party and the Soviet state without lengthy irresolution and wavering. However, the party not only lacked a leader with such authority, but was deeply divided by quarrels and the struggle for supremacy of the pretenders to the dictator's throne. For a time it was a vessel without a captain.

Therefore the Comintern and the Soviet press, following the law of inertia, went on with their hate propaganda against the Baltic states as well as against the whole non-communist world. The propaganda against the Baltic states was even intensified, possibly as a result of the increased resistance of the masses to the Soviet order and the vehemence of the antagonism within the "monolithic" party. So many cases of murder, attempted murder and assault of the correspondents of the Soviet papers were reported in these papers in 1924 that a proclamation was published in the press urging the citizens to organize the protection of the "village and worker-correspondents" from acts of violence threatening them everywhere at the hands of the "enemies of the people" (*Pravda*, 10.3. 1924). An extensive uprising in Georgia in the same year (1924) must also be mentioned, yet another symptom of the increased discontent of the masses with the prevailing order, although this uprising was obviously an act of despair, since there was scarcely room for hope that it might bring about some kind of chain-reaction and spread over wider regions of the Soviet Union.

In the atmosphere of increased tensions in the party, divided by internal strife, the disposition to hazardous venture was given scope which it would not have received in Lenin's time, since the very existence of the Soviet order might thus have been put in jeopardy. Among the rebukes addressed by Trotsky, in his above-mentioned letter to the Central Committee of the Party, there was also the following: that the leaders of the Party had tried to smooth over its *opportunist mistakes by adventures in Estonia and Bulgaria*. By these adventures he means a revolt set on foot in the Estonian capital Tallinn on December 1st, 1924, and an infernal machine plot in the cathedral in the Bulgarian capital Sofia on April 16th, 1925. There is hardly reason to dwell upon the latter completely senseless crime, which entailed the loss of about 150 lives and more or less seriously wounded several hundred persons. The revolt in Tallinn, on the other hand, is well worth a closer examination.

The activity of the communist fifth columns increased in intensity in the Baltic states after the beginning of the year 1924. In communist proclamations, printed in Soviet Russia and smuggled into the Baltic states, vague threats about the imminent "liberation of the working classes" became more and more frequent. These threats and several other pieces of information derived from different sources seemed to intimate that some action designed to effectuate a forcible overthrow of the prevailing democratic order was being contemplated and prepared. Certain indications suggested that some attempt in this direction might be made in connection with a mass trial in Tallinn in which 149 persons indicted of criminal subversive activity were to be court-martialled. The defendants, to whom directions as to how they were to conduct themselves in the court had obviously been smuggled into the prison, behaved from the very start of the proceedings with the most provocative brazenness, which only confirmed the conjectures formed on the basis of the information gathered. In their replies to the question at the start of the proceedings as to whether they avowed themselves guilty of the crimes they were charged with, all the accused exerted themselves to outdo each other in foul language, expressing their contempt for the court and the state. Some of these answers have been preserved for history in a correspondence sent to *Pravda* by its own correspondent from Tallinn and published on November 22nd, 1924. One of these replies will suffice to give an idea of their style and content. "A communist will never avow himself guilty in the court of the bloodhounds of the bourgeoisie, in a court that is nothing but a circus." When the accused who gave this answer was being sent out of the court room by order of the presiding judge, he shouted to the court: "Dogs!" All other replies were in the same style. *Pravda's* correspondent was very much pleased with them. His judgment upon them runs as follows: "The defendants conducted themselves with independence and dignity."

Emboldening themselves mutually by such "dignifield" replies, the accused grew more and more brazen. It was manifest that they had been instructed to profane and soil the proceedings and tear down the authority of the court and state to the utmost of their ability. There would have been no cause for concern in this to either the court or the state were it not clear which foreign Power was backing and emboldening the defendants, and fresh in memory how less than four years earlier Georgia and had been invaded under the camouflage and trumped-up pretext of a grossly simulated, really non-existent "uprising of Georgian workers and peasants".

When one of the accused went to the length of inciting to sedition the soldiers on guard in the court room, the court interrupted the proceedings and decreed that for this crime, committed in the court room itself, he be put on trial at the drumhead court-martial which during the following night sentenced him to death. Only after this sentence, and the fact that it had been carried out during the night, was made known by the presiding judge at the opening of the proceedings on the following morning, did the defendants relinquish the roles prescribed them by the communist underground stage-management, and the proceedings could go on in a normal way.

The sentences which were passed on November 27nd were severe: 39 of the accused were condemned to life imprisonment, 81 to different penalties from 4 years' to 15 years imprisonment, and 11 to different lesser penalties. Seven were acquitted.

One purpose of the brazen demeanour of the accused, as it came to light later, had been to protract the proceedings until December 1st, 1924, the date which had been fixed for an attempt at forcible over-throw of the prevailing democratic order. Since the preparations for this action must have taken several months, this date must have been definitively fixed at least a few weeks in advance. Since, however, according to the elaborated plans, it was to take place in connection with the mass-trial of the 149, it was of vital importance that this trial should not be brought to a close before Dec. 1st. But the sentence of death passed by the drumhead court-martial upon one of the accused had produced such an impression on the others that it proved impossible thus to protract the proceedings. The trial came to an end four days earlier, on November 27th, bringing an unforeseen change in the time-table. However it was not considered so essential as to necessitate a deferment of the action, long planned and prepared in all details.

At five o'clock sharp on the morning of Monday, Dec. 1st, the barracks of all the more important military units, the railway stations, the telegraph office, several police stations, etc., were assaulted by gangs armed with automatic pistols, rifles, and hand grenades. Although the assailants enjoyed the most complete advantage of surprise, nobody having imagined the possibility of such bare-faced action and thus no precautionary measures having been taken for such occasions, most energetic and vigorous resistance set in everywhere spontaneously, and after a very short fight the assailants were put to flight. Only the central railway-station, occupied without hindrance by a gang, took about half an hour of firing to clear. Another gang which had gained entrance to the telegraph office was liquidated before it had had time to begin despatching telegrams. Without doubt the first telegrams to be sent would have been an appeal to the Soviet Red Army to run to the succour of the "Estonian toiling masses risen in rebellion". In order to ensure an instant reply to this request three divisions of the Red Army had been concentrated in good time on the Estonian frontier; this was ascertained by the Estonian military intelligence service. For to bring these divisions up to full battle strength, four younger classes of reservists had been called up in the military district of the 56th territorial division of the Red Army, adjacent to the eastern frontier of Estonia and Latvia.

About fifty per cent of the assailants were captured either during the flight after they had been repelled or in the days immediately thereafter. Not a few later fell into the hands of the police. As it was revealed at the ensuing investigation, the leaders of the gangs, about two hundred and thirty, had been clandestinely sent to Estonia from Soviet Russia, where they had had a thorough military training and been provided with weapons as well as with a detailed plan of action elaborated by Soviet specialists on the tactics of civil war. Every man had been taught letter by letter what he would have to do. About three hundred of the most active members of the local communist fifth column, those considered to be most reliable and appropriate for the task, were, according to the plan, to be added as reinforcement to these specially trained men sent from Leningrad.

On November 30th in the evening the local underlings had been summoned by personal orders to a number of flats in different parts of the town where those sent from Leningrad awaited them. Any possibility of slinking away had been rendered impossible by armed guards placed at all possible outlets. For this very reason even two secret informers of the police who had been among the persons summoned, had found themselves deprived of any possiblity of escaping and informing the authorities of what was going to happen. Weapons and ammunition had been distributed and the long hours of the night had been used to impress upon each his special task in the assault and teach those who needed it how to handle the weapons. Particular emphasis had been laid on the injunction to use weapons most ruthlessly and resolutely.

The assailants had not failed to follow this order. Twenty five persons fell their victims, only one of them, an officer, in the fight against the gang which had occupied the railway-station. The rest had fallen victims of absolutely meaningless murder, several of them shot unawares from behind in the street. One of these needless killings was that of the Minister of Communications, who informed by a telephone call that an armed gang was assailing the railway-station, had in haste set out thither and been shot down.

There can hardly be any doubt that if the gang which had penetrated into the telegraph office had had time to send off the appeal for succour to the Red Army and the assailants been able to keep some part of the town in their hands for twenty four hours or even less, the three Red Army divisions waiting in readiness behind the frontier would have started invading Estonia. For what purpose had they been completed to full war strength and concentrated on the frontier of Estonia by the very day of the revolt in Tallinn, planned and prepared for in all details in Leningrad, if not to march into Estonia as soon as the trumped-up pretext had been raised? However, the soap-bubble of the bogus "uprising of the Estonian toiling masses" had burst, thanks to the spontaneous resistance it met everywhere, and the Red Army divisions had to be sent home without having an opportunity to accomplish the task assigned to them.

One further characteristic detail is worth mentioning: about thirty per cent of those members of the local communist fifth column who had taken part in the assaults and been overtaken by justice, turned out to have been in the service of the Soviets: six in that of the Soviet legation, thirty three in that of the local branches of the Soviet commercial organizations Dobroflot and Zentrosoyuz.

These briefly related facts should be borne in mind when one considers the above-mentioned sentencing to death by drumhead court-martial of one of the accused in the mass-trial. It is, of course, beyond dispute that such a measure is unwarrantable in a state founded on law and justice. A normal sense of justice tells us there can be no justification in sentencing a defendant to death for a speech held during court proceedings, even if addressed to soldiers and other persons present and irrespective of how criminal that speech may be. But the circumstances in which this trial was held were anything but normal. The court was well aware whence the accused had derived their boundless brazenness and impudence: from the assurance that they were backed in their treasonable activity by the might of the Soviet state. The court was aware that in trying to obstruct orderly proceedings the accused were carrying out instructions issued by this Power and helping it to prepare the same fate for the Estonian people as had befallen the Georgians less than four years earlier. All lawful means for maintaining the order of the procedure prescribed by law having proved of no avail with those in the prisoners' box, made fanatical by the support of the foreign Power in question, the court resorted at last to an unwarrantable measure. This is highly regrettable, but the reproaches for it must be addressed in the first place to the Comintern and the Power that was its master and maintainer. The court felt it could not in this instance follow the rule: *fiat justitia, pereat respublica!* (Let justice be done though the republic should fall.) It considered its duty to lie in the observation of another venerable rule: *salus respublicae suprema lex!* (The welfare of the republic is the supreme law).

The miserably failed revolt was described in the Soviet press as a rising of the Estonian workers, driven to despair by insufferable oppression at the hands of a numerically insignificant "white-guardist" bourgeois clique raised to power by German occupation authorities. Literally thus was it referred to in a proclamation of the Comintern published in *Pravda* on December 11th, 1924. There is hardly need for lengthy comment on these outpourings. Suffice it to make but the following short corrections.

Firstly, what the Comintern abusively called a "white-guardist bourgeois clique", was in reality the Estonian national government, established in free, democratic elections. Secondly, far from raising this government to power, the German occupation authorities, as already mentioned, had done their utmost to suppress it: they discontinued the activity of the Estonian Provisional Government, sent its leader K. Päts into a concentration camp, and even after the capitulation of Germany put every kind of hindrance in its way to deprive it of the possibility of organizing the defence of the country against the aggression of the Red Army. And thirdly, as to the pretended "uprising of the Estonian toiling masses", it was irrefutably demonstrated at the investigation that not a single person involved had joined the assailants of his own accord, although thousands of workers were on their way to the factories and workshops while shooting was still going on in several places and the darkness of the early morning offered the best opportunities to any who might have felt an inclination to cast their lot with the assailants. The whole venture was from beginning to end a conspiracy of about two hundred and thirty mercenaries of the Comintern, trained and armed in Leningrad and clandestinely sent to Estonia, where they had been reinforced by about three hundred local supporters with whom neither the Estonian workers nor any other class of the Estonian people had anything to do.

One cannot help wondering how it was possible for Soviet Russian experts on civil war so grossly to miscalculate the chances of the planned revolt in Tallinn? How did they not anticipate that the attempt would not meet with any response on the part of the "Estonian toiling masses" but, on the contrary, would arouse a spontaneous resistance which would nip it in the bud? The answer to these questions is given by Trotsky in his statement quoted above. This attempt was a reckless gamble undertaken by the leadership of the communist party or — may be — some clique among the leaders "to smooth over the opportunist mistakes" made in its grand policy and strategy. The gamblers were, moreover, grossly ignorant of real conditions and of the moods of the toiling masses in the so-called capitalist countries. They believed that conditions actually were more or less as described e.g. concerning Estonia in the proclamation of the Comintern quoted above. They believed that the broad masses of workers would spontaneously join those four or five hundred conspirators sent to raise the standard of rebellion in Tallinn. These assailants were in their eyes only the kindling spark that would detonate the proletarian revolution in Estonia. And last but not least: there were the three Red Army divisions ready to march into Estonia and hasten to the assistance of the "Estonian workers risen in rebellion".

The abortive revolt was followed by a torrent of vituperation against Estonia in the Soviet press well worthy of a place among the records of this kind of art. The following examples might give an idea of their style. In the proclamation of the Comintern quoted above the following words were used about the Estonian government: "The gang of gallows-birds that calls itself the Estonian government". Under the heading: "The Estonian Infanticides" *Pravda* wrote on December 23rd, 1924, that the whole family of a communist, his wife and three children aged from three (!) to nineteen years had been shot. In a report from Tallinn about a trial in which two accused had been sentenced to death for having taken part in the revolt of Dec. 1st, *Pravda* wrote on April 9th, 1925, that drunken plain-clothes men would give evidence in the Estonian courts, to which "information" the comment was added: "The nauseousness and abominations of the administration of justice in Estonia defy description".

Moreover, revilings of the same kind were in fact published about the other Baltic states too. Thus of Lithuania *Pravda* wrote on February 5th, 1925 that prisoners were being tortured by means of electric current and that there had been cases of mental derangement brought about by tortures. At about the same time *Pravda* began to write about the torturing of prisoners in Estonia, too, where "electric baths" were said to be in use (*Pravda*, 1.28. 1925).

Although it is hardly necessary to waste words upon these terms of abuse and horror stories, the following short remarks may still be in place.

As far as the stories about the torturing of prisoners, etc., concern Latvia and Lithuania, I must refrain from passing judgment upon them, since I have not had the opportunity of checking them on the spot and there are no means of arranging a thorough investigation in the prevailing circumstances. However, as far as Estonia is concerned I am sufficiently acquainted with the facts not to hesitate to declare most emphatically that these horror stories were but propagandist fables, customary with communists and reflecting only the rage of the Soviet leaders at the lamentable failure of the carefully plotted revolt in Estonia. Evidently it very soon dawned upon these leaders themselves that this propaganda was only arousing ridicule by its coarse exaggerations. This can be inferred from the sudden disappearance from the pages of the Soviet papers of the stories about the shooting of children after they had figured there under screaming headlines for a week. In reality no torturing of prisoners, whether by "electric baths", or otherwise, was possible or conceivable in Estonia, since no law officer would have dared to make himself guilty of such abominable crimes, which would certainly have been revealed by the free press and provoked interpellations in Parliament.

It goes without saying that those who had taken part in the assaults on the morning of Dec. 1st, 1924, were brought to justice and had penalties imposed upon them for the crimes committed. However, in all these cases the rules prescribed in all civilized countries to secure just proceedings were observed at the bar of the court. Moreover, the following facts should be noted. According to the law the penalty of death could be inflicted upon all those who with set purpose had taken part in the revolt, irrespective of what part they had played in its execution. Nevertheless the court-martial abstained from inflicting the penalty of death on those found to have participated as express messengers or telephone operators, or carters for conveying weapons, etc., and thus to have been prevented from being among actual assailants. More than that: even those who had actually been among the assailants but for some reason or other had not yet made use of their weapons, were not sentenced to death but given other penalties. And again, most of the sentences of long-term imprisonment were commuted and considerably mitigated in subsequent years.

Since the horror stories about the "white terror" after the abortive revolt in Tallinn were without the slightest foundation, it seems more than likely that the same was true of the analogous stories spread by Soviet propaganda about Latvia and Lithuania. Personally, I have not the shadow of a doubt that they were nothing but deliberate lies.

IX

THE STABILIZED CAPITALIST WORLD AND
MOSCOW'S MANOEUVRES

The revolt in Estonia could not but arouse anxiety in the neighbouring states, especially since it was difficult to surmise what ulterior schemes Moscow had been devising in connection with this plot and what surprises it might still have in reserve. Would not the miscarried attempt in Estonia soon be followed by other action elsewhere, aiming at the same ends? As long as the policy and plans of the Soviet government were an unsolved riddle, one had to take such possibilities seriously into account.[1] It was quite obvious that protection against the danger threatening first and foremost the states adjacent to the Soviet Union could be found only in the coordination of their precautions. To discuss the establishment of such coordination and collaboration a conference was convoked in Helsinki on April 25th, 1925. At this conference the same five states were represented which had attended the conference held in the same place in January, 1920: Finland, Estonia, Latvia, Lithuania, and Poland — Lithuania, of course, having sent but an observer. It turned out, however, that the impression made by the revolt in Tallinn had not sufficed to bring about so radical a change in the frame of mind of the states concerned as to induce them to form a defensive alliance for the protection of their independence and territorial integrity. No proposal to such effect was even deliberated at the conference table. A convention on arbitration and conciliation was concluded and it was decided to create a permanent conciliation commission. Since, however, there were no contentions among the four states which

---

[1] The infernal machine plot in Sofia on April 16th, 1925 showed that there was reason to reckon with the possibility of most startling crimes contrived by the Comintern.

were not amenable to solution through the usual diplomatic channels no value to speak of could be attributed to this the only real outcome of their deliberations. Just the same, Moscow did not fail to express its displeasure at the conference, which was labelled "a renewed attempt at the creation of an anti-Soviet block under the guidance of Poland."

The revolt in Tallinn had been schemed and carried out by the Soviet Red Army with a view to creating a trumped-up pretext for the invasion of Estonia by the Red Army. It seemed more than probable that if a new plot were formed by Moscow somewhere else, it would follow more or less the same pattern. The problem of the most effective protection against such surprises was therefore a military one. Consequently it was quite natural for the general staffs of the states concerned to exchange their information on the matter and deliberate about the measures to be taken to ward off the common danger.

One such deliberation took place in Riga on April 1st, 1925, the representatives of the general staffs of Poland, Latvia, Estonia, Finland and Rumania taking part in it, the two latter as observers. The intention had been to hold this conference in complete secrecy. Moscow, however, had got wind of it and the Soviet propaganda machine began to sound the alarm. Disturbed by any collaboration among the adjacent states, the masters of the Kremlin viewed with particular disfavour any joint activity by the Baltic states and Poland. The reasons for this were plain enough. Only a defensive alliance of the Baltic states and Poland could form a military force strong enough to compel Moscow at least to refrain from such adventurous plots as the revolt in Tallinn. If the designers of such plots had to reckon with the possibility of conflicts in which Poland would not stand passively aside, they would have to weigh up the risks more seriously. Therefore the Soviet leaders felt obliged to do anything in their power to prevent such an alliance, and missed no opportunity of putting obstacles in its way.

In its campaign on the occasion of the conference in question Soviet propaganda branded it as "a new military intrigue of Poland in the Baltic area", "an attempt by Poland to attain hegemony in the Baltic area, at whatever cost" and "a military conspiracy against the Soviet Union as well as against Germany". By the way, whenever an occasion offered, Soviet propaganda sought to emphasize that the endeavours of the Baltic states to form an alliance, especially with the participation of Poland, were directed not only against the Soviet Union, but also against Germany. In the same article *(Pravda,* 4.9. 1925) in which the above terms of disparagement were employed, Estonia and Latvia were accused of having trespassed against the peace treaties by having taken part in a conference along with Rumania, which country had unlawfully seized a part of the Russian territory.[2] Latvia especially was warned against making friends with Poland, who was said to covet not only Klaipeda (Memel), but also the Latvian town of Liepaja (Libau) and Yelgava (Mitau). On this occasion Latvia was reminded of the importance to her budget and national economy of her trade relations with the Soviet Union, particularly of Soviet transit traffic through Latvia, and the threat was added that Latvia might lose Soviet transit traffic.[3]

In the meantime, however, a very important change was to come about in the policy of the Soviet government. It was signalled by a sensational leader in *Pravda* on April 26th, 1925 under the heading: "The Stabilization of the Capitalist 'Encompassment' and the USSR", the gist of it being expressed in the following sentences: "A whole series of symptoms lead to the conclusion that international capitalism has now achieved a certain relatively stable equilibrium . . . An

[2] This was a hint at the Rumanian province Bessarabia, lying between the Pruth and Dniester rivers and inhabited mainly by Moldavians, this being but another name for the Rumanians. This province had been ceded to Russia in 1812 by Turkey, under whose rule it had been since 1511. A few months after the Soviet revolution in Russia (Oct. 1917) it was proclaimed an independent Moldavian republic by a Moldavian National Council, and at the end of 1918 incorporated into Rumania at the request of the said National Council. The incorporation was recognized by the Peace Conference in Paris on Oct. 28th, 1920. The Soviet Union, however, never recognized Rumania's possession of Bessarabia and broke off diplomatic relations with her. These relations were not resumed until 1934.

[3] Russian transit traffic through Latvia had been quite considerable in Tsarist time and its importance for the national economy of the country was still more keenly felt in the first years of the independence of Latvia, when the country was suffering from unemployment and other wounds inflicted by the war and revolutionary disturbances. The importance of Soviet transit for Latvia was ruthlessly exploited by the Soviet government, who often threatened to deflect it elsewhere as well as to withdraw orders given to Latvian factories. These threats were not infrequently carried out.

immediate revolutionary situation is lacking... There is stabilization of a kind in our country, too... we too are making headway."

There had been talk about the stabilization of capitalism in the columns of *Pravda* even earlier, but the word "stabilization" had always been used in inverted commas, to emphasize that no true communist could consider a real stabilization of the capitalist system, irrevocably doomed to destruction, to be possible. Even in this leader the stabilization of capitalism was spoken of as but "certain" and "relative" one. However, the traditional inverted commas had been dropped for the first time and it was avowed that a situation immediately favourable for revolution was lacking in the world. The publication of such a leader in *Pravda* signified a very radical change in the policy of the Soviet state.

It was not long before this change began to make itself felt in the policy of the Soviet government towards the Baltic states. The masters of the Kremlin began to invite economic delegations from these states to Moscow for negotiations about developing closer economic relations with the Soviet Union. The Latvian government was the first to receive such an invitation. When the Latvian economic delegation arrived at Moscow, a high official of the Commissariat of Foreign Trade, Y. Yansson, declared in an interview given to *Pravda*, that the economic development of Latvia was possible only through economic collaboration between her and the Soviet Union. Without such co-operation Latvia's economic progress would certainly slacken its speed. (*Pravda*, 10.18. 1925)

In an article published a few weeks later, on Nov. 13th, 1925, the paper declared that a noticeable change in the attitude of the Baltic countries towards the Soviet Union had been perceived of late: a loyal, favourable wind had begun to blow from that quarter. Good-neighbourly relations and peaceful collaboration were said to be sprouting forth. Obviously the Baltic statesman had made up their minds to stop dancing to the tune of the imperialist Powers and forming anti-Soviet plots, declared the paper. It prophesied, moreover, that the example of Latvia would soon be followed by Lithuania and Estonia and even Finland. In fact a Lithuanian delegation came to Moscow in November, a Finnish delegation in December, and a Polish one in January 1926. On all these occasions the Soviet press would draw highly tempting perspectives of the blissful rewards which all these states were to reap from economic collaboration with the Soviet Union.

It requires little reasoning to show how real facts had been turned topsy-turvy in *Pravda's* article about the loyal, good-neighbourly feeling which had begun to flow from the Baltic area. It was not the statesmen of the Baltic nations who had been to blame for the fact that their relations with the Soviet Union had not been as they ought to be and usually are between good neighbours, but the Soviet government, who had been openly encouraging and supporting the subversive activity of the communist fifth columns in these states, going even to the length of instigating a revolt in Tallinn. If a "news chapter had opened in the relations of these states and the Soviet Union", it was only because the latter had found it opportune to change its tactics in relation to the Baltic. And being thus occasioned by temporary tactical considerations, it was quite uncertain how long the change was to last. There was reason to wonder if the old policy of propagating hatred against and encouraging subversive activity and armed plots in the Baltic states would not be resumed at a new turn of affairs in the international situation.

Soon after the visits of the economic delegations to Moscow the Soviet government took a new initiative: at the end of 1925 it opened negotiations with Poland, the Baltic states, and Finland about the conclusion of pacts of non-aggression, neutrality and conciliation. According to the Soviet press, a noble and sincere love of peace had induced the Soviet government to take this initiative, which was declared a guarantee of peace between the states bound by the proposed pacts. *Pravda* even asserted that these pacts would make armed conflicts superfluous by substituting conciliation procedure in conciliation commissions for bloody conflicts. (*Pravda*, 9.29. 1926). In reality these "guarantee pacts", as they were called in the Soviet press, offered no guarantee that the Soviet government would keep them. Instead they created convenient pretexts for raising designedly false accusations against the other contracting parties of having infringed them, and thus seemingly justified aggression against them, since no neutral organ was foreseen to decide equitably whether there were

any **reasons** for such accusations.[4] Arbitration was declared to be unacceptable to the Soviet Union since it claimed that no neutral arbiter
conceivable in a quarrel between the proletarian Soviet state and the
so-called capitalist states. Since the Soviet government thus reserved
for itself the right of interpreting the treaties at its own discretion,
even the proposed convention on conciliation was practically worthless.

Worst of all was the matter concerning neutrality. The obvious aim
of the Soviet government was to create a situation in which the states
which had signed these pacts would have lacked the right to give
succour to one another if Soviet imperialism started aggression against
one of them on some pretext or even without pretext. In other words,
the purpose of the Soviet proposal was to isolate the states which
would sign the pacts and deprive them of the right to form alliances
or unions to defend their territorial integrity and political sovereignty
which combined strength: it thus secured a convenient possibility to
devour them one by one. In this special sense the proposed pacts could
with reason be called "guarantee pacts", since they aimed at offering
a legal guarantee to Soviet imperialism that no signatories would
intervene when another was being swallowed by this imperialism, but
in sheepish passivity must await their own turns to be devoured.

One cannot help wondering what end Moscow was pursuing with
the proposals in question? It is hardly possible to imagine that there
was any prospect of their being accepted by the states to whom they
were made. Therefore it was obvious that these proposals were but
a tactical move pursuing some other end than their acceptance. What
end was it?

There could be no doubt that this move had some connection with
the sensational revision of the prospects of world revolution that had
found its expression in the article of *Pravda* quoted above. It must
have been a stunning shock to the Soviet leaders to avow that international capitalism had attained a state of stable equilibrium and
there was no revolutionary situation in the world.[5] By this admission

---

[1] It is worth mentioning that, as will be shown further on, the ultimatums presented to the three Baltic states in June 1940 by the Soviet government were based
on designedly false accusations that these states had trespassed upon the so-called
Pacts of Mutual Assistance.

[5] The qualifying adjectives and adverbs: "a certain", "relatively", "immediately ',

the whole policy of the Russian communist leaders from April, 1917 on was recognized to have been based on erroneous presumptions. It was equivalent to an avowal of bankruptcy and foreboded the inevitable breakdown of the Soviet dictatorship in a not distant future. The only reason and aim of this dictatorship had been to serve as "the base of the world revolution", as Lenin had emphasized again and again. If now Soviet leaders had to avow that "capitalism", instead of being in its last agonies, had attained a stable equilibrium and there was no revolutionary situation in the world, the breakdown of the Soviet dictatorship could be but a question of time.

As a matter of fact, as a well-informed witness who had had inside information on the frame of mind of the communist big guns, told me in 1938 when I was in Moscow as envoy of my country that the whole leading group of the Kremlin potentates, with the possible exception of a few silliest ones, had been convinced in the years 1925–1928 that the "Soviet experiment" was approaching its inevitable end. But by 1928 the hope had revived again that it might yet be possible to keep the Soviet ship afloat until the period of the "stabilization of capitalism" was over, since the leaders of the "capitalist world" had turned out to be far less clever, consistent, farsighted and energetic than the masters of the Kremlin had surmised them to be. The testimony of the witness in question as to the defeatist mood of communist leaders in those years is corroborated by a series of indirect proofs. One such proof is to be found in the fear of the leading circles of the communist party of the Soviet Union in the years in question that the "capitalist world" had made up its mind to assault the Soviet Union. This fear was reflected in numerous articles in the Soviet press as well as in scores of proclamations issued by various Soviet and Party organizations. Suffice it to advance but a few examples.

In a proclamation of the Central Committee of the Communist Party, published on June 1st, 1927, the broad masses were exhorted: "To be on guard, to look straight into the face of the danger, to be ready to strike back — such is the first duty of the workers and

---

can be overlooked since it is obvious that they were inserted only to mitigate the shock. With the same end in view it was added that "there is stabilization of a kind in our country too, we are also making headway".

peasants of our country." A proclamation in the same tenor was issued a few days later by the Central Committee of the Union of Communist Youth, and on Aug. 1st, *Pravda* wrote in its leader: "To the preparations for war under way among our enemies with the criminal fervour of devils, we must oppose our own preparation."

This fear was by no means a feint and false show made for some crafty tactical purpose. The tone of the proclamations and articles alone was a sufficient proof that it was genuine. There are, moreover, other proofs which corroborate the impression gained from the tone of these writings. Thus, e.g., in the spring of 1929 I heard from the well-known speaker of the German Reichstag, Herr Paul Löbe, on a semi-official visit to Tallinn at that time, that neither he nor any other German politician who in those years after the conclusion of the Rapallo Treaty had often had occasion to meet prominent Soviet leaders, had ever succeeded in persuading them that their fear of an imminent assault of the "capitalist world" upon the Soviet Union was but a groundless scare. There could not be any doubt, Herr Löbe said, that the Soviet dictators really unshakably believed that an aggression against the Soviet Union was eagerly being prepared.

While such a mood of *Götterdämmerung* prevailed in the Kremlin, the efforts of the states adjoining the Soviet Union to form alliances or unions of any kind must have been highly alarming to the Soviet government, especially if Poland was participating in them and, moreover, the general staffs of these states were assembling in conferences. What was this if not manifest proof of the preparation for an assault upon the Soviet Union, being carried on by order of the "international bourgeoisie"? To parry the mortal danger which in their opinion was threatening them, diplomatic manoeuvres, propaganda and other devices of every kind must be resorted to. But negative propaganda against the endeavours to form unions and alliances could hardly be successful. Incomparably better prospects of achieving success could be anticipated if some plausible alternative to the idea of a defensive alliance could be offered to the peoples of the states concerned. And a more promising manoeuvre to this end could hardly have been devised than the proposals for the "guarantee pacts". These pacts were admirably suited for the eulogies of Soviet propaganda that they made armed conflicts superfluous by substituting conciliation procedure for bloody conflicts, though they were not to put any check upon Soviet imperialism that might have interfered with the carrying out of its real schemes. The efficacy of this propaganda could, moreover, be considerably increased by combining it with puffing advertisement of the huge benefits to be derived from economic collaboration with the Soviets.

The five governments to whom the Soviet proposal for the "guarantee pacts" had been made, were from the very beginning well aware of the real aims Moscow was pursuing. However, they did not consider it appropriate to decline these proposals without further ado. In order to enlighten their citizens about the real contents and aims of the proposals and most effectively to parry the campaign of deceitful praise of them which could easily be anticipated, they proposed a number of amendments designed to turn the proposed pacts from hypocritical manoeuvres of Soviet imperialism into real instruments of peace. The most important of these amendments was the proposal to conclude the pacts jointly, "at a round table" and as a system of interdependent treaties in which all the signatories were to retain freedom of action and consequently have the right to assist the victim of aggression in the event of one signatory being assaulted by any other in violation of the treaty. Amended in this way the proposal would have ceased to be a guarantee and encouragement to the aggressor. Another amendment proposed that any disputes eventually arising as to whether a violation of the pacts in question had taken place, as well as all disputes about the interpretation of these and other pacts were to be submitted to arbitration. According to a further amendment the proposed pacts were not to interfere with obligations under the Covenant of the League of Nations. There is no need to dwell upon the rest.

Moscow rejected all these amendments. It made no secret of its negative attitude even to a union of the three Baltic states, Estonia, Latvia and Lithuania, though it was downright grotesque to think that a union of these three small states, with less than six million inhabitants, could be of any danger to the vast Soviet empire. The attempts to form a union or federation of these three states were branded in *Pravda* (6.12. 1926) as "a policy of adventure to which external guardians, England and Poland, had begun to incite them after the plans for erecting a barrier from the Baltic to the Black Sea had broken down". The Baltic states should refrain from such a policy and adopt an attitude of strict neutrality, abstaining from all attempts to set up guardian forces, since the main strength and stability of such small states lies in their absolutely neutral attitude, admonished the paper.[6]

Most important for Moscow was, as already mentioned, to preclude the establishment of closer relations and collaboration between the Baltic states and Poland. Every effort made for the attainment of this aim was denounced as an attempt to create an aggressive anti-Soviet block making for the military encirclement of the Soviet Union. "The masses of workers and peasants of our Union can never tolerate a hostile military alliance of states on our western frontier." *(Pravda,* 5.25.1926). "The Soviet Union would never recognize Polish hegemony in the Baltic area, since this would be another step in developing the bellicose schemes of Poland." *(Pravda,* 8.29. 1926). To obstruct the attempts to establish closer relations between the Baltic states and Poland the Soviet press resorted to the spreading of absurd, trumped-up reports about "Polish intrigues in the Baltic area", "secret agreements of Poland and the Baltic states" etc. In most cases these inventions were launched to the press in foreign countries or were published in the Soviet press in the guise of reports from Berlin, Paris or other foreign capitals. As a typical example of such red herrings a report "from a reliable source in Paris" may be mentioned, published in *Pravda* on June 25th, 1926, according to which Poland, in order to torpedo the negotiations on the "guarantee pacts", had proposed to Finland, Estonia and Latvia to conclude a secret agreement forming a common front against the Soviet Union, promising to assume the obligation to lend military aid to these states in the event of their being assaulted by the Soviet Union. In reality this report, devoid of any foundation, had been "made in Moscow" and launched in order

---

[6] A pathetic question addressed to the Baltic states in the same article deserves to be quoted in passing. "Have our western neighbours not yet gained an insight into our interest in the maintenance of the independence of their sovereign states". Since every citizen of the Baltic states well remembered the revolt of Dec. 1st, 1924 in Tallinn, it was not very easy for the western neighbours of the Soviet Union to be sure of the interest of the latter in the maintenance of their independence.

to torpedo the efforts to establish close collaboration of the Baltic states with Poland.

In Soviet propaganda for the "guarantee pacts" the Baltic states were persistently upbraided for trying to shirk the conclusion of these pacts. They were said to be doing so by order of England and other foreign Powers, "contrary to their own economic and political interests, which can be satisfield only by a policy of peace and friendship with the Soviet Union." (*Pravda*, 5.26. 1926). The part of the villain was always attributed to England, and "the agent of the Entente — Poland" was depicted as a myrmidon of England. "Intriguing against us in the Baltic area without cease, England incites Poland to anti-Soviet plots and holds up the conclusion of the guarantee pacts beetween the Baltic states and the Soviet Union." (*Pravda*, 7.18. 1926).

At the very time when this propaganda campaign round the guarantee pacts was at its height, the Soviet Russian political police, the nefarious OGPU, succeeded in staging a sensational incident which was eagerly exploited in Soviet propaganda for some time. The hero or rather victim of this incident was the Estonian Minister in Moscow, Mr Ado Birk, who, having been relieved of his appointment and being on his way to Estonia, disappeared under mysterious circumstances before he had managed to cross the frontier of the Soviet Union. Three weeks after his enigmatic disappearance an article was published in *Pravda* (7.14. 1926) under the heading "The Former Estonian Minister in the USSR Unmasks the Policy of Estonia", with the name of A. Birk printed under the article. Three weeks later, on August 4, another article was published in *Izvestya* and on the following day in *Pravda*, too, under the heading "Birk Unmasks the Military Preparations of Poland in the Baltic Area". Two and a half weeks later the same papers published an interview which was said to have been given by A. Birk to the press in Moscow.

However, this interview was most peculiar and suspicious in several respects. It was claimed to have been given in the presence of the representative of the Soviet Telegraph Agency *Tass* and some of the representatives of the foreign press in Moscow. One could not help being astonished that neither were the representatives of the foreign press named nor the foreign papers or agencies mentioned whose representatives they were. Not even the number of those anonymous "representatives of the foreign press" who had attended the interview was given. There could not be any doubt that this "interview" was a bluff and a clumsy forgery. This being the case one could not help wondering if Mr Birk had had anything to do with the two articles published in the Soviet press under his name.

There seemed to be so much the more reason for doubt as the contents of the articles as well as of the "interview" were identical with what Soviet propaganda had been and was harping on day by day, moreover in the same jargon; that the Estonian government, being led by the nose by foreign Powers and serving entirely alien interests, was striving to thwart the negotiations for the guarantee pacts; that Poland was striving to establish a united military front of the Baltic states against the Soviet Union by means of surreptitious machinations; that Poland would gain a dominating position in this common front and play the part of a guarantor of the Baltic states, and so on.

After the "interview" Mr Birk was not heard of again for seven months. After having caused a sensation for a few weeks he vanished quite as suddenly as the bomb of his first mysterious disappearance, of the ensuing articles in the Soviet press, and of the "interview" had exploded. It was as if the earth had engulfed him. Even his name was never again mentioned in the Soviet press.

But suddenly a new bomb exploded. On an evening in March 1927 at about 8 o'clock there was a ring at the door of the Norwegian legation in Moscow. A gentleman was asking to see the Norwegian Minister on a most important and highly urgent matter. When the Minister came, it turned out that his visitor was Mr Birk, who broke the following news to him; when in the previous summer he had been about to leave the Soviet Union, he had been stopped from passing the frontier to Finland under the pretext that his Soviet visa for leaving the territory of the Soviet Union was not quite in order; he had to go back to Leningrad where the visa would be amended; when he arrived there, however, he had been kidnapped at the railway-station and since then kept in strict custody in different places in the Soviet Union, deprived of any means of giving signs of life to anybody, the last place of his detention had been a small house in a suburb of Moscow; making use of an unexpectedly arisen opportunity, while taking his daily walk, he had succeeded in escaping from his guard, a somewhat dull Red Army lad. Leaping on a tram-car he had hastened to the nearest foreign legation in order to obtain asylum before guards could be sent to the doors of all embassies and legations to catch the fugitive. He begged the Norwegian Minister to inform the Estonian legation of all this and to offer him asylum until the Estonian authorities could take the necessary steps for conveying him to Estonia.

The Norwegian Minister granted the request and a few days later Mr Birk arrived in Estonia.

Every thoughtful person in Estonia had guessed from the very beginning, especially since the obviously trumped-up "interview", that Mr Birk had fallen victim to some fiendish intrigue and was in all probability being kept in custody in Soviet Russia. It was impossible to believe that he had suddenly turned traitor to his country and become a tool of Soviet propaganda. Since, however, the question whether he had had anything to do with the articles published under his signature in the Soviet press and the alleged interview had to be clarified by competent courts, he was taken into custody on his arrival in Estonia and brought to justice. Having been one of his counsels for the defence, I had the opportunity of acquainting myself with all the details of this unique case. From considerations of space I shall pass over in silence numerous accessory circumstances which would offer first rate material for an exciting crime-story and confine myself to reporting the most essential points. A concise summary of what came to light in the proceedings runs as follows.

For some reason or other strained relations had arisen between Mr Birk and his government. The Soviet political police, well aware of that fact, had begun to throw oil into the fire of the existing tension. Its plan had been to exploit the fact that a man of rather impetuous character, easily seized with suspicions, was then Prime Minister in Estonia. From a mysterious "underground anti-Soviet group", which for a time had been providing the Estonian Military Attaché in Moscow with "valuable" confidential reports about the secrets of the Soviet government, pieces of information began to drop which accumulating awoke serious doubts about the loyalty of Mr. Birk to his country. Fabricating these reports, and forwarding them through the bogus "underground anti-Soviet group" to the Estonian government, the OGPU naturally — and quite correctly — reckoned that they would be submitted to the Prime Minister and bring about the easily anticipated reaction. In fact the Prime Minister turned out to be as susceptible to the aspersions about the disloyalty of Mr. Birk as Othello was to the insinuations about Desdemona whispered in his ears by Iago. At the same time, on the other hand, secret reports reached Mr. Birk that hostile forces, backed by mighty foreign Powers, had managed to throw very grave suspicions upon him in high quarters regarding his loyalty to his state. The intrigue had been staged with such diabolical cunning that Mr. Birk had begun firmly to believe that he was in serious danger of being murdered. The state of his nerves was without doubt to a great extent responsible for his letting himself be frightened out of his wits.

When Mr. Birk had received the official notification of his dismissal, he had been at first somewhat irresolute as to whether to return immediately to Estonia, since the danger of being murdered had seemed to be more real there than anywhere else. He had decided to go first to Finland and to decide there what to do next. Arrived at Leningrad after having been refused passage at the frontier to Finland he had been offered a seat in a motor-car which, however, instead of conveying him to an office in that city to have his visa amended, had driven him to a place near Moscow. It turned out that he had been kidnapped, and remained in that state until the very moment in March 1927 when he had managed to escape. Most of these eight months he had been kept under a strict guard somewhere near Moscow, the last of his abodes having been in a small private house in a suburb of the city. Once, however, he had been conveyed for a few weeks to the Caucasus. The guards attached to him had had to keep a particularly sharp lookout that he might not be able to send any letters or telegrams or in any other way to give signs of life. He had had nothing to do with either the articles published under his signature in the Soviet press, or the peculiar interview. Both had been forgeries. In his last place of detainment his obsession had been the possibility of fleeing and regaining his freedom, since in this place he could hope to reach some foreign legation and find asylum there before he was captured again. Looking for opportunities to flee he had taken long walks in the neighbourhood of his place of detainment every day, accompanied by his guard, until at last, in a dusky hour one day in March a propitious occasion had suddenly presented itself which he had not failed to make use of.

The examination of the case in the court was carried out with all the care and throughness it deserved. Mr Birk was acquitted in all three instances.

All the attempts at creating a common front and some kind of alliance of the five states from Finland to Poland which had been resumed after the revolt of Dec. 1st, 1924, had come to naught in the end. More and more evidence gradually came to light that Moscow had drawn practical conclusions from the change in its assessment of the international situation and the prospects of world revolution, signalized in *Pravda* on April 26th, 1925, and changed its strategy and tactics accordingly. No new revolts or infernal machine plots like those in Tallinn and Sofia followed anywhere. The danger of such disagreeable surprises seemed if not to have disappeared definitively, at any rate to have become immaterial for a period of longer duration. The stimulus towards creating a common front for protecting their independence and territorial integrity from a common danger began therefore to relax in the states in question. On the other hand, the visits of economic delegations to Moscow and the tempting per- spectives of the beneficial results to be derived from economic collaboration with the Soviet Union which were being painted there, could not help but produce an impression. There seemed reason enough to anticipate that such collaboration would prove profitable to the states in question, since it would offer a fair chance of selling the products of their industries in the Soviet Union more easily than in the Western world.

These prospects of economic benefits were with brutal openness exploited by Soviet diplomacy in the pursuit its political ends. Thus *Pravda* wrote in its leader of June 12th, 1926 already quoted: "To put an end to the anxiety about the dangers threatening from the east we have proposed to conclude guarantee pacts; after that we are ready and willing to set about elaborating a definite plan of economic development which would be profitable to both parties; but it is necessary to give up the policy of adventure and accept as a guide the principle of strict neutrality." In other words, if the neighbouring states wanted to take advantage of the economic benefits held out by the Soviet government as the reward of economic collaboration with it, they had to refrain from forming unions and alliances. They were to stand isolated from one another.

Lithuania was the first of the Baltic states to abandon the policy of a common front. Having no actual common frontier with the USSR, Lithuania was less anxious about the danger threatening from that quarter. She strove rather for the Soviet Union's diplomatic and political support in her conflict with Poland, which fettered her attention to such a degree that all other problems seemed to be of less consequence. It was therefore small wonder that the Lithuanians felt but very mediocre interest in the creation of a Baltic union[7] and without apprehension signed — on September 28th, 1926 — the non-aggression pact. The following appreciation was given by *Pravda* on Sept. 29th, to this success of Soviet diplomacy: "This treaty frustrates the schemes of imperialists in the Baltic area and will spur other Baltic states to sign similar treaties. Those who are aiming at creating anti-Soviet blocs can no longer reckon upon Lithuania. The Lithuanian government has shown that the foolish fables about Soviet imperialism are no longer believed by the Lithuanian people".

A few weeks after the conclusion of this pact a *coup d'état,* which has already been mentioned, took place in Lithuania. It seems appropriate to say here a few words about it, so much the more as there is a certain connection between these two events.

The pact in question was concluded by a left-wing government formed after the elections held in May 1926, in which the clerical party, dominant till then, had lost its majority, though remaining still the strongest party. Lacking political experience, the new government was improvident enough to take the initiative in a series of radical anti-clerical measures which roused widespread, acute dissatisfaction in this sternly catholic country. No less dissatisfaction was aroused in nationalist-minded, patriotic circles by the proclaimed intention of the government considerably to reduce the armed forces. The non-aggression pact with the Soviet Union and the emphatic declarations about the Lithuanian—Soviet friendship made on this occasion, as well as the striking weakness of the government, encouraged

---

[7] One of the leading Lithuanian statesman, Prof. Voldemaras, declared openly in 1927 that the idea of such a union was only romanticism.

communists to presumptuous, provocative actions. By all these and a number of other blunders a tension had been created which burst in an explosion: in the night of Dec. 17th, 1926, a group of officers arrested the members of the government without meeting any resistance. A new government with the clerical party as its core was appointed by the President of the Republic. Unfortunately the leader of this new government, Prof. Voldemaras, who had had his finger in the pie of the *coup d'état*, was a man who lacked the wisdom and mental balance required of a statesman worthy of the name. Instead of restoring the lawful, democratic order, he led the Lithuanian state farther and farther into the bog of an authoritarian régime. Although Voldemaras himself was turned out by a subsequent *coup d'état* a few years later, it took about ten years before the first tentative steps towards the re-establishment of a free, democratic order were taken.

The prophecy of *Pravda* that the Lithuanian example would soon be followed by the other Baltic states, came true quite soon, though but in part. On March 9th, 1927 an agreement was reached on a Latvian—Soviet non-aggression pact, which was initialled on that date in Riga. The validity of the Estonian—Latvian treaty of defensive alliance was not cancelled by this agreement. Latvia was highly interested in the conclusion of a commercial treaty with the Soviet Union which would secure her an increased volume of exports to that country as well as of Soviet transit traffic through Latvia, and consequently fuller employment for her industry, railways and harbours. Moscow expressed willingness to grant this, but only on condition that "guarantee pacts" be concluded prior to the commercial treaty. To decline this proposal would be to miss the opportunity of the economic benefits which could be anticipated from the commercial treaty. Refusal would also have provided the communists with an effective and highly dangerous propagandist argument for attacking the government: they would have been able to accuse it of not attending to the vital interests of the country and consequently of "dancing to the tune of the western imperialists". There was therefore hardly any choice for the Latvian government. It had to give in. Moreover, the common front of the Baltic states in the question of the "guarantee pacts" had already been broken by the conclusion of the Lithuanian—Soviet non-aggression pact.

Negotiations about the commercial treaty began immediately after the initialling of the non-aggression pact and were brought to a close by the beginning of June. The treaty was signed on June 2nd, 1927.

The aim of the treaty of commerce was declared in its Art. 1 to be: "to promote the development of the reciprocal economic relations of the two countries and to ensure the most stable conditions possible for the exchange of commodities and for transit trade and also for their subsequent extension". With this alleged end in view the contracting parties established customs reductions on the minimum rates of their custom tariffs, on the assumption that Latvian exports to the Soviet Union would reach the minimum figure of fifteen million roubles or approximately forty million lats, during the first year of the validity of the treaty and the exports of the Soviet Union to Latvia considerably exceed the figure of 1925/1926 exports, viz. about seven million roubles or nearly fifteen million lats. The volume of exports of one of the parties was not to depend upon the volume of exports of the other. Moreover, it was agreed that if the amount of trade between the contracting parties should fail to reach the above-mentioned sums, negotiations would be opened with a view to the revision of the special reductions provided for in the customs convention.

This treaty was doubtless profitable to Latvia, especially in the beginning. This was, of course, quite natural and could not be otherwise. The Soviet Union had to give some economic compensation for the acceptance by Latvia of a political pact in whose conclusion the former was so much interested.

The Latvians insisted upon the conclusion of the treaty for a longer term, it being obvious that it would be almost worthless if concluded for one year or some other short term, after the expiration of which the Soviet Union would be at liberty to withdraw all the concessions made to induce Latvia to accept the non-aggression pact. The Soviet government had to give in: the treaty was concluded for a period of five years.

As to the pact of non-aggression which had been the Soviet government's main concern, being the condition requisite for the conclusion of the treaty of commerce, the outcome was rather bizarre: this pact, though initialled, remained unsigned for the whole five years of validity of the treaty of commerce which came into force in 1927.

The coming into force of the pact and consequently its signing and ratification were made dependent upon the simultaneous validity of a convention on conciliation concerning which, however, agreement was not reached. It was in the interests of Latvia to put off the signing and the ratification of the pact as long as possible, since there could be no doubt that on the very day of the pact's coming into force the Soviet Union would lose all interest not only in prolonging, but also in faithfully carrying out the treaty of commerce.

The actual effect of the treaty on Latvian–Soviet trade, as well as its after-effects, appear from the following table, in which, however, only statistics for Latvian exports to the Soviet Union are given, imports from that country to Latvia giving no occasion for observations.

Exports to the USSR (in mill. lats) and their Proportion in the Total Exports of Latvia:

Years	Total exports	Exports to the USSR	Per cent of the total
1923	162.0	6.0	3.6
1924	169.7	4.3	2.6
1925	179.6	7.5	4.2
1926	188.5	10.2	5.4
1927	221.2	3.8	1.7
1928	261.4	23.5	9.0
1929	273.9	40.1	14.6
1930	247.9	35.1	14.2
1931	163.8	33.1	20.7
1932	96.6	14.2	14.7
1933	81.6	1.2	1.5

This table fully confirms that the treaty was profitable to Latvia. Whereas the average export of Latvia to the USSR in the five years 1923–1927 had been 3.5 per cent of her total exports, it was 14 per cent or four times more in the five years of the validity of the treaty. It is also evident that increased exports to the Soviet Union considerably mitigated the damage caused to Latvian national economy by the world economic depression in the years 1930–1932, since without them the decline of export trade would have been still more serious.[8]

As to Soviet transit traffic through Latvia, it too considerably increased, though by far less than Latvian–Soviet trade. Of course, its average volume, which had been 360,000 tons in the years 1924–1927, rose to 604,900 tons in the years 1928–1932, exceeding the former figure by 68 per cent, as appears from the following table:

Soviet Transit Traffic through Latvia (in 1.000 tons):

Year:	1924	1925	1926	1927	1928	1929	1930	1931	1932	1933
Tons:	339.0	246.7	346.7	508.1	576.8	635.0	629.3	791.4	392.1	257.8

However, the coin had also its reverse side.

The intention of the agreement concerning the volume of trade had obviously been that the *minimum* fixed for the first year of the validity of the treaty was to be exceeded in the succeeding years, since this agreement, according to the Final Protocol of the Customs Conventions, was made "with a view to developing trade between the two countries *to its fullest extent*" (italics furnished), and according to Art. 1 of the treaty of commerce the contracting parties promised to strive "for the subsequent extension of the exchange of commodities". Actually however, as appears from the above table, this minimum was reached but once, in 1929, i.e. in the second year of the validity of the treaty, whereas in the first year no more than 59 per cent, and in the last three years 88, 83 and 35½ per cent respectively were reached.

Still worse was the situation with regard to the pledge that the contracting parties would endeavour to ensure the most stable conditions possible for the exchange of commodities. The actual exchange of commodities during the validity of the treaty bore witness rather to the very reserve of "the most stable conditions possible", as can be seen from the following table:

---

[8] It is easy to compute that if the treaty of commerce had not been concluded and the average exports from Latvia to the Soviet Union had remained 6.5 million lats as it had been in the years 1924—1927, the total exports of Latvia would have begun to decline already in 1929 and amounted in that year not to 273.9, but to 240.3 million lats. The decline would also have been considerably greater in the following years than it actually was.

Exports from Latvia to the Soviet Union (in 1.000 lats):

Years:	1928	1929	1930	1931	1932	1933
Kinds of goods:						
1. Hides, leather and peltry	4,815	5,577	4,718	5,581	544	620
2. Knitted articles	2,637	4,283	1,308	361	1	—
3. Cotton fabrics	108	1,288	1,040	225	236	—
4. Woollen goods	1,758	8,301	5,515	994	1,190	25
5. Yarn and cotton yarn	—	1,828	1,323	1,136	—	—
6. Agricultural machinery	1,320	1,438	663	6	39	16
7. Machines of other kinds	153	147	574	2,551	766	1
8. Superphosphate	1,129	2,187	—	—	—	—
9. Paper	1,455	3,122	1,772	276	1	—
10. Spare parts of railway-cars	87	90	2,779	1,074	244	—
11. Railway-cars	—	6,699	12,425	15,799	10,527	—
12. Bicycles	1,890	1,988	953	235	—	18
13. Other goods	791	707	58	2,663	305	176

As this table shows, only the Soviet purchases of hides, leather and peltry were more or less stable, though also but for four years, after which they suddenly dropped to less than one tenth of those of the fourth year. It is true that the sharp curtailment of Soviet imports of Latvian knitted articles, woollen goods, agricultural machinery and paper in the years 1930 and 1931 was counterbalanced to about four fifths by the increase in imports of non-agricultural machinery and railway-cars with their spare parts. It need not, however, be stressed how harmfully such capricious changes in Soviet imports from Latvia affected the economic life of that country.

The worst surprise occurred, however, when on the expiration of its validity the treaty of commerce was not prolonged. To tell the truth, there could have been little prospect of its being prolonged. It was hardly conceivable that the rather peculiar situation with a pact initialled but not signed and ratified could be extended after the expiration of the validity of the commercial treaty. What however sealed the fate of the treaty of commerce was the fact that the Soviet Union managed to conclude the non-aggression pact with Finland — on Jan. 21st, 1932. A fortnight later, on Feb. 5th, 1932, Latvia had to sign a similar pact which was to come into force simultaneously with a convention of conciliation. This convention was signed on June 18th, 1932.

Denounced by the Soviet government, the treaty of commerce went out of force in 1932, at a time when the world economic depression had reached its lowest point. Already in the same year exports to the Soviet Union decreased to 43 per cent of the preceding year, and in the following year dwindled down to almost zero, the outcome being that they were in 1933 thirteen times less than in 1932 and thirty four times less than in 1929. Many thousands of workers who had been hired for the manufacture of railway-trucks and other goods for the Soviet Union, suddenly lost their jobs, swelling still more the alarmingly expanded army of the unemployed. It was beyond dispute that this blow was deliberately dealt to Latvia in order to aggravate still more the distressed predicament created in that country as in many others by the world economic depression. It was intended as a retribution for the resistance offered by Latvia against the repeated attempts of Moscow at making her "dance to Soviet piping", if it be permitted to use an expression patterned after that slogan so often groundlessly hurled against the Baltic states by Soviet propaganda. This reluctance to comply with Soviet wishes deserved, of course, even greater punishment as, in Moscow's opinion, the treaty of commerce obliged Latvia to gratitude and submissiveness to the Soviet Union.

There is a small detail deserving of attention in the table of Soviet imports from Latvia given above: the considerable increase in these imports in 1925 and 1926, followed by their drastic curtailment in 1927. Motives for these changes are easy to guess. As a means of propaganda for the development of closer economic relations with the USSR, increased Soviet imports were obviously far more effective in any country than the most lavish promises not confirmed by concrete steps. The increase in question was consequently a very suitable complement to the wooing of Latvia "to develop closer economic relation with the USSR". On the other hand, by suddenly cutting down its imports in 1927 to one third of the amount reached in the preceding year, the Soviet Union brought heavy pressure to bear upon Latvia to constrain her to accept the Soviet proposals concerning the so-called guarantee pacts.

Estonia too was being zealously persuaded by Soviet diplomacy and propaganda that her "national economy could flourish only if there were close economic ties between her and the Soviet Union which, however, was possible only in an atmosphere of complete confidence and sincerity" (*Pravda*, 10.8. 1925). After the revolt of December 1st, 1924, it was indeed somewhat difficult for Estonia to believe in the possibility of establishing an atmosphere of complete confidence and sincerity between herself and the Soviet Union. Nor were the Estonians inclined to look upon the Soviet Union as the sole anchor of hope for the establishment of a flourishing economy in their country. Of course, Estonia was sincerely desirous of developing trade and economic collaboration with the Soviet Union, but her experiences in this field during the years since the conclusion of peace having been far from encouraging, she was inclined to be on her guard.

In the preceding chapter there was already occasion to mention how through the deceitful conduct of the Soviet government a number of Estonian businessman lost all the money they had invested in goods exported to Soviet Russia in 1921–1922. Not much better fared it with the Estonian iron-works, which in the spring of 1921 had undertaken to repair a consignment of Soviet locomotives. This deal had been brought about on the initiative of the Soviet government, who had considered the renovation of worn-out locomotives to be the first requisite step in averting a complete breakdown of railway-traffic in consequence of extreme wear and tear of their rolling-stock after long years of war and anarchy. Since it was highly important that these repairs be carried out as soon as possible, the Soviet government had seen fit to engage in this work also the Estonian iron-works who, of course, readily undertook the task. On the insistence of the Soviet negotiators a great number of very detailed technical conditions had been inserted into the contracts, many of them solely, as it turned out later on, with a view to creating more opportunities for alleging that the repairs had not been carried out in precise conformance with the contract and on this basis refusing to accept the locomotives unless reductions of the agreed remuneration were granted. Soviet officials sent to take over the repaired locomotives proved extremely pedantic and ingenious in their inspections. In most cases the Estonian iron-works had to yield to their extortionist tactics and make very considerable abatements. The deal ended with heavy losses to all the iron-works, which considered it wiser to decline any new agreements on the repair of Soviet locomotives.

Yet in the teeth of these sad experiences Estonian businessmen as well as the Estonian government were sincerely desirous to see trade relations with the Soviet Union develop, and let no opportunity pass which they deemed likely to lead to their expansion. They entertained hopes that sooner or later reason would triumph over communist doctrinarianism and the Soviet leaders would realize that the development of trade and economic collaboration was in the common interest of both parties. That it was in the interest of Estonia, was, of course, a foregone conclusion. The production capacity of the Estonian iron-works and textile industry, which by far exceeded the receptive power of the Estonian market, was well suited to the requirements of the Russian market, for whose satisfaction they had indeed been established in the last decades of Russian rule. They were therefore well equipped to render good service to Soviet Russia, especially in the early 'twenties, when she found herself faced with the task of effecting the normalisation of her economic life, thrown out of gear by war, civil strife and the communists' rash experiments. Soviet railways, e.g., were in urgent need not only of locomotives, but also cars and wagons. The lamentable state of the railway-traffic in general and of the rolling-stock in particular being one of the worst bottle-necks in the process of economic rehabiliation, it was manifestly in Soviet Russia's interest to overcome the shortage of railway-carriages and trucks as soon as possible. In this one of the three big railway-carriage works established in Tsarist times for the very purpose of supplying Russian railways with carriages and trucks, the Dvigatel Company Limited, situated in the capital of Estonia, Tallinn, would have been able to render Soviet Russian railways a good service. However, the Dvigatel Company never succeeded in obtaining orders on carriages or trucks from the Soviet Union, although the question was several times brought up for discussion by the company itself as well as by the Estonian government.

No better was the outcome of the proposal repeatedly made by the Estonian government at the request of the farmers' organisations to admit the exports of Estonian milk and other farm-produce to Leningrad. With regard to the fact that the agriculture of northern Russia was not yielding the surpluses required to feed Leningrad, and that disproportionately high costs were involved in the transportation of such surpluses from those Russian regions from which that city was obtaining its supplies, this proposal was advantageous not only to Estonia, but also to Soviet Russia, being economically reasonable and sound. It had been no mere chance that St. Petersburg, as Leningrad had been called until 1914, had long been the natural market for Estonian milk, butter, potatoes and other farm-produce. And the opening of this traditional market to Estonian agricultural exports would have been so much the more well-grounded as it was a notorious fact that Leningrad was usually so inadequately supplied with provisions that frequently even hospitals could not be supplied with milk, let alone the population at large. For all that, as already mentioned, the proposal in question came to nothing.[9]

How is so ill-advised an attitude to be explained? The answer would be that the Soviet government obviously regarded economic, businesslike considerations as less important than political considerations dictated by the basic aim and the very *raison d'être* of that government: the promotion of the communist world revolution. A characteristic fact, though of little importance in itself, is worth mentioning since it is an eloquent example of the disregard of normal commercial calculations by the Soviet government: there occurred cases of the import of salt to Estonia from the Soviet Union at prices which on examination proved to be less than the cost of its conveyance to the Estonian frontier. In view of the attitude this anomaly reflects it seems quite natural that neither were orders for railway-carriages and trucks given to the Dvigatel company, nor Estonian farm products admitted to the Soviet Union, although either deal would have been to the economic advantage of the Soviet Union.

---

[9] Only in 1933, when a catastrophic situation had arisen in the provision of towns with meat in consequence of the slaughtering and consumption of half of the stock of cattle by peasants ruthlessly driven into kolkhozes, a small amount of pork was imported by the Soviet Union from Estonia. Desperately trying to remedy the acute crisis in livestock breeding, the Soviet Union began in the following year to import cattle and pigs, and in 1937 started to import even milk for Leningrad from Estonia. These imports were, however, but a makeshift imposed on the Soviet government by the persistent crisis, manifestly incurable as long as the obnoxious, by all peasants deeply hated kolkhoz-system was being forced upon the recalcitrant peasantry.

The point is that the order for trucks and carriages would have diminished the number of unemployed in Estonia by about fifteen hundred,[10] and the opening of the Leningrad market to Estonian farm-produce would have contributed to the well-being of the Estonian rural population, in both cases rendering the toiling masses of Estonia less susceptible to the subversive propaganda of the communist fifth column. Both were therefore highly objectionable deviations from the true communist policy and consequently to be rejected irrespective of their economic merits from the Soviet point of view.

Needless to say, such an attitude of the Soviet government rendered lively and normally developing trade relations between Estonia and the Soviet Union impossible. This is borne out by the actual development of these relations as revealed in the following table, in which data on exports from Estonia to the Soviet Union are given for the same years as above for Latvia. This period, from 1923 to 1933, comprises about three years preceding the commencement of Soviet propaganda for the development of closer trade relations and economic collaboration with the Soviet Union, as well as a number of subsequent years. Here too, as in the table given for Latvia, data on imports from the Soviet Union to Estonia are omitted as irrelevant. Besides data about total exports to the USSR those for a few main categories of exported goods are given as being rather illuminating as to the character of the Estonian—Soviet trade relations.

[10] Such the number of workers of the Dvigatelworks before the war.

Exports from Estonia to USSR in 1923–1933 (in mill. Ekr.)

Year	Exports to USSR	Per cent of total export	Main categories of export goods		
			Paper	Textiles	Leather
1923	4.1	4.1	3.7	—	—
1924	4.0	5.1	4.0	—	—
1925	10.3	10.7	9.5	0.5	0.1
1926	12.4	12.9	8.0	2.2	2.2
1927	6.7	6.3	6.5	—	—
1928	5.5	4.3	5.2	—	—
1929	2.8	2.4	2.6	—	—
1930	4.3	4.5	3.5	0.2	0.4
1931	3.3	4.6	2.0	—	0.2
1932	0.9	0.4	—	—	—
1933	0.9	1.9	—	—	—

This table shows that exports to the Soviet Union played a far from important part in the Estonian national economy, at any rate a part hardly justifying *Pravda's* grandiloquent assertion that the Estonian national economy could flourish only if there were close economic ties between her and the Soviet Union: their average in the eleven years under consideration was but 4.6 per cent of Estonia's total exports. Moreover, they were capricious, fluctuating in regard to both their amount and their composition. Properly speaking paper was the only article in which the Soviet Union felt a fairly stable interest. It also consituted the lion's share of Soviet imports from Estonia, usually above ninety per cent of the total. Purchases of textiles and leather were of occasional character and, barring the year 1926, insignificant as to their volume. And even the imports of paper fluctuated greatly, rising to the peak of 9.5 mill. Ekr. in 1925, falling to two mill. in 1931 and dwindling to zero in the following year, when the total of Soviet imports from Estonia was less than 0.2 mill. Ekr.

It may be pointed out in passing that this drastic curtailment of Soviet imports, equivalent to breaking off the import trade from Estonia, had been made with the intention of bringing pressure to bear upon Estonia in connection with a law-suit in the Estonian courts. A claim for damages caused by breach of contract having been filed against the Soviet commercial representation in Estonia by an Estonian businessman who seemed to have good prospects of winning the case, the Soviet government threatened to discontinue purchases of any goods from Estonia if the Estonian courts decided that this claim fell under their jurisdiction. To render the threat more impressive and efficacious the Soviet government, without awaiting the final decision of the Estonian courts, actually discontinued all purchases in Estonia. Thus the total of Estonian export to the Soviet Union dwindled down to 188,000 Ekr. which trifle was the value of the goods exported in 1932 prior to the total stoppage. This measure actually proved precipitate since the Estonian Supreme Court decided that the claim did not fall under the jurisdiction of Estonian law. Although by this decision the reason for conflict had been removed and Estonian–Soviet trade was set on foot again, it proved still less lively than it had been before. Of course, as appears from the above table, Soviet imports from Estonia rose in 1933 to 0.9 mill. Ekr. which too was but a trifle. They continued to rise in the following years, attaining their peak, 4.7 mill. Ekr., in 1937, the average for the year 1934–1938 being 3.2 mill. Ekr., i.e. about seventy per cent of the average for the years 1923–1933.

As to the uncommonly high Soviet imports from Estonia in 1925 and 1926, they are manifestly attributable to the same political considerations as the high imports from Latvia in the same years: they were intended as a most efficacious support to the propaganda for closer trade relations and economic collaboration started by the Soviets in 1925. Not only was the paper import suddenly more than doubled, but also certain amounts of textiles and leather were accepted. However, when in 1927 it had become apparent that for all this Estonia remained reserved, refusing to agree to the "guarantee pacts", imports were curtailed in comparison with the peak attained in 1926: by 46 per cent in 1927, by 10 more in 1928 and by twenty more in 1929. The treaty of commerce concluded in 1929 on the initiative of the Estonian government, again somewhat raised the Estonian exports to the Soviet Union: from 2.8 mill. Ekr. in 1929 to 4.3 mill. in 1930. Moscow probably tried at least to some extent to fulfil the vague promise given at the negotiations on the treaty — to take steps towards expanding imports of Estonian industrial products to the Soviet Union. These imports, however, dropped again in 1931 to 3.3

mill Ekr., and in 1932 followed the almost complete discontinuation already discussed.

After all these sad experiences it was no wonder that Estonia, instead of tying her hopes to the improvement of her condition to close economic collaboration with the Soviet Union, was judicious and far-sighted enough to reorganize her national economy in accordance with the requirements of the world market. Since 1924 she had been engaged in negotiation for financial assistance, requisite for the development of her national economy, from the western world. A financial crisis arising in that year in connection with difficulties in the process of economic reconstruction had induced the Estonian government to apply to the League of Nations for advice and help. The outcome of these negotiations was a Banking and Currency Loan to Estonia, brought about under the auspices of the League of Nations in June 1927. It was issued to the amount of £ 700,000 in London and Amsterdam and $ 4,000,000 in New York. This enabled her to carry out a reform of the central bank of Estonia (Eesti Pank) in accordance with rational requirements, and effect the stabilization of her currency.

The foreign loan and the banking and currency reform having eased the process of reorganization of her national economy and its adaptation to the conditions of the world market, Estonia felt no especially urgent need to revise the attitude she had taken towards the so-called "guarantee pacts" proposed by the Soviet Union. The Soviet press ascribed this stubbornness of Estonia to the pernicious influence of Great Britain, to whose "piping" she was said to be dancing. "With the contracting of the loan from the League of Nations Estonia has turned into a half-way colony of the British capital", *Pravda* wrote on January 26th, 1927, when the grant of the loan had already been decided, though the issue had not yet taken place. British capital was said to have made large investments in Estonia's banks, railways, and industry. British influences were said to be responsible for the fact that the negotiations about the "guarantee pacts" were not making headway. On July 16 th, 1927, *Pravda* wrote in an article headed "The British Machinations in Estonia": "It is not altogether fortuitous that negotiations about the loan which have been going for two years have been brought to a close immediately after the breaking off by Great Britain of diplomatic relations with the Soviet Union". In the same article a rumour devoid of any foundation was published, according to which the adviser appointed by the League of Nations to the Bank of Estonia, a British citizen, Sir Walter Williamson, was negotiating with the Estonian government about the erection of British naval bases and fortresses on the Estonian islands Saaremaa and Hiiumaa (Ösel and Dagö). No wonder that there was a downward trend in Soviet imports from Estonia.

Since Estonia was not inclined to give in and the conclusion of the "guarantee pacts" with Estonia was no longer of particular importance to Moscow after it had succeeded in concluding a non-aggression pact with Lithuania and reached an agreement on the conclusion of a similar pact with Latvia, the negotiations with Estonia on this matter fell in abeyance and the question was dropped from the agenda for several years.

We have already pointed to the main reasons why Lithuania without long demur gave in to the overtures made and signed the pact of non-aggression proposed by Moscow. In so doing she also certainly counted upon the economic prospects held forth by Soviet propaganda to the states agreeing to sign the said pact. It was therefore quite natural that a fortnight after the conclusion of the pact an economic delegation was sent from Kaunas to Moscow, as was announced in a Tass-telegram from Kaunas, published in *Pravda* on Oct. 12th, 1926. Obviously the group was sent to seek an agreement upon extended trade with the Soviet Union as well as upon that "definite plan of economic development, profitable to both parties" which according to *Pravda* on June 12th, 1926, quoted above, was to be elaborated after the conclusion of the non-aggression pact.[11] However, they returned from Moscow empty-handed. This could already be inferred from the fact that nothing was published in the Soviet papers about the outcome of the negotiations, and finds its manifestation in the statistics for actual Lithuanian—Soviet trade. They mirror no enlivenment of that trade after the conclusion of the

[11] The Lithuanian—Soviet non-aggression pact was not coupled with an agreement about the amounts of mutual exports and imports, analogous to that which the Latvian government succeeded in obtaining about six months later — doubtless only thanks to very hard haggling, since compliance with it implied an evident departure from the stand taken by the official mouth-piece of the all-powerful governing party.

pact, as is clear from the following table of data on total exports of Lithuania and those to the Soviet Union for the years 1924–1938, i.e. for the whole period for which such data are available.[12]

Lithuanian Exports in the Years 1924–1938 (in million Litas).

Years:	1924	1925	1926	1927	1928	1929	1930	1931
Total exports	266.6	242.7	253.3	245.9	256.9	329.8	333.7	273.1
Exports to USSR	4.6	6.4	2.1	1.1	3.7	1.3	5.2	8.3
Per cent of the total	1.7	2.7	0.8	0.5	1.4	0.4	1.5	3.0

(Continuation):

Years:	1932	1933	1934	1935	1936	1937	1938
Total exports	160.2	147.	147.2	152.3	190.4	208.3	233.2
Exports to USSR	6.7	2.7	7.5	13.1	10.1	11.1	13.3
Per cent of the total	3.5	1.3	5.1	8.6	5.3	5.3	5.7

As this table shows, Lithuanian exports to the USSR, instead of expanding under the vivifying influence of the non-aggression pact concluded in September 1926, shrank in 1927 to about half as against

[12] Exports to Soviet Russia were of such diminutive value in the first years of Lithuanian independence that they were not considered worth specifying in statistical publications. Up to 1924, if there were any exports to Soviet Russia at all, they were included in the column which, under the heading "The Remaining Countries", comprised exports of minimum importance. In 1923, e.g. the exports to "the remaining countries" constituted 43.3, to Gr. Britain 26.9 and to Latvia 16 per cent of Lithuania's total exports. — As to the data for the years 1934—1938, they are added to enable the reader to judge how immaterial was the trade with the Soviet Union to Lithuania for the whole inter-war period.

1926, and to nearly one sixth as against 1925. They rose of course somewhat in 1928, though not to the level of 1924 and 1925, but in 1929 dropped again to nearly the nadir of the year 1927, and remained negligible until 1933. If they rose to a somewhat higher level in 1934 and maintained it until 1938, this was by no means an outcome of the pact of non-aggression or of any definite plan of economic development elaborated in order to promote the interests of both parties, as we shall presently see.

The table adduced also corroborates the remark made in passing in the preceding chapter, that the trade of Lithuania with Soviet Russia was insignificant throughout the entire interwar period. This appears still more clearly from a comparison of Lithuanian exports to Soviet Russia with those of Estonia and Latvia, the figures being placed in juxtaposition in the following table:

The Percentage of Exports to Soviet Russia in the Total Exports of the Baltic states

Years	1923	1924	1925	1926	1927	1928	1929	1930	1931	1932	1933
Estonia	4.1	5.1	10.7	12.9	6.3	4.3	2.4	4.3	4.6	0.4	1.9
Latvia	3.6	2.6	4.2	5.4	1.7	9.0	14.6	14.2	20.7	14.7	4.2
Lithuania	—	3.1	2.7	0.8	0.5	1.4	0.4	1.5	3.0	3.5	1.3

Owing to the insignificance of the volume of Lithuanian exports to Soviet Russia it was not of particular importance whether they were stable or unstable. Still it is worth observing that, as the above table shows, they fluctuated no less capriciously than exports from Estonia and Latvia. No better was it with regard to the assortment of the exported articles. In this respect too, trade was anything but consistent, as may be seen from the following table:

Total Exports to the USSR and the Main Exported Articles
(in million Litas).

Years:	1924	1925	1926	1927	1928	1929	1930	1931	1932
Total exports	4.6	6.4	2.1	1.1	3.7	1.3	5.2	8.3	6.7
Hides and leather-ware	4.3	6.3	1.0	—	2.3	—	—	2.5	0.4
Live stock	—	—	—	0.3	0.1	—	1.2	2.7	—
Pork and lard	—	—	—	—	—	—	—	—	6.1
Hardware	—	—	—	0.4	1.1	0.5	0.9	—	—
Spare parts of agric.machines	—	—	0.7	—	—	—	—	—	—
Linseed	—	—	—	0.3	—	—	—	—	—
Super-phosphate	—	—	—	—	—	—	2.1	1.7	—
Woollen goods	—	—	—	—	—	0.5	—	—	—

(Continuation)

Years:	1933	1934	1935	1936	1937	1938
Total exports	2.7	7.5	13.1	10.1	11.1	13.3
Hides and leather-ware	1.1	1.9	0.9	—	1.1	1.4
Live stock	—	2.8	6.7	7.5	8.6	11.0
Pork and lard	0.7	2.5	2.2	—	—	—
Hardware	—	—	—	—	—	—
Spare parts of agric.machines	—	—	—	—	—	—
Linseed	—	0.03	2.4	1.9	—	—
Superphosphate	—	—	—	—	—	—
Woollen goods	—	—	—	—	—	—

This table reveals that in her imports from Lithuania the Soviet Union paid not the slightest regard to that country's need for even and stable development in her exports. All Soviet purchases in Lithuania fluctuated capriciously from year to year and now and then completely ceased, while some of them, as e.g. the imports of iron screws, castings and other hardware, effectuated for four consecutive years, give the impression of being the result of some whim, for the trifling amounts in question could easily be purchased anywhere else. It may be that the real object here was to provide the communist fifth column with a seemingly plausible subject for eulogizing the Soviet Union as a compassionate benefactor of the Lithuanian industrial proletariat, and thereby to render its subversive propaganda more efficacious.

If the imports of hides and leather-ware on the one hand and of livestock on the other were more stable, and the latter even considerably increasing in volume from 1934 on, this depended on the permanent agrarian crisis in general and the crisis of livestock breeding in particular in Soviet Russia, against which crisis all measures have proved ineffective; certainly no efficacious remedy ever will be found as long as the kolkhoz-system is obstinately maintained. It is significant indeed that this crisis began to grow more and more acute from 1931 on, i.e. from the very year when the forcing of peasants into kolkhozes was instituted with apalling ruthlessness. The effects of this crisis appear with particular clarity in the statistics for agricultural export from the Baltic states to the Soviet Union if the data of all three countries are combined. Since for this purpose the data must be computed in one and the same currency, we have chosen the Latvian Lat for that purpose, and as to the rate of exchange, we have taken 72 Ekr. and 192 Litas as equal to 100 Lats, barring the years 1937 and 1938, when the average rate of exchange of Litas to Lat was 113$^1/_2$ to 100.[13] The usual slight fluctuations in the rate of exchange have of course been overlooked. With regard to the fact that their raw-material is one of the important agricultural products, we have included leather-ware among agricultural produce, though sole-leather, which has constituted a considerable part of the exports of these wares, is a manufactured article.[14] Besides this the agricultural produce in the table below includes livestock — cattle,

[13] V. *The Economic Reconstruction of Lithuania After 1918* by A. Simutis, Columbia Univ. Press, N.Y. 1942, p. 1932, Appendix F: Exhange Quotations in Kaunas.

[14] For the rest it is worth adding that even if one excludes all leather-ware from this table, this would neither invalidate, nor essentially change the conclusions drawn from it below.

horses, pigs, cows-, pork, lard, meat, milk, butter, linseed and clover-seed.

The table runs as follows:

The Exports of Agricultural Produce from the Baltic states to the Soviet Union (in million Lats).

Years	Estonia	Latvia	Lithuania	Sum-total
1924	—	0.6	2.2	2.8
1925	0.1	2.4	3.3	5.8
1926	2.2	2.9	0.5	5.6
1927	—	1.6	0.3	1.9
1928	—	7.1	1.2	8.3
1929	—	8.0	—	8.0
1930	—	5.1	0.6	5.7
1931	—	5.6	2.7	8.3
1932	0.1	0.5	3.4	4.0
1933	1.1	0.6	1.3	3.0
1934	2.1	1.4	5.0	8.5
1935	3.0	2.2	5.1	10.3
1936	4.1	4.0	3.9	12.0
1937	5.0	6.4	8.3	19.7
1938	6.1	5.4	10.7	22.2

The table reveals that the curve of agricultural imports into the Soviet Union rose from 1931 on. The seeming exception in the years 1932 and 1933 is actually one of those which but prove the rule. It is well known that a wholesale slaughter of livestock was the spontaneous reaction of the peasants to the forcible drive into kolkhozes. As Stalin revealed at the 17th Congress of the Communist Party in January 1934, the stock of horses had decreased from 1929 to 1933 from 34 mill. head to 16.6 mill., that of cattle from 68.1 mill. to 38.6 mill., that of pigs from 20.9 mill. to 12.2 mill., that of sheep and goats from 147.2 mill. to 50.6 mill. Rather than hand over their cows, horses, pigs, sheep, etc., without any compensation to the hateful kolkhozes, the peasants preferred to slaughter and consume them. No wonder that imports of leather-ware, which had oscillated between 5.3 and 7.1 mill. Lats in the years 1928—1931, dropped to 0.7

mill. in 1932. After the slaughter of half of the stock of domestic animals, there were more than enough hides in the country for the manufacture of requisite leather-ware, as well as enough meat to eat. It would also have been sheer madness to import livestock from abroad in those years, i.e. to squander foreign exchange on such imports at the same time as the slaughter of the country's own livestock was being carried out on an unprecedented scale. Moreover, extreme economy with foreign exchange was then required in order to cover purchases from abroad of the equipment needed for the overhasty industrialization decreed by Stalin.

The conclusion of the Kellogg or Paris Pact for the Renunciation of War gave occasion for a new diplomatic move to the Soviet government. Since this pact was to come into force when all its fifteen signatories had ratified it, the Soviet Union proposed to Poland, Rumania, Lithuania, Latvia, and Estonia that it should come into force between these states and the Soviet Union as soon as they had ratified it, without awaiting its ratification by all its signatories. This proposal was accepted and the so-called Litvinov Protocol was signed in Moscow on February 9th, 1929 by all the enumerated states save Lithuania, who signed it on April 1st, 1929, in order to avoid doing this together with Poland. Soon thereafter Turkey, Persia, and the Free City of Danzig, too, adhered to the Protocol.

The proposal to put the Kellogg Pact into force was a most convenient occasion to parade the love of peace of the Soviet government. Since this pact was but a platonic profession of high principles, making no provision for adequate means of guaranteeing their actual observance by its signatories, it was scarcely of real value. At any rate it did not put any brake upon Soviet imperialism that could interfere with its schemes.

In 1932, about three years after the signing of the Litvinov Protocol, the Treaties of Non-Aggression, about which so much ado had been made by Soviet diplomacy in the years 1926 and 1927, were at last concluded between the Soviet Union and Finland, Estonia, and Latvia. The Soviet—Finnish Non-Aggression Treaty was signed on January 21st, the Latvian—Soviet Treaty on February 5th, the Estonian—Soviet Treaty on May 4th, 1932. These treaties were to come into force simultaneously with Conventions on Conciliation which the parties undertook to conclude within the shortest possible time. These conventions, which were to form an integral part of the Non-Aggression Treaties, were concluded with Finland on April 22nd, with Estonia on June 16th, and with Latvia on June 18th, 1932.

By the treaties in question the contracting parties guaranteed the inviolability of the frontiers existing between them as defined by the Peace Treaties, undertook to refrain from any act of aggression or any violent measures directed against the integrity and inviolability of the territory or the political independence of the other contracting party, whether such acts were undertaken separately or in conjunction with other Powers, with or without a declaration of war. Concluded for a period of three years, all three treaties contained the usual clause about their automatic prolongation unless notice of termination was given six months before the expiration of the period of validity. Moreover, they could be terminated at any time in the event of an act of aggression by the other Contracting Party against any third Power. (The Lithuanian—Soviet treaty of Sept. 28th, 1926, did not contain this latter clause.)

A new occasion for a diplomatic move in the same direction as the Litvinov Protocol and the Non-Aggression Treaties was offered to the Soviet government by the Conference on Disarmament, in which Moscow had decided to take part, though obviously only in order to exploit her participation for propagandist ends: to denounce the capitalist states as the hotbed from which the danger of military conflicts must spring with the necessity of a law of nature, and to vaunt herself upon her own ardent love of peace. Pursuing such propagandist ends, the Soviet delegation made obviously impracticable and unfeasible proposals such as the one made in Nov. 1927 at the meeting of the Preparatory Committee of the Disarmament Conference: to prohibit all kinds of armament at a stroke.

After Hitler's accession to power, however, Moscow became aware of the danger threatening from that quarter and began to resort to more ingenious and subtle manoeuvres. The Soviet dictators were especially alarmed at the design begot and propagated by Mussolini, to create a directorate of four Great Powers, Great Britain, France,

Italy, and Germany.[15] No stretch of imagination was needed to realize that if such a directorate had been practicable, it would have been anything but friendly to the Soviet Union. No wonder that Soviet diplomacy began to devise schemes to counter the efforts to bring about such a bloc. With this end in view, Litvinov hastened to make use of a draft declaration proposed by the Soviet delegation to the Disarmament Conference and adopted by its Security Committee introducing slight amendments, of course. This draft was a declaration in which "to obviate any pretext whereby aggression may be justified", a definition of aggression, "as specific as possible", was given. While attending the World Economic Conference which opened in London in June 1933, Litvinov proposed to the states who had signed the Litvinov Protocol to enforce the draft of the Security Committee among themselves without waiting for its acceptance by the Conference on Disarmament. The proposal was accepted and two multilateral Conventions for the Definition of Aggression, as well as a bilateral one, were signed in London on July 3rd, 4th, and 5th, 1933 by the Soviet Union and all the states adjoining to it save Finland, who adhered a few weeks later, on July 23rd, viz. Estonia, Latvia, Lithuania, Poland, Turkey, Persia, Afghanistan, and, moreover, Czechoslovakia and Yugoslavia.

The conventions in question were amply praised by Soviet propaganda as a most important and valuable contribution to the cause of peace, brought about on the initiative of the Soviet government. "Bourgeois states are disinclined to say plainly which party is to be considered the aggressor; therefore Soviet diplomacy had to set to and solved the problem with honour", declared Molotov at the seventh Soviet congress on Jan. 28th, 1935. The propagandist effect of this diplomatic move was, however, of but secondary importance. The main aim it pursued was "to create a counterpoise to the pact of four Powers, as the *History of Diplomacy*" puts it (vol. 3, p. 475), i.e. to demonstrate against the design to bring about a directorate of the four

[15] A draft of the Four Power Pact elaborated by Mussolini was discussed by him, MacDonald, and Lord Simon on the visit of the two latter gentlemen to Rome in March 1933, and the Pact, called "Agreement on Understanding and Co-operation", was initialled on June 7th and formally signed on July 15th, 1933. However, it was never ratified and soon came to nothing.

Great Powers. With this end in view Moscow took the initiative in a common action of the Powers who had been set aside by the signatories of the Four Powers' Pact.

It must be pointed out that all the acts of aggression and violent measures committed by the Soviet Union against the adjoining states after the outbreak of the Second World War were in flagrant violation of the Conventions on the Definition of Aggression concluded on the initiative of the Soviet government in July 1933, as well as of a number of other valid treaties.

X

BETWEEN THE DEVIL AND THE DEEP BLUE SEA

How uneasy Soviet leaders were feeling about the danger threatening the Soviet Union from Nazi Germany, was indicated by the lively activity displayed by Soviet diplomacy in seeking counter-measures and still more manifestly by radical changes in their foreign policy which would have been quite inconceivable a few years before. Thus the Soviet Union joined the League of Nations, hitherto heaped with abuse as "a conspiracy formed by imperialist robbers to strangle the life out of the first socialist republic of workers and peasants". It concluded pacts of mutual assistance with France and Czechoslovakia, and French communists were ordered to form a "popular front" with the socialists and radical-socialists, who had always been branded as the most odious traitors and fiendish enemies of the working classes, to be fought to the death.

A sensational change also took place in Moscow's attitude to the Baltic states. Until then the Soviet government had been so intolerant of every kind of collaboration among these states as to refuse to draw up agreements with them jointly, admitting of separate negotiations only, even if the agreements were identical as to their contents. Now, however, the Convention on the Definition of Aggression was concluded in the shape of multilateral agreements, one of which was signed jointly by not only Estonia and Latvia, but also Poland and Rumania. Nine months later, when the non-aggression treaties with the Baltic states — on the initiative of the Soviet government — were extended until December 31, 1935, the Protocols over this act were signed simultaneously by the envoys of the three states in the Commissariat for Foreign Affairs in Moscow on April 4th, 1934. In his speech delivered at this ceremony, M. Litvinov emphasized the deep interest of the Soviet Union in the preservation of the independence of the Baltic states, and declared most decidedly that the Soviet Union had never demanded any revision of the existing treaties and would never do so, since the Soviet state "perceives its State duties to lie not in conquest, not in expansion of territory".

To erect a bulwark against the danger threatening from Nazi Germany, Moscow took the initiative in one further diplomatic action for the protection of the Baltic states. In his *Mein Kampf* Hitler had written: "If we speak of new soil for German *Lebensraum,* we cannot but think first of Russia and her subject border states". Though the expression "border states subject to Russia" was rather ambiguous, it was generally interpreted as referring to the Baltic states. The subjugation and annexation of these states to enlarge Germany's "living space" would have been only the first step in a crusade against the Soviet Union. Such a crusade, however, was fraught with mortal danger to Poland, too. Under this common threat these two states, whose relations had been rather unfriendly till then, now came together for common diplomatic action. At the beginning of January, 1934 Moscow and Warsaw jointly applied to Estonia and Latvia, as well as to Finland, offering them their common guarantee of their independence and integrity. The initiative in this action had been taken by Moscow.

It goes without saying that a guarantee given to the two small Baltic states by these two far mightier neighbours of theirs was, considered *in abstracto,* an excellent thing, to be welcomed with enthusiasm by these states. With regard to the concrete circumstances of the case, however, the guarantees offered, instead of strengthening their security, would rather have rendered it still more precarious, since, being obviously directed against Germany, they would have increased the hostility of the Nazi German government to them and in the event of war would more certainly have drawn the thunderbolt of the onslaught upon them. Estonia and Latvia therefore considered it wiser to decline the offer.

Soon after this move miscarried, Poland made a sharp turn in its foreign policy, concluding a non-aggression pact with Germany for ten years (Jan. 26th, 1934). Thereafter Poland was quite out of the question as one of the guarantors of the independence and integrity of the Baltic states, save in the case of a guarantee in which Germany, too, was one of the signatories. Drawing an inference from the new situation, Litvinov made a tactical move, proposing to Germany in March 1934 to join the Soviet Union and Poland as a third guarantor of the Baltic states. As had been easy to anticipate, Germany declined this proposal. After this Litvinov succeeded in interesting the French Foreign Minister Louis Barthou in his scheme. As an outcome of Litvinov's deliberations with Barthou the French Foreign Office drew up the draft of an Eastern Pact (nicknamed the Eastern Locarno Pact), according to which the Soviet Union, Germany, Poland, Czechoslovakia, Finland, and the Baltic states were to assume the obligation to refrain from supporting acts of aggression by any signatory against one of their number and to consult and concertedly take measures in support of any signatory who might be the victim of such acts. Moreover, the Eastern Pact was to be organically linked to the Locarno Pact, France acceding to it as an additional guarantor and the Soviet Union acceding to the Locarno Pact in the same capacity.

Barthou's plan met with the approval of the British government, on the condition, however, that Germany should adhere to it. The attitude of Italy was on the whole similar to that of Great Britain. Moreover, both of these Powers expressed their willingness to make far-reaching concessions to Germany in the question of the equality of rights in armaments, vociferously claimed by Hitler, as it was obvious that without such concessions the adherence of Germany to the Pact was quite out of the question. All the same Germany refused to adhere to the Pact and Poland followed her example.

For a while the question of the Eastern Pact was dropped, especially as Barthou, who had been the most active promoter of this scheme, was murdered in Oct. 1934. It re-emerged, however, in the spring of 1935, within the compass of the negotiations between Great Britain, France, Italy, and Germany. At the end of March that year Germany expressed her willingness to participate in a multilateral agreement of the states interested in East-European questions, based on the principles of non-aggression, neutrality, arbitration, and conciliation and containing provisions for the summoning of a conference of the contracting parties, at the request of any signatory considering himself threatened with aggression, in order to deliberate on the situation and if necessary on the steps to be taken for the maintenance of peace.

However, only a few days before, on March 16th, Hitler had uni-laterally denounced the armaments clauses of the Versailles Treaty and proclaimed compulsory military service in Germany. The Coun-cil of the League of Nations contented itself with a paper protest against this breach of the said treaty, which actually constituted nothing less than the overthrow of the European order as established by the Versailles Treaties. France and the Soviet Union, feeling their security equally endangered, concluded a pact of mutual assistance (on May 2nd, 1935). Subsequently Germany declared that she would thenceforward consent only to bi-lateral pacts of non-aggression and refuse to be a part of any multilateral non-aggression, arbitration and conciliation treaties. Since the Baltic states continued to stick to their conviction that a multilateral pact guaranteeing their independ-ence and integrity, to which Germany was not a part, would be rather dangerous for their security, the question of an Eastern Locarno Pact was finally dropped.

After Germany had begun her feverish rearmament programme in defiance of the Treaty of Versailles, it would have been lunacy to shut one's eyes to the fact that the danger of a second world war was growing increasingly more real and threatening. As to the three Baltic states, they had to reckon with two facts: on the one hand, that there was no prospect of an Eastern Pact being brought about which would guarantee their independence and integrity, and on the other, that though it would have been an exaggeration to say that Poland had thrown in her lot altogether with Germany, at any rate she had to a considerable degree co-ordinated her foreign policy with that of the Third Reich. Under such circumstances there remained no other choice for the Baltic states, with respect to their foreign policy, than to join closely together and try to keep aloof from the antagonism and conflicts of the Great Powers.

Lithuania, who, as already mentioned, had up to this point given a cold shoulder to the idea of a Baltic Union, now changed her attitude. In the spring of 1934, the Lithuanian government announced to the Estonian and the Latvian governments that Lithuania was of a mind to join a defensive Baltic Union formed of the three states. The conclusion of the Polish—German non-aggression pact was with-out doubt the main goad that had brought about this change. The rapprochement of Poland and Germany could not but arouse anxiety in Lithuania, who had unsettled territorial quarrels with both these mighty neighbours of hers: with Poland about Vilnius and with Germany about Klaipeda (Memel).[1] As long as Poland and Germany had been unfriendly to one another, Lithuania did not need to be particularly anxious about the territorial quarrels with these two states, since there was hardly any reason for apprehending their co-ordinated pressure being brought to bear upon her. Such an eventuality could not, however, be disregarded after the improvement of Polish–German relations, and it was most natural that Lithuania should begin to feel uneasy.

Estonia and Latvia were glad to enlarge their union by admitting Lithuania to it. A Treaty of Good Understanding and Co-operation was signed in Geneva on Sept. 12th, 1934, for a period of ten years. The contracting parties pledged to confer together on questions of foreign policy which were of common concern, and to afford one another mutual political and diplomatic assistance in their international relations. The questions of common concern were dealt with in Art. 3 of the Treaty, which "recognized the existence of specific problems which might make a concerted attitude with regard to them difficult". The Treaty provided for regular meetings of the Foreign Ministers of the three states which were to be held at least twice a year.

Under the prevailing circumstances it was most natural for the Baltic states to do everything they could to establish good neighbourly

---

[1] The dispute about Vilnius has already been mentioned. As to the conflict over Klaipeda, the following short remarks may suffice to give an idea of it. The German town Memel, situated at the estuary of the Nemunas (Niemen) with a strip of land along the river and the coast of the Baltic Sea and a population of about 140,000, was transferred under the sovereignty of Lithuania by a convention concluded with that state by the Allied Powers in 1924. According to the convention the Memel territory was to be an autonomous unit with a democratically elected legislative assembly, the Diet, and an executive branch, the Directorate, under the supervision of a Governor appointed by the Lithuanian government. Since the great majority of the population consisted of Germans and germanized Lithuanians, who were anti-Lithuanian in sympathy, the Diet and the Directorate were almost permanently in confict with the Governor. Germany, who had never acquiesced in the loss of Memel, made frequent complaints to the Council of the League of Nations over pretended violations of the Statute of the Memel territory. German–Lithuanian relations deteriorated after Hitler's accession to power.

relations with the Soviet Union. This was even more natural as Hitler's above-mentioned utterance about the "border states subject to Russia" had not escaped notice there. The anxiety caused by this reference was borne out when a new species of fifth column began to sprout in the Baltic states soon after the accession of Herr Hitler to power: fifth columns which were drawing encouragement and ardour as well as getting financial and other types of support from the German nazi party. In Lithuania, where the formation of such fifth columns was hardly possible, the German national minority being numerically too insignificant, other means were used for subversive activity. There occurred cases of tracts printed in Germany and inciting the peasants to refuse to pay taxes, being smuggled into the country and distributed. Considerably more fertile ground for the formation of nazi-minded fifth columns was to be found in Latvia and Estonia, where there was a rather numerous German minority, in whose ranks, moreover, there were many who had not yet managed to reconcile themselves to the fact that the Baltic Germans no longer constituted a socially and politically ruling class in these recently created national republics. Organizations sympathizing with the German nazi party and spreading its ideology began to shoot up among the Baltic—German youth. This was clearly preparatory work for the imminent incorporation of the Baltic states into Hitler's "thousand year Reich". Among such organizations carrying on subversive activity in the nazi spirit was one called the Baltic Brotherhood, active in both Latvia and Estonia. It was obvious enough that these Brotherhoods were in reality only branches of one and the same organization, controlled by the office of Herr Göbbels in Berlin. The Latvian and the Estonian authorities had to intervene and dissolve them. There were other signs, too, of the preparatory work being carried on for the intended incorporation of the Baltic states in Hitler's Greater Germany, e.g., articles in the nationalist German press in which ill will and animosity against these states were systematically being fanned.

However weighty were the grounds for distrust of Moscow's unalterable schemes concerning the Baltic states, there seemed no doubt that it could not acquiesce in their being swallowed up by nazi Germany, let alone side with Berlin in such an action. The incorporation of these states into the Greater Germany would have been, as already pointed out, but a prelude to aggression against the Soviet Union itself. Therefore the Soviet Union was actually a counterpoise to the danger menacing the Baltic states from Nazi Germany, and there seemed to be sufficient reason for counting upon political and diplomatic support for them from that quarter against the danger in question. It was therefore a most natural course for the Baltic states to apply all means at their disposal toward the establishment of as good relations with the Soviet Union as possible.

With this end in view they continued their endeavours to expand their commercial relations with the Soviet, albeit with no greater success than before. With the same end in view a courtesy visit was paid to Moscow by the Chiefs-of-Staff of the three states in the spring of 1936. It took rather a long time before this visit was returned by Marshal Yegorov — in February 1937. However, this was not to be wondered at considering the sensational events of that year, one of the most critical years in the whole development of the Soviet dictatorship. By this year Stalin had gone so far as to start a wholesale slaughter of Lenin's and his own old brothers in arms. The signal for this was given by a show trial in August, 1936, in which one of Lenin's intimates, the first president of the Communist International, G. Zinoviev, was sentenced to death and executed, along with fifteen other old militants. This trial opened the great purge, which swept over Russia like a tornado, exacting millions of victims either shot in the cellars of the GPU or sent to slave labour camps or "polit-isolators". It was hardly the time for the Marshals of the Red Army to raise the question of a return visit to the Baltic states in the prevailing nervous, terror-smitten atmosphere.

Such a proposal was so much the less opportune as the tension in home politics was occasionally reflected even in the utterances of Soviet leaders on foreign policy, which were of a nature to persuade every Soviet citizen to keep aloof from this slippery ground. Such an utterance was made concerning the Baltic states by one of the Soviet big guns and Stalin's nearest lieutenants, the newly appointed secretary general of the Communist Party, Zhdanov, in his address to the All-Union Congress of the Soviets in Moscow, on Nov. 28th, 1936.[2] His

---

[2] He delivered an address in the same tenor a few days earlier, on Nov. 21st, to the fifth congress of the Soviets of the Leningrad oblast (district) held in Leningrad.

words were reproduced in *Pravda* in a considerably mitigated form, but the world press had taken notice of what he had actually said. According to the Daily Telegraph (Nov. 30th, 1936) his utterance had run as follows: "We wish to live in peace with the Baltic countries, but if these tiny peoples allow big adventurers to use their territories for big adventures, we shall widen our little window onto Europe with the help of the Red Army". This was a highly disagreeable reminder to the Baltic states that the danger threatening from the east was not less than that which threatened them from Hitler's Germany.

This brutal threat was so much the more disquieting as it was quite out of the question that the Baltic states might ever be willing to allow anybody to use their territories for "big adventures". Their heartiest wish and unshakable determination was to keep aloof from any adventures, big or small, and above all from the antagonisms and conflicts of the Great Powers, in order to continue with the creative work in all those spheres of intellectual and material culture in which they had achieved such highly gratifying successes in the few years of their national freedom. The threat flung out by Zhdanov being obviously devoid of any foundation and consequently based on a wilfully — and very clumsily — trumped-up pretext, was but proof that the most disagreeable surprises of any kind might be looked for from that quarter.

The diplomatic representatives of the Soviet Union in the Baltic states sought to dispel the bad impression created by Zhdanov's speech. They assured everyone that the Soviet Union not only had no aggressive intentions against the Baltic states, but quite on the contrary, was the only Power both sincerely willing and able to protect their independence and territorial integrity. What the governments of the Baltic states were thinking as they listened to such reassuring declarations, might best be expressed in the words of Dr. Faust: *Die Botschaft hör' ich wohl, allein mir fehlt der Glaube* (I hear the message indeed, but I lack the faith).

The international situation was in the meantime growing daily worse. The attack of Fascist Italy on Abyssinia showed that there was no reason for entertaining hopes that the League of Nations would be able to prevent military conflicts or to settle them in conformity with the principles and ends proclaimed in its Covenant.

Nazi Germany was feverishly arming, manifestly preparing for an aggressive war to attain the end openly proclaimed by Hitler — the expansion of the German *Lebensraum.* However, the western Powers took no steps to put a stop to this while they were still able to do so. Mussolini was rattling his sword and delivering ranting speeches in which he launched threats against France and boastfully promised to turn the Mediterranean into an Italian *mare nostrum.* It seemed as if the nazi and fascist propagandists were right in their daily proclamations that the democratic Powers, being affected with decrepitude and having lost energy and vigour, were destined to give way to the "young", vigorous Germans and Italians, upon whom, moreover, the totalitarian form of government with its concentration of power had bestowed invincible strength. The world seemed as if by the decision of an inexorable fate to be drifting towards the cataclysm of a horrible great war deliberately sought by Hitler, and no effective measures were taken toward stopping this disastrous development.

The governments and the public at large in the three Baltic states were well aware of the gravity of the situation. It goes without saying that they felt no sympathy for either Hitler or Mussolini. However, in the predicament which had come about, the only reasonable course they could adopt was to take a strictly neutral attitude towards the tensions between the Great Powers, which were growing ever sharper. There is hardly any need to adduce reasons for this attitude of theirs, since any other attitude was hardly conceivable in view of their too insignificant military strength. Their siding with one or the other of the antagonistic groups of the Great Powers could even become a pretext for the aggressive states to set the avalanche in motion, and thus serve as the spark detonating the explosion in an atmosphere filled with inflammable gases. The Baltic states therefore followed undeviatingly the course of strictest neutrality and correctness towards both the Soviet Union and Nazi Germany. Such was also the directive given to me when, at the end of 1937, I was appointed Estonian Minister to Moscow. I observed this directive so much the more strictly as it was in full harmony with my own deepest convictions.

A vexatious incident which had taken place on the Estonian—Soviet frontier in January 1938 and was the first matter I had to settle with the Soviet government when I arrived in Moscow in the first days of February 1938, deserves to be reported, since it sheds light on the strange mentality and modes of action of the Soviet dictators.

The Estonian—Soviet frontier crosses lake Peipus from north to south, cutting it into two halves of about equal size. In order to prevent fishermen and other persons sailing on the lake from passing the frontier-line unawares, this was marked every year before the beginning of navigation by spar buoys, removed again when navigation closed. But fishing was being carried on also in winter, through the ice, and no agreement had been reached with the Soviets about the marking of the frontier on the ice in the winter. To prevent Estonian fishermen from unknowingly and undesignedly passing the frontier, which would usually lead to their being arrested by Soviet frontier-guards and kept in Soviet prisons for a longer or shorter time, the Estonian authorities began to set up boundary-marks on the ice in winter. To obviate eventual frontier incidents as far as possible, the boundary-marks were set up about 550 yards from the actual frontier towards the Estonian shore and fishermen were urgently recommended not to pass the line of those boundary-marks. All the same there occurred cases of Estonian fishermen being dragged away by Soviet frontier-guards, who with this end in view penetrated into Estonian territory, passing the line of boundary-marks set up by the Estonian authorities. The motives for such misdeeds were well known: Soviet frontier-guards were paid premiums for every foreign citizen apprehended on a charge of having passed the Soviet frontier without the required visa. Moreover, such arrests were in all likelihood considered a proof of zeal and rewarded by advancement in rank. Protests made by the Estonian authorities were of no effect, since the reply invariably ran that the arrest had taken place on Soviet territory, and there was no arbiter to decide if this allegation was right or not, since the Soviet government refused to admit any arbitration between the Soviet Union and the non-communist states.

In order to put an end to such annoyances the Estonian frontier-guards were ordered, on the request of fishermen, to make their rounds among the groups of fishing Estonians. One morning in January 1938 two Soviet frontier-guards drove in a sleigh to a group of Estonian fishermen who were fishing some hundred yards to the Estonian side of the boundary-marks. The Soviet frontier-guards had obviously not noticed the presence of an Estonian frontier-guard among the fishermen until they were ordered to stop to be identified. Instead of obeying this order the Soviet frontier-guards turned around, trying to escape and thus gave incontovertible proof that they were fully aware of having unlawfully penetrated into the territory of Estonia. The Estonian guard fired a warning shot in the air and as the sleigh even then did not stop, shot dead the horse. Thereupon the Soviet guards, throwing themselves down upon the ice and taking protection behind the sleigh and the horse, fired off several shots at the Estonians who, returning the fire in self-defence, killed both Soviet frontier-guards.

At the demand of the Estonian authorities the mixed commission for settling frontier incidents, provided for by an agreement concluded in 1927, was convoked. Since the ice was covered with a soft layer of new-fallen snow on which all traces were clearly distinguishable, it proved possible to fix them in all details in the protocol of the mixed commission. The traces showed that the sleigh had come from the Soviet side, crossed the line of boundary-marks set up by the Estonian authorities, penetrating consequently about seven hundred yards into Estonian territory, made for the group of Estonian fishermen, then turned around and driven about sixty yards back in the direction of the frontier, until the horse had fallen down dead. Seven or eight empty cases of the type of cartridge used in the Soviet Red Army, found in the snow around the corpses of the Soviet frontier-guards, as well as the rifles with barrels freshly begrimed with soot in their rigid hands, were so much indisputable evidence that these frontier-guards had been shooting at the Estonian frontier-guard.

The Estonian representative in the mixed commission had taken due care to fix these essential facts in the protocol drawn up by the commission and the riders attached to it, which were signed by the representatives of both parties.

For all that, a protest demanding the punishment of those guilty of having killed the two Soviet frontier-guards and damages for their families was lodged by the Soviet government with the Estonian government a few days before I left for Moscow to enter into office. My first commission in Moscow was to answer the Soviet note. Basing myself upon the protocol of the mixed commission I was able to prove incontrovertibly that the guilt in this highly regrettable incident lay wholly with the two Soviet frontier-guards themselves, and no guilt could be imputed to the Estonian frontier-guard, for which reason the claim for damages was devoid of any foundation. No reply was given to my note by the Soviet government, who obviously had to own that its protest was entirely unwarrantable.

A few weeks later, however, a reply followed, not in the shape of a diplomatic note but in bloodshed in which two fortuitous and absolutely innocent persons fell victims.

On a morning in March 1938, when an Estonian frontier-guard was doing the round in a sleigh driven by his coachman on Lake Peipus from it toward the Estonian coast, a Soviet motor-sleigh, coming whith high speed from the Soviet territory, made towards him. Such motor-sleighs were in use with the Soviet frontier-guards, whereas neither the Estonian frontier-guards, nor private persons on the Estonian shore owned any such vehicles on Lake Peipus. A group of Estonian fishermen who were fishing at a distance of about eight hundred yards saw a motor-sleigh drive over the frontier to a sleigh which was driving on the Estonian side, saw the drivers alight from the vehicles and a couple of minutes later get into them again and drive at a brisk pace over the frontier into Soviet territory. A few minutes after the disappearance of the vehicles beyond the line of visibility a short rattle of firing of some automatic weapon was heard from the direction where they had disappeared.

On the following day the Estonian government received a note from the Soviet government imparting that two persons had driven the day before in a sleigh from Estonian territory into that of the Soviet Union on Lake Peipus and, while attempting to escape when ordered to stop by the Soviet frontier-guards, had been fired at by the latter and killed. From the papers found upon one of the corpses as well as from his uniform it had appeared that he was an Estonian frontier-guard. The Soviet government protested against the violation of the frontier of the Soviet Union by an Estonian frontier-guard.

The evidence given by the above-mentioned fishermen when questioned as witnesses was fully confirmed by the traces left by the two sleighs on the snow-covered ice. The marks showed that a motor-sleigh, coming over the frontier from Soviet territory had made for the sleigh of the Estonian frontier-guard driving on the Estonian side, where there were footprints of the persons alighted from both vehicles to be seen in the snow. There were no traces of anyone having left the spot on foot. Instead the traces showed that both vehicles had driven together over the frontier into Soviet territory. There was, however, no possibility of following out the traces beyond the frontier, since the Soviet authorities this time refused to comply with the Estonian demand to summon the said commission, although — or rather because — the evidence mentioned above was transmitted to them.

In the years which have passed since the outbreak of the second World War, hundreds if not thousands of persons resident in the non-communist, free world, have been kidnapped and dragged away behind the Iron Curtain. Particularly numerous were such cases in France and Austria in the first years after the war. No wonder that general sensitiveness to these abominable crimes has worn blunt. Before the kidnapping and murder of the Estonian frontier-guard and his coachman there had been but two cases of this crime, in which two Russian "white" officers had fallen victim: the leaders of the union of the officers and soldiers of the Russian "white" armies which had fought against the Soviet Red Army in the civil war in 1918—1921, Generals Kutepov and Miller. There was every reason for the Soviet dictators to consider these generals their dangerous foes since the said union, with tens of thousands of members, was using every means to harm the Soviet state and undermine the Soviet order. By getting the leaders of this organization into their hands alive the Soviet leaders could hope that by subjecting them to ruthless torture it might be possible to extort from them important secrets about the activity of the said organization. The Estonian frontier-guard and his coachman, on the other hand, were completely ordinary citizens of a foreign state who had no dealings whatsoever with any organizations seeking the overthrow of the Soviet government, nor was there any reason to suppose that they might be in possession of state secrets of interest to the Soviet authorities. Notwithstanding this they were kidnapped and murdered. And be it noted: there could be no doubt that this crime was committed either by the order or with the explicit consent of the highest Soviet authorities, the habit of acting on their own initiative having been radically purged from the Soviet citizen long before by the terrorist totalitarian order. One could not help wondering what might have been the motive of the highest Soviet authorities in ordering the kidnapping and murder of these two haphazardly chosen, absolutely innocent Estonian citizens.

By way of answering this question suffice it to note the following circumstances.

The crime in question was committed at high noon and the fact that a group of Estonian fishermen were able to witness the most essential part of it, the kidnapping, though from a distance which prevented them from hearing what was spoken and seeing all the details, had not been regarded as a hindrance to its commission. Consequently it had not been considered of importance that there were witnesses to the crime. On the contrary, it had obviously been the express wish of those by whose order it was committed that the Estonian government should not be left in the dark about what had really happened. This inference imposes itself from the fact that the incident was deliberately and defiantly described in the Soviet note in as analogous a manner as possible to the incident in which two Soviet frontier-guards had lost their lives two months earlier. The only deviation from a full analogy was necessitated by the actual impossibility of alleging that the Estonian frontier-guard had opened fire on the Soviet frontier-guards, since if such an allegation had been advanced, it would have appeared so much more inexplicable and suspicious that the Estonian proposal to convoke the mixed commission to investigate the incident was turned down by the Soviet authorities. By deliberately giving a mocking travesty of the previous incident in the description of the new one the Soviet government manifestly sought to insinuate to the Estonia government that it was a revenge for the former one. This retaliation could have but one purpose; to intimidate the Estonian government and the Estonian people, to command respect for the mighty Soviet state according to the well-known maxim of the Roman emperor Caligula: *Oderint dum metuant!* — Let them show hate, provided they fear! In reality this barbarous act, instead of commanding respect, filled the Estonian people with execration towards the Power which considered it appropriate to resort to such loathsome crimes.

However, the vengefulness of the Soviet authorities was quenched and a certain tension which had been perceptible after the mournful incident of January soon faded. Relations between Estonia and the Soviet Union were soon normalised as much as this word was at all applicable considering the increasingly menacing international situation, the ever more intense strain in Soviet home politics, the aggravated xenophobia and the ever more hermetical seclusion from the outer world.

XI

STALIN PREPARING FOR HIS GREAT CHANCE

One thing that struck the eye of every newcomer to Moscow in the late winter 1938 was the propaganda against Nazi Germany being carried on at high pressure. It already screamed forth from numerous placards on the walls of the houses and in show-windows in the streets leading from the railway station to the centre of the capital. One placard which seemed to be most widely spread represented a viper which the vigorous hand of a worker was throttling so hard that the eyes of the reptile, with very conspicuous swastikas drawn upon them, were on the point of being squeezed out. In cinemas films were running which lashed nazi barbarity or showed the peace-loving Russian people, enjoying enviable well-being and happiness under the rays of Stalin's sun, unexpectedly assaulted by enemies bearing the swastika on their uniforms, the assaulters committing horrible cruelties and meaningless destruction, but being soon routed by the invincible Red Army. A series of plays of the same kind were performed in theatres. In both films and plays the propagandist tendency was so importunate and obtrusive that only an utterly unpretending audience might have drawn from them something which, in a very relative sense, could be classed as aesthetic delight. In need hardly be added that the same propaganda was rampant also in the press, the radio and literature.

The practical aim of this propaganda was to prevail upon the masses to acquiesce in carrying the heavy burden of armament without complaint, to be contented with the terribly low living standard, especially with the acute lack of commodities of any kind on sale, to urge them to partake in organizations of civil defence etc. Even the fine arts were engaged in the service of defence propaganda. "Concerts of defence-music" were given in which compositions written in martial rythm or on patriotic themes were performed, and "exhibitions of defence-painting" were arranged in which pictures representing, the famous exploits of the Russian army like, e.g. "Suvorov passing the Alps", etc. were shown. To the same propagandist end even the famous show-trials of the Lenininst Old Guard were exploited to the full. The most odious crime which Bukharin, Rykov, Yagoda and others were charged with in the third great trial of old Bolsheviks in March 1938, was that they had been spies and hirelings in the pay of Germany, Japan, Poland, and England, and undertaken treacherously to open the front to the enemy in the coming war. These charges, to which most of those in the prisoners' box had been coerced to plead guilty, were used to stir up the passions of the masses against the "detestable traitors" and to inspire the patriotic fervour of the people.

The whole attention of the Soviet leaders being concentrated upon on the one hand the violent struggle for power within the Party and the Soviet state, and on the other the perilous international situation, they hardly had any time left for a livelier interest in the three small Baltic states. There was therefore a short interlude of almost undisturbed calm in the relations between these states and the Soviet Union, about twelve months from the spring of 1938 onwards.

In the very middle of this period of lull before the storm I heard for the first time somebody in the diplomatic corps in Moscow give a hint of the possibility of a *rapprochement* of the Soviet Union and Nazi Germany. No space need be devoted here to proving how disastrous such a change in the mutual relations of these two equally aggressive and expansionist states, led by cynical, unscrupulous tyrants, appeared. The *rapprochement* of the two tyrants, conceivable only as a temporary deal, could have no other purport than the partition between them of the main spheres of interest at the expense of other nations, i.e. a free hand to each in subduing the peoples in the respective spheres of interest and trampling their freedom underfoot. The intimated eventuality consequently threatened with mortal danger not only the states situated between the Soviet Union and Germany, but a considerable number of other states too, since there could be little hope of localising the conflict.

The hint in question seemed, however, to be too incredible, since no amount of brain-racking could discover a single fact from which it would have been possible to infer that this development was already imminent or might be anticipated in the foreseeable future. No change could be detected in the manoeuvres of Soviet diplomacy and propaganda. This propaganda went on stressing the imperative need for close collaboration among the peace-loving states and the creation of a system of collective security which would erect insurmountable obstacles to the warlike schemes of the aggressive states, Nazi Germany in the first place. The Soviet Union was, as before, glorified as the only staunch champion of "undivisible peace" and collective security. The propaganda campaign against Hitler's Third Reich and nazism went on unabated. Moreover, it seemed to be past all doubt that a *rapprochement* between the Soviet Union and Germany could not be in the interest of the former. It might have served Hitler's interests, giving him a highly desirable opportunity of making use of a short interlude of friendship with the Soviets to inflict a crushing defeat upon France and England, avoiding the dangers of a war on two fronts. However, there could not be any doubt that as soon as England and France were outfought, he would attack the Soviet Union, when again he would be spared a war on two fronts. Such a perspective was inevitably particularly alarming to the Soviet dictator at a time when the Red Army was seriously weakened by the horrible blood-letting of the Great Purge of the years 1936–1938, to which a great number of higher officers had fallen victims, not to speak of the tension within the Communist Party and the whole of the Soviet Union, which now seemed to have reached its climax if anything could be inferred from what was disclosed at the Bukharin–Rykov trial in March 1938. Considering all these circumstances the intimation in question seemed to be, if not a pure fancy, only a theoretical speculation without any point of support in real fact. Therefore it attracted no attention.

But quite new and disquieting tones sounded in Stalin's address to the congress of the Communist Party on March 10th, 1939. In this address he said that a new imperialist war of one-sided and peculiar character was already going on: "We are witnessing an open re-division of the world and spheres of influence at the expense of the non-aggressive states without the least attempt at resistance on the part of those states.» He reproached the non-aggressive states, primarily England, France and the USA, not only with having rejected the policy of resistance to the aggressors, but even with displaying a certain connivance with them, going to the length of prompting Germany to start war on the Soviet Union. Mentioning especially a furore raised by the British, French and American press about the imminent march of the Germans on the Soviet Ukraine in order to annex it to the Carpathian Ukraine, he said: "It looks as if the object of this suspicious hullabaloo was to incense the Soviet Union against Germany, to poison the atmosphere and to provoke a conflict with Germany without any visible grounds."

The statement that there were no grounds for a conflict of the Soviet Union with Germany was rather sensational, especially with regard to the phrenetic anti-German propaganda in the Soviet Union mentioned above. One could only wonder at the strange fact that this propaganda, carried on with the greatest intensity for several years by the organs of the totalitarian Soviet state, had been so ineffective whereas the spreading, in the foreign press, of a red herring ridiculed by Stalin in the same address as completely devoid of any foundation and downright absurd, was presumed to be able to incense the Soviet Union and to poison the atmosphere to such a degree as to threaten a conflict of the two states.

No less noteworthy was the fact that the speech contained no declaration that the Soviet Union would support the erection of a system of collective security and be willing to assume the obligation to participate in collective actions for resisting aggression.[1]

On the contrary, the states bent on aggression were told that if they would only refrain from trespassing on the interests of the Soviet Union, she would continue to maintain peaceful relations and business connections with them. What was this if not an abandonment of the principle of collective security and the embracing of the · very position of neutrality and non-intervention for which the non-aggressive states were scoffed at and severely censured by Stalin?

The sudden change of policy of the Soviet state came still more clearly to the fore in the following directions to the Party formulated

---

[1] The vague sentence: "We stand for the support of nations which are the victims of aggression and are fighting for the independence of their country", was rather a device to disguise the giving up of the profession of faith in collective security.

in the same address: "To be cautious and not allow our country to be drawn into conflicts by war-mongers who are accustomed to have others pull the chestnuts out of the fire for them; to strengthen the might of our Red Army and Red Navy to the utmost; to strengthen the international bonds of friendship with the working people of all countries who are interested in peace and friendship among the nations." Thus at the very moment when the non-aggressive states were at last overcoming their vacillation and drawing up to collective resistance to the aggressive schemes of Nazi Germany, the principle of this resistance, grandiloquently propagated by the Soviets for several years, was suddenly thrown overboard.[2]

As the long-desired situation now at last seemed to be coming about and most promising prospects for the early victory of the world revolution to have opened, the subjugation of the Baltic states came once more to the fore as in the years 1918—1920, this time, too, as one of the first steps to be taken. Only a fortnight after the delivery of the speech quoted above the first move of Soviet diplomacy followed, the manifest aim of which was to break the ground for that subjugation.

This was a declaration, identical in its contents, presented by the Foreign Commissar Litvinov to the envoys of Estonia and Latvia on March 28th, 1939. This document abounded in pretty words about the spirit of benevolence towards the Baltic peoples felt by the Soviet government, who, it was stated, had constantly laid and still did lay enormous importance upon preserving the complete independence

[2] There is now incontrovertible documentary evidence establishing the fact that Stalin's address was actually meant to announce a deliberate change of the policy which had been professed till then by the Soviet Union. This evidence is to be found in a document headed "Memorandum of a Conversation Held on the Night of August 23rd to 24th, between the Reich Foreign Minister, on the One Hand, and Herr Stalin and the Chairman of the Council of People's Commissars Molotov, on the Other Hand" discovered in the archives of the German Foreign Office captured by the American and British Armies in 1945. Among other toasts proposed in the course of the conversation this document gives the following proposed by Mr. Molotov: "Herr Molotov raised his glass to Stalin, remarking that it had been Stalin who — through his speech of March of this year, *which had been well understood in Germany* — had brought about the reversal in political relations". *(Nazi—Soviet Relations 1939—1941*, published by order of the Department of State in 1948, p. 76).

of the Baltic Republics. The preservation of this independence was said to be conformable not only to the interests of the peoples of these republics, but also to the vital interests of the Soviet state, which was ready to prove with deeds, in case of need, its anxiety to preserve it in its full entirety.

The actual aim of the declaration, however, was the very reverse of these honey-sweet words. The assurances of the deep interest of the Soviet government in the complete independence of the Baltic states were held forth only as a basis for undertaking the complete annihilation of that independence. Pretending to attribute enormous importance to the preservation of the complete independence of these states, the Soviet government arrogated to itself the control of their foreign policy. The gist of the declaration was worded as follows: "No matter what kind of agreements were signed, 'voluntary' or concluded under outside pressure, should they result even only in the abatement or restriction of independence and self-determination, permitting the political, economic or other domination of a third state, and granting the latter any exceptional rights and privileges, either within the territory or in the ports, this would be regarded by the Soviet government as insufferable and contradictory to the stipulations and spirit of the treaties and agreements at present regulating its mutual relations with Estonia (resp. Latvia), and even as a violation of these agreements with all the consequences arising therefrom."

The threat expressed in the last words of the quotation was repeated at the end of the declaration in a still more blatant manner. It declared that the Soviet Union would be unable to remain an idle bystander in open or masked attempts to destroy the self-determination and independence of Estonia or Latvia.

But who was to decide what agreements were to be classed among those which constituted an abatement or restriction of independence and self-determination, or permitted political or other domination of a third state, or what was to be considered an open or masked attempt to destroy the self-determination and independence of the Baltic states? None other, of course, than the Soviet government. Thus the Kremlin pretended to no less than the degradation of these states to the status of Soviet satellites, whose whole policy was to be controlled by Moscow. Notwithstanding this the authors of the declaration had the face to declare that this degradation was to be carried out in the name of the complete independence of these states. In passing it is worth observing that a very convenient pretext for aggression upon these states at any moment considered opportune would have been created by this move: it would only have been necessary to allege that a violation of the agreements regulating their relations with the Soviet Union had taken place and that the Soviet government was acting upon the consequences arising therefrom. — As to the spirit of benevolence towards the Baltic states felt by the Soviet government, there had been adequate demonstrations in the attempt to subdue them by force of arms in 1918—1920 and the plot of Dec. 1st, 1924, in Estonia.

There could be but one reply to the declaration in question. In notes identical in substance, handed to Mr. Litvinov by their envoys in Moscow on April 7th, 1939, the Estonian and the Latvian governments declared that they had never agreed and would never agree, either voluntarily or under pressure, to any restrictions upon the sovereign will of their peoples and the independence of their states; that they reserved to themselves the exclusive right to decide how far their actions were in accordance with their international obligations, and that they could not share with any state their rights and obligations to provide for the defence of their national self-determination and their independence.

It goes without saying that this reply did not suffice to induce the Soviet government, or rather the absolute ruler of the Soviet Union, to abate or restrict his pretensions towards the Baltic states, let alone to waive them. In its manoeuvres during the following months, Soviet diplomacy did everything possible to obtain free scope to swallow up the Baltic states, first from Great Britain and then from Nazi Germany.

The sudden change in policy announced by Stalin in his address to the Congress of the Communist Party and appearing more and more unmistakably in the diplomatic negotiations conducted between Moscow, London and Paris from March to August 1939, was puzzling to all those in the western world who had been listening for years and giving credence to Mr. Litvinov's harangues on "indivisible peace" and the urgent necessity of building up an effective system of collective resistance against aggression. There was, however, hardly anything unexpected or incomprehensible in it to those who had paid due attention to what Stalin had uttered in his numerous speeches and writings, especially since his polemic attacks on Trotsky launched immediately after the death of Lenin in 1924 in order to debar his rival from the leadership of the Party and the Soviet state. In these polemic articles, published in 1924, Stalin had already most emphatically declared that the Soviet Union was to be transformed, as soon as possible, into a base for the further development of the world revolution. Towards this end, Socialism was to fortify itself thoroughly in that country whose duty it was to do its utmost in the raising of revolts and the awakening of the revolutionary spirit in all countries, and even to use armed force against the exploiting classes and their states in the event of necessity.[3] There was, however, a necessary preliminary condition to the victory of the world revolution, which was pointed out by the Congress of the Communist International in 1928, i.e. at a time when no resolution not approved by Stalin could be adopted by that gathering: the world had first to pass the ordeal by fire of a new world war which would render the victory of the communist revolution both possible and inevitable. The armed force requisite for "coming out against the exploiting classes and their states" and supporting the revolts raised and the revolutions awakened to triumph in all countries, had also been built up in the meantime, a huge Red Army and a vast armament industry having been forged into existence in the Soviet Union at the price of almost superhuman hardship imposed on the population. Considering these circumstances, one had to acknowledge that Stalin was acting most consistently when he stopped orating about the urgent need for erecting a system of collective resistance against aggression and began taking steps towards a deal with Hitler in order to remove the last obstacles which had prevented him from unleashing the dogs of war.

[3] Stalin, *Problems of Leninism*, English edition, published in Moscow in 1940, p. 116. It is worth mentioning that the articles in which these ideas were being developed in 1924 have been reprinted in tens of editions and spread in tens of millions of copies in the Soviet Union as well as in other countries. In a letter addressed to "Comrade Ivanov", and published in the Soviet press on Febr. 14th, 1938, Stalin stated that *Problems of Leninism* was by no means antiquated and that its contents continued to be applicable in every respect.

"We are for the support of nations which are the victims of aggression and are fighting for the independence of their country", Stalin had declared in his speech of March 10th, 1939. What he actually did when Hitler unleashed the furies of the second World War, was to plunge the knife in the back of Poland as she offered heroic resistance to the onslaught of nazi aggression and fought desperately for her independence.

In the same speech Stalin had showered scorn and reprobation upon the non-aggressive states for not offering resistance to the open redivision of the world and spheres of interest being carried out by the aggressor states at the expense of the attacked. Now Stalin himself had made a most odious underhand deal with Hitler to divide the whole broad zone of Eastern Europe between the Soviet Union and Germany, from Finland to the Black Sea, into the "mutual spheres of interest" of these two predatory Powers. It should be emphasized that it was Hitler who urged Stalin to attack Poland from the rear as soon as possible and occupy the part of Poland which was to be his share of the spoils according to the secret protocol of August 23rd[4] and that it was Stalin who proposed to Hitler "finally to settle the Polish question" by wiping out the Polish state without leaving any independent Polish rump state.[5]

In his hypocrisy and cynicism Stalin even went to the length of giving his support to the "peace offensive" which was started by Hitler as soon as Poland was crushed. In a joint declaration issued by the Nazi and Soviet governments on Sept. 28th, 1939, "the questions resulting from the disintegration of the Polish state" were declared to be definitively solved by a treaty signed by these governments the same day, and their unanimous opinion was voiced that it would be in the interest of all nations to bring to an end the state of war existing between Germany on one side and England and France on the other. Both governments promised to concentrate their

[4] Cf. Ribbentrop's telegrams to Count Schulenburg of 3.9. and 15.9., as well as especially Schulenburg's talk with Molotov on 10.9. 1939: "I explained emphatically to Molotov how crucial the speedy action of the Red Army was at this juncture." (*Nazi—Soviet Relations 1939—1941*, p. 91.)

[5] Cf. Count Schulenburg's telegram to Ribbentrop of Sept. 25th, 1939, *Nazi—Soviet Relations*, pp. 102—103.

efforts toward reaching this goal and charged in advance England and France with the responsibility for a continuation of war if these efforts should prove unsuccessful. Hitler's peace proposals having fallen on deaf ears, England and France were branded by Soviet propaganda as being guilty of vainly protracting the "imperialist" war. According to the Kremlin's new theory proclaimed by Molotov, England and France had suddenly turned into aggressors.[6]

There could not, however, be any doubt that this official propaganda was pure hypocrisy, Stalin wishing merely to fawn upon his friend and ally, Hitler. It was out of the question that Stalin should desire to see the war between Germany and the western Powers come to an early end. On the contrary, such an eventuality would have been a downright nightmare to him. What he desired was that the war should be as long and devastating as possible — rendering it as easy as possible for the Red Army to inflict the *coup de grâce* on the expiring capitalist world. He was also absolutely sure that the course of war would actually correspond to these wishes of his.[7] Thus there could be no danger of hostilities coming to a premature end, even if Soviet propaganda joined in the chorus of Hitler's "peace offensive".

This did not mean, however, that the Soviet Union could now take up the pleasant position of a *tertius gaudens* passively awaiting events. On the contrary; since the great war offered the long coveted chance of leading the world revolution to victory, the Soviet Red Army intervening at a well-timed moment as the really deciding factor, it was necessary to make all requisite preparations with the greatest haste and energy so as to be well equipped for any emergency which might unexpectedly arise. The first thing to do was to

---

[6] In its leader of July 5th, 1940, *Pravda* went to the length of declaring that — not Hitler, but — the ruling circles in England and France bore the responsibility for the Second World War, as it had been at the instigation of these circles that the peoples of the world had been precipitated into the bloodiest war of history.

[7] In an informal talk after the signing of the Estonian—Soviet Pact of Mutual Assistance, on the night of Sept. 28th, 1939, one of the Estonian delegates asked Stalin's opinion about the chances of the two parties to this Pact escaping being involved in the war. Stalin's answer was that the war would be very long and obstinate. For a number of reasons it seemed to be likely that this time, at least, he was saying what he really believed.

make use of any favourable occasion presenting itself for expanding the sphere of influence of the Soviet Union and, by doing so, to secure advantageous starting-points for the final round in the contest for world domination.

The Soviet government proceeded therefore forthwith to a partial mobilization of its armed forces. Four or five younger classes of reservists had already been called up in the first week after the outbreak of war. This was carried out by personal orders to every reservist — no placards were pasted up at crossways and no proclamation published in newspapers. Nor was any hint of the mobilization made in the press or on the radio. As soon as the divisions were ready for active service in war, their concentration on the western frontier of the Soviet Union, from Finland to Rumania, was begun. The danger of Soviet aggression which had ever overhung the Baltic states now suddenly loomed into the foreground.[8]

An unforeseen incident offered a suitable pretext to the Soviet government for proceeding to the execution of its long-completed plans.

On September 17th, 1939, the very day of the unexpected attack from behind on Poland by the Soviet Union, a Polish submarine *Orzel* had put into the harbour of Tallinn, alleging engine-trouble which had compelled her to call at a neutral port. The vessel was granted the permission to remain in the harbour on condition that she did not leave it before the Estonian authorities had decided on its fate. To secure the observation of this condition armed sentries were posted on board. However, the crew had managed to repair the engine, and, manifestly afraid lest they be interned in Estonia, decided to escape. The sentries having been overpowered by a sudden attack in the night and placed under lock and key, the submarine succeeded in getting out under cover of darkness. The two Estonian sentries were set free and sent away in a row-boat somewhere near the Swedish island of Gotland thirty six hours later.

No information about this occurrence had yet reached me when I learned of it from *Pravda* on Tuesday morning, Sept. 19th. According to a communication of the Soviet Telegraph Agency Tass, pub-

---

[8] According to what Molotov told Count Schulenburg on Sept. 10th, 1939, three million men had already been mobilized by that date. (*Nazi—Soviet Relations*, p. 91)

lished in the press that morning, Polish submarines as well as those of some other foreign Powers were hiding in the harbours of the Baltic states, in collusion with certain persons in governmental circles. On Sept. 18th a Polish submarine which was said to have been interned in the harbour of Tallinn had escaped and bolted, direction unknown. According to Tass there was reason to suppose that the escape had been carried out with the connivance of the Estonian authorities.

Scarcely had I had time to read through the Tass communication when there was a call from the Kremlin that Mr Molotov desired to see me at once. Lacking both information and instructions from my government I could only fortify myself with sang-froid for the forthcoming, surely anything but agreeable conversation.

Mr Molotov began in a rather threatening tone, declaring that the Polish submarine had escaped either with the connivance of the Estonian authorities or with the help of some officers "traditionally sympathizing with Poles and Poland" and acting on their own initiative. The Soviet Red Navy would have to have a look at what was going on in the waters by the coast of Estonia. I replied that as I had not yet got any information and instructions concerning the matter and knew only the version given in the communication of Tass, I was not in a position to decide whether the Estonian authorities could be blamed for the infringement of any agreements in force between Estonia and the Soviet Union or of the rules of International Law. I promised to revert to the question when instructed by my government.

A few days before an official of the Estonian Foreign Office had arrived at Moscow to negotiate a trade agreement for the next year. This was a matter of routine — because of the state monopoly of foreign trade in the Soviet Union, such agreements had to be negotiated every year. This time it was highly desirable to increase considerably both imports from and exports to the Soviet Union. With regard to the fact that the trade of both countries was considerably encumbered by the war now raging in the West, this seemed to be in their common interest, and the chances of reaching an agreement advantageous to both parties seemed to be rather promising in the beginning. At the People's Commissariat for Foreign Trade, where

I had to introduce the representative of the Estonian Foreign Office to the Deputy People's Commissar Stepanov, we were received by the People's Commissar Anastas Mikoyan himself, who assured us in very kindly words of the Soviet government's sincere desire to extend considerably the trade of the Soviet Union with Estonia. However, taking into consideration the extent to which the foreign trade policy of the Soviet Union was swayed by political motives, it seemed to be past all doubt that an abrupt change for the worse would manifest itself in the attitude of the Soviet government after the *Orzel* incident. I was thus really puzzled when I heard that even on the afternoon of the very day of my disagreeable conversation with Mr Molotov about the Polish submarine, no change in the attitude of the Soviet representatives had been evidenced in the negotiations in the Commissariat for Foreign Trade. Contrary to my anticipations the benevolent attitude of the Soviet negotiators seemed not to fade, but to grow still more marked during the following two days. This was so very unusual that I began to be alarmed, since I suspected some mischief behind it.

Agreement was reached on all points on Thursday, Sept. 21st. Exports from Estonia to the Soviet Union and the imports from there were to increase by 350 % as compared with the preceding years. Among the commodities included in the list of imports and exports there were a number of those difficult to import from elsewhere, as well as to export elsewhere. Therefore the agreement seemed to be exceedingly advantageous, though, of course, it was quite natural if two neutral countries whose foreign trade was considerably encumbered by the war, tried to alleviate their temporary common difficulties by increasing their mutual trade. The fair copies of the agreement had been prepared and checked on Friday morning, Sept. 22nd, and the hour had been agreed upon when I was to sign them on behalf of Estonia at the Commissariat for Foreign Affairs. Quite unexpectedly a telephone message from the Estonian Foreign Office informed me that the agreement would be signed by the Foreign Minister, K. Selter himself, who had received and accepted the invitation to Moscow to that end. I saw in this message a confirmation of my worst misgivings: it immediately brought to mind what had happened to the President of Czechoslovakia when, six months before, he had been invited to Berlin by Hitler. I could not understand how the Foreign Minister had been unable to find a plausible pretext for declining the invitation. Since the visit was already settled, revocation of the acceptance was not to be thought of.[9]

[9] I am sorry to say that, as I learned later, Mr Selter himself had brought about the invitation by a hint given to the Soviet envoy that he would not be disinclined to go to Moscow and sign himself the unhoped-for advantageous agreement. Appointed Foreign Minister in May, 1938, without having ever before occupied himself with foreign policy, he lacked experience in this sphere and his judgment in matters of foreign policy left a great deal to be desired. No doubt it was not his doing that during his administration of the office of foreign minister in some circles, insignificant in numbers, but not devoid of influence, those anti-British and pro-German feelings began to sprout on which the British Consul in Tallinn, W. H. Gallienne, remonstrated with him on July 11th, 1939 (v. Brit. Doc., III Ser, vol. 6, pp. 325—327). The reproaches addressed to him by Mr. Gallienne were, however, justified inasmuch as no requisite measures were taken for curbing these circles, and for this the foreign minister was to be blamed. Obviously he had already at that time taken a liking for Hitlerite Germany. It was, of course, symptomatic that almost to the very last day of the war he clung unshakably to the belief in Hitler's ultimate victory. This may also have been brought about by his favourite daily reading, the notorious nazi organ Völkischer Beobachter. His Baltic colleagues in Switzerland, where he was residing during the war, having been appointed Estonian representative to the League of Nations in November 1939, never succeeded in shaking his conviction that Hitler would come out victorious.

XII

PACTS FORCED BY THREAT OF WAR

Mr Selter arrived in Moscow on the afternoon of Sept. 24th. He
was received with the usual honours: the railway station was deco-
rated with the national flags of the two countries and their national
anthems were played by a military band. Mrs Selter was honoured
with a magnificent bouquet of beautiful roses.

Soon after his arrival, Mr Selter was informed that Mr Molotov
would receive him at 9 o'clock p.m.

On the conversation of that night as well as on the negotiations
which followed three days later and led on Sept. 28th to the conclusion of the so-called Pact of Mutual Assistance, I drew up a report
by order of Mr Selter immediately after the Estonian negotiators had
set out upon their journey home. With the most scrupulous accuracy
I could command, though at the same time as succinctly as possible,
I took down all the essential details of the negotiations. This paper,
signed by me on Oct. 1st, runs — with the omission of details of lesser
importance — as follows.

"Having but very briefly mentioned the trade agreement, Mr Molotov at once tackled the matter for which Mr Selter had been invited
to Moscow. What he said was a complete reversal of the declaration
made by Litvinov on April 4th, 1934 to the Envoys of the three Baltic
states. 'The Soviet state has never demanded the revision of existing
treaties and never intends to demand it', Mr Litvinov had proclaimed
on that occasion. Now Mr Molotov began the conversation with the
following words: 'The present situation in the Baltic constitutes a
danger to the security of the Soviet Union, as is made particularly
manifest by the escape of a Polish submarine from Tallinn harbour.
It is indispensable to alter the status quo in the Baltic area in such
a way that the Soviet Baltic Fleet need not feel confined in a menaced
position in the narrow end of the Gulf of Finland. The Soviet Union

has become a powerful state with a highly developed industry, and in possession of a great military force. The status quo which was established twenty years ago when the Soviet Union was weakened by civil war, can no longer be considered as adequate to the present situation and normal. The Government of the Soviet Union cannot any longer tolerate this dangerous situation and has firmly decided to change it.'

"One could not help wondering how one single Polish submarine could constitute such a serious menace to the security of so powerful a state as the Soviet Union, according to Mr Molotov's own declaration, had become. Without stopping at this question Mr Molotov went on:

" 'The Soviet Union needs naval and air bases in the Baltic Sea which would enable it to organize an efficient defence of Leningrad and the area behind it. Suitable places for such bases are to be found on Estonian territory, and Estonia must cede them to the Soviet Union.' Dotting all i's and crossing all t's Mr Molotov added: 'If the Estonian government were to fail to admit of these necessary alterations, the Soviet Union would be forced to carry them out otherwise, employing more radical measures which might prove to be unavoidable. However, the Soviet government wishes to settle the matter by negotiation, and I ask the Estonian government not to force the Soviet Union to take the other course hinted at, a course to which the Soviet government does not want to resort, and which would doubtless be even less desirable to Estonia'.

"In the course of the conversation, especially in the beginning, Mr Molotov time and again mentioned the escape of the Polish submarine from the harbour of Tallinn, asserting that apparently the Estonian government was not master in its own house, and declared the explanations advanced by Mr Selter to be unsatisfactory. He was from time to time seconded by Mr Mikoyan, who in general, however, took but little part in the discussion.

"Emphasizing that the matter was extremely urgent and brooked no delay, since events of incalculable consequence might occur any day, Mr Molotov asked Mr Selter to confer with Tallinn, if he deemed it necessary, and continue the discussion on the following day, Sept. 25th, at 4 p.m., to which proposal Mr Selter agreed.

"Soon after our return to the Estonian legation there was, however, a telephone message from the Kremlin, asking Mr Selter to come back to the Kremlin at midnight since Mr Molotov wanted to hand him the written draft of a pact to be concluded, which would provide a basis for the discussion.

"According to this draft both Contracting Parties were to give each other every kind of assistance, including military assistance, if one of the Parties was menaced or directly attacked by any third European Power, and Estonia was to grant the Soviet Union the right to maintain bases for its Navy in Estonian harbours and a number of aerodromes for its aircraft on Estonian territory.

"Handing the draft to Mr Selter, Mr Molotov explained that it had been drawn up in haste by himself and Mr Mikoyan, since they had considered such a draft would be useful as a basis for discussion and help reach an agreement sooner. Mr Molotov assured us that the Soviet Union did not wish to impose communism nor the Soviet order upon Estonia nor in the least degree to restrict her independence and sovereignty. The social and political order, government, parliament, diplomatic representations, etc., of Estonia would remain unaltered as well as the internal affairs of the Estonian people, with which the Soviet Union would not interfere, he declared. The Soviet Union was mainly interested in the islands of Saaremaa and Hiiumaa (Ösel and Dagö) as they were suitable for naval and air bases. The areas required for these bases could be ceded on lease or concession. Answering Mr Selter's request for a more detailed interpretation of the draft, Mr Molotov at first mentioned that the harbour of Tallinn was a suitable place for a naval base. When Mr Selter pointed out the difficulties and inconveniences which would arise from the establishment of a foreign naval base in the commercial harbour of the capital of another sovereign state, Mr Molotov observed that it was not to be taken for granted that it was the harbour of Tallinn which should be ceded; the desire was that the Baltic Navy of the Soviet Union be able, if necessary, immediately to use certain Estonian harbours as naval bases.

"Stressing that the matter was extremely urgent and brooked no delay, Mr Molotov suggested that Mr Selter might confer with Tallinn over telephone and telegraph in order to be able to sign the treaty without any waste of time. However, upon Mr Selter's emphatic declaration that the matter could not by any means be settled without his oral report to the President of the Republic and the Government and that he would, on his return home, do everything in his power to induce the government to give a definite answer without any delay, Mr Molotov agreed to Mr Selter's immediate return to Tallinn."

In the heart-rending consultation in Tallinn during the following two days the President of the Republic, the Government, and the special commissions of Parliament — those for national defence and foreign affairs — had, after a thorough consideration, to come to the sad conclusion that an attempt to offer armed resistance to the Soviet Union should she use military forces to press her demands, was both hopeless and meaningless. Though it seemed a dead certainty that immediately after Estonia the same demands and threats would be addressed by the Kremlin to Latvia, Lithuania and Finland, there were no chances of these four states joining in an alliance to offer co-ordinated resistance to the aggression which threatened them all. Though it had been stressed in a great number of resounding speeches on festive occasions that these small nations stood a chance of preserving their freedom and independence only if with unswerving determination they defended them with their combined strengh, very little had actually been done in the way of preparing the practical co-ordination of their efforts in the eventuality of supreme danger. All nations in the danger zone were scared out of their wits by the stunning effects of the total war directed for the first time in history by Germany against Poland. Every nation hoped against hope that the raging thunderstorm might pass and its neutrality might be respected if it kept as still as possible.   There was no hope of aid and assistance from abroad.

As to the ability of the Estonian army to withstand the onslaught of the Red Army, it was past dispute that even if an uninterrupted flow of supplies of munitions and weapons from the countries producing them were secured, it would have been a matter of but a few weeks if not days before the enormous superiority of the Red Army in numbers and in armaments broke their resistance. It was, first and foremost, the very question of supplies that completely ruled out the possibility of resistance of any longer duration. Taking into account the enormous scale on which modern battles devour munitions and weapons, one had to reckon with the insurmountable fact that their accumulated stores would have been exhausted in a couple of weeks. Thereafter the rifles and guns would have fallen silent, since there was no munitions industry worth mentioning either in Estonia or in the neighbouring small states, and no possibility of obtaining munitions and weapons from abroad. All the nations which had supplied the Baltic states with war materials in peace time, were themselves feverishly arming, being either already involved in the war or, if not, seeing in this their only chance of escaping involvement. Even communications by sea were actually cut off. To all this must be added that a supply of modern fighters ordered from England and ready for delivery in the summer of 1939, were at the last moment requisitioned by the British authorities, who were themselves in dire need of these planes. The result of this unexpected reversal would have been that the Estonian army would actually have had to fight without a fighter-umbrella, since the Estonian air force, insufficient in both numbers and quality, would have been wiped out of the sky in a few days by the Soviet air force.

In such circumstances, the only result of resistance would have been the sacrifice of the elite of the nation, i.e. of its most dauntless, stout-hearted elements, and mass-deportation of the rest of the population and its scattering to the four winds in Siberia and other gloomy regions of Russia. It would have amounted to the deliberate suicide of the nation. Whatever bitter sufferings and severe trials were in store for the Estonian people if it yielded to the threat of the Soviet government, there was still reason to hope that if its physical existence were preserved, there remained a chance of better times dawning again, bringing with them the restitution of its national freedom. The future does not hold anything for a people which has been annihilated in the meantime. The preservation of the physical existence of the nation was the supreme commandment to follow. In other words — the alternative of national suicide had to be ruled out.

Thus there was no other way than to yield to inexorable fate and surrender to the demands of the Soviet government.

To conduct negotiations with the Soviet government it was decided to send a delegation to Moscow. The only conceivable task and direction to the delegation was to do its utmost to save as much of national freedom as was humanly possible under the circumstances.

The delegation, headed by the Foreign Minister, K. Selter, included the Speaker of the Chamber of Deputies, Professor J. Uluots, and the former Foreign Minister, Professor A. Piip.

The delegation flew to Moscow from Riga on Wednesday, Sept. 27th. It is worth mentioning that when the plane alighted on the Soviet aerodrome Velikie Luki, there was a big plane bearing the emblem of the Third Reich, the swastika, to be seen on the airfield. It took off before long. As it turned out it was von Ribbentrop flying to Moscow for the second time.

The delegation arrived in Moscow at about 6 p.m. Soon thereafter it was summoned to the Kremlin for 9 p.m.

My report gives the following account of the negotiations on Sept. 27th and 28th.

"Molotov, with whom this time, too, was Mr Mikoyan, opened the talks by stating that in the meantime a new disagreeable incident had occurred: a Soviet steamer, *Metallist*, had been torpedoed by an unknown submarine near the bay of Narva."

Here I must put in that none of the Estonian delegates had the least doubt that the whole story about the torpedoing of the *Metallist* was pure invention. Though Mr Molotov did not mention the Polish submarine *Orzel*, there was no mistaking that he was hinting at it. It was however quite obvious that the only reasonable aim the commander of that submarine might have had, had been to get out of the Baltic as soon as possible and therefore to take his course to the west, as was also proved by setting free the Estonian sentries near the Swedish island of Gotland on Sept. 20th. It would have been a completely inexplicable step on the part of the commander of that submarine to turn back from Gotland to the east., proceed right up to the bay of Narva in the eastern part of the Gulf of Finland and there torpedo a Soviet merchantman.[1] Mr Molotov and Mr

---

[3] A clumsy farce had been staged at the same time to confirm the tale of the torpedoing of the *Metallist*, as testified by the Estonian major A. Körgma in a statement made to the Select Committee on Communist Aggression created by the House of Representatives of the US in 1953, and published in the Third Report of that Committee (Washington, 1954). Major Körgma, who was in Sept. 1939 chief of the border guard in the district of Narva, gave the following details in his statement: "Some border guards on their patrol alongside the seacoast west of the

Mikoyan, as well as Stalin himself, could hardly have missed the fact that none of the Estonian delegates believed a word of the story about the torpedoing of the *Metallist,* since they never mentioned it again later. Moreover, a Soviet merchantman *Metallist* was at a later time seen in the Estonian harbours.

Mr Molotov immediately also disclosed the end for which the "torpedoing" of the *Metallist* had been fabricated. He continued:

"This new circumstance obliges the Soviet government to add a new demand to the proposal handed over on Sept. 24th." According to a new draft which was handed over by him, the Soviet Union claimed the right to station army and air forces of up to 35,000 men on Estonian territory, in defence of the naval and air bases, as well as for the defence of internal security. After a discussion, in the course of which the Estonian delegation presented a series of arguments against that proposal, Mr Molotov suggested that Mr Stalin should be asked to take part in the negotiations. Stalin arrived at about 9.15 p.m , taking over the leadership of the negotiations and deciding actually all the questions which arose. He declared that the presence of the armed forces of the Soviet Union in Estonia was indispensable for the effective repulsion of attempts to involve the Soviet Union and Estonia in the war, but agreed at last to reduce the number of troops to be stationed in Estonia to 25,000 men. He agreed also to a clause according to which the Soviet Union was entitled to keep its

mouth of the Narva river observed some time before dusk (a day at the end of September) a steamer moving from east to west and dragging something behind it which appeared to be a barge. Though both the steamer and the barge were clearly visible even without fieldglasses they, nevertheless, were so far from the coast that the name of the ship and its nationality (flag, colour, etc) could not be made out. Suddenly a dull explosion was heard from the sea near the steamer and the barge, after which the barge disappeared, evidently having been sunk. The following day the sea ran high and washed refuse to the shore opposite the place where the above-described incident had taken place: plankings, a door, a panel belonging to some kind of a small telephone exchange, etc. All this could not come from any other source than the barge that had been sunk the evening before, though it seemed most improbable that there could have been a telephone exchange on that barge. The door was not of the kind that is usual on boats. It was evident that these objects had been placed on the barge for some special purpose." (p. 225 of the said Report).

armed forces on the territory of Estonia only during the war that was going on.

"In the following discussions, which were interrupted twice, since Messrs Molotov and Stalin were at the same time also negotiating with Herr von Ribbentrop, the talks turned mainly upon the question which of the Estonian harbours was to be ceded to the Soviet Union. Stalin declared at the very outset that after consultation with his military experts it had been established that the harbour of Paldiski[2] was not in a condition fit for employment in the near future. Of course it is possible, he said, to construct a naval base at Paldiski, but this takes time, and the same is true of the creeks of the islands Saaremaa and Hiiumaa. It is therefore absolutely necessary to the Soviet navy to have the right to use the port of Tallinn, since it is usable in its present state. After a rather long discussion, a seeming compromise was reached, according to which permanent bases were to be constructed at Paldiski and on the islands of Saaremaa and Hiiumaa as speedily as was feasible, but temporarily, until the construction of a base at Paldiski, for a period of two years at the most from the signing of the Pact, the vessels of the Soviet navy were to have the right to put in at the port of Tallinn to take on provisions and fuel and for shelter. A provision to this effect was inserted in a confidential protocol signed simultaneously with the Pact as an annex to it.

"The negotiations closed at about 11 p.m. on Sept. 28th and the Pact along with the confidential protocol and the commercial agreement were signed at a few minutes to midnight.

While the fair copies of the Pact being typed, drinks and sandwiches were served and toasts raised in the course of conversation. It may be of interest to note that when Molotov asked Stalin if it were not advisable to defer the meeting "with the Germans" agreed upon, from midnight to half past, Stalin replied rather disrespectfully: "No, send them word to come at one o'clock — they can wait." When the Estonian delegation left Mr Molotov's study at 1 o'clock a.m., Herr von Ribbentrop and his retinue were waiting in the anteroom.

In the course of the conversation, both Stalin and Molotov assured

---

[2] The small town of Paldiski (Baltic Port), situated on a bay about thirty miles west of Tallinn, had been mentioned in the course of the negotiations on the night of Sept. 25th, as a conceivable alternative to the port of Tallinn.

us that Estonia would never have reason to regret having concluded the Pact. "You will see how unfailingly we Bolsheviks abide by what we have signed. Our dependable Bolshevik word vouches for this. Our words and signatures are something quite different from those of bourgeois statesmen." It was not long the Estonian people had to wait to see how dependable Bolshevik words and signatures were.

The essential provisions of the Pact ran as follows.

The Contracting Parties undertook to render each other assistance of every kind, including military assistance, in the event of direct aggression or threat of aggression on the part of a European Great Power against the maritime frontiers of the Contracting Parties in the Baltic Sea, or against their land frontiers across the territory of the Republic of Latvia.[3] Moreover, the Soviet Union undertook to assist the Estonian army with armaments or other war material on advantageous terms. In return Estonia granted the Soviet Union the right to have naval bases and a number of airfields on the Estonian islands of Saaremaa and Hiiumaa and in the town of Paldiski, on lease at reasonable rates. The exact sites of the bases and airfields were to be assigned, and the limits thereof defined, by common accord.

For the protection of these naval bases and airfields the Soviet Union acquired the right to maintain there Soviet garrisons up to a maximum to be determined by special agreement. As already mentioned, this maximum was fixed at 25,000 men (in the secret protocol).

The reassuring declarations made by Mr Molotov at the beginning of the negotiations were set down in the Pact in the following words: "The enforcement of the present Pact shall in no way impair the sovereign rights of the Contracting Parties nor, more especially, their economic system or political structure. The areas allotted for the bases and aerodromes shall remain the territory of the Republic of Estonia."

One more article deserves mention by reason of the use made of it when the Soviet Union set about swallowing up Estonia, along with

[3] The obligation to render each other assistance was, however, qualified by the confidential protocol which stipulated that the assistance be rendered at the express desire of the other Contracting Party.

Latvia and Lithuania, in June, 1940. This article stipulated: "The two Contracting Parties undertake not to conclude alliances nor to take part in coalitions directed against either of the Contracting Parties."

Scarcely had the Estonian delegation left Moscow when it was the turn of Latvia and Lithuania to have analogous Pacts forced upon them.

Invitations to send their foreign ministers to Moscow "for the reconsideration of their relations with the Soviet Union" had been sent to the governments of these states when negotiations with Estonia were still under consideration. Negotiations with the Latvian Foreign Minister, V. Munters, started on the morning of Oct. 2nd, and with the Lithuanian Foreign Minister, J. Urbsys, on the evening of the same day. Negotiations with Latvia were concluded on Oct. 4th, and the Pact was signed on Oct. 5th. Negotiations with Lithuania took a little more time, since the Lithuanian Foreign Minister, lacking the authority to sign the pact on the terms proposed by the Kremlin, had to return to Kaunas to report the matter to the President of the Republic and the Government and to receive new instructions. There was, however, no alternative, and Lithuania, too, had to sign the Pact. This was done on the night of Oct. 10th.

Latvia had to grant the Soviet Union the right to maintain in the towns of Liepaja (Libau) and Ventspils (Vindau) naval bases and a number of airfields, and to construct a base for coastal artillery on the littoral between Ventspils and Pitrags with a view to defending the Strait of Irbs (Irben) at the inlet into the Gulf of Riga. Analogously to the Estonian—Soviet Pact the boundaries of the areas to be allotted to the Soviet Union, as well as the limited numbers of land and air forces which the Soviet Union was entitled to maintain, at its own expense, on the bases and airfields were to be fixed by special agreement. This maximum was to be 30,000 men. In all other respects the Pact was identical with the Estonian—Soviet Pact, save the stipulation, hardly deserving to be mentioned, that if the Pact was not denounced by one of the Contracting Parties one year prior to its expiration, its validity was to be automatically renewed for a further period of — not five, but — ten years.

The pact with Lithuania differed considerably from those imposed upon Estonia and Latvia, not in its essence, but only in its formal aspect. The difference was already expressed in its title, which read: "The Pact for the Transfer of the City of Vilnius and the Vilnius Region by the Soviet Union to the Lithuanian Republic and of Mutual Assistance between the Soviet Union and Lithuania". The transfer of the old capital of Lithuania along with the region surrounding it to the Lithuanian Republic having been placed first in the Pact, this had been given the appearance of an act of magnanimity the like of which had hardly ever been seen before. The agreement on mutual assistance seemed to be only an equally high-minded appendage to this unselfish act. Having obtained his share of the spoils after the rape of Poland committed in collusion with Hitler, Stalin could indulge himself in playing the role of generous benefactor, yielding a part of the spoils to Lithuania, destined in any case to be swallowed up ere long by his totalitarian empire along with this beguiling present.

Probably with the same end in view, i.e. to sugar over the pact, it was to run not ten years, like the Pacts with Estonia and Latvia, but fifteen. It would have been just as well to agree that it was to run a whole century.

One distinctive feature of the Lithuanian–Soviet Pact, insignificant at first glance, is, however, notable. The points at which Soviet garrisons were to be established were left unnamed in the Pact. Stipulations for this matter were relegated to a special agreement. This peculiarity of the Pact was obviously in connection with a conversation which I had with Messrs Stalin and Molotov on the afternoon of Oct. 4th. A brief account of this conversation will be given a few pages further on.

The Kremlin was anxious to take possession of the areas leased to the Soviet Union and to man them with Soviet garrisons as soon as possible. The pact with Estonia was signed late on the night of Sept. 28th, and on the morning of Oct. 2nd a Soviet delegation composed of high officers arrived in Tallinn to settle technical questions about the implementation of the Pact.

As it turned out, this delegation paid very little heed to what was written in the Pact concluded but a few days before. The Soviet Union had acquired by the Pact the right to establish naval and aerial bases in three specified areas, all of them situated on the periphery of Estonia: the two islands Saaremaa and Hiiumaa, and a small town on the coast of the Gulf of Finland. It had no claim to other areas. However, the military delegation wanted to canton a tank brigade in a small town in the centre of Estonia (Paide), a cavalry brigade and a regiment of motorized infantry in Valk, a town on the Latvian frontier, about seventy miles from the seaboard, and in addition to this it claimed two airfields far up country. The only argument the Soviet delegates were able to adduce in support of these claims was the assertion that otherwise it would not be possible to organize effective defence against sudden attacks. Admitting this to be true it was difficult to explain why Stalin had not included the places in question in the list of areas to be leased to the Soviet Union. Was it conceivable that the military experts of the Soviet Union had not been consulted on the tenor and contents of the Pact in order to make it consistent with the requirements of the art of warfare? In fact, Stalin himself had declared on Sept. 27th that he had consulted his military experts and, for that matter, he was himself by no means ignorant of military matters.

Particularly suspicious and disquieting was the claim to quarter a tank brigade and a motorized infantry regiment in the very centre of the country. Was not the talk that this was quite indispensable for the rational organization of effective defence against unexpected attack only a smoke-screen? Was not the real aim to make all appropriate preparations to facilitate a complete military occupation of the country whenever it might be considered opportune to carry it out?

Neither arguments based on the text of the Pact, nor the readiness to give way in all questions of minor importance proved of any effect with the Soviet delegates, who adamantly insisted on their claims. Already on the second day of the negotiations the leader of the Soviet delegation, Army Commander Meretzkov, declared that he wondered if there was anything left for the Soviet delegation but to go home. At any rate, he said, he would have to apply to the People's Commissar for War, Marshal Voroshilov, for new instructions.

There was no other way out of the impasse than a diplomatic démarche in Moscow. On the morning of Oct. 4th, I received a telegram from my government instructing me to apply to the Soviet government. I was received by Mr Molotov in the afternoon. I handed him a note in which, referring to the unequivocal text of the Pact, I pointed out that the claims of the Soviet delegation were entirely unwarranted. These legal arguments proved, however, of no effect. Mr Molotov did not concede a point. Then I advanced an argument which I had deliberately forborne to insert in the written note, considering it more opportune to adduce it orally. I said: "If the Soviet government abides by its claims, which by far transcend what the Pact entitles the Soviet Union to, this would be not only a serious shock and bitter deception to the Estonian people, but would, at the same time, give a godsent clincher to all those in the world who are evilly disposed towards the Soviets. If you do not withdraw these claims, but insist upon them, the comment of the whole world will be that the Soviet government hastens to break the Pact of Assistance before the ink of the signatures has had time to dry: anti-Soviet propaganda will surely be quick to exploit this to the full by declaring triumphantly: is not this the most conclusive proof that what we have always tried to persuade the world is true, viz. that there is no sense in making agreements with the Soviet government? Has not this government now given incontrovertible proof that it does not honour its own signature under solemn treaties and does not respect the principle of the sanctity of treaties?"

This expostulation of mine did not fail to have its effect. Mr Molotov mused a few seconds and then, lifting the telephone-receiver, called Stalin, telling him that he wanted to see him. As I understood, Stalin replied that he would come himself to Molotov, and a couple of minutes later he entered Molotov's study. I repeated to him what I had said to Molotov. Having, too, mused a few seconds, Stalin pronounced his verdict: "An instruction will be sent to our delegation to refrain from the claim to places in the interior of Estonia." He insisted, however, on one claim which went beyond what had been stipulated in the Pact: that in addition to the places mentioned in that document a narrow strip of the mainland of Estonia right opposite the islands of Saaremaa and Hiiumaa be granted to the Soviet Union. He declared this to be quite indispensable for the securing of lines of communication between the Soviet troops on the islands and their rear. My attempts to contest this argument proved futile. However, with regard to the fact that the strip in question was situated on the periphery of the Estonian mainland and, moreover, in a rather thinly inhabited area, there was hardly any reason to consider this claim as especially burdensome and grievous. Moreover, the Estonian government was not in a position to decline it, and vain attempts to object to it would only have given the Kremlin occasion to charge the Estonian government with lack of comprehension of the need for collaboration with the Soviet government in the joint defence against the common danger. Therefore my government abstained from raising objections to his claim.

Two hours later I was summoned to the Kremlin, where Mr Molotov handed me a copy of the telegram sent to the leader of the military delegation in Tallinn. Though the contents of this document were in keeping with what Stalin had decided, I could not help noting its wording. It read as follows: "We propose you relinquish your claim to Valk and areas up country for airfields and the cantonment of Soviet troops. We order you to content yourself with coastal regions, islands and the area of Paldiski." It caught the eye that whereas the word "order", traditional in military orders in all armies of the world, was used in the second sentence, a somewhat unusual term, "we propose", was employed in the first sentence. I could not but wonder if this was not a hint that what was said in that first sentence was rather a recommendation than a command. As it turned out, the military delegation actually interpreted the order in this very way— either on its own understanding or following some hint given in some other order. Thus, it insisted on being 'provisionally' ceded a small seaside town Haapsalu, in the northwestern corner of the mainland of Estonia, and areas for two more airfields up country. As there were fairly plausible reasons for these requests, the Estonian government found it wise to comply also with them.

None the less, the Kremlin obviously realized after my conversation with Messrs Stalin and Molotov on the afternoon of Oct. 4th, that it would have been more convenient not to include the list of areas in a special agreement. It was obviously easier to strain such a special agreement, especially since it could be left unpublished, whereas the Pact had to be published. This explains why the list of areas leased to the Soviet Union was replaced by a reference to a special agreement in the Lithuanian—Soviet Pact, negotiations for which were still at an early stage on the afternoon of Oct. 4th. As to the Latvian–Soviet Pact, though it was not yet signed on the afternoon of Oct. 4th, its text, drawn up after the pattern of the Estonian–Soviet Pact, had been agreed upon and it would have been inconvenient to raise the question of its alteration at the stage reached.

Thanks primarily to the energy and effectivity of the organs of local administration the rather complicated operation of quartering the Red Army units was effected in a short time without friction or incident.

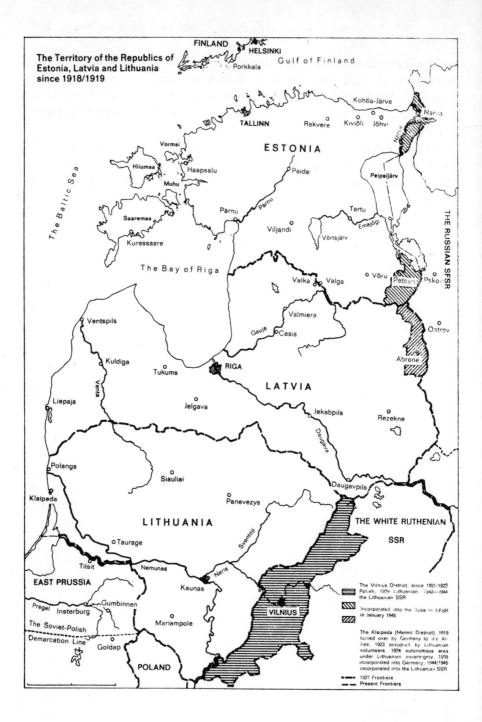

The Territory of the Republics of
Estonia, Latvia and Lithuania
since 1918/1919

FINLAND
HELSINKI
Porkkala
Gulf of Finland

Kohtla-Järve
Narva

TALLINN   Rakvere   Kiviõli   Jõhvi
Vormsi
ESTONIA
Hiiumaa   Haapsalu   Paide
Muhu   Peipsijärv
Pärnu   Pärnu
Saaremaa   Viljandi   Tartu
Kuressaare   Võrtsjärv   Emajõgi

The Baltic Sea

THE RUSSIAN SFSR

The Bay of Riga   Valka Valga   Võru Petseri Pskov

Ventspils   Valmiera
                                Gauja   Cesis   Ostrov
Kuldiga   Tukums   RIGA
                                                    Abrene
Liepaja   Jelgava   LATVIA
                                Jekabpils   Rezekne
Venta
                                        Daugava
Polanga   Siauliai
Klaipeda   Daugavpils

                Panevezys   THE WHITE RUTHENIAN

LITHUANIA   SSR
                        Sventoji
Taurage   Neris
Tilsit   Nemunas
EAST PRUSSIA   Kaunas
                                                The Vilnius District, since 1921/1922
Pregel Insterburg Gumbinnen   Polish, 1939 Lithuanian, 1940—1944
                                                the Lithuanian SSR
The Soviet-Polish   Mariampole
Demarcation Line   Incorporated into the Russian SFSR
            Goldap   VILNIUS   in January 1945

        POLAND   The Klaipeda (Memel District), 1919
                                                turned over by Germany to the Al-
                                                lies, 1923 occupied by Lithuanian
                                                volunteers, 1924 autonomous area
                                                under Lithuanian sovereignty, 1939
                                                incorporated into Germany, 1944/1945
                                                incorporated into the Lithuanian SSR

                                                ▄▄▄ 1937 Frontiers
                                                ---- Present Frontiers

XIII

HONEST FULFILMENT OF AGREEMENTS À LA MOLOTOV

The conclusion of the Pact, and the entry and cantonment of the Soviet troops, coupled with the anxiety caused by the World War, could not but alarm the public at large. People still retained a vivid recollection of the barbarous lawlessness of the first shortlived Communist rule in Estonia in the winter of 1917—1918 and of the bloodcurdling wholesale murders committed at the beginning of the War of Liberation in that part of the country which had fallen into the hands of the invaders for a few weeks. It was also generally known that the same terroristic regime had all the while prevailed and still was prevailing in Russia. Since, however, every thoughtful person realized that there had been no alternative to surrendering to Soviet demands and that there was nothing to do but accept the unavoidable, the panicky frame of mind soon gave way to a resignation which was both tragic and heroic. It was generally understood that the present generation must resign itself to its fate and bow to trials which might prove almost inhuman, only not to endanger the future and the very existence of the nation.

The conduct of the soldiers and officers of the Red Army sent to the naval and aerial bases in Estonia, as well as the friendly attitude the Soviet government towards Estonia after the conclusion of the Pact, contributed much to the calming of minds. The troops sent to Estonia were obviously picked from among the elite of the Red Army. Their discipline was good and their conduct in the streets, in shops, on railways, etc., gave hardly any occasion for criticism. Nor could any flaw be detected in the attitude of the Soviet government towards Estonia after the conclusion of the Pact. The only thing that could not help giving occasion for dissatisfaction and even misgivings was the fact that neither did the Estonian authorities succeed in obtaining the payment of rent for the areas leased to the Soviet Union and especially the compensation due to the owners of real-estate expropriated for the needs of the Red Army, nor were the armaments and other war material forthcoming which had been promised — "on advantageous terms" — to the Estonian army. The question of furnishing certain quantities of war material was broached by the Commander-in-Chief of the Estonian army, General J. Laidoner, while on a visit to Moscow at the invitation of the Kremlin in the first half of December, 1939 — partly since there was actually need for them, partly to try to sound thereby the intentions of the Soviet government. Although most generous promises were given on that occasion by Stalin himself, a group of Estonian officers sent to Moscow to implement the deal had to return home with empty hands after long fruitless talks with half a dozen of the People's Commissariats. However, even in these two questions it was difficult to determine whether the real reason for procrastination and evasion on the Soviet side was the evil intent of the Soviet government or rather the deep-rooted fear of Soviet officials of assuming responsibilities and the unprecented unwieldiness of the over-centralized administrative apparatus of the Soviet state.

If, however, one overlooked these somewhat disquieting aspects, it had to be admitted that the attitude of the Soviet Union towards Estonia was not only correct, but almost as good as Estonia had always desired it to be. No wonder that the anxiety which had arisen in the beginning gradually abated and minds calmed down.

In connection with this, an illusion arose and attained rather wide circulation. There was hardly any thoughtful person in Estonia who sincerely believed that really hearty and unshakable friendship had been established between Nazi Germany and the Communist Soviet state by the Molotov—Ribbentrop Pact. The idea was too far-fetched to be acceptable. The Soviet Union was arming in feverish haste. Why and against whom? Obviously against Germany. An inevitable clash of these two tyrannical Powers was approaching, many concluded. But, they reasoned, the potentates of the Kremlin could not be unaware that the Estonians, as well as the two other Baltic peoples, would consider the annexation of their countries by Nazi Germany to be a national catastrophe. They must therefore also be aware that the armies of the Baltic states would be allies of considerable value to the Soviet Union in the imminent clash. On the other hand the imposition of the Soviet order and of communism upon them would certainly stir their anger and might even drive them into Hitler's arms. Was it not therefore reasonable and wise on the part of the Soviet government to display forbearance towards the Baltic peoples and abstain from subjugating and sovietizing them, and so preserve valuable allies for the imminent life and death struggle.

Such reasoning seemed plausible on the face of things, since it appreared to be confirmed by facts. Moreover, it was emphatically corroborated by official declarations made by Mr Molotov before the Supreme Soviet of the Soviet Union. On Oct. 31st, 1939, Mr Molotov declared: "The Pacts with the Baltic states in no way imply the intrusion of the Soviet Union in the internal affairs of Estonia, Latvia and Lithuania, as some foreign interests would have the world believe . . . These pacts are inspired by mutual respect for the governmental, social and economic system of each of the contracting parties. We stand for a correct and honest fulfilment of the agreements which we have signed on a reciprocal basis and declare that foolish talk of the sovietization of the Baltic states is useful only to our common enemies and to anti-Soviet provocateurs". No less explicitly positive was the declaration made by him on March 29th, 1940: "After the experience of the half year which has passed since the conclusion of mutual assistance pacts with Estonia, Latvia, and Lithuania, it is possible to draw fully definite, positive conclusions concerning the treaties with the Baltic countries. Despite the intimidation practised by imperialistic circles hostile to the Soviet Union, the national independence of Estonia, Latvia, and Lithuania and their autonomous policies have in no way suffered. The execution of the pacts with these countries is proceeding satisfactorily and creating the requisite bases for a further improvement of relations between the Soviet Union and these states."

If the Soviet Union was concocting perfidious schemes against the Baltic states, why should Mr Molotov give such unequivocal public assurances of the intention of the Soviet government strictly and honestly to implement the pacts and emphatically declare rumours about their imminent sovietization to be foolish talk, useful only to anti-Soviet provocateurs?

Such conjectures seemed plausible and were apparently confirmed by facts. Actually they turned out to be dangerous illusions, based on the assumption that communist tyrants were led by the same kind of logic in their reasonings and actions as the statesmen of the free nations. Such is not, however, the case. Communist totalitarianism is expansionist to the backbone. The aim it undeviatingly follows and cannot desist from following, is to expand its domination until the whole world is subjugated. Moreover, the existence side by side with it of the free world constitutes an inconvenience which threatens to sap its very foundations, since the standard of living is far higher and life incomparably easier and worthier of human beings in these free communities, thanks to the wonder-working generative power of human liberty. Communist tyranny cannot admit free intercourse of the peoples in its control with the free world, since the comparison of the conditions of slavery and misery in which they are held with those prevailing in that other world would unceasingly incite them to revolt. It must therefore surround itself with a spiritual Chinese wall, an impenetrable "iron curtain" which renders impossible all contact of the enslaved peoples with the free world.

Why, however, did the Soviet Union more or less correctly stand by the assistance pacts for about eight months and refrain from breaking them and annexing the three Baltic states, though without a doubt this could with ease and impunity have been done at any· time?

The reason for this unusual continence of the potentates of the Kremlin was easy to understand.

If on Oct. 4th I had succeeded in making Mr Molotov take thought and even apply to Stalin himself, it was not, of course, to my power of persuasion that this effect was to be ascribed. The explanation lay in the fact that the Latvian–Soviet Pact was not yet signed, negotiations with Lithuania still at an early stage, and those with Finland not yet begun. Even Molotov, whose mulish obstinacy was generally known, saw at once that by grossly violating the Estonian–Soviet Pact of Mutual Assistance almost the day after its conclusion the Soviet government would make it as clear as could be to all three states in question that the conclusion of analogous pacts would be equivalent to suicide. There was still the possibility that a joint, though improvised action of the four states, which had not been duly prepared, might be brought about in the very nick of time as a desperate measure dictated by the instinct of self-preservation. That the Soviet Union in fact had reason to be apprehensive of such an eventuality was strikingly revealed but three months later in the Finnish Winter War. It is true that the heroic resistance of the Finns was considerably favoured by the exceptionally cold winter and the topography of their country, admirably suited to defence especially in a war against Russian soldiers, the overwhelming majority of whom were not accustomed to this kind of condition. But even making allowance for this one could not but be filled with admiration for the Finnish David who struck such heavy blows at the unwieldy Soviet Goliath. Up to Moscow and still further hospitals were crowded with Red Army soldiers wounded or frostbitten on the Finnish front. Even the victualling of Moscow went wrong (though, of course, partly also in consequence of the uncommonly hard winter), so seriously was the vast Soviet empire shaken by the war with tiny Finland. If the Soviet Union had had to wage not a singlehanded war against Finland, but simultaneously against the three Baltic states south of the Gulf of Finland as well, the feet of clay of the Soviet giant would have begun to totter much more vehemently and it would not be unreasonable to suppose that in such a case Finland would have escaped the harsh peace treaty imposed on her in Moscow on March 13th, 1940, and Estonia, Latvia, and Lithuania might have continued to exist as independent states.

But the Finns had been inured to singular sturdiness and persistency by their unrelenting struggle against the severity of the climate and the scantiness of the soil of their country. They displayed an equally great tenacity in their diplomatic negotiations with Moscow preceding the Soviet aggression as in their exploits on the battle-fields. Although Marshal Voroshilov had boasted that the indomitable might of the Red Army would smash the resistance of any adversary, Stalin preferred to try to get from the Finns without war what he had succeeded in getting from the three states south of the Gulf of Finland: naval bases and airfields on the territory of Finland to serve as Trojan horses which would render it easy to usurp that country too at the proper moment. Tremendous masses of Red Army troops were concentrated on the frontier of Finland — primarily to give the Finns such a fright that they would yield to the demands of the Kremlin, realizing that it would be madness to fight against such odds. But the Finns were not scared. They negotiated very toughly and dragged out the talks. Although the procrastination was getting on the nerves of the potentates in the Kremlin, Stalin considered it expedient to go on with negotiations, hoping that the Finns, "slow on the uptake", would eventually come round and follow the example of Estonia, Latvia, and Lithuania. It seemed, of course, hardly conceivable that Finland would be bold enough to offer single-handed resistance to her gigantic neighbour. Moreover, the High Command of the Red Army did not doubt for a moment that should the Finns prove such hopeless fools as to be unable to listen to reason, it would be a mere trifle to crush their resistance in a lightning onslaught similar to that by which Hitler's armies had overrun and wiped out the Polish state.

It is thus clear that there was no question of tearing up the Pacts concluded but a few weeks ago with Estonia, Latvia, and Lithuania and proceeding to their annexation and sovietization while negotiations with the Finns were still going on. On the contrary, it was most expedient to create the impression that the Soviet government was scrupulously observing these agreements. For this reason, Mr Molotov assured everyone most emphatically in his speech before the Supreme Soviet on Oct. 31st, 1939, quoted above, of the Soviet government's determination "to stand for a strict and honest fulfilment of agreements signed by it". These assurances were actually addressed to the Finns, and designed to induce them to take the same course in their current negotations as had the Estonians, the Latvians, and the Lithuanians. The Finns, however, turned out not to be so gullible as to listen to Mr Molotov's siren song.

The month of November was already nearing its end and the Finns had not yet "come around". Moscow could not wait any longer, since the biting frosts might set in at any moment. On Nov. 26th *Pravda* published an article in which the coarsest abuses were heaped on the Finnish Prime Minister. This was an unmistakable indication that the Kremlin had lost patience and reached the decision to take up arms. Diplomatic moves pointing in that direction followed in rapid succession and four days later the Red Army pounced on Finland without a declaration of war.

Contrary to expectations, the Finnish army proved a much tougher adversary than Moscow had presumed. Instead of winning easy laurels, the Red Army suffered a series of shameful defeats at the hands of the

Finns, by far inferior in numbers but incomparably superior in valour. However, even the most heroic, death-defying bravery and the most glowing patriotic ardour could not disprove the old saw that God is with the heaviest battalions. Inevitably the Red Army managed at last to get the better of the Finns. It was indeed a wonder that the Finnish army was able to resist the furious onslaughts of the Red Army for over three months before its power of resistance was broken.

But whatever turn the trial of strength with Finland had taken, the potentates of the Kremlin did not need to put off the annexation of Estonia, Latvia, and Lithuania any longer after they had broken off negotiations with the Finns and started aggression. Why then did they still delay the execution of designs conceived long ago? Why did they abstain from annexing the countries in question even for three months after the conclusion of peace with Finland? And why did they acquiesce in concluding peace with Finland instead of completely subjugating her by force of arms, as they certainly would have been able to do once the backbone of Finnish resistance was broken by the overwhelming superiority of Soviet force?

The most plausible answers to these questions seem to be the following.

The masters of the Kremlin were well aware of the utter disrepute they had brought upon themselves by the infamous Molotov–Ribbentrop Pact and the heinous crime of the rape of Poland. Their reputation now threatened seriously to jeopardize the chances of corrosive communist propaganda in the world and even involved the danger of the Soviet Union's premature involvement in the great war. It was therefore well advised to display moderation postponing the final swallowing up of Finland and the annexation and sovietization of the three states south of the Gulf of Finland for some while, awaiting a more opportune moment. Moreover, the war with Finland had to a degree scarcely expected shaken the Soviet empire, exposing many serious failings in the Red Army. Before embarking upon new adventures it was expedient to correct the mistakes made and remove the flaws revealed by the reverses suffered on the battlefields in Finland. Thus it was only the firmness and stubbornness of the Finns in their negotiations with Moscow in October and November of 1939 and their subsequent admirable resistance to which the

Estonians, the Latvians and the Lithuanians owed the postponement of the annexation and sovietization of their states for eight months.

In late April, however, there appeared the first disquieting signs of a change in the attitude and demeanour of Moscow towards the Baltic states. They emerged first of all with regard to Lithuania. As a forewarning, the communist underground cells, which had kept rather quiet all this time, began to stir, to provoke incidents and organize strikes of the workers employed in the construction of barracks for Soviet forces. Then, all of a sudden, on May 25th, the Lithuanian government received a note from the Soviet government most alarming because so strange.

According to this note, two soldiers of the Red Army had disappeared from the military bases in Lithuania and the Lithuanian authorities were accused of having abetted the persons responsible for these disappearances by giving the soldiers in question drinks, involving them in criminal activities, and preparing the way for their desertion or disappearance.[1] The Soviet government said that a stop must be put to such "provocative actions", and the necessary steps be taken immediately to search for the missing Soviet soldiers and deliver them to the Soviet military authorities. The note closed with an undisguised threat: "The Soviet government hopes that the Lithuanian government will take the necessary measures to comply with the Soviet proposals and *will not force it to take other measures.*"

The Lithuanian government did everything in its power to investigate the matter without delay. It begged the Soviet government to furnish all available evidence that might facilitate and accelerate the investigation and, in the first place, to indicate the persons and authorities hinted at in the Soviet note as the malefactors and their

---

Cases of the disappearance of Soviet soldiers had occurred before, as is evidenced by the text of the note, which reads: *"two more soldiers . . . recently disappeared."* There could hardly be any doubt that there were among the Red Army soldiers stationed in Lithuania some who were tempted to desert and to try to escape abroad, which in all probability seemed easier from there than from the Soviet Union. Moreover, one should draw attention to the fact that, according to the note in question, the Soviet government was only "sure" that the disappearance of the "two more soldiers" had been brought about by persons who had been acting under the protection of the Lithuanian authorities.

protectors. Instead of furnishing the evidence and the indications requested the People's Commissar for Foreign Affairs, i.e. Mr Molotov, published in the Soviet press on May 30th a communiqué under the heading: "On Provocation by the Lithuanian Authorities" which contained a fantastic story about two Red Army soldiers allegedly kidnapped by unknown persons and exposed to attempts to extort information about the Soviet forces by dint of threats and violence, while detained without water and food somewhere in a basement, one for seven days, the other for three days. One of these soldiers was said to have been taken one night blindfolded out of the basement where he had been detained, conveyed to the town and released there, the other to have managed to escape through a sewer main.

A number of alleged cases of the Lithuanian authorities pestering the Red Army units were also mentioned in the communiqué, which ended with the same threat as had been launched in the note of May 25th: that the Soviet government would be forced to take other measures if the Lithuanian government would not comply with the claims set forth in the note.

Two days before the publication of this communiqué, a first harbinger foreboding stormy weather for Estonia too had appeared. It was a notice from Tallinn, published in *Pravda* on May 28th under the heading: "Political Feelings in Estonia". In this article Estonia was taken to task because of the warm sympathies for England displayed by all classes of her population and the strong dislike of Germany. Such feelings could hardly be considered in harmony with the policy of the Soviet government, which at that time was making show of its friendship and loyal collaboraton with Nazi Germany. The article contained, moreover, explicit reproaches to the "ruling circles" and "political figures" of Estonia, who were criticised for not publishing facts about the trade between Estonia and the Soviet Union and concealing from the public the role of the Soviet Union with regard to Estonia. The publication of such a querulous article three days after the delivery of the above-mentioned threatening note to Lithuania could not but give alarm.

Before long these misgivings proved well-founded. Of course, a settlement of the quarrel with Lithuania by an amicable compromise was more or less inconceivable after the publication of an official statement drawn up in such a tone as the communiqué of May 30th. There was therefore little prospect of averting the imminent disaster by way of the negotiations entered upon by the Lithuanian Prime Minister, Mr A. Merkys, who, complying with the desire expressed by Mr Molotov, went to Moscow for this purpose. In the ensuing negotiations Mr Molotov proved impervious to arguments, facts and explanations, as was usual with him. Indulging in quibbles, he pertinaciously reiterated the charges proffered against the Lithuanian authorities in the above-mentioned note and the communiqué. He addressed captious, really preposterous reproaches to the Prime Minister himself on account of a trivial article he had published, demanded that the Minister of the Interior, General Skucas, and the Director of the Department of Security, Povilaitis, be dismissed as hostile to the Soviets and prosecuted for unfriendly and damaging acts against the Soviet forces. Moreover, he brought forth a new, quite amazing allegation: that Lithuania was organizing a military alliance of the Baltic states against the Soviet Union. The Soviet government *knew*, he said, that Lithuania, Latvia, and Estonia in secrecy, behind the back of the Soviet Union, had concluded a military convention against the Soviet Union. He did not, however, adduce any evidence in support of this assertion, although the Lithuanian Premier categorically denied it. Neither this denial, nor the arguments advanced in its confirmation, made any impression on Mr Molotov. His only reply was that "the assurances of the Lithuanian government with regard to the non-existence of a military convention between Lithuania, Latvia, and Estonia had not convinced him" — as if it were not he himself who had to prove the charges he made but, on the contrary, the Lithuanian Premier who had to disprove those charges, set forth without a shadow of evidence. Mr Molotov was usually very eager to support his statements with arguments of every kind, even of a most sophisticated type. Why did he not adduce any evidence in support of the allegations in question? Obviously because such evidence simply did not exist.

Having failed in his efforts to smooth the conflict which had arisen between Lithuania and the Soviet Union, Mr Merkys returned to Kaunas, on June 12th, leaving behind his Foreign Minister, Mr J. Urbsys. Late on the night of June 14th, the latter was summoned to the Kremlin where Mr Molotov presented him an ultimatum from the Soviet Government to Lithuania — with demands allegedly designed "to assure the proper execution of the Pact of Mutual Assistance", but in reality trampling underfoot this Pact as well as the Treaty of Peace, the so-called Litvinov Protocol, the Treaty of Non-Aggression, etc., and initiating the annihilation of the national freedom and independent statehood of the Lithuanian people. The charges proffered against the Lithuanian government in the above-mentioned note and communiqué, as well as the trumped-up allegations concerning the existence of a military convention between Lithuania, Latvia, and Estonia, were iterated in the ultimatum and supplemented, moreover, with additions which would have been ridiculous, had not the matter been so tragic. Suffice it to adduce but a couple of examples of these additions. The kidnapping and torturing of Red Army soldiers was said to have been carried out "with the purpose of discovering the military secrets of the Soviet state". How the Lithuanian authorities could be foolish enough to expect information of any value about the military secrets of the Soviet state from a couple of privates of the Soviet army, was left to the readers of the ultimatum to puzzle out. The main aim of these "provocative actions" had been, according to the ultimatum, "to make impossible the presence of the detachments of the Soviet Union in Lithuania". With the same end in view, numerous arrests of launderers, canteen personnel and other persons of Lithuanian nationality, who had been serving the detachments of the Soviet army, were said to have been effected — obviously in hopes that if not the kidnapping and torturing of the Soviet soldiers, then such petty vexations would induce the Soviet army to clear out of Lithuania . . . More than that: such provocative acts were said to have been calculated to create antagonism to the Soviet troops and to show that the Lithuanian government was "preparing an attack on the Soviet garrisons settled in Lithuania in accordance with the Pact".

Based upon such allegations, which indeed defy characterization, the ultimatum put forth the following claims:

"1) that the Minister for Internal Affairs, Skucas, and the Director of the Security Department, Povilaitis, be prosecuted as directly responsible for the provocations perpetrated against the garrisons of the Soviet Union in Lithuania; 2) that a new government of Lithuania be immediately formed which would be able and willing to assure the proper execution of the Pact of Mutual Assistance between the

Soviet Union and Lithuania, and would firmly suppress the enemies of this Pact; 3) that a free entry into the territory of Lithuania be immediately assured to units of the Soviet armed forces as well as their settlement in the most important centres of Lithuania in sufficiently large numbers to guarantee the possibility of execution of the Mutual Assistance Pact and of preventing acts of provocation directed against the garrisons of Soviet Union in Lithuania."

"The government of the Soviet Union expects an answer by 10 a.m. on June 15th; if no answer should be received before the specified time, this would be regarded as a refusal to fulfil the above demands of the Soviet Union", was added at the end.

Seeing that barely ten hours were given to the Lithuanian government for deliberating and deciding on the ultimatum, Mr Urbsys asked if the time limit could be prolonged. This request was rejected. Moreover, Mr Molotov added: "Irrespective of what answer the Lithuanian government may give, the Soviet troops will enter Lithuania."

There was no alternative — Lithuania had to submit. In the early afternoon of the same day, June 15th, the submersion of Lithuania by the Red Army began.

The blow dealt to Lithuania was forthwith followed by moves against Latvia and Estonia. Ultimatums in the same tenor were read and handed over to the envoys of these two neighbours of Lithuania — at 2 o'clock and 2.30 p.m. respectively. The only difference was that they contained no stories about the kidnapping and torturing of Soviet soldiers or annoyances to Soviet garrisons with acts of petty vexation. Therefore also no claims were put forward for the prosecution of any civil servants for acts of provocation allegedly committed against Soviet garrisons.

The ultimatums were based on the following contentions.

Latvia and Estonia not only had failed to liquidate their military alliance, which had been concluded before the signing of the Pacts of Mutual Assistance and was said to have been directed against the Soviet Union, but on the contrary had extended it by drawing Lithuania into it. They had even attempted to draw Finland into it as well. As a matter of fact, the ultimatums continued, the Estonian–Latvian military alliance had been inconsistent with the treaties of non-aggression concluded by these states with the Soviet Union in 1932. The Soviet government had, however, indulgently overlooked this inconsistency. It had believed that after the conclusion of the Pacts of Mutual Assistance, Estonia, and Latvia would liquidate their alliance. Contrary to this expectation, Estonia and Latvia had begun to revive and expand it, thus grossly violating the said pacts, which had forbidden the parties to conclude alliances or to take part in coalitions directed against the other contracting parties. The existence of a military alliance between Estonia, Latvia and Lithuania was declared to have become, after the conclusion of the Pacts of Mutual Assistance, not only intolerable but even extremely dangerous and menacing to the security of the frontiers of the Soviet Union.

There is hardly any need to embark upon a detailed refutation of the arguments put forward in the ultimatums. They are really not worth such a refutation, and it would demand more space than we have. In any case what is to be said on this score has been brought forward as concisely as possible by the author of this book in his foreword to a selection of "Diplomatic Documents and Other Evidence", presented to the delegations of the United Nations' Assembly held in Paris in Sept. 1948 and published under the title *The Nazi-Soviet Conspiracy and the Baltic States* (Boreas Puhlishing Company, London, 1948, pp. 12—18). As can be gathered from the brief analysis given in that foreword, all the arguments on which the ultimatums are based collapse helplessly at the least breath of criticism. Suffice it here to adduce but a few illuminating instances.

Among the claims put forward against Lithuania, that for the prosecution of Messrs Skucas and Povilaitis stood in first place. From the repeated emphatic references to it on the part of Mr Molotov himself, as well as of his subordinates, it must be inferred that this claim was considered by the Soviet government to be at least as important as the two others, if not still more important. Therefore it would have been natural to expect the new government formed at the dictation of Moscow's emissary Dekanozov, to take the required steps to bring these two malefactors to trial, since they had been singled out in the ultimatum as directly responsible for the kidnapping, torturing and even murdering of Soviet soldiers. One would have expected a sensational trial after the pattern of the well-known Muscovite show-trials, designed to mete out the deserved punishment to these felons and their accomplices. But strangely enough, nothing was ever done in this matter, although the Soviet authorities in Lithuania had a whole year at their disposal to examine the case and make preparations for a trial before the Russo—German war broke out and the Soviet occupants were driven out of the Baltic states. This was so much the stranger as Mr Molotov, after baldly handing over the ultimatum to Mr Urbsys in the middle of the night of June 15th/16th, had obligingly promised the assistance of Soviet lawyers to the Lithuanian authorities, in case of need, in ferreting out the provisions in the Lithuanian codes under which Messrs Skucas and Povilaitis could be prosecuted.[2] It is worth adding that not a single word has ever been breathed regarding the prosecution of Messrs Skucas and Povilaitis, even in the years which have passed since the re-occupation of Lithuania by the Red Army in 1944. This strange behaviour of the Soviet government admits of only one explanation: that all the horror stories concerning the kidnapping, torturing, and murdering of Red Army soldiers by persons under the protection of the Lithuanian authorities were trumped-up charges devoid of any foundation, quietly dropped as soon as they had served their momentary purpose in the ultimatum.

It was the same with the allegations on which the claim for the establishment of governments, "able and willing to warrant the honest execution of the Pacts of Mutual Assistance" was based. All three ultimatums stated that the Soviet government *considered as established the fact* that Estonia and Latvia had expanded their military alliance, drawing Lithuania into it. In support of this allegation the following three "proofs" were adduced: (1) two periodic routine conferences of the Baltic Entente, held in accordance with the provisions of the treaty by which that Entente had been formed in September, 1934, were branded as "secret" ones, although no secret had been made of the occasions and official communiqués were published on their deliberations; (2) an assertion advanced without a shadow of evidence, that the general staffs of these states had, with-

[2] *Third Interim Report of the Selected Committee on Communist Aggression* of the House of Representatives, Washington, 1954, pp. 333—334: the report of the Lithuanian Minister in Moscow to his government on the scene of the handing over of the ultimatum to Mr Urbsys by Mr Molotov.

out the knowledge of the Soviet Union, intensified their mutual relations; (3) a most harmless trilingual publication "Revue Baltique" edited in collaboration by three Societies of Friendship of the Baltic Peoples, and dedicated exclusively to cultural, social, and economic affairs, was branded as a "special organ of the Baltic military Entente". From the fact that the authors of the ultimatums had to resort either to barefaced distortions of plain facts or to allegations in support of which no proofs could be adduced, there was only one conclusion to be drawn: real and true evidence was completely lacking.

This inference is most convincingly confirmed by the following consideration. There could be no doubt that if the allegation concerning the transformation — "behind the back of the Soviet Union" — of the Estonian–Latvian alliance into a triple military alliance had had any foundation in real fact, abundant complementary evidence of it would certainly have fallen into the hands of the Soviet authorities when the occupation of the Baltic states had been carried out. Even if one makes the hardly probable supposition that all written traces of this alleged fact had been destroyed before the Soviet government got possession of the secret archives of these states, the fact remains that their civil servants with few exceptions did fall into the hands of the occupants. By questioning them it would have been an easy task to lay bare even the minutest details of this alleged "gross violation of the Pacts of Mutual Assistance". It would have been a most natural thing to bring to trial those guilty of this misdeed which, according to the ultimatums, had created a situation "extremely dangerous and menacing to the security of the frontiers" of the vast Soviet empire. However, no one has been prosecuted for this crime in Lithuania, Latvia, or Estonia, nor have any secret documents confirming the allegation in question been published.

The text of the ultimatum to Lithuania also contained, as already mentioned, the time limit for answering it: 10 a.m. on June 15th. As to the ultimatums to Latvia and Estonia, it had been considered more expedient not to insert the time limit in the written text, but to announce it orally. After having read the text, Mr Molotov declared orally that the ultimatum was to be answered within $8^{1/2}$ hours, adding that in case no answer indicating submission was received by the stated time, the Red Army units concentrated at the frontier would receive orders to march into Latvia (resp. Estonia), suppressing any resistance by armed force.

With heavily armed Red Army units stationed in their rear, within their territories, armed resistance by the Baltic states was still less to be thought of than had been the case eight months before, when the Assistance Pacts were being forced upon them. There was no alternative but to bow to the inevitable. Immense masses of the Red Army began to flow in only a few hours after the time fixed for the answering of the ultimatums, and in a few days the entire territories of these states were submerged by the occupation army.

While the first echelons of the Red Army were still passing the frontiers, a plenipotentiary emissary was sent from Moscow to each of the three states to see to it that the new governments to be established would correspond to the purposes of the Soviet government. This was a rather delicate and complicated task, since according to the plans elaborated in the Kremlin, the swallowing up of these states was to be staged in such a way as to create the deceptive appearance to the Baltic peoples having suddenly grown tired of their independent statehood and decided voluntarily to give it up. The potentates of the Kremlin had not yet openly spurned the ideology which had been authoritatively voiced on frequent occasions at international conferences by Mr Litvinov and expressly repeated on April 4th, 1934 in his address to the envoys of the three Baltic states, quoted above: that the Soviet Union considered its duty as a state to lie not in conquest, not in expansion of territory, but in the building of a socialist society. Openly to throw overboard this ideology would have been highly detrimental to communist propaganda, which at that very time had considerable difficulties in its attempts to justify the Molotov–Ribbentrop pact, the heinous stab in the back of Poland, inflicted in collusion with Nazi Germany, and the disgraceful aggression against peace-loving, democratic Finland. The Kremlin had therefore decided to distort the subjugation of the Baltic states into a voluntary renouncement of their national freedom by the Baltic nations themselves. The new governments imposed upon them had to play the crucial part in this travesty. The outer world and even the peoples concerned themselves were to be deceived, at least in the initial phase, into the belief that these governments had been formed in accordance with the provisions of the constitutions of these states and were fulfilling their function according to their laws and the will of their peoples. Actually, however, they were to be mere puppet governments whose task was to execute the instructions given to them by the emissaries of the Kremlin.

This scheme made it absolutely indispensable that the governments be appointed by the highest competent constitutional authorities, i.e. by the Presidents of the Republics. No voice in the selection of the persons to be appointed, however, was to be given to the Presidents. The emissaries of the Kremlin presented them the lists of the new Cabinets and they could only sanction this choice by their signatures. No alterations were admitted, not even the slightest change in the allotment of offices to those included in the list.

In order to force the Presidents to sign the appointment of the Cabinets according to the lists presented to them, disturbances were artificially brought about under the protection of Soviet tanks and seamen in the capitals of the three states. The Soviet personnel participated in these disturbances, inciting and encouraging the scum of the population to lawlessness, whereas the police had been ordered by the occupation authorities to keep aloof. The Presidents found themselves constrained to sign the appointments, since a refusal to do so would have entailed meaningless bloodshed on a large scale without having been of any avail.

Moreover, the lists of the Cabinets had been drawn up in such a way as to deceive all and sundry concerning the real character of the new governments and the part assigned to them. Why such a stratagem had been devised was to come to light before long. If it had been manifest from the very beginning that Moscow's aim was to annex and sovietize these states, there would have been no possibility of succeeding with the devised travesty. It was consequently indispensable, on the one hand, either to abstain from including communists in the list of the Cabinet or to admit them only as a minority, and, on the other hand, to try to enlist in it some venerable and loyal citizens, though preferably such as were rather naive and lacking in political insight.

Thus the list presented to the President of Estonia did not contain a single notorious communist[3], and there was in it a general of the Estonian army and a successful businessman, both known as loyal citizens of good repute. In Latvia but one out of the total number of seven candidates in the list — the minister of the interior — was a communist. The others were persons of middle-of-the-road political views. More unconcealed was the communist element in the Cabinet imposed upon Lithuania. In the very first set of ministers appointed under duress by the Acting Prime Minister, A. Merkys, as the substitute of the President of the Republic[4], on June 16th, there were but two communists out of the total number of seven, with at the same time two loyal citizens held in high esteem by the Lithuanian people. It should be noted, however, that one of the two communist mem-

[3] It is true that concerning one of the members of the Cabinet the police had reason to presume that he had been a secret agent in the pay of the Soviets. However, even he could not be pointed out as a notorious communist, which, besides, he hardly was. It is worth mentioning that a week after his appointment he was removed from his office since it had dawned upon the emissary of the Kremlin, Mr Zhdanov, that the elevation of this sordid fellow, a petty provincial solicitor of very bad repute, to the dignity of Minister of Justice had exposed the whole "pro-Soviet" government to general derision.

[4] A few hours before the arrival of the emissary of the Kremlin, Mr V. Dekanozov, in Kaunas on June 15th, the President of the Republic, A. Smetonas, had left the capital, going abroad in order to escape being forced to lend a semblance of legality to the illegal acts aiming at the annihilation of the independence of Lithuania which could be anticipated. According to the Constitution the task of substituting him in his duties devolved upon Mr Merkys, who, though he had resigned with his Cabinet, continued in office as Acting Prime Minister until the appointment of a new Cabinet. The powers of such a substitute of the President of the Republic being strictly limited, Mr Merkys did not have the authority either to designate a new Prime Minister or to charge anyone with the formation of a new Cabinet. Only in the event of the death or the resignation of the President did all his powers devolve upon the Prime Minister, among them also the power to appoint a new Cabinet. There is hardly any need to mention that the Kremlin did not pay any heed to these constitutional subtleties. In an official communiqué published by the Lithuanian Information Bureau on June 16th, it was stated that "under the present circumstances the Government considers the departure of Mr Smetonas as his resignation from the duties of the President of the Republic", and that consequently all the powers of the latter had devolved upon Mr Merkys. Even if such a decision really had been made, it would have been null and void, the government having no authority to make such decisions. Actually no such decision was ever made by the government. The communiqué in question was simply a forgery.

bers of the Cabinet was appointed Prime Minister and automatically assumed the duties of the President of the Republic. In this capacity he appointed on the following day, June 18th, a third communist as Minister of the Interior. By the end of June, three more having been appointed, the Cabinet was completely dominated by communists.

One disquieting trait in the described manipulations with the establishment of the pro-Soviet governments could not help attracting attention: the importance attributed by Moscow to the securing of the ministry of the interior to reliable communists. Both in Latvia and Lithuania, as already mentioned, communists were appointed to this post. In Estonia this office was entrusted to a left wing socialist, who, however, was known to have been on visiting terms with the Soviet legation. For safety's sake, a reliable communist was immediately appointed his deputy, and in a few days all the higher posts in this department were filled with dependable communists. The same happened in Latvia and Lithuania: in a few days the police force and the whole apparatus of the ministry of the interior were transformed into strongholds and branches of the communist party, which in its turn was but an obedient tool of the occupants.

To what end these measures had been taken was to come to light before long. In the meantime, however, most definite assurances were given by the members of the new governments to the effect that no encroachments upon democratic liberties, constitutional order and the sovereign rights of the states were to be apprehended. "The solid friendship between the great Soviet Union and the Republic of Latvia will ensure the independence of the Latvian state; the Government will see to it that the constitution of the Republic of Latvia is fully enforced in accordance with the free will of the people", declared the new Moscow-chosen Prime Minister, Prof. A. Kirchensteins, on June 20th, i.e. the very day when the new Cabinet of Ministers "had formed itself" as the odd passage ran in the unsigned announcement of the formation of this Cabinet published in the official gazette. "The basic elements of our governmental system remain unchanged", declared also the communist Minister of the Interior of the Republic of Lithuania, Mr Gedvilas, on June 21st. "The Red Army came to our country with no purpose of changing our system of life or of carrying out any kind of occupation, but to protect us from the danger of war and to help us maintain our independ-

ence". Identical assurances were given in Estonia, too: "The consoli-
dation and maintenance of political independence now and in the
future is the supreme task of the government", declared the Prime
Minister of Estonia, J. Vares, and the newly appointed Commander-
in-Chief of the army in their interviews on June 24th, and 26th respectively. The electoral manifesto of the government coalition, published on July 6th, even went to the length of vituperating the deposed government, which was branded as "Plutocratic", for having
endangered the independence of Estonia, while the new "government
of the people" was praised for having dispelled this danger.

Countless lulling assurances were also given to the effect that "nobody threatens legally acquired property" (the Lithuanian Minister
of the Interior on June 22nd), "nothing will be expropriated, nothing
taken away; all rumours to this effect are spread by malevolent elements hostile to the people" (the official organ of the Estonian puppet
government *Rahva Hääl* on June 25th), "it is a lie spread by irresponsible rumour-mongers that collective farms are to be set up in
this country, — this is not going to happen, we do not want them"
(speech of the Estonian Minister of Social Welfare on July 15th), etc.,
etc. It must be emphasized that all such reassuring declarations made
by the leaders of the new governments had been either approved or
directly drawn up by the plenipotentiary Soviet emissaries, who
checked all such official announcements of the members of the
governments.

XIV

VIOLENCE MASQUERADING AS LEGALITY

The declaration of the new government read over the radio on June 22nd by the Estonian Prime Minister J. Vares contained the announcement that the government would raise the question of dissolving the Chambers of Parliament as not representing the will of the people, and of holding new elections in order to secure really popular representation. At a Cabinet meeting held on July 4th, the Minister of the Interior, Mr Unt, announced that the elections were to take place on July 14th—15th, since he had received an order to this effect from Mr Zhdanov. A note written in Russian in Zhdanov's hand contained this order along with the following: the highest authority with regard to the elections, the Supreme Electoral Committee, was to consist of two members appointed by the Minister of the Interior, two representatives of the Communist Party, one of the trade unions, and one of the Central Statistical Bureau; the decisions of this Committee were to be final, no appeals to courts being admitted.[1] Since, as already mentioned, the Department of the Interior had been turned into a stronghold and branch of the Communist Party and the non-communist board of the Central League of the Trade Unions turned out by force and replaced by a new, self-appointed board consisting of communists, five out of the total number of six places in the Supreme Electoral Committee were to be secured to communists.

According to the Electoral Law in force in Estonia, elections were

---

[1] According to the Electoral Law in force, all infringements of this law could be appealed against to the Supreme Electoral Committee, and the decisions of this Committee referred to the Supreme Court of Justice. Thus the lawfulness of the elections was guaranteed by the control of the High Court of Justice. Now this control was to be completely abolished.

to be proclaimed not less than 35 days before the first day of voting. Consequently, if proclaimed on July 4th, they could not be held before August 8th. Therefore there was no possibility of holding lawful elections on July 14th unless, of course, the Electoral Law was changed and the term of 35 days replaced by a shorter one. Mr Unt had tried to bring home this impossibility to Mr Zhdanov, but failed in his attempt. Brushing aside all arguments Mr Unt put forth, and leaving unheeded the hint of the possibility of an eventual amendment of the Electoral Law, he had abided by the order in question. As was to become clear before long, he had no authority to change it, since it turned out to be a command of the Kremlin given simultaneously to all three puppet governments. Official declarations that the elections to the Diet were to be held on July 14th were published by the Latvian and the Lithuanian governments on July 5th, and by the Estonian government on July 6th.

However, the electoral laws in force were considered to be inappropriate for achieving the ends devised by Moscow. Their recasting was carried out with express rapidity in decrees issued by the puppet governments, who actually had no authority to alter any laws whatsoever.

In Lithuania a new Electoral Law was published in the Official Gazette on July 6th. This "law", drafted after the pattern of Soviet electoral laws, openly monopolized the nomination of candidates to the communist party, since it provided that the candidates were to be nominated at "county meetings of the working people" where, however, according to a decision of the Supreme Electoral Commission, only labour and other organizations dominated by communists were entitled to bring motions regarding the candidates to be nominated. In Estonia and Latvia, such coarse measures to exclude non-communist candidates from election had been considered inappropriate. Other more subtle, stratagems were to be resorted to. With this end in view, a great number of alterations, exactly corresponding to the orders given by Mr Zhdanov to the Estonian Minister of the Interior on the night of July 3rd, were made in the Electoral Laws: the abolition of the control of the High Court of Justice over the elections and the exclusion of members independent of the government from the highest electoral organ, all the members of which were now to be appointed by the government. It need hardly be remarked that the appointment of the members of the said organs only formally and not in substance differed from what Mr Zhdanov had ordered. Actually the governments only sanctioned the appointments made in conformity with Mr Zhdanov's ukase.[2]

Unnaturally short terms for the nomination of candidates was the first — and the least indecent — measure taken for debarring non-communist candidates from the elections.

In Latvia, the decree covering the elections was published on July 5th and the time limit for the nomination of candidates was 8.00 p.m. on July 10th; in Estonia the decree was published on July 6th and the time limit was July 9th at 12 midnight. These short terms were, however, not to put any difficulties in the way of the candidates envisaged by the occupants, i.e. to communist candidates. With this end in view, the requisite steps had been taken in secrecy, before the publication of the election decrees, in order to make possible the nomination of the communist candidates at short notice after the proclamation of the elections. This is clearly manifest from the fact that the same issues of newspapers in which the decrees concerning the elections were published on July 5th (in Latvia) and July 6th (in Estonia), contained also electoral programmes signed by the communist party and a large number of other communist-dominated organizations. If these numerous organizations had had time to elaborate a common electoral programme and to amalgamate into a "Working People's League" the designation given to these electoral blocs in all three states *before the elections had been announced*, there could hardly be any doubt that the lists of their candidates had been drawn up and other appropriate steps taken beforehand to permit these immediately to comply with the rather complicated formal rules. As to the political groups independent of the government, there seemed to be every reason to anticipate that it would be either quite impossible or at least very difficult for them to reach agreements regarding the selection of proper candidates and to carry out all the formalities ordained by the decrees for the nomination of candidates within the un-naturally short term given. There was all the more reason to anticipate this as a frenetic campaign of intimidation of the population was simultaneously launched, calculated to

---

[2] A proclamation or imperial order, having the force of law (in former Russia).

stun the patriotic elements and to paralyze their will to resist and their energy. All over the country thousands of agitators and organizers were at work. The country reverberated with meetings at which threats and condemnations were hurled at all non-communist elements, who were denounced as enemies of the people, "Plutocrats", instigators of war and accursed abetters of English and French war-mongers and imperialists. Public counter-propaganda was made absolutely impossible. Candidates independent of the government and their sympathizers had merely to hold their tongues. They were given no chance of organizing a single election meeting, of printing appeals or publishing them in the press. Nor could they directly address a single word to the whole people over the radio.

Public order and personal security were in abeyance, for the whole machinery of the police had been thrown into confusion and the police themselves exposed to terrorization. Alongside the police, a red militia composed of the worst riff-raff, a so-called "People's Self-Defence", was organized — doubtless according to instructions emanating from Moscow, since a similar "militia" was created simultaneously in all three Baltic states. All day and night powerful Russian artillery and armoured vehicles rumbled heavily along the streets of Tallinn, Riga, Kaunas, and other towns, undoubtedly with the purpose of creating a depressing and paralyzing effect on the patriotic population.

Yet in spite of all this and although everybody was fully aware of the absolute illegality of the elections, patriotic circles had nevertheless decided everywhere to put up their candidates. In Latvia, where the system of proportional representation was in force, lists of candidates independent of the government were put up in all the five electoral districts, twelve lists in all. In Estonia, where the eighty members of the Chamber of Deputies were to be elected by a majority of votes in eighty constituencies, the patriotic element had managed to reach agreement and nominate only one common independent candidate in each constituency. The lists of candidates (in Latvia) and the letters of nomination of candidates (in Estonia) had been drawn up with particular care as to formal requirements set forth in the regulations enacted by the governments, since it was easy to anticipate that any slight informality would be used as a welcome pretext for discarding the list and disqualifying the candidate. Therefore it was hardly possible to detect any flaws in these documents which might have been used for such pretexts.

To overcome this difficulty proved, however, a mere trifle to the inventiveness of the electoral stage-managers sent from Moscow.

Like a thunderclap from a cloudless sky, a decree was suddenly issued by the Latvian Central Electoral Commission on July 8th, ordering all candidates to present the programme for which they stood, along with the proof that the programme had been brought before the electorate. Unless this condition was fulfilled, the candidate would be disqualified. No space need be devoted to exposing the complete unlawfulness of this decree, it being manifest that the said Central Commission lacked any authority to enact such regulations. Since, however, even this was not an absolutely safe means of getting rid of non-communist candidates, an ordinance of the Minister of the Interior, prohibiting printing-offices from taking orders for printing works in connection with the elections and delivering such works already produced to anybody without the assent of the Minister, was published in the same issue of the Official Gazette, along with the decrees in question. It would be superfluous to add that only the lists of independent candidates were hit by this ordinance, all printing-offices being closed against them, whereas the "League of the Working People" was granted full freedom to produce as many printed propagandist works as it chose.

All legal possibilities of bringing their programmes before the electorate having been in this way cut off for the non-communist candidates, the electoral bloc of the Latvian democratic political parties took a desperate step: the programme of the candidates was printed clandestinely and pasted up on the walls of houses under cover of darkness. The only result of this act was the sealing up of the premises of the bloc along with the confiscation of all the copies of the printed programme discovered there, followed before long by the arrest and deportation to Russia of the leader of the bloc.

All the twelve lists were discarded "for formal defects", the main defect consisting in the programmes of the candidates "not being brought before the electorate". One single list remained — that of the Working People's League.

There can hardly be any doubt that the emissary of the Kremlin,

Mr Vishinsky, was the initiator of the disgusting trick by dint of which all the lists of non-communist candidates were discarded. As to Estonia, a slight variation of the same trick was resorted to, and it is positively known that the idea of it was given, or rather the application of it was dictated to the puppet government by Mr Zhdanov.

On the evening of July 9th, three hours before the expiration of the term set for the nomination of candidates, when the nomination had actually already been closed, the government, summoned in all haste, enacted a decree, again ordered by Mr Zhdanov, by which the Electoral Law was supplemented as follows:

"In order to prevent the elections from being exploited to further purposes injurious to the Estonian Republic or people, each candidate has to announce his electoral programme by 2 p.m. on July 10th at the latest; candidates not complying with this decision will be disqualified; the present decree is put into force by telegraph."

Giving this order, Mr Zhdanov had no doubt calculated that save, perhaps, a few exceptions, it would be practically impossible for the non-communist candidates to comply with this new, unexpected demand. Of course, there seemed to be every reason to believe that in most cases the notice of it would reach the candidates too late for them to be able to formulate and file the programme in time. Moreover, to make quite sure, steps had been taken simultaneously to frighten the candidates into withdrawing their candidature. All candidates who could be reached over the telephone were urged by persons pretending to be speaking on behalf of the communist party to refrain from standing for election and in threatening words warned against the grave mischief they would incur by ignoring this warning. A number of candidates were called upon late that night by unknown persons armed with pistols, who threatened them with certain death if they did not not withdraw their candidature.

However, it turned out that Mr Zhdanov's calculations this time, too, had been brought to naught: neither the trick with the shockingly short term for complying with the unexpected, new, bewildering demand, nor the attempts to frighten the candidates by brutal threats had produced the desired effect. The telegraph and telephone operators had done their very utmost to reach the candidates early in the morning, and with the assistance and advice of national leaders the candidates had managed to formulate and file their programmes in time. No more than seventeen candidates had yielded to threats and refrained from standing for election — "voluntarily" as it ran in the official statement published on the morning of July 11th. In view of the prevailing conditions these seventeen withdrawals were not to be wondered at, — rather was it to be wondered that such cases were not considerably more numerous. Only four candidates had failed to file their programme, the reason being, in all probability, that the notice of the decree had reached them too late.

On the following morning, July 10th, the Supreme Electoral Committee sent a directive to the district electoral committees which ordained: "If the electoral programme presented is worded in too general terms, or is obviously intended to dupe the voters, the district electoral committee shall decide on the electoral platform of the candidate, after having considered the substance of the question." To give a hint of what the Committee desired the district committees to do, a reference to section 38 of the Electoral Law was added, which ordained that letters of nomination not complying with the provisions of the Law were to be invalidated.

It goes without saying that this hint was well understood by the district committees. Surely the communist members of these committees, i.e. their overwhelming majorities, had been informed in plain words by the communist party what they had to do. All the non-communist candidates were disqualified, only the candidates of the Working People's League remained — one in each constituency. The only non-communist candidate not disqualified need not be taken into account, since he was detained on the first day of the elections in consequence of a charge of forgery of a bill and accordingly dropped out as a rival. No doubt the charge hanging over him was the only reason for the leniency shown to him by way of exception — obviously in jest.

As to the bases for disqualification, the committees had not taken much trouble to invent any which, at least at first glance, might not have appeared laughable. A single example may give an idea of them — the following one by which the disqualification of a number of candidates was effected in Virumaa district: "In this electoral programme liberty of speech, of the press, of holding public meetings, etc., is demanded for all citizens, consequently also for enemies of the

State and of the people. This runs counter to the rulings of the Electoral Law, according to which the elections may not be exploited for purposes injurious to the Estonian Republic and the Estonian people." Some of the motivations are even more ridiculous than this.

In Lithuania, as already mentioned, the question of candidates competing with those of the Working People's League never arose, since the nomination of candidates had been openly monopolized to communists after the pattern of Soviet electoral laws. Now in Estonia and Latvia, too, all candidates independent of the puppet government had been eliminated.

Although the elections had become a meaningless game, seeing that a single candidate remained in each constituency (in Estonia) or a single list of candidates in each electoral district (in Latvia and Lithuania), the electoral campaign continued with the same frantic madness. By Moscow's order the government took every possible step to ensure that participation in the elections and the number of votes cast would be as great as possible. Threats, lures, deceit, and all other imaginable means were resorted to in order to prevent the great mass of voters, seized with a spirit of protest, from staying at home instead of going to the polling booths and thus spoiling the whole *mise en scene*. On the days of election, motor-cars were sent to the homes of the voters to drive them to the polling booths; so-called "movable polling booths" were set up in order to make circular tours to hospitals, almshouses, etc. With the same end in view, a whole series of opportunities for falsifying the elections were created under the pretext of "simplifying" the electoral law. In Estonia, e.g., almost unlimited possibilities of extorting ballots by dint of fraud, threats, pressure etc., were brought about by the cancellation of the rule that the ballot paper had to be handed in at the poll by the voter personally. Abolished was also the rule that the voter had to present a document sent him along with the ballot and testifying that he was on the list of enfranchised citizens entitled to vote in the district. Instead of this the Supreme Electoral Committee decreed on July 9th that a passport or any other official document would suffice. Thus only the identity of the voter was to be established somehow or other by some document, no proof being required that he had the right to vote in the district in question or that he was an enfranchised citizen at all. Yet, even this was not enough: at the very time of voting the Supreme Electoral Committee sent a telegram to the precinct electoral commissions, ordering them to allow even such persons to vote who had no document of identification whatever to show, if only some of the members of the commission declared that they knew them personally. This made it possible for communist agents to be sent under false names to vote in several precincts in collusion with the communist members of the precinct commissions. There was abundant evidence that all these opportunities for fraud were exploited to the full. Of course, to what end had they been created if not to turn them to account?

According to official reports, these efforts at ensuring as high a participation in the elections as possible had met with brilliant success: in Lithuania 95.1, in Latvia 94.8, in Estonia 84.1 per cent of all those who had the right to vote were said to have voted, and the percentage of ballots cast for the candidates of the Working People's League was said to have been 99.19 in Lithuania, 97.8 in Latvia, and 92.8 in Estonia. At none of the elections held in these states before had such high numbers been attained, and Soviet propaganda was very proud of this achievement.

However, even if the numbers in question had been true and unadulterated, there still would have been no reason for boasting on that score. "Shirking the elections would be a very imprudent step to take: in the present situation passivity could be viewed by us as hostility towards the working people; only those opposed to the working people will remain passive", wrote e.g. the official organ of the Estonian puppet government *Rahva Hääl* in its editorial of July 14th. Threats of the same tenor were launched in newspapers and orally at innumerable meetings in all three countries. "Persons who do not vote are enemies of the people; there is no longer a place for such persons in working Lithuania", wrote e.g. the Lithuanian daily paper *Vilniaus Balsas* in its editorial of July 9th, and on the election day, July 15th, the communist Acting President of the Republic wrote in another paper: "Only the enemies of the people may stay at home and not participate in this victory march of the Lithuanian people." (*XX Amzius*, July 15th.)

Those who did not wish to be dismissed from their posts, deprived of every chance of finding work, or subjected to all kinds of persecution, including imprisonment and death, had naturally to avoid being put on the list of »enemies of the people». How would it have been possible to shirk the elections in larger numbers under such circumstances?

A further point of interest is that in Latvia the government ordered the voters to march in groups to the polling places. This applied to government workers and army units as well as to employees in factories, offices, shops or anywhere else. The same has been reported from Lithuania. Cf. two remarkable letters from Latvia and Lithuania in *Pravda* on July 15th, in which it was recounted with stirring enthusiasm how workers from several factories marched to the polls to vote "in organized columns", headed by porters and bands — *note, on a Sunday morning!* Is it not clear as noonday that this marching in organized columns was nothing but another form of forcing the "free electors" to the polls? What worker would have dared to oppose the order to appear in the "organized column"?

However, one cannot help doubting whether any trust is to be put in reports published by the puppet governments which, by order of the emissaries of the Kremlin, had to commit the disgusting frauds exampled above. Are there not ample grounds for suspicion in regard to the numbers given in the official statements about the participation in the elections and the ballots cast for the candidates? Not only are such doubts well-founded, — there is abundant positive proof that these statistics have been adulterated.

Neither threats nor other measures taken had been able to produce the effect desired by Moscow. The cynical overriding of right, fairness and decency in staging the electoral parody had so deeply agitated people's minds and evoked feelings of such irrepressible loathing that hundreds of thousands had preferred the risk of persecution to taking part in that repulsive spectacle. Forgery had therefore to substitute what threats and other measures taken had proved unable to produce. The genuine percentages of the participation in the elections and of the votes cast had to be "adjusted" or, in other words, to be falsified.

Already at that time, in July 1940, it was an open secret that falsifications had been committed on a large scale by the subordinate electoral organs as well as by the supreme or central organs, by order of the puppet governments. Now this fact has been established by testimonies under oath by a number of refugees from the Baltic states interrogated as witnesses by the Select Committee on Communist Aggression of the US House of Representatives.

In order to pave the way for these manipulations, the counting of the ballots was done behind closed doors, although the provision of the Electoral Law, according to which it should take place in public, had not been abolished. There were no obstacles to the falsification process demanded by Moscow, the communists and their fellow-travellers dominating the electoral precinct commissions, the non-communist members of these commissions being terrorized by the atmosphere of lawlessness let loose in the country and the threats launched day by day against all those who dared oppose "the victory march of the working people". "The local communists received orders to show the participation in the elections at 90 per cent", testified one witness concerning the elections in Estonia, and another added: "In the countryside, where it was easier for people to abstain from voting, often only 40—60 per cent of the voters went to the polls." Summarizing the testimonies of witnesses, the report stated: "In cases where the precinct commissions had reported the truthful balloting figures, the district committee 'adjusted' the numbers upward. Thus many precincts ended up with a participation of 100 per cent, although actually only 50—60 per cent of voters had attended the polls." (*Third Interim Report* ... p. 275).

There is no doubt whatever that the same method of forgery and falsification applied at the Estonian elections was employed also in the cases of Latvia and Lithuania. Judging by a number of perfectly credible positive statements, its application was still more extensive and cynical in these countries than in Estonia. Thus, e.g., with regard to Latvia, accounts by reliable witnesses state that at many polls batches of envelopes containing ballot-papers were dropped into the ballot-boxes by the communist chairmen of the electoral commissions before sealing the boxes.

As to the percentage of ballots cast for the candidates of the "Working People's League", the following facts ought to be taken into consideration.

Privacy of voting was practically non-existent at the polls. Alongside the communist members of the commissions there were sitting everywhere politruks[3] of the Red Army who kept a keen eye on the

---

[3] Political commissars.

20

behaviour of all voters and took written notes. To use the corner separated by a screen for inserting the ballot into an envelope before handing it in involved the greatest risk of being included in the list of suspects or "enemies of the people". At the same time it was almost impossible without using the screen to cross out the name of the candidate or to write something on the ballot-paper, substitute some other paper for it, avoid placing the ballot-paper in the envelope or express in any other way the desire to vote against the candidate without being noticed by the commission members. In such circumstances the greatest admiration is due to the 43.400 citizens in Estonia who yet dared to indicate in some way or other their condemnation of the candidate and of the comedy of the "elections" à la Soviet. According to the official information, 43,399 votes were declared invalid, and all such annulled votes signified that the votes had been against the appointed candidate. Actually a good many more voters dared to vote against the candidates, as a certain number of electoral committees declared valid a great number of ballots — many thousands of such — concerning which there could be no doubt as to the intention of the voters to oppose the candidates (e.g. ballots on which the name of the candidate had been crossed or cut out, to which the word "against", "no good", etc., had been added, etc.). Many ballot-papers showed remarks couched in very sarcastic and caustic terms, expressing the voter's utter detestation of the humiliating spectacle and their profound contempt for the candidates and the communist rulers, who were regarded as traitors to their country.

The computation of votes had not yet been completed before a campaign was started, simultaneously in the three states, and obviously by order of the Kremlin, for their transformation into Soviet republics and incorporation into the Soviet Union. "Spontaneous" demonstrations were staged and meetings held in the squares in the Baltic capitals, at which these unexpected new demands were raised. They were declared to be the expression of the respective people's wills, and the "parliaments" hastened to execute "the will of the people". No explanation was given why the question of these very important political changes had never been touched upon, let alone brought up for discussion in the electoral campaign which had closed but a couple of days before. Neither the electoral platforms of the

"Working People's Leagues", nor the speeches of the representatives of the new governments appointed at the dictation of the Kremlin, had contained a word to this effect. Exactly the reverse: as already mentioned, and as can be proved by a number of characteristic quotations, most definite assurances of the opposite purport had repeatedly been given by the high officials of the governments. The very few cases of deviation from this official line were branded as acts of provocation. Moreover, there is absolutely conclusive evidence that the demands in question emerged for the first time when the election was over. It is to be found in the editorial of the official organ of the Estonian puppet government, *Rahva Hääl*, on July 18th. In this editorial it is said in so many words that *"a new slogan had been brought to the fore at the demonstrations on July 17th*: the formation of the Soviets of the working people and the transformation of the bourgeois Republic of Estonia into an Estonian Soviet Socialist Republic, a member of the Soviet Union." To lay still more stress upon this announcement the editorial repeats: "This was the new slogan of the demonstrations of July 17th." Thereby it is incontrovertibly documented that the slogan in question emerged for the first time two days after the election was over.

At the very same time, on the evening of July 17th, when "the will of the Estonian people" concerning the transformation of Estonia into a soviet republic and her adherence to the Soviet Union was being fabricated at a big meeting held in Liberty Square in Tallinn, the Soviet emissary Zhdanov told the head of the puppet government, Vares, that Estonia would have to join the Soviet Union, and the newly-elected "parliament" be convened by July 21st to pass resolutions to this end as well as to apply to the Kremlin for the admission of Estonia into the Soviet Union. The same order was at the same time issued to the puppet governments of Latvia and Lithuania.

All three sham parliaments met at the same hour, at noon on July 21st. They had four identical questions on their agenda and four declarations, identical as to their tenor, were adopted. By the first of these resolutions the states in question were proclaimed soviet republics in which all power was said to belong to the working people, represented by the Soviet of workers' deputies. By the second it was decided to petition the Supreme Soviet of the Soviet Union for the admission of these new soviet republics to the Soviet Union as constituent republics. By the third all large industrial and transportation enterprises, as well as all banks and mines were nationalized, i.e. declared henceforth to be the property of the state. By the fourth all the land, along with all natural deposits, forests, lakes, and rivers, was declared to be the property of the state. In the last mentioned declaration a maximum area of land allowed to each "working peasant" was fixed — 30 hectars (=74.13 acres). All land exceeding this maximum was to be added to a State Land Reserve out of which landless peasants and those holding small areas were to be provided with additional land. The land up to 30 hectares which was left to the "working peasants", as well as that which was to be apportioned to landless people or to those holding insufficient land was declared to be held by them in perpetual tenure. Nobody, consequently, was to own land as property.

All these declarations were to such a degree identical not only as to their purport, but also in their phraseology that there could be no doubt that they had been translated from the same original, surely drawn up in Moscow and sent from there to the three puppet parliaments. In order to provide a seeming, though very shabby and transparent justification for the acts by which the "parliaments" were to proclaim the abolition of the national sovereignty of their states and their transformation into dependencies of the Soviet empire, the declarations depicted the social conditions which had been prevailing there till then as downright hellish, to express it in one word. How wide a gulf separated this fantastic picture from the reality can be seen e.g. from the fact that chronic unemployment was said to have been the fate of the working people in town and country in all three states, whereas not unemployment, but on the contrary, scarcity of hands had become a problem in Estonia and Latvia. About forty thousand seasonal workers came every year, in the second half of the thirties, to Latvia and about six thousand to Estonia, mainly from Poland, though partly also from Lithuania. We shall not dwell here upon the question why there was still a certain amount of excess population in the rural districts of Lithuania. Be it but briefly said that it was a part of the wretched legacy left by the incompetent and corrupt Russian administration which the Lithuanians had had to endure for 120 years. It goes without saying that the grievances caused by Russian misrule could not be redressed overnight by the resuscitated sovereign Lithuanian state, although the progress made by it in the department of national economy as well as in all other spheres in the interwar period was astonishingly gratifying and rapid. Considering this rapid progress, there could hardly be any doubt that it was but a question of a few years before the excess population would disappear in Lithuania too as it had disappeared in Latvia and Estonia. The allegation that unemployment was "the only fate of the working people in town and country" was consequently an unwarranted, demagogic exaggeration even with respect to Lithuania, let alone Latvia and Estonia.

Some details of the declarations on land also deserve attention. By grant of land to those in need of it and a series of other measures for the benefit of the "working peasants" promised in the declarations, e.g. annulment of arrears in tax payments, repeal of unjust taxes etc, the prospect was held out that an end would be put to "starvation and misery among the peasants, an end to these constant companions of the political and economic rule of Capitalism". Oddly enough, however, the most characteristic institution of the communist agrarian order, the system of collective farms (the kolkhoz-system) did not figure in the declarations among the beneficial innovations to be carried out as soon as possible. Instead of this, all three declarations on land contained a sentence obviously translated from a common original sent from Moscow which ran as follows: "Any attempt to seize the farmers' private property or to compel the working peasants to join collective farms against their will shall be decisively prevented, since any such attempt would be detrimental to the interests of the state and the people." Thus in the Estonian declaration. The Latvian declaration differed slightly inasmuch as instead of the pledge "decisively to prevent any attempt to compel the working peasants to join collective farm" it contained the threat of heavy penalties to those who should make themselves guilty of such attempts. Whether this divergence had arisen casually or had been made on purpose, and, if so, for what purpose, cannot be ascertained.

There is hardly any need to enlarge upon the reasons why any intention of compelling the peasants to join the collective farms was forsworn in such a showy manner. The time was to come soon enough when the kolkhoz-system was to be forced upon the peasants of the Baltic states without any regard to the fact that the individualistic outlook, characteristic of peasants in general, was much more deeply ingrained in them than in the Russian peasants, since they had never known the collectivist system of communal ownership of land under which the latter had lived for centuries. For the moment, however, the masters of the Kremlin considered it more expedient not to render the complicated task of the political and social transformation taken in hand still more knotty by throwing these peasants into despair and provoking their desperate resistance in the period of transition from a democratic to the communist Soviet order.

The nationalization of land was eulogised by Soviet propaganda as the true agrarian reform, carried out in the interests of the "working peasants" and for the benefit of the whole nation, whereas the great land reforms carried out in the early 'twenties were cried down as miserable half-measures without any real value and even downright detrimental to the people in general and the peasants in particular. Actually, however, there was no real need for an agrarian reform in the Baltic states, since it would not be an exaggeration to say that the agrarian order created by the reforms of the 'twenties was almost ideal. What had remained to be done was to continue the never-ending daily work of correcting small flaws and, above all, systematically and untiringly to modernize and render increasingly effective the agricultural production of the country by the common efforts of the free co-operative and other associations of farmers supported by the purposeful assistance of the organs of public power.

After the passing of the declarations, each of the three "parliaments" appointed a commission to draw up a constitution for the newly proclaimed soviet republics, the "Stalinist constitution" of the USSR being, of course, the obligatory pattern to follow. Furthermore, each "parliament" elected a delegation to be sent to Moscow to submit the application for the admission of the three new soviet republics into the Soviet Union as "constituent republics".

By then, the time had come to do away with the Presidents of the Republic of Estonia and Latvia, who were still formally at their posts, though they were actually under house arrest, bereft of any possibility of exercising their constitutional powers and even of making this fact known to their peoples.[4] No doubt the occupants had considered

---

[4] As already mentioned, the President of the Republic of Lithuania, A. Smetona,

it to be in their interest to have them still nominally at their posts, the reason being, in all probability, that this might help to maintain the misconception that the sovietization of the Baltic states and their incorporation into the Soviet Union was being effectuated in a lawful way by the decision of their constitutional organs and consequently by their own free will. After the passing of the declarations in question there was no longer any need to keep the Presidents even nominally in their offices. On the evening of July 21st the Estonian puppet government, acting, no doubt, by Zhdanov's order, asked the President of the Republic to resign. Willingly complying with this demand, the President signed an order to this effect, stating in it, moreover, that on the strength of the Constitution the powers of the President of the Republic would devolve upon the Prime Minister J. Vares. However, the reference to the Constitution not being to Mr Zhdanov's liking, the order of the President was suppressed and the act of his resignation was laid before the Chamber of Deputies, which "accepted" it and appointed Mr. Vares the provisional substitute for the President of the Republic.[5] Nine days later the President was deported to the Soviet Union. The same fate befell the President, or rather dictator, of the Republic of Latvia, K. Ulmanis, at about the same time. No authentic information about the fate of the two Presidents has been discovered. About the Estonian President, K. Päts, a rumour went abroad in the early summer of 1956 that he was back in Estonia — an ailing old man. In the annotations to the reprint of the works of an Estonian author published in January 1957, the laconic dates "1874—1956" have been put after his name. Since he was born in 1874, there cannot be any doubt that the latter date is that of his death.

It goes without saying that the requests for the admission of the Baltic soviet republics into the Soviet Union were most willingly granted by the Supreme Soviet of the Soviet Union. On August 3rd

---

had left the country in the nick of time and the powers of the President were arrogated in a patently unlawful manner by the communist leader J. Paleckis.

[5] Though this is hardly requisite, it may be mentioned that even a Chamber of Deputies issued from decent elections, held in accordance with valid laws, would not have had any authority either to "accept" the resignation of the President of the Republic or — still less — to appoint a provisional substitute for the President.

Lithuania, on the 5th Latvia, and on the 6th Estonia were admitted as the 14th, 15th, and 16th soviet republics respectively.

"The sixth of August is a great historical date — the birth of the 16th Soviet Republic. Only a few days ago there were but twelve republics in the USSR. To-day there are sixteen.[6] Time works for Socialism. History has not yet closed her account", wrote *Pravda* on the morning of August 7th.

This time, too, the masters of the Kremlin had considered it expedient to make a parade of their special generosity to Lithuania: certain districts of the Byelorussian Soviet Republic with a predominantly Lithuanian population were ceded to the Lithuanian "sister-republic" by the Byelorussian Soviet Republic. That this act of magnanimity, quite unusual for Soviet mentality, would have been spontaneously conceived by the organs of the Byelorussian Soviet Republic, is not to be thought of. It had certainly been ordered from the Kremlin — obviously to allay in a manner the grief felt by the Lithuanian people, proud of their glorious past, at the early, tragic loss of their but recently recovered sovereign statehood. It is, however, more than dubious whether any Lithuanian has found any comfort in this gift.

[6] The fourth of the new Soviet Republics was the Karelian—Finnish Republic which, however, was dissolved a few years ago.

APPENDIX

EVENTS AFTER 1940

by Evald Uustalu

The preceding treatment of the history of the Baltic States by August Rei, the late former President of the Estonian Republic, is concluded by the incorporation of the Baltic area into the Soviet Union. However, many dramatic events took place before the Second World War came to its end, and there have been some important developments during the aftermath. They all belong intrinsically to the recent history of the Baltic peoples and should therefore not remain unrelated. This the present additional chapter will seek to do.

There are two reasons why this account must be kept as brief as possible. One of them is the notion that a full treatment of events following the incorporation of the Baltic States into the Soviet Union would probably be somewhat premature. There are still too many things of which we have only incomplete knowledge. A second and decisive reason is that a detailed treatment, on about the same level as used by the author of this book, would require more space than we have at our disposal. We shall try therefore to keep to essentials.

SOVIETISATION OF ECONOMIC LIFE

Incorporation of the Baltic States into the Soviet Union did not mean any sudden break in those developments set in motion immediately after the Soviet occupation troops had arrived. A detailed plan for sovietisation had been drafted in Moscow upon the conclusion of the Pacts of mutual assistance with the Baltic States, and this plan was rigidly adhered to by the Kremlin emissaries who were sent to direct the process on the spot.

The first measures of sovietisation concerned the economy. The declarations of the newly elected communist Baltic Parliaments nationalising industrial enterprises and proclaiming all land, forests, lakes, rivers and mineral wealth the "property of the people", were immediately followed by corresponding actions. In some fields these actions even anticipated the Parliamentary declarations, and in general very little heed was paid to the individual feelings. However, intrusion into the existing land holdings made an exception. Although the aim of the Soviets was without doubt from the outset collectivisation of agriculture it was obviously deemed a matter to be handled cautiously. In any case not all land was taken away from the farmers but only those parts which exceeded 30 hectars. The rest remained in "perpetual tenure" which, however, could no longer be sold or bought. However, certain things soon became apparent which seemed to indicate what the bolshevist land reform was aiming at. One was the size of the new farms which were to be created from the expropriated lands. Their size was to be 10 hectares in Latvia, where the soils were better, and 12 hectares (30 acres) in Estonia. Farms of this size were too small in the Baltic climate to support a family and this reform did not therefore seem to be intended as permanent. It looked more like a measure to create a large pauperised peasantry as a first step towards collectivisation. A like impression is given by the new taxes, which were increased about ten times, and the introduction of compulsory deliveries of farm products to the state at exceptionally low prices. Nevertheless as compared with the handling of nationalisation of industry and business this could be described as a very cautious procedure indeed. The authorities obviously feared that immediate collectivisation would cause a stoppage of all food supply and even bloodshed.

No such precautions were deemed necessary at the nationalisation of private industry, banking and trade. Since this affected a relatively smaller number of people, the authorities did not feel the necessity for any restraint. The nationalisation of industry commenced at the beginning of July 1940, several weeks before the Parliaments passed the appropriate declarations. At first trustees or commissars were appointed to industries, who were placed in complete control of the factories regardless of the fact that as a rule they had no kind of experience in industrial management. This could not fail to have disastrous results in many cases. The general ruling was that all enterprises with 10 or more workers were to be nationalised. This limit, however, was not always observed as in many cases even workshops with the owner as sole worker were expropriated. This happened for instance with many repair shops for agricultural machinery, which after the Soviet pattern were converted into Machine and Tractor Stations.

The fate of the former owners of nationalised industries was a very sad one. At first they were required to stay on without pay until the books were audited, and had then to leave and never enter the premises again. As former "capitalists" they could not find employment elsewhere either, and as even their personal bank accounts had been seized as the property of their former enterprises, the result was in most cases utter misery. Although they had not committed any crime or taken part in any political conspiracy, they were now dependent upon such occasional work as they could get or on the charity of their friends. And the possibilities to help were small indeed as all bank accounts were at first frozen and then, in January 1941, nationalised except for 1000 roubles, of which, however, only 100 roubles could be withdrawn a month. Also all valuable effects in banksafes and at pawnbrokers were nationalised.

The nationalisation of banking, insurance companies and publishing houses took place simultaneously with industry. Owing to the character of their business this process had a much smaller impact on the general public than the nationalisation of agriculture and industry. On the other hand everybody was affected by the expropriation of trade, which had a decisive influence on the distribution of food and consumer goods. Although the declarations of the communist Parliaments had said nothing about the nationalisation of trade, commissars were appointed also to all large commercial enterprises. As shop assistants were rarely considered to be politically qualified for such duties the commissars in trade were taken mostly from the ranks of messenger boys and warehouse workers. The result was an incredible confusion in trade which reigned from July until the end of September 1940. Only after the shops which no longer belonged to anybody had been literally bought out by eager customers, among whom the Soviet-Russian army personnel were most conspicuous, the Government issued a decree arranging for the transfer of larger commercial enterprises to public ownership. In Latvia enterprises whose yearly turnover exceeded 100,000 lats were regarded as large enterprises, while in Estonia no clear rules were given, so that the nationalising committees were at liberty to put anyone on the list. Also the former owner of a business firm had to surrender his entire property including his private bank account without any compensation. They were allowed to keep only their clothes and furniture, provided these were not sold at executive auctions to pay the taxes. Thus although at this time the existence of private shops was still entirely lawful in the Soviet Union, certain members of this profession lost their means of existence entirely. By a decision of the Communist Party former owners of business firms were also forbidden to be employed in their former enterprises, which placed them in precisely the same situation as the industrialists.

Also all larger transport companies were nationalised. Shipping was expropriated immediately after the occupation although respective decrees were not issued until the beginning of October 1940. The idea was obviously that some ships might obey the order of the authorities to enter some Soviet port. This hope proved to be vain in spite of the penalty of 25 years forced labour for failure to obey this order. Larger motor transport companies were nationalised along with industrial enterprises. No compensation was paid and former owners were left with the obligation to pay off any debts outstanding. Nor did smaller transport enterprises and owners of private cars get away so easily. A Government decree made all owners of private motor vehicles liable to undertake "public carting", which authorised the authorities to order any car for journeys of any length without informing the owner or paying for petrol. This of course was tantamount to a special tax on car owners, who had no chance of escaping this additional burden as it was forbidden to sell, to give away or rent out a private car for longer periods than three months without the permission of the Transport Board.

Also houses whose useful floor space exceeded 220 square metres in five Latvian and four Estonian larger towns, and 170 square meters elsewhere, were nationalised by a special law towards the end of 1940. As all rooms, including kitchens, larders, pantries, bathrooms, and cloakrooms were regarded as useful space, even comparatively small houses were expropriated. Their size could in fact be minimal in cases where several houses whose combined floor space exceeded the limit belonged to the same owner. In this case all the houses were expropriated no matter how small they were. Neither did flats in co-operative housing societies escape nationalisation. By a supplementary Government decree former owners of nationalised houses could be, and in many cases actually were, evicted and placed in cellar flats which because of a steady improvement of housing conditions during previous years had been vacant a long time.

Expropriation was also the aim of the Soviet finance policy. The Russian rouble was introduced as means of payment on equal terms with the local currencies at a very unfavourable rate to the latter. In Estonia for instance the kroon was to equal 1.25 roubles while its real value had been between 10 to 15 roubles. After January 1, 1941, the rouble became the only valid legal tender.

ACTIVITIES OF THE NKVD

However, neither the deterioration of economic conditions nor the general confusion of life were the greatest problem of the day. It is quite possible that even those most heavily discriminated against, who certainly belonged among the more enterprising and industrious part of the population, would somehow have found a new start had their personal integrity and safety been guaranteed. But precisely the lack of security and protection against the Soviet secret police became the biggest problem. And this was a problem which concerned not only the officially discriminated people. Gradually it became a problem for everybody and at the end there were hardly any exceptions at all. Before the first year of the Soviet occupation was over many a former fellow-traveller was on the run from the Soviet secret police or had disappeared for good. As an example of this category of newly-made Soviet citizens we might mention the Estonian People's Commissar of the Interior, comrade Maxim Unt, who had at least in the beginning been one of the Russians' most trusted local henchmen. At one time he had even been Acting President of the Estonian Republic and as such in charge of the country while other top men were in Moscow attending the session of the Supreme Soviet and requesting the incorporation of Estonia into the Soviet Union. Only a few months later comrade Unt vanished without trace and he has never been heard of since.

The Soviet secret police, at that time known under the initials NKVD, had arrived in the Baltic States simultaneously with the Red Army and occasional arrests were made by it as early as June 1940. However, at first its activities were on a rather modest scale although they increased considerably in July. People started to vanish never to come back and the "knocks on the door" at early hours of the day started, becoming at last a steady feature in the life of the Baltic people. The level of 200–300 arrests a month in each of the Baltic States, which seemed to be the maximum capacity of the local branches of NKVD, was achieved at the beginning of November. At that time there also occurred a definite turn for the worse in the legal position of the Baltic people. On November 6, 1940, the criminal, civil, and matrimonial legislation of the Russian Federal Republic was retroactively set in force also in the Baltic States. The most ominous stipulation in this decision of the Supreme Soviet was of course its retroactivity. This meant that many deeds and doings which had been entirely lawful according to the laws of the independent Baltic republics had now become criminal. For instance every soldier who had fought against the Soviets in 1918–20 was now a criminal, as was every judge who had tried a case of subversive activities of the communists against the independence of the Baltic republics. Of course a lot of other activities had now become criminal too. It seemed hardly possible that there was anybody who in one way or other had not trespassed against some of the laws of the Russian Federal Republic.

This situation gave a free hand to the NKVD to impose its terror on the Baltic peoples. By the time it was unleashed this organisation had had plenty of time to prepare the lists of its victims. They were officially called "enemies of the people" and as such were considered all leading members of political parties, higher civil servants, prominent members of the Home Guard, persons previously employed in the diplomatic service, judges, public prosecutors, army officers, policemen, ministers of all religious denominations, persons of aristocratic descent, industrialists, ship-owners, merchants, owners of large houses, representatives of foreign firms, relatives of persons who had escaped abroad, relatives of persons who had been sentenced for political crimes under the Soviet regime, and persons who had close contacts with foreign countries. The list of people who had to be considered as being *eo ipso* "enemies of the people" contained in all 29 different categories to whom NKVD was to devote special attention.

This attention found its expression in a steady flow of arrests and trials by a three-man jury whose sessions were held in seclusion and where even the accused were not always present. In no instance was the privilege of legal defence or the right to call witnesses granted to the accused. Neither is there known any case which resulted in the acquittal of the accused. This could not happen in practice as sentences were decided on the "confessions" of the accused and the persecution methods of the NKVD had been developed to such perfection that they could hardly fail to produce the signature of the accused to his "confession". After the Russians had retired before the onslaught of the German *Wehrmacht*, mass-graves were found in each of the Baltic States with bodies bearing hideous marks of torture. The number of such bodies found was 1355 in Latvia, 1400 in Lithuania, and 2 185 in Estonia. These were victims of the NKVD who had died under torture or for some reason had been shot on the spot.

The routine procedure was to condemn the arrested to 25 years forced labour and to transfer them to prisons or to camps of "corrective labour", called also Stalin's slave-labour camps. Also this category of NKVD victims was biggest in Estonia, probably because there had been more time for their evacuation. The names are known of 5976 prisoners who were transported to Russia besides 1100 other names recorded as "vanished without trace". The latter were either in graves whose site could not be found or had been sent to Russia without their names coming to records. The figures of the prisoners sent to Russia might easily have been bigger by a few thousand had not some large transports been overtaken by the sudden advance of the Germans in August 1941.

However, all these individual arrests could still handle only a fraction of the people whose disappearance was thought to be necessary for the subjugation of the Baltic peoples. To achieve satisfactory results the NKVD had decided to use special operations which by their sheer size, as well as by their intentionally brutal execution, usually produced a sufficiently strong terrorizing effect. The special tool for this kind of work in the arsenal of the NKVD was mass-deportation.

DEPORTATIONS

Mass deportations as a means of repressing opposition had been developed into an extremely effective political weapon during the

Stalinist era in the Soviet Union. Two very desirable aims could be achieved by it at one stroke: large numbers of dissenting and therefore dangerous people could be rendered harmless, and at the same time a shock could be administered to all those not directly affected. It was therefore perhaps only natural that preparations for such an operation in the Baltic countries were initiated long before this area had come under Soviet sway.

On October 10, 1939, the same day as a banquet was held in the Kremlin in honour of the Lithuanian delegation who the day before had put its signature to the Pact of Mutual Assistance with the Soviet Union, an ominous document was signed by General Serov, commissar of 3rd grade in the NKVD. This document, classified as "extremely secret", was an instruction to the NKVD officials who were sent to the Soviet military bases in the Baltic States. Its title was "The Deportation of Anti-Soviet Elements from the Baltic Countries". It was a long and thorough exposition of seven chapters. After an introduction dealing with the general situation and stressing the great political importance of the operation, the instruction discussed the briefing of the personnel, which documents should be issued to the deportees, the manner in which the deportees should be fetched from their homes, how the separation of the men from their families should be handled, how the convoys should be arranged and how the loading of deportees at railway-stations should proceed.

The instructions were followed in all detail during the execution of the first mass-deportation from the Baltic countries which started in the night between the 13th and 14th of June 1941. The lists of deportees had been prepared during the previous winter by committees of three (so-called *troikas*) of which in every county there had worked one with an overhead central committee for each of the three Baltic States. These lists contained 21,114 names for Lithuania, 16,205 for Latvia and 11,157 for Estonia. However, although the pursuit went on several days, not all could be found. Many had already started to avoid the vicinity of their homes, especially at night time, and some had the good luck to escape at the last moment. So the 662 box-cars which were sent away from Latvia contained only 15,081 persons (thereof 3332 children under age of 16), and the 490 railway carriages from Estonia 10,205 persons (of whom 3018 were children under the age of 15). Also the deportee trains from Lithuania are considered to have contained fewer people than were listed. But neither had the authorities been able to provide freight cars in the required quantity. In consequence carriages which should have contained 25 people each were loaded with 30 and even 40 persons, which increased the inconveniences considerably 'on journeys taking in some cases several weeks. Among the terminals of the trains were according to the schedule issued by the same General Serov on June 13, 1941, such remote places as Jenissei, Karaganda, Novosibirsk and Barnaul, to name but a few somewhat better known places.

This deportation came in fact as the shock to the Baltic peoples it had been intended to be. This effect was in a great degree achieved by the way it was executed. August Rei, the former President of Estonia, has in another connection given a good description of its execution, which we would like to render as it stands. He writes:

"The accomplishment of the deportation actually began on June 13, about noon, when the aforesaid committees of three ordered all owners of lorries to put these at the disposal of the militia (police) in the evening. The persons who were appointed to execute the deportation — members of the Communist Party, militiamen, officials of the NKVD and some Communist sympathizers among the workers — were also convened to some specially selected halls or buildings for the evening. These men manned the lorries in groups of four, received a list of deportees whom they were to fetch and were sent out on their errand at about 1 a.m. on June 14. The lorries drove to the houses of the deportees, two of the men stayed outside, two entered the house carrying arms. The deportees were informed that they were to leave immediately for Russia and ordered to dress and come away. Depending on the discretion of the deporters, in some cases they were allowed only 15 minutes to get ready, in others up to two hours. In some instances no luggage was allowed, in others a family could take with them up to 100 kilogrammes of clothes and food. Thereupon the deportees were ordered to climb onto the lorry and driven to a railway station where cattle wagons with barred windows awaited them. The wagons had a hole in the floor which was to serve as a toilet convenience. At the stations the men were parted from the women and placed in separate carriages. Up to forty people were crammed into one carriage, which were so full that the people had to take turns to lie down to sleep on the floor. The doors of the 'loaded' wagons were locked from the outside with iron bars. The trains were surrounded by NKVD-men and soldiers of the Red Army and stayed at the stations for three days until the NKVD prepared their despatch. During all this time the deportees got neither food nor water to drink. A few had taken some food with them but nobody had known that even water would not be available. Fainting with thirst in the hot summer sun, people stretched out their hands from between the iron bars clamouring for food but more often for a drink of water. All their prayers were of no avail, the guards refused to open the doors or to allow even a mug of water to be handed in through the windows. Some people lost their reason from heat and thirst, a number of infants died, pregnant women gave premature birth to their children on the filthy floors of the cars — but these things meant nothing to the guards. Even the corpses and the demented were not removed. Only several days later, when the trains had already crossed Estonia's frontier, the doors were opened for the first time and some thin soup and water distributed to the prisoners."

The echelons with the deportees were despatched from Estonia as goods trains, at the lowest velocity. As apparent from the duplicates of the train manifests, which were subsequently found at the stations of embarkation in Estonia, three echelons with 148 carriages went via Narva and seven echelons with 342 carriages via Irboska. On these train manifests the People's Commissariat for Interior Affairs of the Estonian SSR was mentioned both as the sender and the receiver, the goods were designated as "people, 30 per carriage" and a note at the bottom stated that the freight would be paid by the sender.

The duplicates of the train manifests showed that the deportees were sent to the district of Novosibirsk in Siberia (233 carriages), the district of Kirov in Northern Russia (120 carriages), Babynino (57 carriages) and Starobielsk (80 carriages)... The men were sent to one place, the women and children to another. At the stations of destination the deportees were informed that the men were to be considered as arrested and would be placed in forced labour camps, while the women and children, as a rule, were to be viewed as "banished" and would be assigned to work at kolkhozes, factories, etc., under the supervision of the local militia.

The merely "banished" women have been able to write a few letters to their relatives, but no news has ever come from the arrested and convicted men. Indirectly it has been ascertained that a large number of them died in the winters of 1941 and 1942, either from under-nourishment or exposure.

The Soviet—German war broke out one week after these deport-ations and there was no time left to continue the scheduled program. Instead the authorities tried with improvisations. These gave best re-sults in Estonia, owing to a stop in the German advance for a couple of weeks. This enabled the NKVD to deport under the guise of cons-cription about 22,200 men from the northern half of the country. These men were sent to work in lumber camps around such remote places as Kotlas, Karaganda, Omsk and Petschora, where in some camps about 25 % of them perished during the next winter through undernourishment, hard work and very primitive quarters which the inmates themselves had to erect on their arrival in the woods. That should prove the true nature of their "mobilization", although the survivors later were actually called into service in the Red Army. Along with the conscripted men also members of the standing army and different service personnel, such as railwaymen, chauffeurs and medical staffs were sent to Russia. Under these headings were re-corded the loss of 7400 persons in Estonia and about 13,000 in Latvia. It has been calculated that altogether 124,467 persons had been either executed, deported or forced to leave for Russia from the Baltic countries during one year of Soviet occupation in 1940—1941. Of these losses 59,732 fell on Estonia, 34,250 on Latvia and 30,485 on Lithua-nia.

WAR EVENTS IN THE SUMMER OF 1941

Nazi-Germany attacked Soviet-Russia in the early hours of the 22nd of June 1941. Lithuania, bordering on Germany, became involved from the very first moment and the reaction of the Lithuanian people was to rise in open revolt against the Soviet authorities. This was an un-equivocal reply to the Soviet propaganda claim that Lithuania had voluntarily renounced its national independence and willingly joined the Soviet Union. A Provisional Lithuanian Government was formed, the insurgents occupied Kaunas radio station and units of the former Lithuanian Army, which now had been incorporated into Soviet forces, revolted at Vilnius and Varena.

This was obviously an unpleasant surprise not only to the Russians but also to the Germans, who seem to have hoped that all nationalist activity had been stamped out by the Soviets. The nationalist uprising of the people obviously did not suit the political plans of the Third Reich at all. In their dogmatic and stupid policy the Nazi authorities found it necessary to counter it by an order to their military commanders to check the activities of the Lithuanian government and put a stop to the independent political activity of the Lithuanian people. This was done in due course and the Lithuanian government was forced to discontinue its functions on August 5th, 1941.

The Russian troops had been driven out of Lithuania within three days and during the first week of July Latvia was also firmly in German hands. Of the three German Army Groups on its Eastern front the Northern one under Field Marshal von Leeb was the weakest. It comprised only three armoured divisions and 23 infantry divisions of which but three were motorised. However, the Russian forces opposing them were not strong either. At the frontier in East Prussia the Soviets had only seven infantry divisions while their main forces were stationed deep inland around Kaunas, Vilnius, Šiauliai and even further back as far as Pskov. Such a dislocation gave the Germans an easy start. Only north of Kaunas had they to ward off some counter thrusts which, however, did not hinder them from reaching Daugavpils (Dünaburg) and Liepaja (Libau) in Latvia already on June 26th and 28th respectively. Riga fell to the Germans on July 1st, and Pskov in Russia on July 9th.

As the beaten Red Army units withdrew in easterly and northeasterly directions the Germans could already cross the Estonian frontier on July 7th. They found the country practically clear of the enemy up to a line running from the East along the river Emajõgi, through the town of Viljandi (Fellin) in central Estonia to the sea at the town of Pärnu (Pernau). To the south of that line only one Red Army unit near Viljandi is known to have made opposition to the small German advance detachment. In the Baltic area the German *Wehrmacht* practically lost battle contact soon after having passed Riga and did not encounter the enemy again before reaching the aforementioned line right across the middle of Estonia.

This situation was, at least partially, the result of the partisan activity of the local population. The insurgence against the Soviets which had broken out in Lithuania simultaneously with the German attack had in Latvia been well ahead of the German advance. In Estonia it had time to assume such proportions that the Germans found on their arrival the national flags flying everywhere. This was the feat of the local partisan units which were known also under the name of "Brethren of the Forests". These were bands of armed men of very variable size and organisation. Some of them consisted of only a few men of the neighbourhood, who had sought refuge in the forests from the arrests and deportations. Others, however, numbered several hundred men and were organised by former army officers into units under military discipline. Depending on their size and leadership the activity of these units consisted of self-defence against the mere harassment of the local authorities, but some of them were also able to take on regular NKVD and Red Army detachments. Although the partisans in these encounters seldom got the upper hand they were never complete losers. This, together with a steady harassment of the boshevist communication lines, probably had some influence on the Russian decision to give up a large area without fight.

But the Red Army forces in the northern half of the Baltic countries were also comparatively slight at the beginning. The Germans, however, did not use this situation for a quick advance for reasons as yet not convincingly explained. In any case the German advance stopped completely for two weeks on the line Pärnu—Viljandi—Tartu (Dorpat), which they reached between the 8th and 10th of July. The most probable explanation is that the Germans did not venture an advance with their weak forward units in spite of the lack of any notable opposition from the Red Army. But even after the bulk of two German infantry divisions had crossed the Estonian border on July 11th and 14th, they made only a local thrust in the central part of their front. The general offensive was not resumed before the end of July and by then the opposition had stiffened beyond recognition. New Red Army units had arrived from Russia with better morale and fighting qualities. So the German attack which had started from the vicinity of Tartu was able to push a wedge northward and reach the Gulf of Finland at Kunda on August 7th only after some heavy fighting. And turning thereafter eastward the capture of Narva took them another ten days.

Although their way of retreat to the East had already been cut off by the fall of Kunda, the Red Army units in Estonia continued to fight hard, at first on the mainland until they lost Tallinn on August 28th, and later on the Estonian islands. The German conquest of Saarema (Ösel) was completed only on October 5, and that of Hiiumaa (Dagö) on October 21st.

This protracted struggle between two opponents of almost equal strength (the Soviets had since the end of July five divisions in Estonia, of which two were motorised) was for the local population a time of hard trial, though the hardships caused by the military actions were considered a lesser evil than the constant hunt by the regular NKVD Army units. These were moreover aided by so-called "destruction battalions" formed of the local bolshevist elements. This was the time when deportations of able men in the form of four consecutive conscriptions were carried out and when everything was sent eastward for which transport could be found. After the land connection had been severed communications with Leningrad were effectively maintained by the Soviet navy and merchant marine, which the Germans were unable to stop, having as yet no navy in the Gulf of Finland.

To escape deportation whole families were now starting to seek refuge in the forests, where an unaccounted number of fugitive camps came into being. It is known for instance that in the Virumaa county alone over 100 such camps were in existence. The majority of these camps were small but such with two and three hundred inhabitants were not uncommon, and there were also a few camps numbering 500 men, while one camp around the out-of-the-way village of Kautla is known at one time to have housed about 2000 people.

All these camps were organised more or less after the same pattern. A nucleus of unarmed men, women and children were guarded by those who had been able to get hold of arms. The only way to procure arms had been to venture surprise attacks on community centres and on small bolshevist detachments. Succeeding in taking at least one gun it was already much easier to take more the next time. In any case this improvised hide and seek in the woods proved a rather effective means of self-defence for the population. Although no match for an attack by regular NKVD forces, even the two thousand people in the Kautla camp were able to extricate themselves from the NKVD grip, thanks to the offensive tactics of its guarding partisans. A motorised bolshevist column was attacked immediately upon its arrival in the vicinity of the camp and before it had time to surround the area. This action, with heavy casualities to both sides, was led by a small detachment of Estonian volunteers in the Finnish Army, who at different times, mostly during the Winter War, had fled over the frozen Gulf of Finland on their skis. They had been parachuted after the outbreak of the Russo-German war back into Estonia and had joined this particular community of the "Brethern of the Forests".

GERMAN OCCUPATION

By their fight against the Soviets the Baltic people had demonstrated their opposition to the power which had destroyed their independence and also against the communist way of life in general. The number of those among the indigenous population who had embraced the teachings of bolshevism, and actively supported the Soviet order, was rather small. At the same time the great majority of the Baltic people were inspired by the hope that the downfall of the Soviet regime would mean the restitution of their independent states. These hopes ended in frustation. In Latvia and Estonia the Germans were even able to avoid the establishment of national Governments, which had so inconveniently surprised them in Lithuania. The leaders of Nazi Germany had decided to consider the Baltic States as part of the Soviet Union which had now become their war booty.

The German Baltic policy became evident at an early stage. The first indication had been the non-recognition and the later supression of the Lithuanian Provisional Government. Next the Latvian military units which had been reorganised after the outbreak of the Russo-German war were dissolved in July 1941. They had to surrender their weapons under threat of death penalty, and it was prohibited to wear Latvian uniforms. And also the Estonian partisan forces which had fought valiantly at Emajõgi and in the territory south of it were disarmed already at the beginning of August. Before their dismissal a "Victory parade" was organised on the market place of Tartu on July 29th, 1941. After that the majority of the partisans handed over their arms and returned home. Only one volunteer battalion led by a former Estonian Army officer, but under German command on regimental level, continued the fight. In other sectors of the German front line in Estonia two more volunteer battalions were organised under similar conditions. All these volunteer battalions were sent home after the conquest of Estonia had been completed. Obviously their existence was considered to be a certain risk to the realisation of the Nazi German political plans in the Baltic States.

These plans were far-reaching indeed. As revealed at the postwar Military Tribunal in Nürnberg a memorandum dated April 2, 1941, stated as German war aims in the East the conversion of the Baltic countries into a German settlement area. This was to be achieved by assimilation of "racially most suitable elements" and by transfer of the bulk of the educated classes to Russia, and by settlement of German, possibly also Danish, Norwegian, Dutch, and even British farmers. Accordingly a General Instruction to the Reich Commissars in the occupied Eastern Areas, issued before the outbreak of the Russo—German war, declared that the aim was to transform Estonia, Latvia, Lithuania and White Ruthenia into part of the Greater German Reich by germanising suitable elements, by settling there German races and by banishing undesirable elements.

Although these extensive plans came to nothing, a good start was made at once. After a relatively short period of military government, a German civilian administration was introduced. It was composed exclusively of German citizens and was headed by Alfred Rosenberg, who on April 20, 1941, had been appointed Commissioner for the "Central Control of Questions Connected with Eastern European Regions" (sic!). On July 17, 1942, he became the Reich Minister for Occupied Eastern Territories. Under him resided Reich Commissar *Ostland* in Riga, who in his turn had the command over Commissar-Generals *(Generalkommissare)* in the capitals of each of the Baltic States, and in Belorussia. The areas under their sway were called General-Districts *(Generalbezirke)*, which in their turn were subdivided under the leadership of Area commissars *(Gebietskommissare)* and County leaders *(Kreisleiter)*. All these functionaries were aided by a horde of so-called "Special leaders" *(Sonderführer)*.

Parallel to this administrative system there existed another which was established by the National Socialist Party. This arrangement made the German administrative system very similiar to the Russian one. Nor was the third component missing — the notorious political police. As was the case in the Soviet Union, the German Security

Service *(Sicherheitsdienst)* often wielded greater power than the administrative agencies, and its initials — SD — became with time no less intimidating than had been those of the NKVD.

Although all political decisions as well the executive power were in the hands of the German authorities they found it opportune to cause the formation of indigenous administrations *(Landeseigene Verwalt-ungen)* in the form of Directorates, also called Self-Governments, in each of the Baltic countries. At the head of these bodies with only advisory functions stood leaders of the Self-Governments, also called first directors, who were supposed to lead a team of directors conducting the work of different administrations which roughly corresponded to the former ministries of the independent Baltic republics. In reality the Directorate possessed no power whatsoever. It had no decisive say in questions of food supply or rationing, compulsory services and deliveries, wages, military and labour service, or in any other field of administration governing the daily life of the people. All these questions were decided by the Reich Commissariat *Ostland* or by the General Commissariats in each of the General Districts. The directors of the so-called Self-Governments were only expected to be helpful in carrying out decisions in the making of which they had had no say at all.

The incapacity of the Directorates to influence policies and decisions became incriminating in connection with political arrests, internment in concentration camps, and deportations to forced labour in Germany. Even acts of genocide which took place on the territories of the former Baltic republics, in all probability without their knowledge, could and have been put on the account of their political sins.

In any case the Directorates turned out to be more or less subservient institutions and fairly malleable to the German wishes. These circumstances became especially significant in connection with compulsory drafts to military and labour service which the Germans proclaimed on December 19, 1941, August 27 th, 1942, and March 23rd, 1943. The regulations issued on these days by Reich Minister Alfred Rosenberg, and proclaimed at different dates in each of the Baltic countries, ordered a conscription of able-bodied men in the occupied eastern territories for service either in labour battalions or in the German armed forces.

As these measures were obviously in conflict with the rulings of international law the Germans circumvented this problem by designating the draftees as voluntary assistants *(Hilfswillige)* to the *Wehrmacht*. This naturally did not alter their character as a compulsory conscription although there were also genuine volunteers to the German Army. A considerable number of Estonians and Latvians had volunteered since the summer of 1941 for the so-called "Defence Battalions" *(Schutzmannschaften)* later renamed Police-Battalions. According to official pledges these battalions should have done service only in their respective home countries but were almost at once dispatched to Russia. There they were at first mostly used to fight Soviet guerillas in the rear areas but later on to an increasing degree also for regular combat duty in various parts of the German front line from Leningrad to the Black Sea.

The Lithuanians succeeded in restricting the German drafts both to military and to labour service to comparatively small numbers. The evasion of German conscription was especially effective after the creation of the Supreme Committee for the Liberation of Lithuania. The Lithuanians consented only to the formation of local military command posts which were organised by the Lithuanian Self-Government. These were needed to give protection to the populations against the Soviet parachutists and bands of escaped war prisoners. Later on, in the spring of 1944, the Supreme Committee gave its consent also to the formation of 14 battalions of so-called Local Detachments, altogether about 4000 men. It was hoped that these formations would become a nucleus of a new Lithuanian Army. This force stood under the direct command of General Plechavicius, who had got from the Germans in addition to the usual pledge that these battalions would not be used outside Lithuanian territory also an unequivocal promise that all further attempts to recruit Lithuanians for any other formation whatsoever would be abandoned. Neither of these promises was kept. In consequence the Supreme Committee withdrew its consent and General Plechavicius ordered the units to disband. This called forth an instant German reaction in the middle of May 1944. The General and his chief of staff were deported to Germany as prisoners while the battalions were surrounded and disarmed. The men as far as they were not able to flee to the forests, as some entire units actually did, were sent to Germany and used as ground staff on airfields while their officers and noncommissioned officers were put into concentration camps.

Under these circumstances the Germans did not have any chance to organise in Lithuania special shock-troop contingents which in Estonia and Latvia came into being under the name of "Legions". It is not unlikely that the idea of organising larger military units among the Baltic nations came to the Germans when they noticed the good fighting qualities of the volunteer *Schutzmannschaften* and Police-Batallions. Soldiers from these battalions also formed the nuclei of the Estonian and Latvian Legions, while the rank and file was filled by compulsory draft. The formation of the Legion in Latvia was ordered by Hitler on February 10th, 1943, and the draft was carried out in March and April of that year. The conscription in Estonia took place during the same months. Although the draftees theoretically had a choice between joining the Legion or labour companies, the lamentable service conditions in the latter, as well as the heavy pressure exercised in recruiting offices, resulted in more than half the recruits volunteering for the Legions. The Estonian Legion came eventually to comprise about 5000 men while the Latvian Legion which absorbed also later conscripts swelled to a strength of two divisions.

The decision to volunteer for the Legions instead of being placed in labour companies proved a fateful choice for those concerned. The Estonian and Latvian Legions were organised as regular Waffen-SS formations. As such they got the training and armament of elite troops but were later also used with the usual ruthlessnes. In consequence there were not many survivors in the battalions initially organized. The chances of survival were somewhat greater for the later replacements who instead, after the war, had to undergo the degradation of being treated by the allies as war criminals. Although they technically of course were members of the German SS organisation, it was understood only much later that the Estonian and Latvian Legionaries were not volunteers at all but mobilised men, and unlawfully mobilised at that.

Of the young men who were put before the cruel choice in German recruiting offices in the spring of 1943, those in Estonia had an alternative, albeit a problematic one. Estonia is separated from Finland by a gulf which at places is no more than 20 to 40 sea miles wide. This was no serious hindrance for decided young men, provided the Gulf was frozen over, as it normally is for a couple of months each winter, or again a boat was available. In summer time it was even possible to cross the Gulf in a rowboat in one night except for about two months around midsummer. The nights do not get dark at that time of the year and a sentence of forced labour awaited those caught in an attempt to flee the country. In spite of these risks and the difficulties of finding boats, about 5000 men and many of their families succeeded in evading the German coast guards and their patrol boats on the sea and reaching Finland between April and December 1943. Over 2600 of these young men volunteered for the Finnish Army, where they were eventually organised into one infantry regiment, while about 400 men joined the Finnish Navy and served on its various ships until the end of the war. After several months' training the infantry regiment did regular front line duty on the Carelian Isthmus, where it also fought with valour during the great Soviet offensive June 1944.

The great majority of Estonian volunteers did not, however, stay in Finland until the end of the war. After the Soviet offensive had reached the Estonian frontier at Narva at the end of January 1944, a strong urge to return home, and to help to defend it against the Bolshevists, made itself felt among the Estonians in Finland. The Finns found themselves compelled to comply and over 1950 Estonian volunteers returned home in August 1944.

Although the Estonians coming from Finland had received the German amnesty for their "desertion" in advance through Finnish intermediation, they were met with open distrust. The Germans had use for only one battalion while the rest, all fully trained men and the majority of them probably the most experienced forest fighters the Germans had at their disposal at this moment, were scattered over a number of training camps. There they remained until the German retreat without having been of any use to their country or for that matter to the German war effort either.

ATTEMPTS AT RE-ESTABLISHMENT OF LITHUANIAN
AND LATVIAN INDEPENDENCE

Several attempts were made during the German occupation to re-establish the independence of the Baltic nations. Some of them sought to achieve this aim with German cooperation, while other attempts were made by conspiracy in opposition to the German authorities. Nearest to success came the very first try of them all. The formation of a Lithuanian Provisional Government, proclaimed by Kaunas radio station of June 23, 1941, under the leadership of Colonel Kazys Škirpa, former Lithuanian envoy to Berlin, was a feat of the Lithuanian underground organisation called the Lithuanian Activist Front. This was an all-embracing powerful movement whose political centre had been founded in Berlin on November 17, 1940. Aware that Nazi-Germany's plans were inimical to the Lithuanian cause, it was decided to proclaim the re-establishment of independence as soon as possible after the outbreak of the war between Germany and the Soviet Union.

The uprising was triggered at the proper time and after two days of bloody fighting with Soviet garrison troops the Lithuanian insurgents succeeded in taking full control of Vilnius and Kaunas as well in most of the provincial towns. It is estimated that over 100,000 men took part in the revolt and that it cost about 12,000 casualities, over 4000 of them killed. Their sudden action had, however, created a situation which allowed the formation and proclamation of the Provisional Government and the subsequent restitution of Lithuanian institutions throughout the country.

However, the standing of the Provisional Government proved to be extremely difficult. It was not recognised by the German authorities, who ignored it for seven weeks. On July 25th, 1941, the formation of a German Civil Administration was announced and eventually, on August 5th, 1941, the Lithuanian Provisional Government was forced to discontinue its activities altogether. This left the Lithuanian underground in a situation which in many ways was worse than that during the Soviet occupation. The Activist Front had been disbanded at the formation of the Provisional Government and it proved extremely difficult in the circumstances to replace it by a new clandestine organisation. However, after some time several resistance groups came into being, many of them organised along the lines of former political parties. Gradually these groups were gathered into two ideological centres, of which one was a Liberal-Nationalist-Socialist coalition under the name of "the Supreme Lithuanian Committee", the other the Christian-Demoratically orientated "Council of Lithuania". After strenous talks between both these organisations, beginning in June 1943 and lasting five months, they succeeded in reaching an agreement on a merger and the "Supreme Committee for the Liberation of Lithuania" was founded.

The new leading body of the resistance movement consisted of representatives of nine political parties and organisations. It held its first meeting in Kaunas on November 25th, 1943, and elected Professor Steponas Kairys chairman. Professor Kairys represented in the Committee the Social Democratic Party, he had been one of the signatories of the Act of Lithuanian Independence and had later served as minister of supply and food and been member of Parliament. The other eight members of the Supreme Committee represented the Christian Democratic Party, the Peasant Populist Union, the Lithuanian Nationalist Alliance, the Lithuanian Labor Federation and three resistance organisations, the Lithuanian Front, the Freedom Fighters Alliance and the Resistance Unity Movement. Of these representatives Professor Antanas Tuménas had been Lithuanian prime minister and minister of justice, Juozas Audénas had been the minister of agriculture and Professor Adolfas Damušis minister for industry. The Committee thus carried great political weight among Lithuanians and during the following five months it was able to direct in its initial composition and with great authority the activities of all resistance groups in Lithuania. Its impact on the conscription has already been mentioned. But the Committee was able to impose its influence also in many other ways. It issued orders and general appeals which were distributed throughout the nation by way of a clandestine press. There were eight printed newspapers, regularly published and of nationwide distribution, and several local ones, mostly duplicated. On February 16th, 1944, Lithuanian independence day, it issued an appeal to the nation giving also instructions and warnings to the population. At that particular moment transfer to Germany threatened a large number of men between 15 and 55 and women between 16 and 45 years of age. On other occasions the Committee fought the German colonization plans, which were of much greater actuality for Lithuania than for the other Baltic countries. Although the Lithuanian Provisional Government had annulled the Soviet nationalisation decrees this had not been recognised by Germany. As in the entire German-occupied eastern area all properties which had belonged to the Soviets were considered German war booty. However, this general principle was applied more thoroughly in Lithuania than elsewhere. Besides industrial and business enterprises also farms were taken away from their owners and given for management to German colonists brought into the country in ever increasing numbers. Against this policy the Supreme Committee organised an effective resistance. The Committee also took steps to help the Jews who had been herded into ghettos and methodically exterminated, but unfortunately with very little success.

The Supreme Committee tried also to organise regular contacts with the outside world. This activity led eventually to disaster. In April 1944 an envoy of the Committee arrived in Tallinn on his way to Sweden. This time was much too late to cross the Gulf of Finland over the ice and rather early to go by boat. Having thus got stuck in Tallinn for six weeks he was caught in the net of the Gestapo, who precisely at that time were undertaking a big hunt for Estonian patriots. The Lithuanian envoy was discovered and brought back to Kaunas. This catch originated a chain of arrests among the members of the Committee, who were all caught in the end, although Professor Kairys, who on his attempt to flee to Sweden had fallen into German hands in Liepaja, was able to hide his identity. He regained his freedom from a German prison in Bavaria after the arrival of Allied forces. In the same way freedom came to two other members of the Supreme Committee, who had fled to Germany and eventually been caught there.

Although the Supreme Committee was at once reconstituted by other representatives of the same political parties and organisations, its activities became steadily more restricted until it was eventually wound up during the second Soviet occupation. But even so it managed to make public two more declarations, on May 25th, and September 30th, 1944, both of them directed against the Soviet occupation.

The Supreme Committee for the Liberation of Lithuania, of an entirely new composition, was reconstituted in Berlin already on October 3rd, 1944. The founders were three of the representatives of the old Committee who had received written authorisation to do so. In May 1945 the Committee was joined by several of its original members released from the German prisons after the arrival of the Allied armies. At that time the Committee was already residing in Wuerzburg, Bavaria, from where it was transferred to the United States of America ten years later.

✳ ✳ ✳

In Latvia the main attempts to re-establish national independence were made by the so-called Self-Government. A member of the Directorate, Alfreds Valdmanis, proposed in two consecutive memorandums, presented to the German authorities on November 11th and 30th, 1942, a mobilisation of the Latvian Army to fight against the Soviet Union in exchange for the restoration of Latvian independence under German guarantee. Latvia would cede to Germany also certain prerogatives in respect of customs duties and armed forces. However, there should be an agreement that the Latvian army would fight only on its own borders. These proposals were rejected outright by the German Commissar General, who replied that the Latvian demands were impossible and that he would not even forward them to his superiors.

These proposals of Director Valdmanis were of course not made without the knowledge of his colleagues, who repeated his propositions at a meeting held with the German Commissar General on January 29th, 1943. The latter was told that the recruitment of "volunteers" in Latvia could yield only poor results unless Germany guaranteed that the Latvian soldiers would be fighting for a free and independent Latvia, that the private property nationalized by the Russians would be returned to its owners, and persecution of Latvian patriots would be discontinued. However, even this appeal was disregarded by the Commissar General and the Germans proceeded with their draft without the consent of the Latvian Self-Government.

The German attitude towards restoration of independence in the Baltic States remained adamant to the very last. This was shown even by certain political developments after the Latvian Self-Government had been dissolved and its members had left the country. Residing in

Germany the former leader of the Directorate, General Oskars Dankers, proposed in December, 1944 the formation of a Latvian National Council with a National Committee as its executive organ. Although this plan was tantamount to the establishment of a Latvian provisional government in exile the German authorities gave their blessing to this scheme. However, it soon became obvious that their consent was not sincere but intended to serve only propagandistic aims. After the National Council had been formed and had held its first meeting in Potsdam on February 20th, 1945, electing a National Committee under the leadership of General Bankerskis, SS-General Behrend was suddenly attached to the Committee as an "advisor". The more correct designation would have been "supervisor", as the members of the National Committee residing in Courland promptly realised. In that part of Courland which was still in German hands, General Behrend was the government while the National Committee had become his "advisory body".

In this situation the Latvian military and political leaders in Courland arrived at the conclusion that the only possible solution would be a conspiracy to replace the National Committee by a Latvian Provisional Government. Such a body was actually formed under the leadership of Colonel Roberts Osis. At its first meeting in Liepaja on May 4th, 1945, it was decided to convene a People's Council. The intention was that such a body composed of representatives of soldiers and civilians in Courland would invest the provisional government with executive authority. Alas, it was too late for such a scheme. The meeting of the Council called for May 8th, 1945 never took place. The day before, on May 7th, news of Germany's unconditional surrender had reached Liepaja.

From this development it is obvious that these Latvian nationalist circles, which had up to then sought to re-establish their independence with German consent, had changed their tactics and started to realize their aims by other means. There existed, however, other nationalist Latvian circles who from the very beginning had set their confidence in conspiratorial ways. These circles were gathered around The Latvian Central Council, an underground organisation composed of representatives of the four largest political parties in the last Parliament *(Saeima)* and of some members of the Presiding Board of *Saeima*, altogether seven members. The constituent parties were the Social

22

Democrats, the Agrarian Union, the Liberals and the Latgallian Christian Peasants. Chairman of the Council was Professor Konstantins Čakste from the Liberal Party.

The Latvian Central Council was of the opinion that cooperation with the German occupation regime was to be rejected, acting on the belief that the war would end in the same way as had the First World War. Such a situation, which would leave both Germany and the Soviet Union weakened, would, it was believed, allow the country to regain independence with the aid of the Western Allies. According to this conception the Central Council in March 1944 prepared a memorandum signed by 189 prominent Latvians, and addressed it to influential political leaders in the western countries. In Latvia itself the Council made preparations to recruit a Latvian Army. To this end a military Committee was set up to keep contact with Latvian military leaders who sympathised with the political views of the Council. Among these sympathisers were even some commanding officers of the Latvian Legion, but its strength lay in a special military unit set up by the Germans to fight Red Army units parachuted into the German rear in Latvia. This unit had also as one of its tasks to make reconnaissance raids behind the Russian lines. Headed by General Kurelis the unit carried out its assigned tasks, but its true aim was to evade major engagements and to keep its forces as much intact as possible until it could be used as nucleus for a new Latvian Army. These tactics did not remain a secret for long. The Germans got wind of the intentions and on November 3rd, 1944, the unit was encircled and disarmed. The commanding general was taken to Germany as prisoner but his 545 men were sent to Sutthof concentration camp and his officers court-martialled. Eight of them were executed.

In Sutthof concentration camp there were at that time already several members of the Council who had been arrested earlier, among them their chairman, Professor Čakste, who died there. Also another prominent member of the Council, Dr Paul Kalniņš, the leader of the Social-Democrats, was in German custody from September 1944. As the last president of the *Saeima* Dr Kalniņš was according to the Latvian constitution Acting President of the Republic. For this reason the Central Council had deemed it advisable that he should go to neutral Sweden. This Dr Kalniņš tried to do, but the motorboat carrying him had been intercepted on the open sea by the German Navy. Dr Kalniņš survived the war by only a few months.

Also the leaders of the churches of Latvia stood not only for the protection of Christianity against National Socialism but also for the restoration of Latvian independence. This had as consequence extensive persecutions of the Latvian clergy. In October 1944, the Lutheran Archbishop, the Orthodox Metropolitan, and three Catholic Bishops were all seized and deported to Germany. The Germans also imprisoned three Catholic priests, of whom one died in a concertration camp.

ATTEMPTS TO REGAIN INDEPENDENCE IN ESTONIA

In Estonia no initiative for regaining independence originated in the Self-Government. The reason may have been either that it knew from experience that there was no chance of success, or that the Estonian Directorate was more docile and pro-German than its Latvian counterpart. Instead several attempts in this direction were made by Estonian nationalist circles, to which belonged practically all leading Estonian personalities who had survived the Soviet occupation. From their part came all initiatives, which fairly well exhausted all possible approaches, legal as well as illegal, to the restoration of the Estonian Republic.

The first attempt to this end came from a group who had gathered around Professor Jüri Uluots, the last Premier of the Estonian Republic. At a very early date, practically as soon as the last shots had been fired in the battle fought in and around the city of Tartu, first steps were taken to sound out the German intentions. A statement was prepared and handed over to the local Field-Commandant of the *Wehrmacht*, the only German representative who could be reached in the circumstances. In this statement Professor Uluots offered his good offices to create an Estonian government which would lead the work of the communal administrative organs and other institutions already re-established in the area occupied by Germany. Further the statement envisaged the formation of an Estonian Army of those partisan units which had fought in and around Tartu.

The statement was delivered by Professor Uluots to the German Field-Commandant on July 29th, 1941, the very day when the parade of the partisans on the market place of Tartu marked the end of their activity. The Field-Commandant at first refused to accept the document at all but consented eventually to forward it. A few days later the general commanding the German 18th Army, Lieutenant-General von Küchler, arrived in the Estonian provincial town of Viljandi. For the eventuality that Professor Uluots' statement might be obstructed somewhere in the "official channels" a replica of it was presented to General von Küchler by an Estonian partisan officer on a special mission from Tartu.

Although no official reply was ever received to this statement the necessary information reached the initiators in a roundabout way a fortnight later. A German novelist, H. F. Blanck, well known in Estonian literary circles from the time before the war, but now serving in the *Wehrmacht* as "special leader" *(Sonderführer)*, came to Tartu paying visits to his old acquaintances. Among them was the Estonian novelist K. A. Hindrey, who had translated Professor Uluots' statement into German. Herr Blanck had all the answers to the memorandum, which made dubious the assumption that Hindrey's part in the preparation of the statement could have been unknown to him. What he had to tell was utterly discouraging, giving at the same time a distinctive warning. Germany will not tolerate, he said, the creation of any national governments in the occupied eastern territories. Nor does Germany need any contribution to its military forces. The extensive plans and operations of the German High Command would only be hampered by armies of other states under their own commands. Any attempt to create national governments and armies is playing with fire and extremely dangerous for all those who get involved.

This warning was very clear indeed, as it was already known what had happened to the Ukrainian National government: they had landed *in corpore* in Sachsenhausen concentration camp. Also news of the curtailment of the activities of the Lithuanian Provisional Government had reached Tartu. All this added up to a politically hopeless situation. It was obviously impossible to regain independence with German consent and neither could this aim be reached in opposition to them. Estonia had escaped the murderous Soviet occupation only thanks to the German conquest and only German armed forces stood in the way of its return. Active and effective resistance to the

German occupational authorities would thus only have increased the chances of such an alarming eventuality. A solution to this problem, if there was any at all, seemed to be moderate resistance seeking only to keep the will for independence alive until some unforseen turn in fortune would make the idea realisable.

This policy did not exclude further careful soundings for possible change of mind in Germany. An occasion to do this was given, oddly enough, by an initiative of the foreign minister of the Reich. Seeing the German draft in Estonia was not going well, von Ribbentrop instructed the German Commissar General in Estonia in October 1943 to make certain proposals for cooperation to Professor Uluots. These proposals consisted mainly of a suggestion to form an Estonian Committee which would make an appeal in support of the draft and in exchange would get some advisory competence in the local administration. To these suggestions Professor Uluots could only reply that he had no authority to decide on questions of such far-reaching national importance and that he must get permission to discuss the matter with leading Estonian personalities. Having received the authorisation to do so he called a meeting attended by representatives of the four political parties which had been represented in the last freely elected Estonian parliament, and also representatives of churches and various organisations of business and industry.

The meeting, which lasted for three days, from October 21st to 23rd, 1943, decided to reply negatively to the proposal of von Ribbentrop as far as it concerned the formation of a committee and the appeal for participation in the fight against the Soviet Union. Concerning the draft the meeting declared, however, that in the interest of the fight against communism in so far as it concerned the Estonians, it was important for the Estonian people to get an opportunity of organising themselves on a constitutional basis, that is, to reestablish the independence of the Estonian republic.

With this reply, consisting of only three short paragraphs, dated October 29th, 1943, and addressed to the Reich's foreign minister von Ribbentrop, was enclosed an extensive exposition of the Estonian case. This carefully worded and rather long document (over six large pages in print) was addressed to the German Commissar General for

Estonia and it explained the reasons why the Estonian national leaders had on deliberation come to such a decision.

This document was given no gracious reception by the Commissar General. Declaring that he had no intention of forwarding such a document to Germany, the Commissar threw it in a burst of anger into the waste-paper basket in the presence of professors Uluots and E. Kant, who had come to present the reply. Although this document was later sent directly to Berlin through other channels, it did not evoke any result or reply.

This encounter ended Estonian attempts to re-establish national independence with German cooperation. There remained now only conspiracy. To this no new initiatives were necessary. There had already long existed an underground circle in Tartu which from the very beginning had approached the problem in opposition to the German authorities. Somewhat later a similar resistance group had arisen in Tallinn. On their initiative a large underground organisation took shape at the beginning of 1944. This was a coalition between the political parties whose activity had been suppressed in Estonia since 1934, but which still proved to be very much alive. On March 23rd, 1944 the Republican National Council of Estonia was founded, in which besides the Agrarian Party, the Smallholders Party, the National Centre Party and the Social Democrats also the resistance groups of Tartu and Tallinn had two representatives each. The chairman of this twelve man body was Professor Karl Liidak.

The political concept of the Estonian Republican-National Committee coincided in all essential points with that of the Latvian Central Council. The differences were mostly only tactical. The resistance group in Tartu had already established rather close contact with the Estonian envoy in Helsinki and through him to Stockholm and London. Steady contact was maintained also with those Estonian nationalist circles who were anxious to regain independence with German cooperation and intermittently and *ad hoc* also with the Latvian Central Council. After the creation of the Republican-National Committee the correspondence to and from abroad increased considerably, which put the German security on their track. So already in April, 1944, the SD succeeded in making a catch. One of the outbound agents carrying a pouch with correspondence was intercepted, and that started a chain of arrests. These hit not only the members and supporters of the Republican Committee but also several persons from the circle around Professor Uluots.

Although seven of the Republican Committee's twelve members were able to get into hiding in time, and were successful in evading arrest until the end of the German occupation, their chances of carrying on with meetings and operations were reduced almost to nil. The result was an almost complete cessation of the Committee's activities until the middle of June, when contacts with the outside world could be re-established. From then on the emigrant circles in Finland and Sweden began to take a greater part in the activities of the Committee. A more or less regular fortnightly traffic by fast motorboats was organised over the Baltic from Stockholm, and at the same time the Committee now had a transmitter at its disposal. In July there was founded in Stockholm the Foreign Representation of the Republican-National Committee of Estonia. Four members of this Foreign Representation were at that time residing in Stockholm and two in Helsinki.

In July a Manifesto was released in Estonia which declared the political aims and the policy of the Committee. The Manifesto aroused wide attention also abroad. In Stockholm it was read at a press-conference attended by practically the entire Swedish press and by almost all foreign correspondents residing there. In July the Council also printed and distributed among the population two of its "Directives". The first one aimed at stiffening resistance to the advancing Soviet forces, while the second gave directives as to what to do before, during and after the arrival of the Red Army. At the time of their release the South-eastern part of the country was already in the hands of the Russians.

At this stage some alterations became necessary in the composition of the Council. Considering the seriousness of the situation it was decided to follow the advice of the Foreign Representation and extend the Committee's membership to the group which in its attempts to re-establish independence had tried to keep itself within the bounds tolerated by the Germans. Professor Uluots, however, who worked in close contact both with the Council and with its Foreign Representation did not himself become a member. As Premier of the last lawful government of Estonia, he was according to the constitution Acting President of the republic, and in that capacity authorized to instal a new government. The Republican Council decided to use this possibility in the hope that it might afford a chance of establishing independence in the interval between the German retreat and the arrival of the Soviets.

To realize this plan the membership was augmented in August 1944. One of the two new members elected then was Otto Tief, a lawyer and member of the Smallholders party. He replaced Professor Liidak as chairman of the Republican-National Committee. The immediate reason for this change was the fact that Tief was not wanted by the police as had been his predecessor. A second reason for electing Tief was agreement in the Committee that he should preside over the new government, whose personal composition was also agreed upon already in August. In consequence of this agreement five ministers-designate who did not already belong to the Committee now became members. It was decided that the proclamation of the government should follow at the earliest opportunity to facilitate the establishment of its authority in the country.

An immediate consequence of these preparations was that the Defence Minister designate joined one of the so-called Estonian Border Guard regiments as an officer. This completed the preparations as far as was in the Committee's power. The military force which it could count upon comprised six Border-Guard regiments, formed in February 1944 of the mobilized men and led by Estonian officers, together with two battalions of the Estonian volunteer regiment in the Finnish Army, which had now come back to Estonia. These "Finnish" battalions, whose loyalty in the first order belonged to the Republican Committee, could be used as shock troops.

Although comparatively negligible, these forces were in fact many times stronger than those with which the Estonian Government had met the Russians at the beginning of the War of Liberation in 1918. Many members of the Committee could remember that, and at the same time they counted on that overwhelming support which Professor Uluots enjoyed among Estonian soldiers and civilians alike. Lifelong impartial observers of Estonian political life have offered the opinion that no other political leader in its entire history has ever had a more complete command of the loyalty of the nation than had Professor Uluots during these fateful months before the return of the Soviet occupation. All this perhaps explains why the members of the

Committee hoped against hope that their venture in proclaiming a new Government of the Estonian Republic might succeed.

However, the Red Army which invaded Estonia in 1944 could not be compared to those poorly disciplined, poorly armed and indifferently led troops which had attacked in 1918. Neither did the Germans give any chance to the Estonian Government to establish itself. Quite the contrary. The military police opened fire on any group of Estonian soldiers who dared to move against their orders. And this applied to anybody organising any action outside the German command. In the small town of Haapsalu on the Estonian west coast, which had acquired temporary importance as one of the loading harbours for troops retreating to the islands, an Estonian "uprising" was put down with singular ferocity and quite unnecessarily. Practically the only favour from the Germans was the announcement to Professor Uluots one day in advance of the decision to abandon Estonia. On the evening of September 17th an officer sent by the German commanding general at the Narva front appeared in his house and announced that the evacuation was going to begin the next morning.

Having received this message Professor Uluots made a last attempt to induce the German authorities to transfer the power to a lawful Estonian government. The answer was still a straight no. In this situation Professor Uluots on September 18th, 1944 signed in his capacity as Acting President of the Estonian republic an order nominating a new Government of the republic. Its members met on September 19th, issuing a declaration which announced that it had assumed the responsibility of the government but that owing to circumstances it might be forced to leave the country to continue the struggle for independence from abroad. At the same time the declaration also announced that the Republican-National Committee had been disbanded. The Government also sent a message to the Estonian envoys in Stockholm and London, who passed the information to the diplomatic representatives of other states in their places of residence and in London also to the British Foreign Office. The next day there appeared the first issue of the Official Gazeteer *(Riigi Teataja)* containing the text of the order by which the Government had been nominated, while the printing and distribution of the Government's declaration was stopped by the destruction of the city's power station the following night. There was nothing more the Government could do. It was obvious that the capital would very soon be occupied by the Red Army and it was highly improbable that Estonian units in any considerable numbers would be able to withdraw into the western parts of the country. In this hopeless situation the Government suggested that Professor Uluots should leave the country in order to avoid being taken by the Russians. This he did on September 20th, 1944, arriving safely in Sweden the next day.

The Government left Tallinn on the morning of September 22nd, only three hours before the Red Army entered it. Although a motorboat from Sweden was to have fetched the members of the Government from the Estonian west coast its departure had been delayed and when it arrived at the appointed meeting place on September 29th, this area had already been occupied four days by the Red Army. All the members of the Government thus fell into the hands of the Russians except those two who had been in Sweden at the time the Government had been formed and one who had left Estonian together with Professor Uluots. Our knowledge of the doings of the Estonian Government during these last critical days emanates from the Secretary of State, who managed to extricate himself in the last moment and had the good luck to meet the motorboat coming to fetch the Government.

Professor Uluots died soon after his arrival in Sweden. The three ministers in the Government of Otto Tief who had reached Sweden had a certain importance later on in connection with the efforts to establish an Estonian exile government. According to the Constitution there were two ways to form a lawful government. First the Constitution provided for a body consisting of certain functionaries of Parliament, the Courts and the Army, which could elect a new Acting President. But according to other stipulations of the Constitution this office could also pass to the oldest member of Government. Both these ways were used in the establishment of the exile government, although questions have been raised as to the correctness of each of these readings of the Constitution. The objection against the first alternative has been that as all its original members are dead or away, the electing body could be constituted only by way of representation, which is not foreseen in the Constitution. The objection to the succession of the oldest member of the Government derives from doubts as to what is the correct reading of the pertinent stipulations, which are contained in two different chapters. The result was that at one moment two rival Estonian exile governments were established. Actually, however, only the one which was based on the oldest member theory and emanating from the exile government proclaimed in Estonia on September 19th, 1944, has remained in existence.

SOVIET RECONQUEST

The experience of one year's Soviet occupation had left such an intimidating impression on the minds of the Baltic people that its return was considered the worst that could happen. This explains the sudden change of attitude of the population, at least in Estonia and Latvia, towards the German occupation at the end of the year 1943 and at the beginning of the next. At that time the Red Army offensive reached the borders of the Baltic countries. But before they improved relations had become pretty bad indeed. Animosity against the occupation authorities had been nurtured not only by conscription but also by an ever deteriorating food-supply situation. The official food rations were clearly insufficient to sustain life, so that people turned to the black market and took the consequences when found out. Nor was the notorious German *Herrenvolk* mentality easy to bear. However, many of these griefs vanished as soon as the Soviet reconquest of the Baltic area became a serious menace. With this the critical attitude changed to active support of the German war effort.

The catastrophe, however, could no longer be averted even though the German drafts started to give better results. On November 15th, 1943 the Latvian Self-Government endorsed the draft which ultimately comprised eighteen annual classes. The mobilisation proclaimed on November 22nd, 1943 by the Commissar of the Reich for Eastern territories for men born in the years 1915–1924 was in Estonia extended by the leader of the Estonian Self-Government in January 1944 to comprise all men born in and after 1904. In Estonia these proclamations started to give results after a radio speech by Professor Uluots. In this speech, or rather in an interview on February 7th, 1944, he supported the mobilisation in accordance with a decision taken at a meeting of the representatives of the Estonian political parties a few days earlier.

Altogether about 45,000 men in Estonia responded to the appeal and they were organised into six so-called Border-Guard regiments. Although inferiorly armed and poorly equipped these regiments had the great advantage of being led by former Estonian Army officers. All previously formed military units had had Estonian command only up to battalion level, all higher staffs being manned by Germans. So even the staff of the Estonian Legion had consisted exclusively of German officers. But even now the Germans were wary of extending the Estonian command beyond regimental level. They thus went back on their promise to organise the Border-Guard regiments into the divisions for which even staffs had been organised. Instead the Border-Guard regiments were kept apart as far as possible, and every regiment got an influential German liaison officer, with frequent misunderstandings and even open animosity as a consequence. More serious incidents, however, were held in check by the impending Soviet reconquest.

In Latvia one part of the new draftees were included in the existing organisation of the Latvian Legion. In consequence its effects increased to 34,000 men in combat units, and to about 20,000 in auxiliary formations. The combat troops were organised into two divisions of which one later fought with great bravery in the bridge-head of Courland. This bridge-head was the only part of the Baltic territory to remain in German hands until capitulation on May 8th, 1945. About 24,000 Latvian soldiers became Russian war-prisoners there. The greater part of them had been transferred to Germany in spite of their sometimes active opposition, with many desertions as a result. According to one incomplete survey of the German *Ostministerium* there were on January 24th, 1945, in all 104,000 Latvian soldiers in East Prussia. The same survey gives as the numbers of Lithuanian and Estonian soldiers respectively 36,800 and 10,000, which figures must be considerably below their real number.

The Soviet conquest of the Baltic countries had begun with the arrival of the Red Army at the Narva river on January 20th, 1944. The Russian offensive which had begun on January 14th, 1944 at Leningrad had pushed the 18th German Army back on this river, where the front came to a stop for another six months. The front-line cut the beautiful Swedish built 17th century town of Narva in two, soon reducing it to a heap of ruins. The Red Army also made quick inroads into Latvia and Lithuania. In the former country Russian forces reached the Gulf of Riga at Tukkums on July 29th, 1944, causing severance of land connections between the German main forces and the Northern Army Group. In Lithuania the Red Army crossed the eastern boundary at the beginning of July and occupied Vilnius on the 13th of that month. On July 28th, the Germans gave up Kaunas and by the middle of October the occupation of the country was practically complete. Aside from this powerful main offensive the Soviets also took the whole of south-western Estonia up to the river Emajõgi. The town of Võru fell to them on August 14th and the southern half of the city of Tartu on August 25th, 1944.

After these developments the Baltic people could not have much hope of avoiding another Soviet occupation. Although the Germans were able to re-establish land connection with their main forces by a counter-offensive executed between the 16th and 20th of August, their position in the Baltic countries had become untenable. The corridor which they had re-established at Tukkums was also only a narrow one and conspicuously insecure. The decision to pull out from Estonia was executed in good order and it began on September 18th. Most of the German forces extricated from Estonia were, however, trapped in a bag in Courland. The Red Army reached Klaipeda (Memel) on a broad front on October 10th, 1944, and 26 German infantry and two armoured divisions were cut off. By that time Estonia was already firmly in Russian hands. Tallinn had been taken on September 21st, and Pärnu on September 24th. The conquest of the Estonian islands was completed soon afterwards, except the Sõrve pensinsula, the southernmost tip of Saaremaa, which remained in German hands until November 23rd, 1944.

AFTERMATH OF THE WAR

The first weeks and months after the Soviet conquest was a nightmare for the population. The advance of the Red Army was followed by a wave of robbery, looting, rape and killing. Under the pretext of looking for arms, homes and people were searched and deprived of all valuable objects, even officers taking part in looting.

The population had no means of protecting themselves from the terror of the brutalised soldiery. To complain to the police was worse than useless as such complaints could easily turn against the plaintiff as "defamation of the Red Army". Neither were summary executions lacking. In Lithuania for instance 600 people were summarily shot in Zarasai, in northeastern Lithuania, 700 in Šiauliai, and 400 in Kaunas. It is also reported that at the same time all inhabitants of three parishes in Lithuania were deported to Russia. And that was only the beginning. At least six country-wide deportations from Lithuania are known: in July–September 1945, February 1946, July–December 1947, May 1948, March and June 1949. It is estimated that in this way altogether about 245,000 people were taken from Lithuania.

The background to these harsh measures was of course the fact that the actual fighting did not cease in the Baltic countries after their occupation by the Red Army. Not all Lithuanian, Latvian and Estonian soldiers laid down their arms at the collapse of the German front. Their units of various size established themselves as guerillas in the forest and some of their bands were still operating ten years later, although their activity in Estonia and Latvia practically ceased in connection with the collectivisation of agriculture in 1949.

This active resistance movement was largest and best organised in Lithuania. Already in April 1945 the strength of the guerilla forces was estimated at about 30,000 men, who two years later were organised into the Lithuanian Freedom Army. The activities of this force enjoyed wide support among the population and its ranks swelled with new recruits. In consequense Soviet colonialism in Lithuania was effectively checked for several years. Gradually, however, losses in action, dwindling supplies of arms and ammunition, and above all the collectivisation of farms, made the position of the guerillas untenable. At last the demobilisation of the Freedom Army became unavoidable. This was carried out in 1952. At this time the losses of the Freedom Army were estimated at 30,000 men and those of their adversaries, the MVD forces which was the new name for the dreaded police organisation formerly known as NKVD, at about two and half times as much. With the demobilisation of the Freedom Army the resistance movement did not cease completely. This happened after the abortive Hungarian rising in 1956, when the Baltic countries could be considered as completely "pacified".

In Estonia the partisan activities were liveliest between the years 1944 and 1946. In these years they were considered so dangerous that a restriction in motor traffic was found necessary. Motor vehicles were allowed to travel in certain parts of the country only in groups of 10 to 20 and accompanied by armed escorts. Nor could all local authorities reside in their community centres but had to be withdrawn into nearby towns. To impose their authority the Soviets in the winter of 1946/47 organised large-scale round-up operations under the name of tactical army maneouvres. Two Soviet infantry divisions, reinforced by armoured units, were detailed for this duty and regular battles were fought in forest areas along Lake Peipsi as well in the counties of Võru- and Pärnumaa. The inevitable outcome was that all larger partisan units were dispersed and their permanent camps destroyed. The decisive blow against the armed resistance in Estonia was, how- ever, the collectivisation of agriculture. This deprived the partisans of their supply bases and reduced their activity to small proportions in- deed. The kolkhoz peasants were so strictly controlled and their food supplies so limited that they were unable to help the partisans, much as they otherwise would have been prepared to risk it. In spite of all some kind of guerilla activity existed even in Estonia until the Hungarian rising of 1956. This destroyed the last hopes of any help from the western democracies. After that the last partisans gave up and surrendered themselves to the authorities. It hardly surprised anyone that the repeated offers of amnesty to those who surrendered were never honoured. All the surrendered partisans, as far as is known, were arrested and deported after spending a period of legal residence in their homes.

Although organs of the Soviet civil administration had followed the Red Army after a only few days delay, it took in these circum- tances considerable time before any order could be restored. Towards the end of September all men born in 1908—1920 were mobilised into the Red Army. At the same time identification cards were issued which were valid either for three months, one year or five years, showing the owner clearly to what extent he was trusted. By then the MVD had also started its operations. At least in Estonia it used a different method as compared to that applied during the first occupation. Screening commissions of three to four members were appointed to every county with orders to investigate into the past, as well into the political views of the inhabitants, and to decide who had to be arrested and deported. These commissions moved from one commune to another and every inhabitant from twelve years upward had to appear before them for interrogation. Having visited all communes of a county the commission returned to the commune it started from and began its work over again. The results were recurring waves of arrest and a thorough purge of opponents to the regime. As the great majority of the people belonged to this category everybody had to be afraid, which of course was the intended effect. The "purges" went on until the end of Stalinist era in Russia, about nine years later.

But these new methods of the MVD were rather slow to produce results or at least the authorities seem to have thought so. They were therefore completed with full scale deportations, of which the biggest one was arranged in connection with the collectivisation campaign. This violent drive to found kolkhozes was introduced by Communist Party Congresses in all three Baltic republics in December 1948 and January 1949. The process of collectivisation had been remarkably slow indeed (for instance in Estonia only 6.5. per cent of the arable land had been collectivised up to then) but after the congresses it assumed the velocity of a hurricane. As a result in May 1949 already 72 % of farms in Estonia and 75 % of those in Latvia had joined kolkhozes. Such spectacular results were achieved by mass deportation in all three Baltic republics in March 1949. Although the exact numbers of people involved are not known, it is estimated that altogether 330,000 people were taken away from the three Baltic republics. On circumstancial evidence it is estimated that between thirty and forty thousand people were deported from Estonia, which brought the total number of deportees from that country during the second Soviet occupation to 75,000. The respective overall figures for Latvia and Lithuania are estimated at 136,000 and 245,000.

Deportations in connection with the collectivisation drive marked the end of the aftermath of the war. Although some wholesale deportations occurred even later in the years 1950–1954, these were on a smaller scale and were considered as more or less routine measures and a necessary corollary to a communist regime. The final score of losses of the Baltic peoples is estimated to be in round figures about 570,000, of which 140,000 fall to the Estonians, 144,000 to the Latvians, and 285,000 to the Lithuanians.

Although circumstances as far as personal security was concerned remained until the end of the Stalinist era such that nobody could count on being able to sleep the whole night in his own bed, there nevertheless occurred a certain stabilisation after the deportations of March 1949. The severely decimated Baltic peoples could in their heavily war damaged country again start to look around for a means of survival in the harsh and hazardous climate of Stalinist Russia.

FATE OF THE DEPORTEES

The people who had to pay for the relative improvement in conditions in the Baltic coutries were those who had been deported either to so-called "Camps of corrective labour", as they were officially termed, or to remote places in the Soviet Union as "settlers". The Baltic people were scattered over a vast area reaching from Archangel in Europe to the mouth of Lena river in Siberia. The length of their stay there did not at all depend on their sentence but mostly on the time of their arrest and trial. Most of the survivors were released in virtue of the Amnesty law of 1955. The punishment, the banishment of the Baltic people lasted thus from five to thirteen years whatever was their sentence. The standard sentence for political opponents of the regime seems to have been 25 years of corrective labour camp, which of course was many times over their life expectancy in these institutions. The majority of the inmates perished in fact in consequence of inhuman living conditions and bad treatment. The greater part of the survivors could return to their home-countries after the amnesty law, while a minority has been withheld in the vicinity of the slave-labour camps or places of exile as "free settlers".

The conditions in the slave-labour camps, which is by far a more suitable designation for these institutions than their official name, are fairly well known by now. There even exists a literary report from Soviet sources (by Aleksandr Solzhenitsyn, *One Day in Ivan Denisovich's Life*). Apart from sheer extermination by overworking the inmates with a twelve-hour day and insufficient food, the aim of these camps seems to have been to force the people into submission by degradation. This secondary aim was to provide for the eventuality that some of the inmates should survive. To make them "ripe" for life under the Soviet regime they were submitted to systematic degradation, which is a general phenomenon of Soviet penal system. The most cherished and effective method was to appoint criminal offenders as overseers to political prisoners. This means, which was succesfully used also in Hitler's concentration camps, was anchored even in the Russian law for corrective-labour camps (See Chapter IX: 87).

But there is no doubt that the principal aim of the slave-labour camps was extermination. Most convincingly it is shown by the percentage of the inmates who died there. But there is also other evidence. A study of the question by the International Confederation of Free Trade Unions has established that the diet at the camps of corrective labour was clearly under the minimum requirements for sustaining life even without work in a temperate climate. While this minimum requirement is set at 1800 calories a day the diet of the slave-labour camps gave the inmates only 1292 calories. The majority of the camps to which the Baltic deportees were taken were situated moreover to the north of the polar circle, which made their life expectancy short indeed. It has been variously estimated that the average span of life of a deportee under camp conditions was from two to five years and that only exceptionally robust people were able to survive longer. The only conclusion to be drawn from these facts is that the primary aim of the "camps of corrective labour" was the extermination of the prisoners in a way most profitable to the regime.

Besides deportees who were sentenced to detention in the camps there was a large category of deportees who were regarded as "voluntary settlers". In their individual fates were still greater differences than in those of the inmates in the different camps. Some transports of the "voluntary settlers" were set down in places where all prerequisites to produce food were lacking. Of those unfortunate people only a very few survived. It seems that at least in one concrete case their survival depended upon the minimal difference between those who had enough energy left to collect roots in the forests for their soup and those who tried to live on soup cooked of grass. The majority of the voluntary settlers, however, came to more civilised surroundings such as lumber camps and kolkhozes in remote places. The vast majority of survivors who eventually could return to their home-countries belonged to those fortunate people. But they were few. It is estimated that four fifths of all those who were deported during the second Soviet occupation have not returned and will never return.

The slave-labour camps in the Soviet Union have survived the Stalinist era. Although they were officially abolished after Stalin's death the authorities saw quite soon the necessity to reorganize them. The reason for this might well have been that a state of the type of the Soviet Union needs such kind of institutions to preserve its establishment. Another reason was in any case the inability to recruit workers into the industries and mines previously founded by slave-labour in the high north and in Siberia. To attract voluntary workers to these areas they were promised higher wages, better lodgings and richer food supplies but with only very little result. Voluntary workers failed to show up in sufficient numbers and at last a new system of "detention camps" had to be organized to keep production going.

From one of these camps there exists a quite recent report. In 1967 an American of Russian descent, Alexander Dincens, was released from the camp at Potma, a place about 310 miles east of Moscow. In 1962 Dincens had fallen in a trap set for him by KGB (the new initials of the Russian security police) during his visit to Russia. On urgent begging of a Russian officer whom he had met travelling by train he had exhanged some American dollars against roubles. For that he got a sentence of five years in detention camp.

In Potma area there had been along the railway line in a distance of about twelve miles 19 different camps. In Dincens' time these camps had about 40,000 prisoners belonging to all nationalities of the Soviet Union. There had been separate camps for political and criminal prisoners with their different living conditions. As compared with the Stalinist camps physical torture is not any more in use, and neither are the prisoners suffering from hunger, cold, poor sanitary conditions or physical exhaustion. The internees even get paid for their work. But what makes life a hell also in these new kind of camps is psychological terror. This emanates from a changed system of surveillance. In Stalinist camps surveillance was exercised by a guard of NKV-soldiers and a net of agents and informers recruited among the prisoners. But as the latter were relatively few they were usually found out quite soon and thus unable to do much harm. Under the new system the guard is "neutral" and in many cases even helpful in purchasing food, tobacco and spirits from outside the camp area. Instead the surveillance is now arranged by compelling the majority of prisoners to become informers.

The method how it is done is simple but quite ingenious. The prisoner is one day called to the camp-commandant and informed that his term of detention might be substantially shortened if he would consent to cooperate with the administration. His duties are said to be easy ones consisting only of controlling the cleanlines in the barracks, that the lights be but out a right time at night, etc. Hearing this the prisoner does not see any reason to refuse. After some time, however, he is recalled to the commandant and told that he has performed his duties satisfactorily and that his term of detention has been shortened by so and so many years. But at the same time his duties are extended comprising now also an obligation to report on the conversation of his fellow prisoners. In the first place the commandant wants to know who among the prisoners are critical of the political order in the country, who plans escape, etc. If the prisoner complies even to this proposition but fails to report, which the majority of victims think to be the easiest way out of the trouble, his next meeting with the commandant will be of a quite different sort. He is then told that owing to the neglect to perform his duties his term of detention has been lengthened by so and so many years and if he does not improve himself this could become still longer. After a few of such meetings with the commandant the term of detention may have become ten or more years instead of the three or five years to which the prisoner had been sentenced originally. The prisoner might even get the idea that in not complying to the wishes of the commandant he will never get out of that place. The result is that everybody is a possible informer and that every prisoner must distrust anybody else.

Worst inflicted by this system are of course the political prisoners who in their majority are young intellectuals who are used to discuss politics. They are also those who feel their punishment utterly unjust as they have not made any revolt against the government but only claimed rights to which the citizens of the Soviet Union are entitled according to its constitution. For them life in these new detention camps often becomes unendurable and many of them commit suicide.

The regime in the camps for criminal elements is said not to be quite as severe. The majority of the inmates in these camps are young men and women of whom from time to time whole train-loads arrive into the camp area. These camps have also an exceptionally flourishing corruption. The guard-crews take a lively part in it, their most conspicuous line being a trade with young girls.

THE SOVIET SOCIALIST BALTIC REPUBLICS

The boundaries of the Soviet Socialist Baltic republics do not coincide with those of the independent Baltic States. The Supreme Soviet of the Russian Soviet Socialist Federal Republic included by its decrees of January 15th and 16th, 1947 about 2500 square kilo-metres of Estonia and over 1800 square kilometres of Latvia in its territory, while that of Lithuania had been increased already in 1940. It had then received the Vilnius area from Polish territory, about 9300 square kilometres in all.

Also the administrative division of the Baltic republics has been changed. After the collectivisation in 1950 the 11 counties of Estonia, 19 of Latvia and 23 of Lithuania were replaced by 39, 58 and 87 rayons respectively, after the Russian pattern. The introduction of the division into *Oblasts*, however, remained only provisional. Lithuania had been divided into four Oblasts in 1950 and Estonia and Latvia into three *Oblasts* each in 1952, but this three-tier admistrative division was abolished already in 1953. It had caused a tremendous increase in the numbers of civil servants, which anyhow surpasses many times that of the independent Baltic States. The smallest administrative unit in the Baltic Soviet republics is the village-soviet, of which since 1954 there are 320 in Estonia, 708 in Latvia and 1224 in Lithuania. Before the 1954 reform their numbers were much greater, 641, 1229 and 2774 respectively.

As is generally known, political power in the Soviet Union does not rest either with the Government or with Parliament but is firmly anchored in the Central Comittee of the Communist Party, or rather in the Bureau of this committee. In practice this means, however, that the power is in the hands of the secretaries of the Central Committee. Accordingly also the Central Committees of the Baltic communist parties and their bureaus and party secretaries are of much greater consequence than the Supreme Soviets of these republics and their councils of ministers, i.e. the governments. The Baltic communist parties are moreover not independent parties at all, as their names might suggest, but only territorial sections of the Communist Party of the Soviet Union. To the Baltic sections of the party thus belong all those party members who reside in these republics, including party members among the Red Army personnel. In consequence only about one third (as in Latvia) or about one half (as in Estonia) of the members of the Baltic communist parties belong to the indigenous population. Thus only 213 delegates of 650 at the Latvian Party Congress in 1966 were Latvians while 207 were Russians and the rest of other nationalities of the Soviet Union. The same relation exists in the composition of the important Central Committees. The 111 members of the Estonian Central Party Committee elected at the party congress of 1966 included only 26 Estonians. Among the rest 45 were Russians of Estonian extraction and 26 pure Russians. The all-important posts of the First Secretaries of the Central Committees are in all three Baltic republics occupied by persons of Baltic extraction who have come or been sent to the Baltic countries after the war. All the Second Secretaries of the Baltic communist parties are genuine Russians and it is assumed that it is they who have the real power.

Another fiction of long standing is of course that the communist party is an instrument by which the proletariat executes its dictatorship. In fact the workers have only a small say in the decisions of the communist party. This is so in the Soviet Union as well in its Baltic republics. According to official statistics, referring to January 1, 1967, of the total party membership in Latvia for instance only 27.8 per cent were workers and 10.8 per cent kolkhoz members while a whole 61.3 per cent were political functionaries, employees, etc. As it is well known that even the groups of workers and kolkhoze members include individuals in leading position with corresponding high salaries (kolkhoze chairmen for example) it is fairly clear that the communist party has become a convenient tool in the hands of the functionaries to govern the toiling masses. The workers have no means at all to control those who have power in the Soviet Union.

The communist parties of the constituent republics of the Soviet Union of course cannot have any independent policy of their own.

Basically they only execute the decisions of the Central Committee, and of the Party Bureau in Moscow. And when from time to time there occur divergencies in policy, the local party organs and their functionaries are at once made to toe the "right party line". This is how the notorious "purges" originate.

The Baltic republics have up to now seen two large purges. The first hit Estonia in the years 1949—1951. The First Party-Secretary, Karotamm, half of the other party-secretaries, the Chairman of the Council of Ministers, i.e. the prime-minister, and more than half of the other members of the government, as well the Chairman of the Præsidium of the Supreme Soviet i.e. the President of the Estonian Soviet Republic, were all removed from their posts. Some of them, among others two members of the government, were deported to slave-labour camps whence they obtained release only after the promulgation of the general amnesty. The President of the Estonian Academy of Sciences was likewise imprisoned. All the functionaries involved were accused of "bourgeois nationalism", which is the Soviet designation for all deviations from the party line in favour of the interests of national minorities. No Russian has ever been accused of this crime.

Basically the same kind of crime caused the purge in Latvia in 1959. The First Secretary of the Latvian Communist Party, Kalnberzhins, and a Vice-Chairman of the Council of Ministers, Berklavs, as well a number of Trade-Union and Komsomol leaders came forward with certain demands. They insisted that the immigration of Russians into the Latvian republic should be restricted, and therefore opposed the development of heavy industry which had required a massive influx of workhands from Russia. Instead they recommended concentration on light industry for which the local workers reserve would have been sufficient. Coming out with these demands the leading Latvian party functionaries had without doubt before their eyes the situation in the oil-shale mining area in North-East Estonia, in whose population the Russians dominated heavily. Besides trying to avoid the creation of the same situation in large areas of Latvia the demands suggested also increased teaching of the Latvian language, Latvian history and geography in schools.

These demands drew down a thorough purge among the Latvian communist leaders. Kalnberzhins, Berklavs, and the Chairman of the

Council of Ministers were deposed and with them about 800 other functionaries. Berklavs and some others were moreover sent away from Latvia for residence in central Russia.

The authority of the constituent Soviet Republics is thus clearly very limited. Nevertheless the central committees of the local parties, or rather their bureaus and party-secretaries, are the highest political authorities in each of the Baltic republics. The bureaus of the central committees usually include also the chairmen of the councils of ministers, i.e. the prime ministers. Their governments, however, are essentially only executive organs bound to follow decisions taken in the bureau of the central committee. The supreme soviets as well as the chairmen of their præsidiums, i.e. the presidents of the Soviet Baltic republics, are practically only decorative institutions without any real power. It is very possible that this utter helplessness to influence policies which he could not approve, was the main reason for the suicide of the first "President" of the Estonian Soviet Republic, the doctor and poet Johannes Vares-Barbarus, on November, 29th, 1946.

As in every other way the Soviet occupation has also thoroughly changed the national make-up of the population. There are no greater changes in total numbers although the losses in the years 1940—1952 are estimated at 305,000 inhabitants for Estonia, 502,000 for Latvia and 730,000 for Lithuania. These figures contain also the refugees who left the Baltic countries before the arrival of the second Soviet occupation. It is estimated that on this occasion about 65,000 Estonians, 115,000 Latvians and 70,000 Lithuanians left their countries, preferring life in exile to life under the Soviets. In spite of these losses the official census of 1959 shows an increase in population in each of the Baltic republics. The increase for Estonia is 63,000, for Latvia 103,000 and for Lithuania 136,000 people. These figures indicate the extent of Russian immigration and the proportional decrease of the indigenous population. While in 1940 the proportion of Estonians in the population of their independent republic had been 88.2 %, that of Latvians 75.5 %, and that of Lithuanians 84.4 %, these proportions were in 1959 72.9 %, 62 %, and 79.3 % respectively. The percentage of Russians in the last mentioned year was 23.9 % in Estonia, 30.9 % in Latvia, and 10.3 % in Lithuania. The respective pre-war figures had been 8.2 % in Estonia, 12 % in Latvia, and 2.4 % in Lithuania.

Since then these figures have of course changed so that the census due in the Soviet Union now should show a substantially different picture. In all probability the percentage of Russians and other nationalities of the Soviet-Union will have increased as the population of the Baltic Republics is now bigger than a natural increase would warrant. Another indication is the increase in urban population after 1959 as foreign elements in Balticum mostly settle in cities. As a consequence these republics now show the highest percentage of urbanisation in the entire Soviet-Union. So in 1965 the share of urban population was 63 per cent in Estonia, 62 per cent in Latvia and 45 per cent in Lithuania. This is a big increase as compared with the 1939 year's figures which for Latvia were 35.3 cent, for Estonia 34 per cent and for Lithuania 23 per cent. The influx of foreign elements does not of course count for all this increase. In 1964, according to official data, the share of Estonians in their cities and towns was 61.92 per cent while 30.76 per cent were Russians, 2.03 per cent Ukrainians, 1.46 per cent Belorussians and 3.83 per cent other nationalities. In Latvia the corresponding figures were 51.64 per cent Latvians, 34.46 per cent Russians, 2.96 per cent Belorussians, 2.21 per cent Ukrainians, 3.24 per cent Poles, 3.08 per cent Jews and 2.41 per cent other nationalities. Of the population of Lithuanian cities and towns were 69.11 per cent Lithuanians, 17 per cent Russians, 6.56 per cent Poles, 2.39 per cent Belorussians, 2.33 per cent Jews and 2.61 per cent other nationalities.

These changes in the national composition of the population cannot fail to reflect also in the cultural life of the Baltic peoples. The Russian influence is easily recognisable in every field of cultural activity and this trend is supported in every possible way by the authorities. Just to give some examples we could mention that the movement for language reform which aimed at innovations towards a greater versatility, and which was especially lively in Estonia, has been stopped. Instead the borrowing of expressions from Marxist jargon and from the Russian vocabulary has been propagated as much as possible, even imposed by order of the respective authorities. Authors are also encouraged to start writing in Russian instead of their own language, a campaign which has found a wholehearted supporter in Brezhnev, the General Secretary of the Communist Party of the Soviet Union.

The universities in the Baltic republics have been down-graded. They have lost their research functions, which were transferred to the Science Academies. All Theological Faculties have naturally been closed. Some other faculties have also been separated from the universities and re-established as independent institutions. So for instance in Estonia the faculties of agriculture and forestry as well that of the veterinary sciences were reorganised as an independent Academy of Agriculture. Changes in other fields of higher education are, however, not great. Engineers are trained in Polytechnical institutes, teachers in pedagogical institutes, composers and musicians in conservatories. At the end of the nineteen-fifties there were in all these institutions of higher education altogether 12,000 students in Estonia, 16,000 in Latvia, and 24,000 in Lithuania.

During the subsequent years the number of students has increased further. According to official statistics there were in 1965 for instance in Estonia altogether 19,874 students in all institutions of higher education. Of them 6,032 were studying at the Tartu University, 8,535 at the Polytechnical Institute, 3,030 at the Academy of Agriculture, 1,638 at the Pedagogical Institute, 318 at the Arts Institute and 321 at the Conservatory. However, the number of graduates from these institutions does not seem to be quite in proportion to these figures. Thus only 8,404 students took their degrees at the Tartu University between the years 1950 and 1964. The number of graduates at the Polytechnical Institute in Tallinn was 5,275 during the same period, 3,996 at the Estonian Academy of Agriculture (since its foundation in 1951), 3,907 at the Pedagogical Institute in Tallinn (founded in 1952), 528 at the Estonian Art Institute, and 390 at the Tallinn Conservatory.

The schools were reorganized in the years 1945—1947 according to the Soviet school system. As a special favour and in order to facilitate a more thorough study of the Russian language the eleventh school-year could be retained in secondary schools, which in Russia have only ten forms. The Russian language also takes a very prominent place in the curricula of the schools and starts already in the second school year. Instead there is no special place in the curriculum for teaching the history and geography of the childrens' own republic.

All they get to know about it is the small share allotted to them in the general history and geography of the Soviet Union. Of all schools 38 % in Latvia and 35 % in Estonia have Russian as the teaching language. As an experimental school-type there has existed now for a couple of years an amalgamated school type for both Russian and local children. In these schools the pupils are generally taught in two separate groups in their mother tongue but a few subjects are common and these are taught in Russian.

The churches are hard pressed by the official anti-religious propaganda and periodically recurring persecutions. They had lost many of their clergymen already during the first Soviet occupation. In Lithuania 42 priests had been murdered or deported and the losses of the Latvian churches included three Lutheran pastors killed and ten deported, twelve Catholic priests killed and twenty-nine deported, three Orthodox priests killed and nine deported. In Estonia the losses during the first Soviet occupation were two pastors murdered, seventeen deported and six drafted into the Red Army. Five of the Estonian Orthodox clergymen were murdered, 12 deported, and six drafted into the Red Army.

After the commencement of the second Soviet occupation in 1944 the situation of the churches deteriorated considerably. Many pastors and priests had left the country, among them the Archbishop, Bishop, and 74 pastors of the Estonian Lutheran Church as well the Metropolitan and 22 priests of the Orthodox Church. The deportation from Latvia of the Archbishop of the Lutheran Church, of the Orthodox Metropolitan and of three Catholic Bishops by the Germans has already been mentioned. The number of the pastors who remained was further decimated. For instance of the 95 Lutheran clergymen who remained in Latvia in 1944 five were killed and 35 deported. Of the 260 pastors who in 1939 had served the Lutheran congregations in Estonia only 63 remained in 1952. Before going into exile the Estonian Lutheran Archbishop had appointed a caretaker of the Church who, however, was not allowed to take up his duties. Instead another pastor was appointed acting Bishop by the Ministry of Home Affairs of the Estonian Soviet Republic. After one year he was, however, deported to Siberia and another pastor appointed in his place, who was later promoted to Archbishop. He held this post until October 1967, when he retired because of "ill health". According to some reports the health of the Archbishop was bad indeed after a visit to Moscow. It is generally believed in Estonia that he had been there closely questioned about his doings on the foreign visits which he undertook as official delegate to international church congresses in various parts of the world during his long tenure of office.

The Catholic Church in Lithuania suffered still greater losses. Of the 1022 pre-war churches only about 500 remained open in 1963. Of 14 Lithuanian bishops and 1439 priests (in 1939) only one bishop and 400 priests were still in service in 1948. Since the beginning of the second Soviet occupation the Lithuanian Archbishop M. Reinys has died in prison, Bishop Borisevicius and 78 priests have been executed while two bishops and 180 priests have been deported. Later, however, a certain increase in the number of clergymen has been noticed. In 1956 the authorities had permitted the Lutheran Churches in Estonia and Latvia to hold theological courses under the surveillance of the Communist Party. As a consequence there were according to official Soviet data six years later again one bishop, 115 pastors, 15 deans and 20 candidates in the service of the Latvian Lutheran Church. In Estonia the Lutheran congregations were served in 1966 by one bishop and 110 pastors. Also one of the Lithuanian theological seminaries has been permitted to function in a restricted degree. Although enrolment to it has been limited to 50 students the number of Catholic priests in Lithuania was again about 800 in 1963. But there was only one bishop in office. Two new bishops had been ordained in 1955 but one of them was arrested in 1961. In 1956 two deported bishops returned from their exile but were not permitted to carry out their duties.

Also the bishops of the Latvian Catholic Church have been persecuted with special energy. The Catholic Metropolitan of Latvia died in 1958 and of the two auxiliary bishops appointed by him one was deported and the other died under mysterious circumstances in 1960. Thereafter the Latvian see was vacant until 1964, when a prelate was permitted to visit Rome and was appointed Administrator of the Riga and Liepaja dioceses and promoted to the rank of bishop.

The Orthodox Churches of Estonia and Latvia are incorporated in the Russian Orthodox Church and administered by the Patriarch of Moscow. Of the three bishops, 138 priests and 23 deacons of the Estonian Orthodox Church only one bishop, 55 priests and 6 deacons were in service in 1966.

As an overseer for all religious denominations and as their contact organ with the authorities each of the Baltic republics has a Board of Religious Affairs. Its chairmen are as a rule appointed from among the members of the communist party.

Atheist propaganda in Estonia and Latvia is primarily aimed at the Lutheran Church. Numerous professional agitators are employed for this task but also scientists, teachers and students must take part in antireligious propaganda unless they want to be considered hostile to Soviet society. Practicing Christians are moreover ineligible for teaching posts or any other work which has some connection with youth activities.

Besides the individual atheist propaganda among pre-school age children, schoolchildren and their parents there exist special atheist schools and universities which arrange seminars and courses on this subject. At all establishments of higher education exist also atheist clubs which arrange lectures, discussions and so called atheist competitions. Such an atheist competition arranged at the Poly-technical Institute in Talinn, Estonia, in 1968, was for example to invent the best anti-religious joke.

AGRICULTURE, TRADE AND INDUSTRY IN THE SOVIETISED BALTIC REPUBLICS

After the reoccupation the Soviet agrarian policy was reintroduced. The most outstanding feature of the Stalinist economic policy was that the agriculture had to bear the brunt of the costs of industrialisation of the Soviet Union. This made the lot of the peasants a heavy one indeed. In the Baltic countries to start with the maximum acreage of farms was further decreased in 1944, being now fixed at 25 hectares. At the same time the prices for the excessive obligatory deliveries in kind to the state were fixed so low that they hardly ever came up to the production costs. The aim was to force the farmers into kolkhozes. The process began in Estonia in 1947 and the next year in Latvia. At first it aimed at "voluntary" joining, but this giving very meagre results it switched on the forcible collectivisation in 1949. The new policy was called "liquidation of the kulak class" and its main instrument was mass deportation. "Kulaks" were all farmers who employed hired labour on a seasonal or annual basis. The "liquidation" policy brought immediate results and in December 1949 already 82 % of the farms in Estonia, 90 % in Latvia and 50 % in Lithuania had joined kolkhozes. In the years 1950—1954 the number of kolkhozes initially founded (3017 in Estonia, 4035 in Latvia, and 6 000 in Lithuania) was drastically reduced through amalgamation, so that in the last-mentioned year their number was 914 in Estonia, 1448 in Latvia and 2266 in Lithuania. At the same time the collectivisation went on, and in 1954 embraced already 98 % of all farms in each of the Baltic republics. Later the number of the kolkhozes further decreased, partly by continued mergers but also by their transformation into state-owned farms, the so called sovkhozes. At the end of the year 1961 there were for instance in Latvia 984 kolkhozes, of which 16 were fishermen's kolhozes, and 162 sovkhozes. In 1964 there were in Lithuania 1865 kolkhozes and 232 sovkhozes.

Through mergers the number of farms in Estonia has been reduced from almost 800 in 1960 to 393 in 1972 (209 kolkhozes and 184 sovkhozes). In the agricultural organisation the so-called Machine-Tractor Stations had a most important function. Their prime responsibility was to work the kolkhoze fields with agricultural machinery but at the same time they functioned also as institutions of technical and political control. The numbers of Machine-Tractor Stations in 1955 were 69 in Estonia, 120 in Latvia, and 135 in Lithuania.

This arrangement was in force until the great agricultural reform carried out in 1958. Introducing the reform Khrushchev, the new omnipotent leader of the Soviet Union, mentioned as the main reasons that the quality of the work done by the MT-Stations had been poor, that this kind of organisation was an obstacle to progress, and that the provision of agricultural products through MT-Stations was more expensive than other more direct methods. The MT-Stations had namely functioned also as collectors of agricultural products as their work was paid for in kind. This had caused great differences in the remuneration which the members in different kolkhozes received for their work. It has been calculated that in consequence of this system workers in kolkhozes with better quality soils had received up to 26 times more pay for one so-called "normal" day's work than workers in kolkhozes with poor soil. This meant that in some backward kolkhozes workers did not get any pay at all and were dependent for their upkeep entirely upon the private plots to which each household (family) was entitled. The agricultural production of these private plots is very substantial as according to official data they delivered in Estonia as late as in 1966 16.2 per cent of the cattle and 23.6 per cent of all milk bought by the government purchasing centres. According to the Latvian regulation of February 27th, 1948, each kolkhoze household could keep two cows, two calves, one breeding sow with young hogs, 10 sheep and an unlimited number of poultry. In practice however, the private plots did not exceed 0.5 hectares and the number of cattle was limited to one milk cow and one calf. But even so 16 per cent of all cows, 11 per cent of hogs, and 33 per cent of poultry in Latvia belonged to kolkhoze members privately.

The Stalinist system of provision with agricultural products had been very complicated. It had consisted of four different ways of collection. First there were the obligatory deliveries in kind for which the prices were lowest and only seldom came up to production costs. The second mode of collection consisted of payments in kind to the MT-Stations for the work done on kolkhoze fields, and the third way state purchase. But it was the fourth way which was instrumental in producing huge differences in the income of different kolkhozes. It was called "contracted purchase" and the prices, which were higher for every category previously mentioned, were highest for this fourth category. Moreover — and most important of all — there were progressive premiums to win on all products delivered over the contracted quantities. Hence the great inequality in the incomes of kolkhozes.

This complicated system of provision was replaced in 1958 by a single state purchase for fixed and yearly adjusted prices. At the same time the MT-Stations were abolished and their machinery sold to the kolkhozes. This system proved advantageous to the latter, which seized eagerly the opportunity offered. In the summer of 1958 for instance in Estonia already 530 kolkhozes out of a total of 807 were working with their own machinery.

By this reform the situation in agriculture started to improve in the Baltic republics. This also stopped the trend to get away from the countryside, which had been one of the major problems for the authorities. Seeing that work was worth while the people remained in the kolkhozes, which gradually started to improve. A few years later foreign correspondents visiting Baltic countries also noticed this. Their reports pointed out with some amazement that the Baltic people seem to have managed to make the Soviet agricultural system work, or at least work better than it did in Russia. These observations were, however, made after the agricultural sector had received additional incentives by Khrushchev's followers in the leadership of the Soviet Union. If the last eye-witness reports from Estonia are to be believed the kolkhozes there are now doing fairly well. This is shown also by the statistical data on the fulfilment of state plans in 1966, which give as the kolkhoze workers' average wages calculated per "normal work-day" three roubles ninety-two kopeks.

Also the state-owned farms, the sovkhozes, are now doing much better than before. In Estonia for instance all the 168 sovkhozes had worked with profit after the year 1965, and were therefore allowed to convert to the new self-management system in the middle of 1967. At that time only 222 sovkhozes in the entire Soviet Union had received this privilege. The essential advantage of this system is that instead of a large number of detailed planning directives only basic indices are prescribed by the authorities. Although the total sum of the wages is fixed by the Ministry of Agriculture the sovkhoze managers may give wage raises to workers with higher qualifications up to 30 per cent of their fixed wage rates. It is possible that this system may help to improve the situation of the sovkhozes, which at present are criticised because of their excessive production costs and low profitability. The production costs in 1958 were calculated for instance in Estonia at 8.4 roubles for one centner of rye or wheat in the kolkhozes and 10.66 roubles in the sovkhozes (the state purchase price at the same time being 8.5 roubles). The production costs were also higher in sovkhozes for potatoes (3.9 roubles as against 4.88 roubles) for milk (10.4 roubles as against 14.19 roubles), bacon (104.4 roubles as against 112.16) etc.

☆ ☆ ☆

Soviet trade is still characterized by a scarcity of consumer goods and shops which sell them. Although lately a certain improvement has occurred people have still to watch for the occasion when certain goods, or goods of certain quality, are available. As a rule the stocks of these bargains are quickly depleted, people buying with the intention to barter things against other items which somebody else has had the good luck to get hold of. But of course the list of the goods now continuously on sale has increased considerably during recent years. Not to speak of the immediate post-war years this list was a very short one as late as 1958. Black rye bread, spirits, tobacco, some expensive kinds of tinned food, cotton fabrics, shoes of cloth, expensive furniture and wireless sets were the only items which had been then steadily on sale for a number of years. Anything else was to be had only occasionally. In restaurants in these years you could count only on spaghetti — for anything else you had to have good luck. But the number of restaurants as well as the diversity of their menus has changed very much for the better. Also the number of shops has increased and many of them have been modernised, functioning now as supermarkets. But back in 1955 there had been for example in Estonia altogether only 2300 shops, one quarter of the number during the country's independence.

The shops, as well the restaurants and cafés in cities and bigger towns belong to different state-owned trusts with headquarters in Moscow. The distribution of all consumer goods is in the last instance supervised by the Soviet Union's Ministry of Trade. But supplies of raw materials to industry, as well as the marketing of finished products, are handled by the Board of Technical Supplies and Marketing which belongs under a different Ministry. Agricultural supplies again are handled by an agency called Agricultural Equipment, which is governed by a third Ministry. Although the activities of all these agencies are supposed to be coordinated by the State Planning Commission the system is too complicated to ensure smooth operation. And this organisation does not comprise the entire Soviet trade either. Most of the trade outside cities and towns is handled by cooperatives which have their central organisations in each of the Baltic republics and an All-Union headquarters in Moscow. These "Republican Cooperative Central" organisations also own industries, mostly in the food processing branch. They may also sell agricultural machinery and fertilizers and sometimes function even as agents of the government in the purchase of agricultural products.

Besides the state-owned trusts and the cooperative organisations there exists even a third form of trade in the Soviet Union, which could be characterised as a kind of free trade sector. On the one side there exists a chain of quasi free-trade shops which take in and sell used consumer goods on commission for people who are unable or unwilling to do it themselves. On the other side there is the so-called "Kolkhoze market". In every city and town as well as in a number of smaller places kolkhozes and their members may sell on these markets their surplus products after their obligatory deliveries to the state have been exacted. The prices on these markets seem to be governed by demand and supply and are as a rule above the prices fixed by the state. All prices in the Soviet Union are excessive measured by Western standards but the difference in foodstuffs is not nearly as high as it is for other consumer goods.

The share of the so-called "kolkhoze markets" in Soviet trade in foodstuffs is considerable, although it is difficult to ascertain exactly how big. However, according to official Soviet statistics for the year 1955, the share of the kolkhoze-market in Tallinn was 14.6 per cent of all trade in foodstuffs in that city.

Soviet statistics seldom divulge such information as this, and of course it gives no clues as to the extent of the economic exploitation of the Baltic republics. However, one calculation made on the 1955 annual statistics has shown that the net taxation amount in Estonia was at least 3,348.4 million roubles. This figure, however, does not contain the taxes collected in the form of obligatory deliveries in kind from kolkhozes. There was no way of calculating these with any exactitude. Of the amount of net taxation 1,000.1 million roubles (or about 19.6 per cent of the Estonian national income) was invested in Estonia while the rest, or 2,148.4 million roubles, plus the unknown share of the deliveries in kind from the kolkhozes was taken out of the country. These figures thus indicated that even without taking in account the export of agricultural products, about 38.4 per cent of the Estonian national income was taken out of the republic in the form of taxation.

There are also other indications of the extent of Soviet economic exploitation in the Baltic countries. According to a calculation made on Estonia considerable quantities of foodstuffs were sent elsewhere in the Soviet Union. Thus of the 141,000 tons of fish caught in Estonia in 1963, at least 115,000 tons were taken away, of the 56,700 tons of meat produced that year, 25,700 tons were sent away, and so were

11,700 tons of butter of a total production of 15,900 tons, about 10,000 tons of sausages of a production of 18,000 tons, and about 2,900 tons of cheese of a production of about 4,000 tons.

The background to this export is of course the fact that the production of foodstuffs per ·capita is much greater in the Baltic republics than in other parts of the Soviet Union. In 1962 the per capita catch of fish was 87 kg in Estonia, 79 kg in Latvia but on the average only 18 kg in the Soviet Union. The production of butter per capita in the same year was in Estonia 12 kg, that of meat 79 kg, and that of milk 648 kg, while the average in the Soviet Union the figures were only 9, 42 and 286 kg respectively.

The same phenomenon is seen in industrial production. Of about 5,300 million kW hours of electric energy produced in Estonia in 1963 only about 600 million kW hours remained in the republic, of the 615,000 tons of mineral fertilisers there remained according to plan only about 100,000 tons, of the 526,000 tons of cement only about 340,000 etc. Nor can the proportions be any different in the case of window-glass, of which in 1963 two million square metres were produced: according to Soviet newspaper reports there has been a constant scarcity of this ware in Estonia. The same can be said of paper, of which in the year 1963 98,700 tons were produced. This list could possibly be continued with all other commodities produced in Estonia. Only to give one more example we could mention that the furniture industry in Estonia, which in 1963 produced goods to the value of 25.8 million roubles, could keep only the equivalent of 9 million roubles.

The background is also here a bigger per capita output than the average in the Soviet Union. Were the export of surplus products a question of trade, it would be a profitable business indeed. Unfortunately it is not; the products have to be given away with no compensation at all. That this is pure exploitation of one part of the Soviet Union in favour of another is clear from the facts. The wages of the workers in the Baltic republics are the same as they are elsewhere in the Soviet Union, the commodities and food are no cheaper or more abundant than elsewhere, and flats are definitely not better or more spacious (4.5 square metres as official minimum per individual in 1964) than in other parts of the Soviet Union. Neither is clothing better than in Russia, possibly only cleaner and sometimes of exceptional quality for those who have relatives abroad and are receiving gift parcels from them. The only things received in exchange for all the exported goods are new tools and new factory installations which could be considered as compensation only where the people who produce goods with them could in any way profit from their better and more refined machinery. Up to now this has not been the case and for this reason the otherwise so watchful Soviet propaganda has never been able to explain how the Baltic republics are compensated for the products which on Moscow's orders are taken away from them. The only explanation offered is the maxim that the more progressive republics have to "aid" the backward ones and that this is the way the Soviet economy functions. This of course sounds very much like a confirmation of an extensive exploitation of the Baltic republics especially as much of the export, practically all the agricultural production, goes to Leningrad, which according to this explanation would thus be a "backward" area. That this city can hardly be classified as such is clear from the supply situation there, which according to eye-witness reports is superior to those prevailing in the Baltic republics.

❊   ❊   ❊

The rehabilitation and development of industry in the reoccupied Baltic republics was one of the chief targets of the Stalinist five-year plans. The plan for 1946—1950 envisaged an investment of 3.5 million roubles in Estonia, 2.05 million roubles in Latvia and 1.5 million roubles in Lithuania. The big share of Estonia is explained by the importance attached to the oil-shale industry there. This industry, as all other important industries in the Baltic republics, was subordinated directly to the All-Union ministries in Moscow and the authorities of the local republics had thus nothing to do with their management. The Baltic republics remained responsible only for the industries producing consumer goods with limited production and processing food stuffs.

The responsibilities of the authorities of the constituent republics were, however, widened somewhat in connection with the decentralisation of Soviet industrial organisation by the creation of the Regional Economic Soviets (Sovnarchoses). But both before and after the reform the aim has been maximum economic exploitation of the Baltic republics. The big investments there thus concerned in the first place industries whose products are taken out of the republics. This is not only true of the big industries subordinated to All-Union ministries, but also of factories subordinated to the republican authorities. Tinned food-stuffs, for instance fish conserves, which were and are produced in great quantities in the Baltic republics, were almost never available there for ten and many more years and are scarce even today.

The bulk of the products from All-Union subordinated industries are naturally sent directly to other parts of the Soviet Union, especially to Leningrad. Such is the case with the production of the electro-industry in Riga, which during Latvia's independence had reached a high standard of development. The production of electrical gadgets and instruments has been stepped up and its production has been increased four times. The Tsarist Russian ship-building installations in Tallinn, which between the wars lay idle, were refurnished and set to work for the Soviet navy. Also the big railway factories in Riga and Tallinn under Tsarist Russia, have been rebuilt and now furnish rolling stock for the Soviet railways. To provide fertilizers for Soviet agriculture the big phosphate factory near Tallinn has been extended by factories for sulphuric acid and superphosphate. The last mentioned factory started its production in 1956.

The biggest increase has however been achieved in the power industry. The production of oil-shale in Estonia, which before the war had been two million tons a year, had already reached a production of nine million tons by 1960 (according to plan it should have produced 12 million tons that year). Oil-shale is used as fuel for a "Baltic Electric Power Plant" in the oil-shale mining area, which started production in 1960. This also provides Latvia and Lithuania with electric power. In 1963 its capacity was 800,000 kW. Oil-shale is also used as raw material for gasworks, of which the first one with a capacity of 400 million cubic metres was opened already in 1948. The production of this as well of another later built gaswork went at first entirely to Leningrad but was later, when that city started to get cheaper natural gas, led off even to Tallinn and other cities. Hydroelectric works have been erected at Narva and Kaunas, while the new power station at Riga is based on peat fuel. Of these the first one was planned for 120,000 kW capacity.

According to the statement of a communist party secretary the volume of industrial production in Latvia had already by 1954 increased elevenfold as compared with the time of the country's independence. In Estonia the claim of a tenfold increase was made in 1960. Although such claims in the Soviet Union never quite match the facts the progress of industrialisation has obviously been considerable. The industrialisation of Lithuania, however, has proceeded at a much slower tempo.

The industrial capacity of the Baltic republics is not negligible even measured by standards of the over-all production figures of the Soviet Union. The prime minister of the Latvian Soviet Republic, V. Ruben, was thus able to state in January 1968, that his country is producing 29 per cent of all railway-cars made in the Soviet Union, 23 per cent of radios, 12 per cent of washing machines and 11 per cent of electric bulbs. At the same time he made the claim that Latvia's industrial production has increased 23-fold during a period of 28 years.

Unfortunately this development does not give the Baltic people' any advantages. Their standard of living has not improved in the least but deteriorated as compared with the situation during their independence. This is easily demonstrated by a comparison of the buying power of their wages. While a worker for instance in Estonia in 1939 was able to buy for his monthly wages 38 kilogrammes of butter, the corresponding figure for a Soviet worker was only 18 kg in 1955. The differences were even bigger in some other commodities, so for instance in sugar, where the relation was 170 kg against 55 kg, in pork 84 kg against 27 kg, etc. Where a worker in independent Estonia could buy 1.5 men's suits of good quality for his monthly earnings in 1939, he was only able to pay for one half of a poor suit in 1955. While in 1939 he could buy seven pairs of leather shoes in 1939 he would get only 1.8 pairs in 1955.

Although things have improved somewhat since 1955 the prices are still very high, especially for commodities. In 1964 women's shoes cost 20 to 50 roubles, a woollen dress 30 to 40 roubles, nylon stockings 3.5 roubles, men's suits 60 to 70 roubles, shoes 25 roubles, a shirt 12 roubles. Compared with wages it is easy to see that the standard of the working population cannot approach the west European level. In 1965 a skilled worker in Estonia earned on the piece work basis 60 to 80 roubles a month, while only a few highly specialised workers came up to 100 roubles. In this, however, the miners in the oil-shale industry were an exception as their pay according to newspaper reports was 113 to 126 roubles a month. But there are many general workers whose pay also according to newspaper reports was only 40 roubles a month in 1965. An average monthly wage for a female worker is 55 roubles but occasionally (for instance in a machine building factory in 1964) they earned according to press reports 74 roubles a month in 1965.

During the following years wages have shown a slight increase. The salary of a general worker in 1968 was between 60 and 100 roubles for males and 50 to 80 roubles for females. Qualified workers, such as for instance lathe-operators, earned between 100 and 120 a month. The pay of the kolkhoze peasants showed still great variations in different kolkhozes being between 25 and 100 roubles a month (i.e. 2.50 to 4 roubles a day). Even remunerations as high as seven roubles a day have been reported from some exceptionally successful kolkhozes. The pay of kolkhoze directors is of course higher being as a rule between two- and three hundred roubles a month. Research scientist are also paid as much while a university professor gets between 600 and 1000 roubles. Also senior army officers get 800 and 1000 roubles a month. Better off are only officials of the communist party and some writers, artists and actors. Thus it is known for instance that party secretaries in charge of a district get 1500 roubles and that a few writers and artists in favour may get as much as 2000 roubles a month. At the bottom of the wage ladder are the charwomen, whose pay is about 30 roubles a month.

In between these income groups are of course a great wealth of rather finely differentiated wage categories. The wages of lower employees are between 40 and 60 roubles and those in medium positions 70 to 100 roubles. Teacher's salaries vary between 85 and 150 roubles depending on the type of the school and on the length of their service. A doctor begins with 90 roubles a month and may get as much as 150 roubles. An engineer earns the same salary if he is not an inventor or industrial manager. As to the salary of the last-mentioned category no data have been available.

As the rent for flats is low (0.80 to 0.13 roubles per square meter) even the lowest incomes do not present special difficulties as to the procurement of food. The prices of food have in most cases remained on a reasonable level being for instance for a kilogram of rye bread 0.14 roubles, for that of potatoes 0.10 roubles, of butter about 3.50 roubles, of pork 1.80 to 2 roubles, and of sugar about 0.78 roubles. One liter milk cost 0.26 roubles in 1968. But the purchase of clothing can be a problem for some income groups. In 1968 a men's suit cost 45 to 150 roubles, shoes 10 to 45 roubles, shirts 4 to 22 roubles, and a nylon shirt was not to be had under 20 roubles. But the real problem for an ordinary wage earner was purchase of consumer durables. In 1968 the price of a bicycle was 60 to 70 roubles, of radios 42.50 to 80.50 roubles, of refrigerators 150 to 225 roubles, of a TV-set 354 roubles, and of automobiles 4000 (Moskvich) to 5300 (Volga) roubles. Comparing these prices with the monthly earnings of ordinary workers and employees it is clear that the purchase of these commodities requires really hard saving or may in some cases be unattainable.

It is understandable that these circumstances must in the long run have had a harmful effect on industrial production. Seeing that he cannot profit from his efforts the worker is bound to lose interest in bigger and better production. That is probably also the reason why the recent reforms in industry seek to share a small part of the results of increased production with the workers. One industry after another has been switched to the new system initiated by Professor Liberman. Although the results of this reform have not become fully clear, it is officially maintained that the eight industries which in Estonia worked on the basis of the new system in 1966 have increased their production by 13 per cent, their productivity per worker by 15 per cent, and their profits no less than 35 per cent. Nevertheless the new system seems to be but a half measure which can hardly bring any radical change. The industrial output in Estonia is said to have increased by 8.4 per cent in 1966 as compared with 1965, but the increase in monthly wages has been only 4.6 per cent. However, on the occasion of the golden jubilee of the October Revolution the five-day working week was introduced in the entire Soviet Union.

SOME RECENT DEVELOPMENTS

It is not easy to write of recent developments in the Soviet Union. The events and sudden changes can and usually do make any description obsolete before it is published. What seems to be a certainty today may be an error tomorrow. The only way to avoid such pitfalls is to generalize. As one such general observation we could suggest that the decisions of the Soviet leaders seem in great measure to be influenced by one of Lenin's pamphlets entitled "One step backward — two forward". This would be a good description of Soviet politics if we only knew where the Soviet leaders are headed and which steps are thus forwards and which are backwards. Very few outside the Soviet Union, and still fewer inside it, believe nowadays that their goal is still to achieve communism as it has been taught in the past. In this the Chinese are probably quite right. However, following the developments in the Soviet Union since Stalin's death we can ascertain a certain trend towards liberalisation. In spite of repeated lapses there has certainly occurred a relative liberalisation of Soviet life although it cannot yet be measured by any western standard. The people and their doings are still closely watched, the communications, especially those to and from abroad, are still censored, and the political pressure on people is still constant and heavy. But on the other hand the reactions of the authorities to dissident opinions are not quite as frequent as they used to be, and even criticism of the existing order is said sometimes to remain unpunished, especially when the culprit has been intoxicated.

The relative liberation is perhaps most perceptible in cultural fields, but everybody knows of course what happened to the Soviet writers who overstepped the bounds. There is no law which would indicate where the dividing line of the permissible goes, and probably there never will be any as long the Communist Party is in power. Khrushchev once divulged in his impulsive way a very important maxim of the Soviet government. He said that laws on these would only give the "enemies of the people" a shield behind which they could creep. Probably this is a necessary maxim in a state where three per cent of the population seek to govern the rest.

As things are now there are no great risks if the authorities relax the grip somewhat. All the old revolutionaries are long dead, and so are the more enterprising people who were prepared to take risks. Those of the older and middle-aged generation who have survived, are only glad to be left alone. "You cannot live twelve years under constant threat of being awakened in the middle of the night and taken away, and want to start it all over again now when at long last you are left alone to live your life in your own small way." So a middle-aged man in one of the Baltic republics put it recently as an explanation of his way of thinking.

The state of things at any given moment is moreover no guarantee that it will be the same tomorrow. As soon as the authorities decide that the political situation demands it, a sterner regime is at once introduced. This is how the lapses in the general trend away from Stalinism occur. The cause may be internal or foreign, the remedy is always the same: annulment of certain liberties and favours, a stepped up surveillance and increased political pressure in the desired direction.

The harsher climate which hit the Baltic republics in April 1968 is for example thought to have been caused by current events in Czechoslovakia. Up to the time of writing no other explanation has been suggested. Such lapses have occurred now and then, but they have so far remained only temporary phenomena and in the long run the trend has led towards greater tolerance. The big watershed in the post-Stalinist era has been of course the amnesty law of 1955. After that the deportees started to return, singly or in small groups. The bulk of the survivors returned during the following two or three years, although not all. A certain number have had to stay in the vicinity of the corrective labour camps as settlers. But even for those who returned their old country did not look quite the same. Not only were there now myriads of Russians living everywhere, causing an acute shortage of dwellings. Families were pressed together into incredibly small quarters and improvements were very slow in coming. Thus when in 1967 queues were organised for those awaiting assignment of accommodation in Estonia, top priority had to be given to families who had lived at least eight years in flats with three square metres of floor space for every individual. Overcrowded dwellings and a close surveillance by the secret police has made life hard to endure even if it must have been a lot easier than living as exiles in some forlorn place of arctic wilderness.

The so-called "thaw period" was not half so intensive in the Baltic republics as it was in Russia. In the Baltic countries it arrived rather late and proved to be quite chilly. This period also made it clear to people inside and outside the Soviet Union that the Baltic countries were no longer politically and ideologically the most progressive parts of the Soviet Union. From the "thaw" period on all pressure on authorities for more liberalisation has come from Russia and actions initiated in Moscow and Leningrad have brought only much weaker echoes in the Baltic republics.

The reaction of the authorities to every kind of unauthorised self-expression has nevertheless been as severe in the Baltic republics or even more so than in Russia. The ghost the authorities have most feared and against which they have fought most relentlessly, is "bourgeois nationalism". The "bad" influences coming from abroad have got only secondary attention. For instance, the first secretary of the Estonian Communist Party reminded as late as March 1967 that the party cadres have "to condemn every expression of bourgeois ideology, especially every tendency to nationalism. We must develop decisive attacks on bourgeois ideology and reveal the reactionary character of that ideology". On the same occasion the party cadres were also told to give special attention to writers, artists, composers and actors. We should "inspire them with intolerance against tendencies towards pseudo-innovation and ensure that they do not abandon party principles and social realism in literature and art".

To press home these orders which initially of course had come from Moscow, the Estonian artists were told in their Congress in April 1967 that they should drop "the abstractionist buffoonery" of the West and renounce "extremist experiments and sterile quests". Even art critics on this occasion got their share of scolding. They were told they no longer consider the Leninist principles and that they were incapable of Marxist analysis of art. The chairman of the Estonian Artists' Union who had to deliver these tirades, however, was supported only by the secretary of the Soviet Union Artists' Union, who called upon the artists to keep the party line even when going in for modernist and innovatory styles. The artists themselves, as much they had the possibility to address the Congress, discussed mainly practical problems such as scarcity of studio space, shortage of materials, etc. They nevertheless also found opportunity to point out that due to lack of contacts abroad they had no means of keeping themselves informed about what was happening in art outside the Soviet Union.

Tallinn, where this congress was held, is however one of the best informed places about the events in the outside world. The people there are able to watch the Helsinki TV programs, which are easy to follow because of the great similarity of the Finnish and Estonian languages. One actually begins to understand it simply by listening to it for a few months.

Some influence on the mood of the population in the Baltic republics has probably also come from the numerous tourist visits. A lot of Baltic people have close relatives abroad, who in recent years in increasing numbers have started to visit their old home countries. Since 1965 also an increased number of people in the Baltic republics have received permission to visit their relatives abroad. According to official report permission for such visits was granted to 250 people in Estonia during the first four months of 1967. It was also announced that in May that year 350 persons were abroad, and that 500 applications were waiting to be decided when these 350 travellers had returned.

The possibility of foreign travel is one of the most cherished favours the people of the Baltic republics know. It was therefore a great shock when the bureau which handled the applications for visits abroad was suddenly closed down in April 1968. Fortunately the close-down was only a provisional measure.

Finally a few lines about the youth problem. Generally speaking these problems in the Baltic republics are identical with those of the so-called "fourth generation" in Russia. Although the Baltic youth is only the first soviet generation, they are basically as apolitical as their Russian counterparts. Although both are said to be patriotic there is the vital difference that the patriotism of the Baltic youth is resented, while that of the Russian one is not. The latter is also dubbed as "Soviet patriotism" which is considered to be good, while the patriotism of the minorities is bad. An interesting phenomenon connected with these questions, however, is that the Soviet authorities do not seem to believe in the patriotism of the Soviet youth, or at least in their "Soviet patriotism". This became quite evident in connection with the recent court actions against young Soviet writers.

On the other hand the authorities seem to believe very much in the patriotism of the Baltic youth and to be only afraid that this is more a "bourgeois nationalism" than "Soviet patriotism". In this they may be quite right, as *inter alia* the poor showing of the Baltic Komsomol organisations has demonstrated. For instance in 1967 a general review of the Komsomol organisation in Estonia was arranged in the form of change of membership cards. On this occasion 35,000 members of a total of 105,000 failed to show up during the first four months and had probably to be expelled. Some members of the Estonian Komsomol Central Committee were sacked that year, while its secretary general had been fired already in 1966. The youth actually pays very little heed to what the political leaders are saying. They want to live their own lives and to look to their own interests. Their personal interest is also their main reason for joining the Komsomol organisation, as membership carries with it certain privileges in education and so on.

At the side of this pragmatic view the youth is very interested in all things Western and fancies tremendously its whims. Western jazz is no longer a bone of contention as the Soviet officials have long ago given up the fight against that kind of "bourgeois decadence". Now they are busy trying to protect their youth from a hippie vogue. Also juvenile criminality seems to be a serious problem. It is reported from Tallinn that since the beginning of 1968 a satirical play has been staged about this problem. Although the piece with a peculiar title ("Criminal tango and very decent people") by a young Estonian playwright is said to be without literary merit, and that even the production has no artistic value, it has become a smash hit especially with young people. The reason is obviously that the shady sides of soviet society are presented in a lively and funny way. The chief character in the play is a boy of seventeen who as a schoolboy had wanted to become a doctor. But learning that the doctor's pay after six years of university studies is only 70 to 80 roubles a month, and never going to exceed 120 roubles, he becomes a lorry driver where his initial pay is already higher. In this way he falls into bad company, which gives the author a chance to present a whole gallery of "anti-social' types, including hippies and criminals.

There is no doubt that the youth has a good time looking at the buffoonery as a change for the barrack-like order around them. Military order applied to every walk of life, and from the cradle to the grave, is perhaps the nearest description of the communist social order which could fully be understood by a westerner. Presumably for the same reason the youth in the Soviet Union is not particularly enthusiastic about that order. This problem could one day become a major crisis if the authorities continue cutting off all possibilities for the youth to vent their feelings. Such a policy cannot fail to create powerful and dangerous tensions which must explode one day. And the explosion will be the bigger the more time the tension has to gather.

METHODS OF COLONIZATION AND RUSSIFICATION NATIONAL RESISTANCE IN THE BALTIC STATES

The present minority policy of the CPSU was constituted in 1961 by the Party Programme which states the following: "The deeply rooted communist system creates a new phase in the relations of nations inside the Soviet Union which is characterized by futher national contacts and the achievement of their final complete unity". The Programme also talks about "wiping out national differences, chiefly the linguistic ones". A culture "common to all Soviet people" shall develop, which encourages the general knowledge of the Russian language as a "common language of cooperation of all peoples of the USSR". Thus Russian should become the "second mother tongue" of all non-Russians and serve to pave the way for the disappearance on non-Russian cultures and traditions. The permanent contact should thereafter lead to a final merger of the non-Russian and Russian peoples.

The Party Programme was commented on by several contributors. The Soviet author Y. Kravzhev stressed that communists were against the perpetuation of national differences and that "small nations must melt into the larger ones". V. Savchenko explained that "today's national relations may be the beginning of tomorrow's amalgamation." According to another author, A. Isupov, in the Soviet Union the "convergence and amalgamation of nations" is a factor of development which "encourages the emergence of one single nation with one single language". The writer P. Podyatshich thought that in the USSR "we could see today the process of assimilation of small nations".

The 1961 Programme and the ensuing comments, here quoted from official Soviet sources, are documents forming the basis for the ideology of communist policy of denationalization and russification of non-Russian peoples. They are the theoretical basis for the practical policy of assimilation as it has been carried out with various methods systematically for years.

In Soviet practice, the main part in national politics is played by the systematic colonization of non-Russian republics with the help of Russian and other non-indigenous elements. This development is of great importance as it is today the chief means of russification. Russian colonization is designed change gradually the national composition of non-Russian republics and to turn the natives into a minority in their own countries.

These large-scale population reorganizations are due to many causes: First of all, to military and political aims. Russian Communist Party officers and administrative civil servants are permanently stationed in these republics in order to carry out political supervision over these non-Russian republics. Soviet military troops, particularly officers and their families, are overwhelmingly Russian. This is meant to strengthen security in border territories.

Secondly, Russian colonization is encouraged by rapid industrialization. This is carried out by the central Ministry of Industry in Moscow. That really means that the establishment of any new factory in the various republics is determined centrally in Moscow. The central Ministry in Moscow then appoints most of the plant managers and engineers — mostly Russians. Workers are also transferred from Russia to the new factories, and soon their families follow. Natives usually form only a small part of the workers and the technicians. This is caused partly by lack of native labor, as Moscow often builds factories unessential to the economy of the republic in question.

The result of this systematic channelling of Russian workers to non-Russian factories is that many non-Russian towns and cities, particularly in the Baltic States and in the Ukraine, today show a Russian majority. In Riga, Tallinn, Kiev, Kharkov and Baku, the majority of the population is Russian.

Based on official sources, it can be stated that in Latvia, for instance, in the sixties Russian immigration (artificial growth of population) amounted to nearly 13,500. In comparison, natural growth was only

8,800, and even of this some 40 per cent were Russians and other non-Latvians. It is estimated that in the future more than 40 per cent of the Latvian industrial labor force will have to come from Russia and White Ruthenia. These figures are ominous for a small country with a population of 2,364,000. The fact of the systematic introduction of Russian manpower is also acknowledged by Russian statisticians.

Thirdly, in some non-Russian territories, particularly in the Baltic area, special circumstances play an important part: In these areas the standard of living is much higher than in most Russian territories — the atmosphere and way of life is West European. The Baltic States, which were occupied by Russia 32 years ago, are still called by many Russians "Soviet foreign countries." They attract many Russians, who move into the Baltic area on their own initiative.

Apart from the huge Russian occupation army in the Baltic republics, at least 1,000,000 Russians have moved to these small countries. The result of this mass colonization is reflected in the 1970 census. According to this census the ethnic composition of the so-called Estonian Soviet Republic is the following: total population is 1,356,000, of which Estonians comprise 68.2 per cent (against the former 88.2 per cent 1939), Russians 24.7 per cent, and others, in the main Slavic peoples, 7.1 per cent. Corresponding figures for Latvia are: total population 2,364,000, of which Latvians are 56.8 per cent (against 75.5 per cent of the pre-war figure), Russians 29.8 per cent, and others 13.4 per cent. The total population of Lithuania is 3,128,000, of which Lithuanians form 80.1 per cent (against the former 84.4 per cent), Russians 8.6 per cent and others 11.3 per cent. The total population of all three Baltic republics is 6,848,000, of which titular nationalities form 69.7 per cent, Russians 19.1 per cent and other non-indiginous nationalities, in the main Slavic peoples, 11.2 per cent.

If this situation continues unabated it can lead to similar conditions which can be found in Soviet Karelia where 68.0 per cent of the population is Russian and only 12.0 per cent Karelian.

☆ ☆ ☆

Today there is no actively organized national opposition in the Baltic States. The effectiveness of the Soviet police state has thus far precluded this. Nevertheless, there are continued manifestations of resistance to Soviet rule in the Baltic republics as attested inter alia to by local publications of *samidat* (underground Press). These type-written publications contain critical comments, informations on arrests, poems of resistance, etc, which appear at irregular intervals despite the efforts of the KGB in suppressing them.

The Moscow underground "Chronicle of Current Events" No. 25 in 1972 reported the existence of an Estonian National Front which seeks a referendum on the self-determination of Estonia. Its program is carried by a new underground journal, *Eesti Demokraat*, published in May 1972. At the same time a letter from a group in Estonia was smuggled out for publication in Estonian newspapers abroad. The letter protests against the russification policies, the general lack of freedom and the Russian occupation of the Baltic countries. It states: "The Baltic question must be discussed widely in the Press and raised in the U.N.".

In addition Soviet newspapers constantly attack manifestations of "bourgeois nationalism" in the Baltic republics as well as in the other non-Russian republics. This national resistance to russification is particularly strong among the intelligentsia and students. Poets and writers who have shown "bourgeois nationalist" tendencies lose their privileges and their works are barred from further publication. Similarly, students and scientists who have voiced oppositional views are barred from universities and research institutes.

The Baltic peoples' resistance to russification is seriously worrying Moscow, more especially their opposition to the ever increasing influx of Russian and other Slavic peoples into the Baltic republics. Moscow has responded to this by ordering the local communist parties to suppress this opposition. Thus, August Voss, First Secretary of the Latvian Communist Party, called on party propagandists to combat "nationalist tendencies" and to emphasize "the need for a united and integrated Soviet nation." (*Pravda*, March 12, 1972) He also stressed the need for "peaceful co-existance and cooperation among ethnic groups."

In Estonia, the Communist leadership on March 6th, 1972, referring to the 24th Congress of the CP last year which condemned "evidence of nationalism, chauvinism and ethnic bigotry", convened a special meeting of its Central Committee to issue guidelines against Estonian antagonism to Russian settlers..

Recent isolated outbursts of national resistance in the Baltic countries are the following:

The russification through mass immigration has become now so evident that even local communists are beginning to revolt. A protest letter by 17 Latvian Communists in the beginning of 1972 was smuggled out of Latvia and sent to Communist Party leaders in Romania, Yugoslavia, France, Austria, Spain, Sweden and elsewhere. The 17 Communists charge Moscow with "forcible colonization" of Latvia, Lithuania and Estonia with Russians, White Ruthenians and Ukrainians. They complain that the organizational bureau of the CC of the CPSU for Latvian affairs assigns all leading posts to Russians. New large industries are being constructed and existing plants expanded without regard to local economic considerations in order to facilitate the "massive influx of Russians". The same purpose is also served by establishing large bases for the Soviet armed forces on Latvian soil.

The 17 Communists recall the fate of E. Berklavs, former first secretary of the Riga city Party committee, Vice-Chairman of the Latvian SSR Council of Ministers, and member of the Latvian CPCC Bureau, who attempted to stop this russification during the Khrushchev era, when Khrushchev himself flew to Riga to quell the dissatisfaction in the Central Committee of the Latvian CP. Berklavs was relieved of his posts, deported, and scores of other national Communists were purged from the Party. Since then all the important posts have been taken by either non-Latvians or russianized Latvians. The authors of the letter appeal to the Western Communist parties to intercede on their behalf against Moscow. They ask that the foreign Communist leaders "unmask and boycott" the leaders of the Soviet Communist Party, if Moscow does not stop its russification policies.

In the beginning of 1972, 17,000 Catholics in Lithuania signed a letter to the central government in Moscow and to the U.N., protesting against denial of freedom of worship.

At the end of April 1972, several students of the Tallinn Polytechnical Institute were expelled for participating in an anti-Soviet demonstration during the world icehockey championships. Hundreds of students had rushed out into the streets after the games to celebrate Soviet defeat by Czechoslovakia.

In May and June 1972, four persons burned themselves to death in
Lithuania, in protest against the Soviet occupation of their country.
A riot followed the funeral of Roman Kalanta, a student who had
burned himself in a public park in Kaunas for political reasons.
Thousands of people, mostly young, protested against Russian domination, and chanted "Freedom for Lithuania". They started fires, and
fought police and the army with sticks and stones. The riot lasted
for two days and was only suppressed after heavily armed Soviet
internal security and parachute troops had been flown in from the
Russian SFSR. Hundreds of demonstrators were arrested.

Approximately 150 students were arrested in Vilnius, Lithuania,
during an international handball tournament in June, 1972. The
students had jeered at Russian players, cheered non-Russian players,
distributed patriotic leaflets during the games, and had hoisted
Lithuanian national flags in the streets. Similar events had taken place
in Tallinn. Now, according to new rules made by Moscow, cities that
cannot control their audiences will lose the right to host All-Union
contests.

What is most remarkable about the recent outbursts of sporadic
resistance is the role of youth, of those who were born and raised
under Soviet rule and have no memories of the independence. The
Baltic peoples hope for the restoration of all their rights and of the
independent Republics of Estonia, Latvia and Lithuania. They hope to
regain their rightful place in a free European community of nations.

LITERATURE

Aspects of Estonian Culture. (Editorial Board: Johannes Aavik, . . .) Boreas Publishing Co, London 1961.

Audénas, Juozas (editor), Twenty Years Struggle for Freedom of Lithuania. Supreme Committe for Liberation of Lithuania, New York 1963.

The Baltic States 1940—1972. The Baltic Committee in Scandinavia, Stockholm 1972.

Balys, Jonas, Lithuania and Lithuanians. F. A. Praeger, New York 1961.

Berzins, Alfreds, The Unpunished Crime. A Case Study of Communist Takeover. Robert Speller & Sons, Publishers, New York.

Bilmanis, Alfreds, A History of Latvia. Princeton 1951.

Bilmanis, Alfreds, Latvia under German Occupation, 1—2. Washington 1942.

Bilmanis, Alfreds, Latvian—Russian Relations. Documents. Washington 1944.

Bukšs, Michael, Die Russifizierung in den baltischen Ländern. München 1965.

Chambon, H. de, La tragédie des nations baltiques. Paris 1946.

Die Deportationen im Baltikum. Estnischer Nationalfond, Stockholm 1966 (Stenciled.)

Eliaser, Elga, Estonia Past and Present. Estonian Information Centre, Stockholm 1959.

Estonian Events. Bimonthly Newsletter. Dr. Rein Taagepera, School of Social Sciences, University of California, Irvine, Calif. 1970—.

Estonian War of Independence 1918—1920. Reprint of a summary prepared by Estonian National Historical Committee in 1938—1939. Eesti Vabadusvõitlejate Liit, New York 1968.

First Conference on Baltic Studies. A Summary of Proceedings. University of Oklahoma, Washington 1969.

Second Conference on Baltic Studies. A Summary of Proceedings. Norman, Oklahoma 1971.

Freivalds, Osvalds, De internerade balternas tragedi i Sverige år 1945—1946. Daugavas Vanagi, Stockholm 1967.

Frihet vid fritt hav. Junikommittén, Stockholm 1966.

Graham, Malbone W., The Diplomatic Recognition of the Border States. University of California Press, Berkeley, Calif. 1939.

Ha de rätt att leva? H. Gebers Förlag, Stockholm 1943.

Harrison, E. J., Lithuania's Fight for Freedom. Lithuanian American Information Center, New York 1952.

Hellmann, M., Grundzüge der Geschichte Litauens. Darmstadt 1966.

Horm, Arvo, Estland fritt och ockuperat. Tiden, Stockholm 1944.

Hundra miljoner fångar. Natur och Kultur, Stockholm 1953.

Iliste, Ivo, Sovjetunionens brott mot mänskligheten. In: Friheten möter Chrustjov. Baltiska Kommittén, Stockholm 1959.

Jackson, J. Hampden, Estonia. (Second edition with a postscript on the years 1940—1947). George Allen & Unwin Ltd., London 1948.

Juhkam, Martin, The Church in the Chains of Communist Dictatorship. The Baltic Committee in Sweden, Stockholm 1968 (Stenciled).

Jurgela, C. R., History of the Lithuanian Nation. New York 1948.

Kaelas, Aleksander, Das Sowjetisch besetzte Estland. Estnischer Nationalfond, Stockholm 1958.

Kaelas, Aleksander, Baltikum i Sovjetsfären. Utrikespolitiska Institutet, (Broschyr-serie nr 9), Stockholm 1960.

Kaelas, Aleksander, Human rights and genocide in the Baltic states. Stockholm 1950.

Kaelas, Aleksander, The worker in the Soviet paradise. Boreas, London 1947.

Kaelas, Aleksander, Estland efter andra världskriget. Utrikespolitiska Institutet, Stock-holm 1951.

Kalme, Albert, Sovjets blodsdåd i Balticum. Natur och Kultur, Stockholm 1948.

Kalme, Albert, Total Terror. An exposé of genocide in the Baltics. Appleton-Century-Crofts, inc., New York 1951.

Kalnins, Bruno, De baltiska staternas frihetskamp. Tiden, Stockholm 1950.

Kalnins, Bruno, The Position of Minorities in the Soviet Union. Bulletin of Baltic Studies, No. 8, Lincoln, Nebraska 1972.

Kant, Edgar, Jüri Uluotsa memorandum Eesti seisundi kohta 29. juulist 1941. (The Statement of J. U. about the standing of Estonia of 29.7. 1941). In: Eesti riik ja rahvas teises maailmasõjas (Estonian State and People in the Second W. W.). VI. EMP, Stockholm 1959.

Kareda, Endel, Estonia in the Soviet Grip. Boreas, London 1949.

Kareda, Endel, Technique of Economic Sovietisation. Boreas, London 1947.

Kareda, Endel, Estonia, the Forgotten Nation. Estonian Central Council in Canada, Toronto 1961.

Klesment, Johannes, Kolm aastat iseseisvuse võitlust võõra okupatsiooni all (Three Years of Struggle for Independence under the Foreign Occupation). In: Eesti riik ja rahvas teises maailmasõjas (Estonian State and People in the Second W. W.) VII. EMP, Stockholm 1959.

Kodumaa küsimusi (Problems of the Home Country) I. Eesti Rahvusnõukogu (Esto-nian National Council), Stockholm 1959. (Stenciled).

Kristian, A., The Right of Selfdetermination and the Soviet Union, London 1952.

Küng, Andres, Estland — en studie i imperialism. Bokförlaget Aldus/Bonniers, Stock-holm 1971.

Laaman, E., Eesti iseseisvuse sünd. (The Birth of the Independence of Estonia). Re-print Kirjastus Vaba Eesti, Stockholm 1964.

Landsmanis, Arturs, De misstolkade legionärerna. Stockholm 1970.

Lidandets väg. Baltiska 14 juni-kommittén, Stockholm 1949.

Maandi, Helmut, Ten Years Ago. In: Minevikust tulevikku — From the Past to the Future. Estonian Student Association Põhjala, Stockholm 1954.

Manning, Clarence A., The Forgotten Republics. Philosophical Library, New York 1952.

Meissner, B. Die Sowjetunion, die baltischen Staaten und das Völkerrecht, Köln 1956.

Mihkelson, Johannes, Estonian Labour in chains. Lund 1955.

Mägi, Artur, Das Staatsleben Estlands während seiner Selbständigkeit. Stockholm 1967.

Mägi, Arvo, Estonian Literature. The Baltic Humanitarian Association, Stockholm 1968.

Nazi—Soviet Relations 1939—1941. The Department of State, Washington, D.C. 1948.

Nerman, Birger, Balticum skall leva. Natur och Kultur, Stockholm 1956.

Newman, Bernard, Baltic Background. R. Hale, London 1948.

Newsletter from Behind the Iron Curtain, Vol. I-XXVI. Estonian Information Centre, Stockholm 1947—1972.

Nodel, Emanuel, Estonia — Nation on the Anvil. Bookman Associates, Inc., New York 1963.

Nurk, Harald, Nii elatakse Eestis — olukord arvudes. (Such is Life in Estonia — Situation in figures). In: Rahvuslik kontakt (National Contact) 1968: 3.

Olberg, Paul, Tragedin Balticum. Natur och Kultur, Stockholm 1941.

Olberg, Paul, Tragödie des Baltikums. Europa-Verlag, Zürich/New York 1941.

Olberg, Paul, Balticum. Fantasi och verklighet. Baltiska Kommittén, Stockholm 1946.

Olberg, Paul, Rysslands nya imperialism. Natur och Kultur, Stockholm 1940.

Oras, Ants, Baltic Eclipse. V. Gollanch, London 1948.

Oras, Ants, Estonian Literature in Exile. Eesti Kirjanike Kooperatiiv, Lund 1967.

Oras, Ants, Slagskugga över Baltikum. Natur och Kultur, Stockholm 1949.

Oras, Ants, Mörke over Baltikum. Höviks forlag, Oslo 1949.

Oras, Ants, Viron kohtalonvuodet. Gummerus, Jyväskylä 1958.

Orr, Charles A., Stalins slavläger. Fria Fackföreningsinternationalen, Bryssel 1952.

Page, S. W., The Formation of the Baltic States. Cambridge, Mass. 1959.

Pelékis, K., Genocide, Lithuania's Threefold Tragedy, Schw. Gmünd 1949.

Perlitz, Harald, Estlands kyrka under sovjetväldet. Stockholm 1943.

Pick, F. W., The Baltic nations. London 1945.

Pullerits, Albert, Estonia; population, cultural and economic life. Tallinn 1937.

Purre, Arnold, Eesti saatusaastad (Years of Fate of Estonia) 1945—1960, III. EMP, Stockholm 1965.

Pusta, K. R., The Soviet Union and the Baltic states. New York 1943.

von Rauch, Georg, Geschichte der baltischen Staaten. Kohlhammer Verlag, Stuttgart 1970.

Raud, Villibald, Estonia. A reference book. The Nordic Press, Inc., New York 1953.

Rei, August, Balticum och Sovjetunionens säkerhet. Baltiska Kommittén, Stockholm 1943.

Rei, August, The Drama of the Baltic Peoples. Kirjastus Vaba Eesti, Stockholm 1970. Appendix: Events after 1940 by Evald Uustalu.

Rei, A., Nazi—Soviet Conspiracy and the Baltic States; Diplomatic Documents and other Evidence. Boreas Publishing Co., London 1948.

Rei, A., Soviet Deportations in Estonia (Stenciled).

Rutkis, J. (editor), Latvia — Country and People. Latvian National Foundation, Stockholm 1967.

J.-Scheynius, Ignas, Den röda floden svämmar över. Natur och Kultur, Stockholm 1945.

Siiras, Jaan, Viro neuvostokurimuksessa. W. Söderström, Porvoo/Helsinki 1942.

Silde, Adolfs, The profits of Slavery. Latvian National Foundation, Stockholm 1958.

Silde, Adolfs, Resistance Movement in Latvia. Latvian National Foundation, Stockholm 1972.

Silde, Adolfs, Die Sowjetisierung Lettlands. Münster 1967.

Soviet-Occupied Estonia 1967. Monthly Reports. Estonian National Council, Stockholm 1968. (Stenciled).

Spekke, A., History of Latvia. An outline. Stockholm 1957.

Suduvis, N. E., Allein, ganz allein, 1964.

Survel, Jaak, Estonia Today. Boreas, London 1947.

Svabe, Arveds, Lettlands historia. Lettiska Nationella Fonden, Stockholm 1961.

Swettenham, J. A., The tragedy of the Baltic states. London 1952.

Tarulis, A., Soviet Policy Toward the Baltic States. University of Notre Dame Press, South Bend, Ind. 1959.

These Names Accuse. Nominal List of Latvians Deported to Soviet Russia in 1940—41. Stockholm 1951.

Third Interim Report of the Select Committee on Communist Aggression, House of Representatives, Eighty-Third Congress, Second Session. United States Government Printing Office, Washington, 1954.

Uluots, Jüri, Grundzüge der Agrargeschichte Estlands. Tartu 1935.

Uustalu, Evald, The History of Estonian People. Boreas Publishing Co, Ltd., London 1952.

Vaitiekunas, Vytautas, Lithuania. Assembly of Captive European Nations, New York 1965.

Valters, M. Das Verbrechen gegen die baltischen Staaten. Nice 1962.

Vardys, V. S., Lithuania under the Soviets. New York 1965.

Vardys, Stanley, Soviet colonialism in the Baltic States 1940—65. Baltic Review 1965/29.

Vardys, V., Captive Lithuania 1944—1962. F. A. Praeger, New York 1965.

Watson, H. A. G., The Latvian Republic. London 1965.

Weiss, Hellmuth, Die baltischen Staaten. In: Die Sovjetisierung Ost-Mitteleuropas. Alfred Metzner, Frankfurt/M 1959.

Wieselgren, Per, Från hammaren till hakkorset. Stockholm 1942.

Zundé, P., Die Landwirtschaft Sowjetlitauens. In: Wissenschaftliche Beiträge zur Geschichte und Landeskunde Ost-Mitteleuropas Nr 58, Lahn 1962.